The Politics of Safety

The Politics of Safety

The Black Struggle for Police Accountability
in La Guardia's New York

. . . .

SHANNON KING

The University of North Carolina Press Chapel Hill

© 2024 The University of North Carolina Press
All rights reserved
Set in Charis by Westchester Publishing Services
Manufactured in the United States of America

Library of Congress Cataloging-in-Publication Data
Names: King, Shannon, author.
Title: The politics of safety : the Black struggle for police
    accountability in La Guardia's New York / Shannon King.
Other titles: Black struggle for police accountability in La Guardia's
    New York
Description: Chapel Hill : The University of North Carolina Press, [2024] |
    Includes bibliographical references and index.
Identifiers: LCCN 2023044350 | ISBN 9781469676166 (cloth ; alk. paper) |
    ISBN 9781469676173 (pbk. ; alk. paper) | ISBN 9781469676180 (ebook)
Subjects: LCSH: New York (N.Y.). Police Department—History— 20th
    century. | African Americans—New York (State)—New York—
    Social conditions—20th century. | Racism in law enforcement—
    New York (State)—New York—20th century. | Police-community
    relations—New York (State)—New York—20th century. | Police—
    Complaints against—New York (State)—New York—20th century. |
    Public safety—New York (State)—New York—History—20th century. |
    BISAC: HISTORY / African American & Black | HISTORY /
    United States / State & Local / General
Classification: LCC F128.9.B53 K56 2024 | DDC 974.7/100496073—
    dc23/eng/20231002
LC record available at https://lccn.loc.gov/2023044350

Cover photo of woman with victim of police brutality from Joe Schwartz
Photo Archive via Getty Images.

Contents

Illustrations

Introduction

· ·

The Harlem police force had been augmented in March, and the unrest grew.
Perhaps the most revealing new item, out of the steady parade of reports of
muggings, stabbings, shootings, assaults, gang wars, and accusations of
police brutality, was the item about six Negro girls who set upon a white girl
in the subway because, as they all too accurately put it, she was stepping on
their toes. Indeed she was, all over the nation.

—James Baldwin

"I had never before been so aware of policemen, on foot, on horseback, on
corners, everywhere, always two by two," remembered James Baldwin,
Harlem native and novelist, describing his arrival home to Harlem in early
June of 1943, a month before the passing of his father and two months before the Harlem Riot of that year. Two years before, crimes of theft and physical assault by Blacks upon whites, especially youth and women, especially
in areas bordering Black and white neighborhoods enraged white New Yorkers. This precipitated a moral panic. Soon Mayor Fiorello H. La Guardia
and Police Commissioner Lewis J. Valentine received a flood of angry letters from white New Yorkers, and an army of white dailies, especially the
New York Times, dubbed this series of crimes a "crime wave." Whites' hysteria about Black crime, the complaints of patrolmen about Black people, and
the white press's exaggerated crime news drove the mayor and Valentine
to wage a war against "Negro thugs" to wipe out the crime wave, a war that
lasted well into the postwar era.[1]

What happens if we center crime discourse and policing in our investigation of Black politics during the La Guardia era beyond the large-scale
Harlem uprisings of 1935 and 1943? This question does not ignore the uprisings or their socioeconomic and political dimensions. It does, however, consider police brutality as something significantly more than a catalyst that
sparked the uproars. *The Politics of Safety* foregrounds police violence as
an analytical category that operated on two interrelated registers—as an
act of blatant police brutality and a more nuanced but equally dangerous act

of unequal protection to tell the lesser-known story of Black activism and the politics of safety during the La Guardia era.

Drawing from an array of sources including letters, newspapers, organizational records, and municipal, state, and federal records, *The Politics of Safety* examines anti-Black violence, crime, and policing during La Guardia's three terms as mayor of New York City to ask several questions: How did the La Guardia administration respond to the uprisings? How did it respond to calls for police accountability and equitable policing? How did Blacks experience and make sense of racial violence? How did whites, Blacks, and the police respond to and define crime? What roles did the media play in shaping public perceptions of Black criminality? Considered collectively, how did public discussions of crime, policing, and violence shape urban crime policy in Black neighborhoods during the Great Depression and World War II eras?[2]

In eight chapters, *The Politics of Safety* reveals the experiences of Black New Yorkers with, responses to, and debates around crime and police violence. The book traces the development of Black New York's first movement against police violence, a response to the police occupation of Harlem and other neighborhoods across the city after the Harlem uprising of 1935. I argue that the expansion of Blacks in predominantly white public and residential areas, their pursuit for equality and police accountability, and Black-on-white crime shifted public debates on policing and crime from Blacks as victims of police brutality in the mid-1930s to Blacks as purveyors of crime by the early 1940s. In the process of this shift, there were two overlapping and interrelated developments: Black New Yorkers initiated various campaigns around crime and policing for the safety of the Black community that challenged police brutality, demanded equitable police protection, and deracialized crime news that tethered Blackness to street crimes; and white New Yorkers, public officials, and the white press converged to build a political movement and an argument to protect the safety of white New Yorkers from Black criminals—real and imagined—by expanding and reestablishing the city's racialized police apparatus.

After the Harlem uprising of 1935, the mayor commissioned an interracial group of civil liberties, labor, social reform, and religious leaders to investigate the causes of the uproar. Both the riot and the work of La Guardia's commission rocked the state of racial politics in Gotham City and exposed the mayor's complicity with police violence and municipal neglect. Following the uprising and the complaints of whites, especially the propertied classes, about widespread crime in the district, Valentine detailed police patrols to Harlem that Blacks described as a "police army of occupation." This discourse about the threat of Black crime reoccurred throughout the La Guardia era in Bedford-Stuyvesant in late 1930s and throughout the early 1940s as prelude to and aftereffects of the 1943 uproar.

Police occupation of Black neighborhoods ostensibly to fight crime—but mainly to protect white people—not only sanctioned police violence against Blacks but also made plain the divergent and unequal ways the police protected Black and white neighborhoods. As they watched the police assigned to white areas bordering Black ones, Blacks complained about the laxity of police protection in their own communities. But more than complaining about unequal protection, Blacks organized anticrime campaigns around crime prevention and punishment. Waged simultaneously, Black "law-and-order" politics and anti–police violence campaigns had an uneven impact on the moral panic in the early 1940s. The city's concerns about white New Yorkers overshadowed Black activism. As the city ignored Black anticrime campaigns, white New Yorkers maneuvered Blacks' calls for police accountability to both criminalize Black protests and launch their campaign for police expansion to fight Black crime. After the Harlem uprising of 1943, unlike the first, there was no investigation and report. "Negro hoodlums" —La Guardia, Valentine, and even Black leaders, such as the NAACP's Walter White, agreed—triggered the uproar.

For more than a decade, scholars historicizing the period from the Gilded Age to the end of the Prohibition era have produced work on the criminalization of Black communities, drawing on the interwoven relationships among the criminal justice system and popular and academic discourses on crime, race, gender, and the economy. Building on this work, *The Politics of Safety* pays close attention to intraracial crime and the Black community's responses to it, yet it prioritizes the Black community's discussions around and responses to Black crime and policing in view of white mobilizations around Black crime and the reproduction of a white-generated crime discourse during the Great Depression and the World War II era.[3]

Over the last several years, historians of the carceral state have focused on policing. This scholarship has assiduously interrogated the inner workings, ideologies, and overall politics of police departments and their embeddedness in federal, state, and local governments.[4] *The Politics of Safety* uses the uprisings of 1935 and 1943 to frame Black activism and debates around safety. The book engages how liberals policed Black communities and how street crime and uprisings shaped the relationships among the New

York Police Department, the criminal legal system, and white and Black New Yorkers. While extant scholarship has focused mainly on the post-1945 era, I foreground the Great Depression and World War II eras, as well as expand upon and deepen historical work that covers but does not concentrate on the 1930s and 1940s. More specifically, I illuminate how La Guardia, Valentine, and the New York Police Department (NYPD) used liberalism, proceduralism, and color-blind policies as a shield against allegations of police violence.[5]

Recently, scholars outside the discipline of history have written on intracommunity Black crime to explain mass incarceration in the late twentieth century. Political scientist Michael Fortner and legal scholar James Forman Jr., for example, have located the carceral state in Blacks' efforts to stop crime and protect Black citizens. While Fortner frames Black activism as the engine that sets the stage for the Rockefeller Drug Laws of 1973, Forman centers Black politicians and Black law enforcement in Washington, D.C., as self-identified expressions of the legacy of the civil rights movement. *The Politics of Safety* foregrounds an earlier period than that which Fortner and Forman focus on and considers Black protest against police brutality, proffering a more robust examination of Black politics around punishment than the former. At the same time, I place Black New Yorkers' anticrime politics, like the latter, in the context of the broader political aspirations and demands of the Black community, as it sought greater inclusion in municipal politics and equitable treatment in New York City.[6]

· · · · · ·

The Politics of Safety underscores the limits of New Deal liberalism, uncovering how the La Guardia administration, white citizens, and white media formulated an anti-Black crime discourse and policy that sanctioned police repression.[7] Liberalism in this work refers not only to New Deal programs but also to "racial liberalism," a political project where white public officials and white leaders advanced the political equality of Blacks while at the same time "sustained a common interest in upholding order and maintaining the racial status quo."[8] During the Progressive era, liberal race relations experts, Black and white, used statistics to counter claims of Blacks' biological criminality yet fastened on to cultural arguments to explain Black crime. At the federal level, proponents of "liberal law and order," responding to the uprisings in Detroit, Harlem, and other urban centers during World War II and the postwar era, claimed that white racism in the South, the lack of civil rights, and deprivation caused Black crime. Despite the divergent explanations, the argument that race and Blackness were the common denominators to explain crime remained the status quo.

The Great Depression devastated most in New York City, but few more so than its Black citizens. Across the city, one in six lost work and among Harlem's Black population, one in four. The marginal ground Black New Yorkers made in the industrial labor force during the Great War and throughout the 1920s quickly petered out. According to a 1933 study by the Milbank Memorial Fund, less than 25 percent of all families earned less than $1,200 in 1929. By 1932, about 60 percent earned less than that amount.[9] The labor movement offered little support. Only weeks after the stock market crash in October 1929, Elmer Anderson Carter, editor of the *Opportunity*, complained that the American Federation of Labor had "not only failed to unionize the Black workers; it ha[d] failed to unionize the white workers." According to its president, William Green, "the Federation c[ould] not effectively carry the gospel of unionism until workers [were] ready to hear and act." The combined impact of the Great Depression, indifference and racism in the labor movement, and employers' steadfast commitment to an economic policy that regarded Black labor as "the last-hired, first fired" spun Black New Yorkers into an unforgiving social, economic, and political quagmire.[10] Mayor James John Walker's anemic response, ignoring recommendations to cut city spending and selectively aiding Democrats affiliated with Tammany Hall, worsened the city's economic predicament. It would take former congressman Fiorello H. La Guardia to lead the city to better times.

Mayor La Guardia's political agenda and sensibilities had anticipated and built upon President Franklin Delano Roosevelt's New Deal programs. In 1922, La Guardia proposed a reserve fund for a large-scale public works program to counteract potential economic downturns, but naysayers claimed that it would be too costly.[11] A decade later, La Guardia would prove them wrong. Because of the relative success of the programs, such as the Federal Emergency Relief Administration and the Civil Works Administration, many Americans, New Yorkers especially, expected intergovernmental cooperation. La Guardia, like the Roosevelt administration, understood the Great Depression as a crisis of multidimensional proportions. In April 1934 and over the next ten months, he made numerous trips to Washington, D.C., to secure grants and loans for the completion of—and sharing plans for—various municipal projects, including the Eighth Avenue Independent subway line, schools, hospital buildings, parks, housing projects, tunnels, and a viaduct. Because La Guardia excelled at articulating this vision and executing it through New Deal programs, many New Yorkers, as historian

Mason B. Williams writes, "came to view the goods and services now provided by the public sector as 'rights' of urban citizenship."[12]

No different than their fellow New Yorkers, Blacks expected unencumbered access to the services and public goods that the city rendered through New Deal programs. Yet from the start, they had complained about the administration of the programs, especially work and home relief. According to a New York Urban League report, Blacks were "confined to the lowest paid and unskilled positions regardless of their experience and fitness."[13] In late December 1934, Rev. Adam Clayton Powell Sr. held a protest at Abyssinian Baptist Church. Myles A. Paige, chairman of the North Harlem Community Council, conducted the meeting that included an array of civic and religious speakers, including Powell and Richard B. Moore of the Communist Party. They spoke about the "discourteous and unfair treatment accorded Negro applicants for aid" in Districts Twenty-Six and Twenty-Eight. At the end of the meeting, they adopted a resolution requesting the removal of Mildred Gordon, assistant director of the Emergency Home Relief Bureau; Victor Suarez, administrator of the Twenty-Sixth Precinct; and Sophie Schupack, case supervisor of the Twenty-Eighth Precinct, and sent the resolution to La Guardia and other state and municipal officials of the relief administration.[14] The protest at Abyssinian Baptist Church was one of many campaigns against racial discrimination not only in the administration of relief but also in other areas of local government, as well as in the housing and labor markets in the private sector. These demonstrations, led by coalitions of religious, civil rights, Black nationalist, and left-leaning organizations, represented Black New Yorkers' expression of their community rights, exemplified by the "Don't Buy Where You Can't Work" campaigns in the early 1930s.[15]

Beyond housing, jobs, and relief, Black New Yorkers also complained about police brutality and used a range of strategies to protest it. Thus, the uprising was more than a response to a singular episode of police violence and the Depression. Their demands for police accountability and equitable access to New Deal programs in the aftermath of the March 19 uprising built upon previous iterations of activism against state-sanctioned violence and economic and social deprivation before La Guardia took office.[16]

Policing the Crisis

In New Deal New York, anti-Black racism and various notions of Black criminality operated as modalities of liberal governance and civic discourse. To understand the La Guardia administration's response to Black street crime and calls to stop it, I interrogate street crime as a "criminal phenomenon." By doing so, I analyze street crime not merely as an act of deviancy but more so to illuminate how media and the police and sometimes the courts defined crime and gave meaning to it. As Stuart Hall, Chas Critcher, Tony Jefferson, John Clarke, and Brian Roberts have argued in their classic, *Policing the Crisis: Mugging, the State, and Law and Order*, "The culture and institutions of social control [a]re as much part of deviant or criminal phenomena as those who committed crime," and they "played an active role, not only in the control of antisocial behavior but in how that behavior was labeled, defined, and publicly understood." The white press and the La Guardia administration configured and directed the public's perception of crime and employed it to serve their own agenda. Once La Guardia took office, his task included not only bringing the city out of the Depression and later the war effort but also persuading New Yorkers that his vision of democracy served all citizens regardless of their political, racial, ethnic, class, and religious identification. La Guardia's open support of labor, his own Italian and Jewish ancestry, and his fusion administration furthered progressive politics in the city but also complicated them.[17]

The mayor had to mitigate not only the tide of anti-Semitism coming from white New Yorkers, including the Klu Klux Klan, but also sentiments of it rooted in socioeconomic conflict within the Black community, particularly among some Black nationalist organizations.[18] Black activism during the Italo-Ethiopian War in the mid-1930s also exacerbated tensions between Blacks and people of Italian descent in the city. La Guardia tried to manage this, while also defending his administration and the New Deal from those who believed he used public spending to control the masses—the working class, Blacks, Jews, and other marginalized groups. In different ways, these all challenged his political authority, including his relationship with the city's Republican and Democratic parties. La Guardia's "war on crime" presented its own problems. As a vocal reformer, La Guardia and Valentine tried to transform New Yorkers' vision of the criminal legal system, particularly its police department, from one based on collusion and corruption, as represented by the city's power political machine Tammany Hall, to one embodying professionalism and law and order. La Guardia often faltered, especially when his efforts to reform the police clashed with police authority to use coercive force.[19]

White New Yorkers challenged this vision when they argued that La Guardia's response to the uprising and Black youth crime thereafter was not only inadequate but also a political maneuver to protect Black criminals to secure the "colored vote" and to advance his own political ambitions. In that way, white New Yorkers doubted La Guardia's commitment to their own safety, as well as his own advocacy of a reformed and anti-corrupt criminal legal system. Thus, La Guardia and Valentine's aggressive responses to Black youth crime represented not only their "capacity to practice authority, but also their ideological and cultural power to signify—give events social meaning—and to win society to their 'definition of the situation.'" La Guardia's administration reoriented his crime policy to, in part, fulfill white New Yorkers' demands for safety but also to win over the city to how his administration defined safety and law and order to establish hegemony that had been undermined throughout his three terms.[20]

Regarding Black New Yorkers, Mayor La Guardia effectively checked their protests by engaging in a politics of disregard, denial, delay, and blame.[21] Throughout his three terms, La Guardia managed Blacks' grievances by disregarding their complaints and demands for municipal accountability. When the mayor confronted these issues, he often denied that there was any substance to these complaints and demands or undermined them by blaming Black parents and criminalizing Black youth. La Guardia's commission itself was an expression of racial liberalism, as it acknowledged the grievances of Black Harlem and created an interracial commission to investigate the uprising. The mayor's reluctance to disclose the report, which detailed widespread racial discrimination in the city's economy and his administration's exclusionary and inequitable treatment of its Black citizens, revealed racial liberalism's commitment to fortifying the racial order. At the same time, the La Guardia administration's decision to police the crisis exposed the punitiveness of liberal governance. Over his three terms, the mayor chose to implement some of the recommendations outlined in the report. Yet under the pretext of preventing disorder, Police Commissioner Valentine deployed police patrols to Harlem for well over a year, defending the criminalization of Black youth and sanctioning police violence.[22] The surveillance and punishment of Black Harlem and Black neighborhoods across the city were not solely the outcome of top-down decisions by the La Guardia administration, however.[23]

During the hearings in 1935, white civilians and white business groups asserted that Black crime—not Jim Crow conditions and police violence—precipitated the uproar. Thus, white conservative and liberal social scientists used statistical discourse to link race and crime. Similarly, white citizens, the white press, and the NYPD used a vernacular discourse on Black criminal behavior to tether race to crime. Like the La Guardia administration, white citizens, the criminal legal system, and the white press were "active" in how Black youth crime was "labeled, defined, and publicly understood." Though the mayor met with Black leaders publicly promising police accountability, the La Guardia administration followed the directives of white New Yorkers and white public officials. This structured the racial dynamics of policing under the La Guardia administration, as Black New Yorkers and migrants moved into predominately white neighborhoods to escape and circumvent excessive rents and overcrowded housing in Harlem.[24]

In the mid-1930s, Blacks moved to all areas of the city, but a preponderance chose to begin their new life in the Bedford-Stuyvesant neighborhood in Brooklyn. Whites in Bedford-Stuyvesant, like their white counterparts in Harlem before World War I, tried unsuccessfully to impede Black property ownership and contain the expansion of the Black community. The rapid growth of Black Bedford-Stuyvesant, often called Brooklyn's "Little Harlem," and occurrences of Black street crime sparked a moral panic among whites, prompting whites to call for more police in the neighborhood. Blacks in the 1930s and 1940s were prey, therefore, to the whims of white New Yorkers' imagined and real fears and outcries about Black crime, which were expressions of their broader grievances about Blacks moving into white residential space and access to New Deal programs. Consequently, policing Black neighborhoods was a matter of not only Black street crime but also whites' perception of Black people as a physical, political, and residential threat to the safety of the white community, as well as the city's racial order with whites at the top and Blacks at the bottom.

In the early 1940s, the mainstream press's front-page stories of "crime waves"—a manufactured political and racial construction presaging conservative calls for "law and order" in the 1960s—precipitated a moral panic among white New Yorkers. White New Yorkers' outrage stemmed from the news of street crime, but it was also a backlash to Black communities spreading into white ones in the midst of wartime conditions and deprivation. The white press's crime reportage depended on the authority of their sources. The police and at times the judiciary defined and gave meaning to "crime" through the execution of their authority and at times through their commentary to the public *through* the media. Consequently, the white press played an instrumental role in the production—the framing, interpretation, and distribution—of crime news. The white press deployed the term "mugging" to describe street robbery, though the police rejected it as a legal concept. Nonetheless, the epithet "mugging" accompanied by "thugs" and "hoodlums" reproduced and reinforced the relationship between crime and

Blackness.[25] This grammar of crime news, fortified by white civilians' and public officials' outcries about Black crime, simultaneously tied crime to Black youth and urban space. At the same time, white civic associations, churches, public officials, and judges across the city in the late 1930s and 1940s, especially in Bedford Stuyvesant, Brooklyn, echoed white Harlemites' crime formulation in the mid-1930s—that the expansion of Blacks into white neighborhoods generated anti-white crime.[26]

Whites' complaints for police protection were matched by patrolmen's own contrived grievances about La Guardia restraining their authority to use coercive force. Tensions between the police and the mayor erupted when he directed the police not to use their batons during various demonstrations, especially the taxicab strike in 1934. The taxicab companies but also police rank-and-file complained about the mayor's intervention. La Guardia's first police commissioner, John F. O'Ryan, echoed these complaints privately to the mayor but also during grand jury hearings. Coming on the heels of criticism of police corruption and excessive use of force by the National Commission on Law Observance and Enforcement and the Hofstadter Committee, La Guardia's actions further compromised the NYPD's legitimacy and authority.

The Politics of Safety unearths the NYPD's discourse on police discretionary constraint that helped shape public discussions on crime and urban crime policy. The police's "preoccupation with minority crime," historian Edward J. Escobar writes, "meant that the department's subsequent history became inextricably intertwined with that of the minority communities."[27] That relationship meant that the political viability and legitimacy of the police relied on the control and punishment of Black citizens. Crucial to police legitimacy was its authority to define and explain crime and its structural relationship to the new media. To model "objectivity," the press relied on "authoritative statements from" the NYPD—not only Valentine but also the rank and file, who were primarily responsible for manufacturing and spreading the myth that La Guardia prevented them from fighting crime in Black neighborhoods. As significant, the police's explanations of crime—that is, whom they marked and targeted as a threat to civil society—were often accepted at face value by New Yorkers. Consequently, the police's articulations of crime effectively established the public's perception of crime, and therefore, their definitions of crime shaped citizens' interpretations of crime and the content of crime news in the city.[28]

In New York City, police manipulated arguments against police brutality by telling white and Black citizens that La Guardia circumscribed their "autonomous police discretion" to use coercive force to stop Black crime.[29] In their telling, in exchange for the Black vote, La Guardia promised Blacks that he would punish police officers for stopping Black crime and using lethal force to apprehend Black criminals. The NYPD's fiction of discretionary restraint corroborated white civilians', neighborhood associations', churches', and judges' racist constructions of the Black community and propelled them to demand aggressive punishment of Black crime and the Black community.[30]

Collectively these overlapping campaigns of the police, the white press, white citizens, and the La Guardia administration created an anti-Black political culture of punishment. This politics of punishment increased police surveillance of Black neighborhoods bordering white ones, created the groundwork for Black neighborhoods to become occupied territories, and condoned police repression. White New Yorkers' "crime talk," that is, public talk, jokes, and rumors about crime in the press and among victims of crime, over the course of time aided in spreading the discourse of Black youth crime. The police's narrative of discretionary restraint fostered a powerful argument about the threat of Black violence to the safety of white New Yorkers, setting off a reciprocal position from public officials, the white press, and white civilians. The consensus among them was that punishment and the unhinged discretion of the police to use force were the sole solutions to the threat of Black crime. The consensus gave license to the mayor, the police commissioner, and the criminal legal system in general not only to repress Black New Yorkers and Black residential areas but also to expand the city's racialized police apparatus.[31]

The Politics of Safety

The Politics of Safety brings into focus Black New Yorkers' simultaneous demands for safety from police violence *and* crime. We know much about Black protests for better housing, economic justice, and equal access to New Deal programs, the Double V campaign, and the uprisings but much less about Black activism around what I call "the politics of safety."[32] I introduce and use the phrase to refer to Black activism against police brutality *and* for equitable policing, as well as the various arguments and political activity Blacks employed to bring about safety. The politics of safety centers Blacks' efforts to prioritize the protection of their bodies and communities from harm and illuminates how debates around police violence and Black crime coexisted and shaped Black New Yorkers' articulations and vision of safety beyond the definitions given them by the state. In the late nineteenth and early twentieth centuries, Ida B. Wells's anti-lynching campaign, where she started a social and cultural movement against "lynch law" while advocating armed self-defense, represents one of the most significant expressions of the politics of safety. Of course, Black efforts for safety were not without their contradictions. As historian Kali Gross observes about Black Philadelphians' response to crime among Black women in the late nineteenth century, "Though Black reformers packaged their rhetoric in the language of protection, their actions doubled as an effort to contain" what they considered disreputable behavior. The same was true among Black New Yorkers. Consequently, Blacks' notions of respectability, class, and gender dynamics shaped their efforts to protect their community from harm, defend the race's integrity, and redefine "mainstream notions of Black morality."[33]

In New York City, Black New Yorkers—such as Victoria Earle Matthews and the White Rose Home for Working Class Negro Girls; Grace P. Campbell, who worked as a probation officer and before that for the National League for the Protection of Colored Women; and Samuel Battle, the first Black police officer in the city after the consolidation of the five boroughs in 1898—established a tradition of Black politics around safety in the early twentieth century. Harlem councilman Adam Clayton Powell Jr., the National Association for the Advancement of Colored People, the Communist Party, the Black press, and civic and grassroots organizations across the city forged the politics of safety through their daily confrontations with the city's criminal legal system.[34]

This politics drew upon an array of tactics, including litigation, moral suasion, self-defense, demands for more Black police officers, juvenile justice, and political, social, and economic reform.[35] As the Mayor's Commission's report detailed, anti-Black police violence was an unofficial policy of the NYPD. Throughout the remainder of the 1930s and the 1940s, in spite of the NYPD's claims that the mayor restrained police discretion to use brutal force, the police occupied and brutalized Black neighborhoods, as white New Yorkers, parroting the police, called upon the mayor and Valentine to unshackle aggressive policing. By situating Black resistance within the context of everyday forms of police violence, *The Politics of Safety* highlights how police policies, later formalized as stop and frisk and no-knock laws, have long been part of the NYPD's arsenal of punishment. The NYPD had long criminalized public and private space in Harlem and continued to during the La Guardia era. But white New Yorkers' demands for police protection and safety entrenched and sanctioned what historian Heather Ann Thompson has termed the "criminalization of urban space." Contextualizing policing beyond "riots," police murder, and Black protest to state-sanctioned violence broadens our understanding of the geography of police violence and spotlights the long and violent reach of policing.[36]

The Politics of Safety also centers Black protest against intraracial crime. Black New Yorkers interpreted Jim Crow policing, that is, the inequitable protection, surveillance, and punishment of Black people, as a variant of anti-Black violence.[37] As legal scholar Randall Kennedy has written, "deliberately withholding protection against criminality is one of the most destructive forms of oppression that has been visited upon African Americans."[38] After the Civil War, Blacks served in police departments to "protect African Americans from the endemic white violence and terrorism that characterized the Reconstruction era."[39] Black New Yorkers understood "law and order" as neither limited to calls for punishment nor the presumption that police work naturally entailed crime prevention and crime fighting. Blacks envisioned a form of policing oriented toward the community that prioritized public safety. In contrast, whites leveraged policing to maintain all-white neighborhoods and to contain and punish Blacks. Black New Yorkers perceived crime in their neighborhood as a problem of police racism and neglect as well as a problem of social and economic inequality and neighborhood and familial responsibility. Historian Khalil Muhammad has described this kind of Black criminal justice activism among race relations experts and social scientists as "writing crime into class," noting that "structural inequality . . . became the primary basis for explaining Black criminality."[40] Accordingly, Black New Yorkers' criticisms of La Guardia's failure to release his commission's report and implement its recommendation represented a call for the mayor to advance not only an economic agenda to improve Blacks' housing and employment situation but also a criminal justice agenda to reform police discretion and curtail crime among Black New Yorkers. Thus, as legal scholar James Forman Jr. has argued, they "adopted . . . an all-of-the-above strategy," calling for law enforcement *and* "for jobs, schools, and housing."[41]

And yet Black New Yorkers supported anticrime policies and agencies, including the Juvenile Aid Bureau, an agency attached to the police department; municipal and state regulation of switchblades; harsher sentences for repeat juvenile delinquents; and legislation to penalize negligent parents.[42] At the same time, Blacks distinguished "adequate policing" from police violence. Indeed, in their explicit expressions of "law and order," they supported the enforcement of the law, even as they called for the safety of Blacks while in police custody. Understanding Black New Yorkers' community-oriented articulation of "law and order" helps to historicize "law-and-order politics." This approach historicizes and denaturalizes how law and order has been mainly deployed as an anti-Black political instrument of punishment, and more significantly places it within a longer history of bottom-up responses to crime, responses committed to community safety through investment in housing, schools, hospitals, and employment.[43]

As Blacks called for "law and order," they refused to paint their community as a bastion of crime or worse—to conflate Blackness with criminality. At the same time, Black New Yorkers' class dynamics, as well as efforts to protect their neighborhoods' reputation, shaped their arguments for safety from crime and police violence. These community dynamics were played out in public forums, in Black churches and other forms of Black associational life, within the Black press, and in the city's courtrooms and police precincts. In defense of themselves, Black activists, journalists, and civilians throughout the 1930s and 1940s challenged the white press's racist reportage on crime across the city. Thus, along with movements for political, economic, and social reform and equity, Black political struggles for safety were waged on three fronts: protest and mobilization against police brutality, demands for equitable police protection, and campaigns to deracialize crime by urging the white press to detach race and crime from its crime reportage. Though often in tension, these interrelated struggles in different ways aimed to bring about safety for the Black community.

The Politics of Safety foregrounds Black activism, policing, racial liberalism, and the Harlem uprisings of 1935 and 1943 to place them in the context of widespread anti-Black violence during the La Guardia era. By focusing on Black politics of safety, I shed light on the intertwined relationships between the NYPD, the white press, and white citizens against Black residential patterns and Black crime and raise questions about the roles of white anti-Black violence in the liberal North. White-led movements for punishment and the expansion of the police apparatus, like liberal and conservative law and order policies during the 1960s and thereafter, were as much about white efforts to contain and undermine Black freedom as they were about Black criminal activity. *The Politics of Safety* reveals the complexities of Black politics, moving beyond struggles for better housing, jobs, and education, as well as spotlighting how Black New Yorkers' criminal justice agenda has been driven by a community-oriented ethos of law and order emerging out of their political and economic objectives, the reduction of harm, and the safety of the Black community.

Although civil disorder is not a core component of the book, it does play a critical role in understanding Black politics of safety during the La Guardia era. Throughout the book, I use the terms "riot" and "uprising" interchangeably because debates about "riots" shaped municipal and national politics during the 1930s and 1940s. I consider, however, the term "uprisings" more apt to describe the Harlem uproars in 1935 and 1943, since these occasions of collective violence erupted in a political context and in response to institutionalized patterns of economic discrimination, political negligence, and police violence.[44]

Part I

1 Lawless Policemen

....

"Police! Police!" screamed Mrs. Zerlena Chavis, who lived with her husband in Harlem on 559 Lenox Avenue on July 22, 1928.[1] "Catch that man. He broke into my house and beat me."[2] Clarence Donald and two other Black men had burst into Chavis's home and assaulted her and her husband. As Donald darted out of the building, near 139th Street and Lenox Avenue, Patrolman Charles Kubeil, who heard Chavis's plea, attempted to apprehend Donald, who tried to "wriggle free and shouted for help."[3] Then, Harlemites surrounded officer Kubeil and tried to liberate Donald from the officer's hold. Three other police officers tried to protect Kubeil as well as manage the swelling crowd which grew to more than 2,000 people. By the end of the uproar, reserves arrived from two police stations, and a riot squad with rifles battled with the Black community for about an hour and a half. The *New York Age*, the Black weekly, minimizing the outburst, explained that "the trouble all grew out of the unruly actions of a trio of boisterous rounders, who had been absorbing extra potations of Harlem gin."[4] The *New York Amsterdam News*, another Black weekly, told a different story of how the conflagration began. Officer Herman Destella, who arrived after the commotion, struck a Black woman after she brazenly scolded the police officer: "Shame on you . . . beating that man [Donald] like that for nothing." After Destella hit the woman, her friend "knocked [Destella] out flat," according to witnesses. Because of her courageous protection of Donald, Harlem exploded in defense of her.[5]

As news of the uprising spread across the country, only the white dailies focused singularly on the violence of the Black community. In "2,500 Negroes Fight 150 Harlem Police," the *New York Times* sketched a narrative of the violent negroes and the vulnerable police. As Donald attacked Kubeil, "several negroes standing near by joined the affray. They sent their fists and feet flying at the fallen patrolman," and as other patrolmen arrived to save him, they "too became the target of the attack."[6] The *New York World* condemned the violence of Black Harlem and warned that "the leaders of the Negro race in that great community of colored folk should not allow [the violence] to pass unnoticed."[7] From the viewpoint of the white daily, "There is not the slightest excuse for interfering with officers in the discharge of their duties, in Harlem or anywhere else, and it will not be tolerated." The *New York World* recounted the details of the riot, portraying the New York Police Department (NYPD) and the courts of the city as models of law and order. Accordingly, the editorial notes, "Police Kubeil was acting within the line of duty in arresting Donald for arraignment; nor was there the slightest reason to suppose that Donald would not have this day in court and be fairly tried."[8]

The *New York World*'s curious faith in Kubeil and the courts was out of step with the tales of police violence and pervasive corruption staining the city's criminal justice system.

The *New York World* and Black press's commentary on the street battle between the police and Black Harlem exposed the contrasting interpretations of law and order and Black politics around safety. The white press, white public officials, and white citizens used law-and-order rhetoric to undermine Black New Yorkers' efforts to legitimate their concerns about their safety. In an editorial, "Control the Police," the *New York Amsterdam News* interrogated the white paper's demands on Black leaders. "What does *The World* conceive an officer's duty to be? Is it an officer's duty to club a defenseless man who has his hands up? And when a woman bystander voices her horror at such cruelty, is it an officer's duty to threaten to club her also?" The Black weekly made bare how the white press and the police used police proceduralism, as an element of law and order, to mask anti-Black violence.[9]

Less than a year later, President Herbert Hoover created the National Commission on Law Observance and Enforcement to investigate duplicity in the nation's criminal legal systems. Well before this investigation, however, the city had battled police corruption and violence, especially the abuse of defendants while under interrogation, known as the "third degree."[10] During the Progressive era, public and academic debates on the third degree raised questions about police discretion and the use of force. Under public scrutiny, and sometimes municipal reform, NYPD brass complained about the low morale of the rank and file who warned that banning the third degree would unleash crime or trigger disorder across the city. Forecasting crime and the victimhood of citizens *and* the police, the police's defense of excessive force, buoyed by criminologists and public officials, effectively checked any legitimate campaign to reform the NYPD. By tying police discretion to the maintenance of safety for citizens, the police shifted debate from the necessity of police reform and the suppression of the third degree to crime fighting and protection. The Wickersham Commission, despite drawing attention to New York City's criminal justice system's dogged commitment to the practice of lawlessness, vindicated this line of reasoning in 1931. Indeed, throughout the three terms of the La Guardia administration, this discourse of police victimhood and the fear and threat of a crime wave prevailed over Blacks' complaints of police brutality.[11]

Throughout the 1920s and 1930s, police violence and injustice in the city's criminal justice system constituted a normal feature of the Black experience. This chapter follows Black New Yorkers' experiences in the city's nefarious criminal justice system before Fiorello H. La Guardia's mayoralty. Black activism against police brutality came in the form of protest journalism, ad hoc organizations, and litigation. These mainly liberal avenues of protest laid the groundwork for more progressive critiques of the NYPD and more significantly community-oriented approaches to policing, such as "community policing." As they waged campaigns against the third degree and police brutality in general, Blacks encountered a liberal criminal legal system that stubbornly accommodated some of their demands without bringing about any substantive measure of police accountability. Judges and district attorneys (DAs) upheld the racial status quo and deferred to police authority. Yet despite widespread corruption in Gotham City's courts, African Americans' abiding faith in democracy and refusal to accept anything less propelled them to use the court as a legitimate vehicle for racial redress.[12]

In 1922, the arrest of Luther Boddy, a Black nineteen-year-old who killed two police officers in Harlem, made national news after he divulged upon arrest and in court that he was a repeat victim of the third degree in the Thirty-Eighth Precinct on West 135th Street. Several months after Boddy's arrest and conviction, the police killed Herbert Dent, an eighteen-year-old African American in the same precinct. The police claimed that Dent, while in custody, tried to liberate himself by snatching the gun of the arresting officer. The *New York Age* and its editor, Fred Moore, after unearthing evidence casting doubt on the police department's testimony, demanded an investigation into Dent's death. The Black community's campaign against police violence, namely, the third degree, emerged from its conceptualization of law and order. While condemning criminal behavior, Black leaders argued that the community conferred the police with the power to enforce the law and that punishment belonged to the judiciary—not the police. Although this critique failed to bring about substantive police accountability, it was a searing commentary on excessive force and an articulation of Black advocacy for the safety of the innocent and criminal. After weeks of editorials in the *New York Age* and letters directed to the police officials, District Attorney Joab H. Banton promised to conduct an inquiry regarding the death of Dent, but after months of correspondence, Banton's promise appeared to be a ruse.

Throughout the remainder of the 1920s, the Black press among others led the charge against police brutality and played a pivotal role in exposing police interrogation methods in the aftermath of the uproar in Harlem in July of 1928. Anticipating the Wickersham Commission's condemnation of the unlawful police method yet going beyond its colorblind critique, the *New York Amsterdam News* criticized the third degree and police brutality more broadly, comparing police violence to lynching and white terrorism. Black activism around safety, therefore, was not only oppositional to the city's discourse of law and order but also more progressive than the Wickersham Commission's condemnation of the third degree.

"Figment of the Imaginations of Newspapermen and Magazine Writers"

Throughout the mid- to late 1920s, as a result of widespread corruption in the criminal justice system, the problem of "lawless law enforcement" loomed large across the nation, especially New York City. Because of the growth of the Prohibition state, especially the administration and enforcement of dry laws, police abuse and corruption fomented considerable discussions among public officials, police and lawyer associations, criminologists, and others. These debates interrogating the role of politics and police discretion were a continuation of related concerns raised decades before, especially during the Progressive era. Inspired by Rev. Dr. Charles H. Pankhurst's condemnation of the spread of vice in midtown Manhattan and the New York police force's complicity in it in 1892, the New York State Senate created the Lexow Committee, named after state senator Clarence Lexow in 1894. The Lexow Committee emerged, in part, because of the expansion of the Republican Party's power and the decline of the Democratic Party's electoral gains after the 1893 depression. With the support of the Republican-controlled state legislature and the city's Chamber of Commerce, Pankhurst's campaign against Tammany Hall, the city's powerful Democrat-controlled political machine, exposed the depths of police corruption, though it had minimal impact on police reform. The political organization, Society of St. Tammany, was founded in 1786 and incorporated in 1789. Tammany Hall was a decentralized political organization, operated by ward captains, and its ties to graft and collusion extended through government, business, and culture. In the late nineteenth and early twentieth centuries, Tammany's power, like other political machines, was vested in the millions of European immigrants coming into the city seeking employment, social welfare, and economic security, and the machine effectively fulfilled these needs.[13]

The NYPD's power developed from its relationship with the political machine. The city's police force not only protected the machine's voters and repressed its adversaries during elections but also licensed and often facilitated the criminal activity of Tammany's associates across the city's institutional life. As urban historian Robert Fogel has described them, "big-city police" departments "operated mainly as adjuncts of the ward organizations." Because police power was decentralized, dependent mainly on the captain and ward boss, the patrolman on the beat had considerable autonomy. With the license to use force to subdue a would-be perpetrator, the police had the authority to define crime and, therefore, determine whom to detain, arrest, and criminalize. Within the confines of the machine, as Fogel notes, "the police decided whether or not to permit agitators to speak, protestors to march, and laborers to picket, and if so, judged whether or not the protests remained orderly. They also determined whether or not to intervene in racial, ethnic, and religious clashes, and if so, at what point, on whose side, with how many men, and with how much force." Consequently, autonomous police discretion was principally the authority to criminalize and punish according to the officers' personal, political, religious, ethnic, gender, and racial biases. Policing and police, therefore, were embedded in the city's racial order. Racial difference as much as law and order dictated how the police enforced the law.[14]

On August 12, 1900, Robert Thorpe, a plainclothes policeman, manhandled May Enoch, a Black woman, on Forty-First Street and Eighth Avenue. Acting on the premise that a Black woman on the street at that time of the night was a sex worker, Thorpe attempted to arrest her as Arthur Harris, her common-law husband, jumped to restrain Thorpe. In the physical exchange, Harris fatally stabbed him, precipitating the New York Race Riot of 1900 three days later. White mobs attacked Black pedestrians and the Black neighborhood, mainly between Thirty-Fourth and Forty-Second Streets on Broadway and Seventh and Eighth Avenues. But white civilians were not alone. This episode of white anti-Black violence was also a police riot. As Frank Moss, attorney and compiler of the pamphlet *The Story of the Riot*, stated, "In many instances of brutality by the mob policemen stood by and made no effort to protect the Negroes who were assailed. They ran with the crowds in pursuit of their prey; they took defenseless men who ran to them for protection and threw them to the rioters."[15]

During the four-hour riot, the police's appetite for revenge spared not men, women, or children. A police officer told Rosa Lewis, her husband, and other tenants to go into their apartment building, 332 West Thirty-Seventh Street. She explained that all followed his order, but as she reached the foot of the staircase, "the officer, who had rushed into the hallway, struck me over the back with his club." Irene Wells, 239 West Twenty-Ninth Street, was treated similarly by an officer who struck her across her right hip, as she tried to take her three children into the apartment building. The police also beat Blacks in their custody. At about two in the morning, six policemen charged into John Hains's apartment and accused him of shooting a gun from the window. He stated, "They found an old toy revolver, which was broken and not loaded, and could not shoot if it had been loaded, and said that that was the pistol I had used." Arrested, Hains was "struck by one of the officers in the station house in front of the sergeant's desk, and in his presence, without any interference on his part." The same police officer who beat him charged Hains before the judge, and Hains pleaded innocent. The judge sentenced him to spend six months in the penitentiary, and he was sent to Blackwell's Island (Roosevelt Island) and released ten days later on August 25.[16]

After appealing to and unsuccessfully receiving any support from public officials, the Black community formed the Citizens Protection League (CPL) and pursued justice in the courts where none was found. Black citizens obtained lawyers, and Black leaders such as W. H. Brooks requested Mayor Robert A. Van Wyck to investigate the riot. The mayor stalled until the acting mayor asked the police board to investigate the role of the police force in the melee. Like Van Wyck, the commissioners "delayed, knowing full well how such cases deteriorate by delay, and after several weeks announced that they would investigate." Moss, the CPL's attorney, judged that the "'investigation' was a palpable sham."[17] Despite the outcome, the police board, the courts, and the mayor all eventually fulfilled the official and legal procedures required of them. The city's criminal legal system worked—just not for its Black citizens. Black New Yorkers, customarily overpoliced and underprotected, understood and pointed out the variance between the responsibilities of the police and their behavior. As the 1900 race riot demonstrated, police power was entangled in the city's criminal legal system. Political corruption and anti-Black violence worked hand-in-hand. Gotham's criminal legal system protected the discretion of police to use lethal force to repress Black citizens at all levels of law enforcement. With the authority to define crime and with the support of public officials, police officers on the beat administered racial violence on Black New Yorkers without recourse. Although Gotham City tolerated anti-Black police violence, police discretion to use excessive force did not go unchallenged.

During the late nineteenth and early twentieth centuries, journalists and criminologists labeled police abuse of prisoners while under custody the "third degree."[18] The third degree comprised the variety of methods law enforcement used to compel defendants to confess to a crime or provide information about the commission of crime. According to city lore, the late nineteenth century was the heyday of the third degree, and its most celebrated practitioner, Thomas Byrnes, was the legendary chief of the city's Detective Bureau. Born in Ireland in 1842 and joining the police force in 1863, for years Byrnes had been insulated from criticism because of his respected detective work and in part because of his relationship with journalists, who helped create his reputation as a model of modern law enforcement.[19] In 1893, in an editorial titled "He Rules through Fear," the *New York Times* described Byrnes as a "power for good."[20] A staunch defender of the third degree, Byrnes continued to praise its effectiveness even after he retired. In October 1908, he described the third degree as "any method by which you can reach a man's mind through his imagination. Each case that comes before the chief of the detective bureau requires treatment different from any other." For Byrnes, the third degree was just another tool for the police to guide criminals in a journey of self-discovery of their own guilt. This view would not go unchallenged, however.[21]

Across the nation, public condemnation of the third degree precipitated a counterattack by criminal justice officials. Criticism of the third degree sullied the legitimacy of the police and undermined their authority and, therefore, threatened police discretion. To defend the police's image, in 1910 the International Association of Chiefs of Police (IACP) denied the existence of the third degree, projected the blame upon detectives, and claimed that the practice was anachronistic. At its 1910 convention, the IACP adopted a resolution protesting, "There has been recent unjust criticism of the police in the United States in a revival of the oft-repeated allegation that there prevails a practice of maltreating prisoners for the purpose of securing admission of guilt."[22] Beyond defending their image, the police chiefs endeavored to protect the autonomous police discretion of the cop on the beat.[23] In New York City, the tale of Stephen Boehm, a white young man convicted of second-degree murder, attracted public scrutiny to the abuses of the NYPD in the spring of 1910. On the stand, Boehm explained that the confession "was wrung from him after rough handling and short rations." The judge charged, "If what you told your lawyer took place there is no language I could use which would be strong enough to express my abhorrence and condemnation of it."[24] The *New York Times* interviewed Police Commissioner William F. Baker about the ethics of using the third degree. Baker claimed that its use required "absolutely no punishment, physically or mentally" but admitted that the "ignorant person" necessitated greater physical persuasion. He asserted, "The brutish-minded person can be affected only by brutish treatment."[25] But despite some public outcry, as well as the varied views of magistrates, the NYPD, no different from other police departments across the nation, effectively defended the use of the third degree as an essential weapon of fighting crime.[26]

After complaints of police abuse, Mayor William Jay Gaynor, a former State of New York Supreme Court justice, began reforming the police department in 1909.[27] The mayor placed the deputy commissioner directly under his guidance, reprimanded police officers' overuse of clubbing prisoners, and ordered the eventual removal of nightsticks. In spring 1911, Gaynor's reforms triggered a crime crisis and incited complaints from a swath of the law enforcement community. On March 22, Magistrate Joseph E. Corrigan sent a letter to the metropolitan dailies contending that the city was in the midst of a "crime wave" since the mayor had removed the nightsticks and that the police officers were "demoralized and terrified." He protested "the great alarming increase of crime and of the still more alarming decrease in its detection and punishment." According to the magistrate, "The men feel that they and not the criminals are hunted, that (as many have told me) 'if a man can keep out of trouble he is doing well,' and that the only safe and sure way to do this is to 'look the other way' when a crime is being committed."[28] Corrigan noted that the patrolmen felt like the weight of an entire criminal justice system had turned on them—from the police chief to the mayor—to protect criminals. The safety of the beat cop, therefore, was threatened by not only the criminal but also the police department and the mayor. He continued, "It is to this condition of the force that all the other evils must be attributed. When a policeman feels that he has not the support of the dominant authority, that the word of any convicted crook will be taken in preference to his, and that he must submit to a beating at the hands of the criminal or a complaint under the Mayor's orders, it is idle to hope that he will even attempt to do police duty."[29] The next day, Chief Magistrate William McAdoo held a meeting with other magistrates at 300 Mulberry Street, once the headquarters of the NYPD, and the building most associated with Thomas Byrnes. All but four of the magistrates signed a letter that "earnestly disapproved" of Corrigan's censoring of "the executive branches of the city government" and agreed with the mayor that Corrigan's comments "make the police force insubordinate or indifferent to their duty."[30] The letter affirmed the judiciaries' commitment to "harmony" with Gaynor, though it avoided any direct criticism or correction of Corrigan's sentiments.[31]

Thereafter, Governor John Alden Dix vetoed the Grady bill, which was brought to the New York State Assembly by Senator Thomas F. Grady, the Democratic minority leader, and passed in mid-June. The anti-mugging bill prohibited the police from photographing suspects of crime until they were convicted. To photograph, measure, and question prisoners before a conviction, police would have to get the consent of a magistrate. More critical to the question of police discretion, it charged with oppression any officer who engaged in excessive force either to detain a person or to obtain information from a person while under custody. If convicted, the officer could be sentenced from six months to a year in prison. Although it ostensibly centered on "mugshots," the bill challenged police discretion at the point of arrest and endeavored to punish the police for the third degree. The governor met with a group of police commissioners across the state, including Deputy Commissioner George S. Dougherty of Manhattan, Frank J. Cassada of Elmira, James W. Renx of Schenectady, Michael Regan of Buffalo, and James L. Hyatt of Albany. They complained that if the bill became law, it would "greatly handicap them in the matter of securing evidence."[32] The governor vetoed the bill to protect police discretion and tied citizens' safety to the authority of the police to the use of force. Dix asserted, "It is the first duty of the State to protect from criminals the lives and property of citizens . . . [and the bill] subjects officers to unnecessary and groundless accusations in case of alleged violence or persecution."[33] This reasoning against taming police discretion generated a narrative that continues to this day, that is, that to reform the police is to threaten their own and citizens' safety. The governor's advocacy of protection "for the lives and property of citizens" operated as a cover to thwart police reform. Safe police equaled safe citizens. This logic solidified a police ideology, a tale that police use of coercive force was a prerequisite for crime prevention and crime fighting. Dix's veto was supported not only by the city's and the state's law enforcement but also by James W. Garner, political scientist and editor-in-chief of the *Journal of the American Institute of Criminal Law and Criminology*, who noted, "In our judgement, the abuses of the so-called 'third degree' practice have been greatly exaggerated."[34] The debate about the lawlessness of the third degree among criminologists, journalists, and criminal justice officials continued into the twenties and thirties. But even as time changed and the third degree came under national scrutiny, the narrative persisted that the restraint of police discretion to use coercive force invited "crime waves" and lowered the morale of the rank-and-file of the NYPD.[35]

The protection of police discretion and especially the refashioning of the third degree as an innocuous tactic that prevented crime set the tone of public debate on police use of force during the Prohibition era. In Grover Whalen's first week as the city's new police commissioner in December 1928, his anti-crime drive against speakeasies, especially the edict to his police officers that "they will find a great deal of law in the end of a nightstick," brought the issue of the third degree to center stage of public opinion and the city's politics. Whalen promised to rid the city of criminals by targeting bootleg bars and vice dens.[36] While some welcomed the police commissioner's commitment to and verve for crime fighting, especially those within the business community, many others were critical of his open policy of police aggression. At a tribute to the new police commissioner on January 22, 1929, Gilbert Hodges, the president of the Advertising Club, introduced Whalen with a police badge on his coat and a nightstick for a gavel. Whalen wanted to send the threat of violence to the criminals, because they were, he stated, "cowards at heart." But once Whalen's police force began raiding places without warrants and directing that aggression toward workers, the American Civil Liberties Union (ACLU), noting the difference between criminal activity and workers' rights, protested the mistreatment of garment workers while on strike in March.[37]

Arthur Garfield Hays and Morris Hillquit first sent a letter of protest to Whalen on February 23 and then sent another to the city's Bar Association, requesting that Whalen's "lawless tactics" be "publicly condemned." Staking its claims on the primacy of the nation's constitutional rights, the letter claimed that Whalen and the NYPD were engaged in blatant lawless misconduct. The letter to Whalen prudently made it clear that Hays and Hillquit supported his efforts to enforce Prohibition laws, naming explicitly the "gangsters and speakeasies," but protested the commissioner's means to that end. The letter especially pointed out Whalen's flagrant claim that he would "deal with 'crooks and gangsters on the assumption that they have no constitutional rights.'" The complaint specified Whalen's sanctioning of violent assaults on alleged criminals. Though the well-publicized raids and arrests brought praise from the press, they often resulted in a pattern of false arrests evidenced by magistrates discharging defendants after the arrests. The letter also criticized the police commissioner's assertion that a man with a criminal record was "public property." Once a convict had served his time, he had paid his penalty, they asserted. While it was directed to Whalen and the NYPD, the letter aimed to address issues beyond New York City and the treatment of alleged criminals. The letter made this explicit to Whalen, stating, "Your position in so far as it is in denial of those rights is of vital importance not only locally but nationally, because the principles announced by the head of the New York City Police Department are usually observed by that department as well as imitated elsewhere in the country." Building on the national reach and influence of the NYPD, the letter also asserted that the ease with which a community accepts the unlawful, and unconstitutional, punishment of criminals might be turned toward "any group with which the police find it difficult to deal lawfully." The letter stated, unequivocally, "Our experience all over the country shows that it is only too easy to apply similar lawless methods against strikers and radicals, against negroes and aliens—indeed, in the case of any against whom prejudice can be aroused."[38]

In March, Hays and the American Civil Liberties Union (ACLU) continued with their campaign against Whalen's police-sanctioned lawlessness. Speaking at a meeting of the Young Israel of Brooklyn, a synagogue, on March 11, Hays stated that "there is a movement on foot by the Whalen crowd to get permission to arrest the 'potential criminal.'" Hays's condemnation of Whalen's tactics was concerned not only with the innocent. Even those with a criminal record, he averred, should receive support, should be given a chance. The next day, the ACLU sent Whalen another letter, signed by Hays, Dorothy Kenyon, Morris L. Ernst, and Walter Frank, objecting to the more than 1,200 arrests of garment workers on strike over the last four weeks. The letter asserted that the police had no legal reasons to make the arrests and that the police's arrests were premised on the presumption of guilt. When asked for a response about Hays's letter by journalists, Whalen suggested that his public expressions and the NYPD's emphasis on employing the nightstick were mainly symbolic. The stick-up man and thug feared the "aggressive type of policeman." According to Whalen, police abuse did not happen. The third degree was a "figment of the imaginations of newspapermen and magazine writers."[39]

By the time the report *Lawlessness in Law Enforcement* of the Wickersham Commission had circulated across the nation in August 1931, the NYPD's pattern of "lawless law enforcement" had already been a tradition—celebrated, condemned, and tolerated. The investigation reported that the practice of police violence, particularly the phenomenon known as the third degree, was practiced nationwide. Notably, the *New York Times*, among other white dailies covering the results of the Wickersham investigation, pointed out that "the report singled out New York City for the most attention, as one of the worst spots where brutal methods have been used relentlessly . . . with almost the expressed sanction of the highest city authorities."[40] While previous discussions of the third degree derived from news headlines by police reporters, the evidence on New York City in the report came from interviews with former public officials and the research of the city's prominent legal organizations, such as the New York County Lawyers Association, the Association of the Bar of the City of New York, and the Voluntary Defenders Committee of the Legal Aid Society.[41]

A section of the commission's report was devoted to describing the practices of the third degree in different cities. The section on New York City claimed that the third degree was widespread. The Wickersham Commission described Gotham's criminal justice system as thoroughly corrupt. "The investigators were repeatedly told . . . that the courts know that some of the prosecutors are crooked and the prosecutors know that some of the courts are crooked and both know that some of the police are crooked, and the police are equally well informed as to them," explained the commission. The commission reported that the city's mayors and police commissioners, naming specifically Mayor James J. Walker, former police commissioner George V. McLaughlin, and then-current police commissioner Whalen, had sanctioned the infamous interrogation method. The city's head officials, the commission noted, supported this behavior in order to shore up the morale of the police force. Revisiting the complaints directed at previous attempts to blunt police discretion, the commission wrote, "The New York police are said to be influenced by what they say happened during the administration of Mayor Gaynor, about 20 years ago." Gaynor "issued strict orders against the avoidable use of clubs in arrests. The result, it was said, was a substantial impairment of the zeal and efficiency of patrolmen." The report continued, "Many responsible persons . . . expressed the fear that a let-up of harsh police methods to-day might result in an increase of criminal activity," as it had twenty years before.[42]

While the commission acknowledged the reasoning behind these claims, it asserted, nonetheless, "This argument does not point to any need for the third degree, but only to caution against restricting the police too severely in using force if they deem it necessary to effect an arrest." Despite some support for the third degree, many public officials now believed that it abridged the constitutional rights of the citizens, harming defendants physically and psychologically, and ultimately sullied not only the reputation of the police force but also the city's criminal justice system. Yet by narrowly prioritizing the harm of the third degree, taking for granted that the police employed force against the unlawful, the Wickersham Commission wittingly or not vindicated the New York Police Department's discourse to use excessive force at the point of arrest. The commission, using color-blind language in its conceptualization of police misconduct, ignored its own evidence that the police used the third degree and arrests as acts of racial subordination and repression. This kind of criminal justice reform would not bode well for African Americans. As the ACLU's letter to Whalen emphasized two years before, "It is only too easy to apply similar lawless methods against strikers and radicals, against negroes and aliens."[43]

"So Tired of Being Beaten Up All the Time"

Black New Yorkers were especially attentive to these discussions and had long shone a light on this form of police violence. In 1922, the arrest and imprisonment of Luther Boddy, a nineteen-year-old who fatally shot two police officers in Harlem, turned national attention toward the NYPD and the excesses of the third degree. On January 5, Detective Sergeants William A. Miller and Francis J. Buckley accosted Boddy about the shooting of a Black police officer, Jasper Rhodes. Boddy told them that he had no information about Rhodes, and they detained him and led him to the police station. A few blocks from the station, near 222 West 135th Street, Boddy fatally shot Miller and Buckley, and escaped first to Montclair, New Jersey, to see his mother and then to Philadelphia. On his way to Philadelphia, Boddy disguised himself in a woman's wig and dress during his taxicab ride from Newark to evade the NYPD's dragnet but also to hide a large, identifiable scar on his face, from his right ear to his lip. Once in the City of Brotherly Love, he hid in the home of his mother's friend, Mrs. Martha Hopkins. On the ninth, John Coleman, a lodger in Hopkins's home, notified Rev. Charles A. Tindley, pastor of the Calvary AME Church, who contacted Amos M. Scott, Philadelphia's first Black magistrate, and he called the police station. Accompanied by the police, Scott entered the home, and they found him in bed.[44]

The grand jury charged Boddy with murder in the first degree, and on January 23 the trial was held before Judge Isidor Wasservogel of the Supreme Court of the State of New York. On the thirtieth, the jury convicted Boddy of first-degree murder for killing Buckley and sentenced him to die in the electric chair the week of March 13. Upon arrest, Boddy admitted that he shot the officers because he feared being beaten at the Thirty-Eighth Precinct police station. He stated, "Of course in New York City what they mean by taking you over to the station house is, they take you over and kick you around for two or three hours. I had had that done to me several times."[45] At the trial, his attorney asked him about his first experiences with the police. Boddy recalled a pair of plainclothes men breaking into his room and shepherding him to the police station and recounted the multiple times he had been taken to the station, beaten, and discharged without arrest or coming before a magistrate.[46] After his conviction, now at the Court of Appeals of the State of New York in early February, Boddy once again testified to the frequency of arrests, beatings, and unlawful actions he endured at the hands of the police at the Thirty-Eighth Precinct. In one case, he remembered being taken into a locker room, where he was "punched a few times" and then placed in the center of seven or more police officers. Describing the interrogation, after the initial pummeling, he was seated in a chair, and "there was an officer on each side of me, one in front and one in the rear, and they had about a foot of rubber hose nailed onto a piece of broom stick, and I was beaten over the head with that." Police infamously used the rubber hose because it did not break the skin, and therefore it was deniable in court. He said the police "struck [me] in the head with a blackjack, and my scalp was opened up for about half an inch." Asked how long he endured this, he stated, "Well, it seemed like all day to me, but it really was only half an hour." His attorney asked him if he had been taken to a judge, and he stated he had not and was simply released. According to Boddy, the police rarely followed police procedure, so the police neglected to bring him before a judge and sometimes, before they released him, they often beat him again.[47]

As Black and white reformers, journalists, and civil rights activists condemned Boddy's crime, they also denounced the New York Police Department for its excessive abuse of Boddy. As the *Chicago Defender* made clear, "The death of the police officers, unfortunate as it was, had, however, brought forcibly to attention the growing practice of New York policemen and detectives of unmercifully beating people placed under arrest, or taken into the station for 'questioning.'"[48] Even protest organizations that were in fervid disagreement were in accord about the brutality of the NYPD. Marcus Garvey's *The Negro World* and the NAACP's *The Crisis* lambasted the NYPD. The *Negro World* printed an editorial where an author who undersigned as "New York American" charged that Boddy killed the two detectives because he was "SO TIRED OF BEING BEATEN UP ALL THE

TIME."[49] William Edward Burghardt Du Bois, in the March issue of *The Crisis*, indicted society for "laugh[ing] at him, insult[ing] him, hat[ing] him" and criticized the police and characterized the case "as one of the greatest outrages of our present police system."[50] Despite widespread outcries among Harlemites, as well as a consensus among Harlem's Black political leadership about the unlawfulness of the third degree, the State of New York electrocuted Luther Boddy around eleven o'clock in the late evening on August 31 at Sing Sing Prison.[51]

On June 27, as Boddy awaited the electric chair, another Black youth, Herbert Dent, eighteen years old, fell victim to the brutalization of police while under custody at the infamous Thirty-Eighth Precinct. Some of the dailies reported he died from the beating in the police station, others that he died at Harlem Hospital. Assistant District Attorney John R. Hennis conducted a preliminary investigation and exonerated the police officers, who explained that Dent tried to grab the gun from the holster of Wesley C. Redding, a Black detective. According to Hennis, detectives Edwin C. McGrath and Stanley F. Gorman, both white, struggled to control Dent, who "tried to shoot [Redding]. . . . They had been unable to get the weapon away from the prisoner until he was subdued."[52] The *New York Times* and other dailies recounted a suspicious tale of Dent's association with Boddy's gang of hold-up men. According to the police, Frank Foselli, a rent collector and victim of a robbery by "three negroes," pointed out Dent, known in the streets as "Tin Can," and two others to Patrolman Patrick McHugh of the Thirty-Eighth Precinct. On April 7, McHugh attempted to arrest the men and was shot in the left side of his head, making him the fifth police officer "shot by negroes" since September. The *Evening News* claimed that Dent was the shooter and that the court indicted him for assault and robbery. On the evening of June 27, a Black man divulged to Redding that Dent was at a saloon at Fifth Avenue and 132nd Street. After the arrest, Redding took Dent to the police station, fingerprinted him, and commanded him to sit down. As the detective took off his coat, Dent caught a glimpse of his exposed gun, which was "sticking out of its holster on his right hip." As Redding sat "at Dent's right the negro stepped back quickly, reached behind Redding's back, grasped the pistol butt and gave it such a jerk that it broke the strap and came out in his hand." Thereafter, they engaged in a whirlwind of a scuffle, and "rolled over and over on the floor in a desperate fight for the pistol, which the detective could not wrest from the prisoner's hand." Redding finally yelled for help, and detectives McGrath and Gorman arrived to rescue him.[53]

The *New York Age* questioned the police's justification for killing Dent, as well as demanded an investigation of the case. From July to December, Fred R. Moore, the weekly's editor, used the newspaper to wage a campaign against the third degree and for justice for Herbert Dent. On July 1, the weekly inquired, "Are the Police Unnecessarily Brutal in Treatment of Prisoners at the West 135th Street Station?" The *New York Age* briefly recounted some of the same details of case, but it also revealed the community members' views of the Thirty-Eighth Precinct. According to Harlemites, "In the immediate neighborhood of the station house," it was "a common happening for them to be aroused and disturbed by sounds of severe beatings administered to prisoners at this station. And it is alleged that these beatings are administered not only to male prisoners but that women are handled in the same manner." That morning, a Black woman called the precinct at around three to complain about being awakened by "sounds of blows and by moans and groans of the victim." The police told her that the noise would stop, but the pounding and clamor did not, so she called again.[54] The Black weekly also questioned Dent's ties to Boddy, particularly the dailies' references to other cases of Blacks harming police officers. The *New York Age* recommended that local authorities or the State of New York investigate the case, so that it could distinguish "the police officers who do not pursue these brutal tactics, and cause them to stand clear in the eyes of the public from the group of men . . . whose brutal and ruthless methods have made their names synonymous with unnecessary cruelty."[55]

Throughout the remainder of the month, the *New York Age* continuously demanded that police officials investigate the Dent case. The editorials focused on two related issues. First, they pointed to the Dent case as an outrageous example of excessive force and brought up the incredulity of the detectives' justification for killing Dent. The Black weekly interrogated the feasibility of Dent unfastening Redding's gun, because "the holsters . . . are supposed to be fitted with safety catches that prevent the removal of the gun until that catch has been released," and asked, "How then, . . . , could Dent have gotten Detective Redding's gun from the holster before the officer knew anything about it?"[56] By mid-July, "An officer . . . ha[d] informed THE AGE that the safety catch on the holster prevented the prisoner from getting the gun."[57] The *New York Age* also argued that the violence was excessive and that it was unreasonable to believe that Dent required more than a pair of armed police officers to subdue him. It reproduced three photographs of Dent's head with arrows pointing to wounds on his forehead, throat, and left eye. The *New York Age* described the police behavior as "savage," "brutal," and unjustified and revealed that other stories of police violence had begun to come to light.

Second, the Black community framed its activism for Dent and criticisms of the Thirty-Eighth Precinct through its own conception of law and order. The Black weekly pronounced police violence as an "epidemic," highlighting multiple occasions of brutal behavior throughout the city, including among white police officers and white citizens.[58] Among Black Harlemites especially, the *New York Age* admitted, "It is the subject of rumor that other bodies have been taken from the precinct building under circumstances which savored of secrecy and gave rise to suspicion that police brutality had claimed other victims to which no publicity was given."[59]

Beyond its reportage of Harlemites' fear and distrust of the Thirty-Eighth Precinct, the *New York Age* interviewed Harlem's leadership that vehemently condemned police brutality. The district's businessmen were "a notable exception," for while "most of them have unqualifiedly denounced the cruel and brutal methods of the police," they were afraid that those same methods might be used on them. Harlem ministers remembered a time of favorable relations between the police and the Black community. "Police conditions," they asserted, "in New York were never better than under the Gaynor regime." Gaynor was the same mayor who threatened police discretion to administer the third degree. A decade later, though, Harlemites confronted similar conditions yet bereft of a mayor willing to reform the police department. The ministers' defense of Dent stressed the importance of New Yorkers' adhering to the rule of law, especially the police. Rev. J. W. Brown, the pastor of Mother African Methodist Episcopal Zion Church, believed that the photographs of Dent should anger the humanity of anyone, regardless of their race, creed, or color. Brown's criticisms of police violence stemmed from his ideas of law and order. As he noted, "the law of the land has made provisions for the dealing with criminals and the protection of life and property of its citizens and the observance of law and order." For Brown, this meant that justice "should be meted out to [criminals] throughout the courts and not at the hands of heartless murderers."[60]

Walker Memorial Baptist Church's Rev. J. D. Bushnell, president of the Baptist Ministers Conference, held similar views and defined policing from the perspective of public safety. Police aggression weakened trust between citizens, and rather than reduce crime, it inspired not only fear but also self-protection as an act of self-preservation. From Bushnell's purview, "First of all, it should be understood that the department of the police exists for law and order. And that an officer of the law is sworn to perform his duty even at the peril of his own life. But the officer of the law should not be allowed by the department to brutally handle his prisoners. The citizens appoint these officers, and both officer and citizen should be agreed as to the preservation of the best law and order that a community can afford."[61] Bushnell avowed that public safety was foundational to policing and that law and order, in part, constituted a pact between "officer and citizen." This community-centered framing of policing and law and order reflected political and scholarly criticisms of the third degree that asserted that public distrust of police threatened law and order.[62] But Black Harlem's ideas of law and order also derived from their own daily encounters with police misconduct and violence. At various moments since the turn of the century, especially in 1900, 1905, 1909, 1911, and 1914, Black New Yorkers in the Tenderloin and the San Juan Hill districts and later Harlem had argued that safety constituted a critical aspect of their civil and community rights, and that if police refused to protect them, they were not unwilling to arm themselves for self-protection. During and after the Great War, white mob violence and police repression were widespread across the nation, especially during the "Red Summer" of 1919 and in Tulsa, Oklahoma, in 1921. In Harlem, New Negro activists such as Hubert Harrison, W. A. Domingo, and others used these tragedies to connect Blacks' clashes with the NYPD with Blacks' confrontations with white terrorism and police violence around the country.[63] At a pivotal moment of racial consciousness, Harlemites, including the community's liberal ministers, remembered these violent clashes with law enforcement. Captain Ward of the Thirty-Eighth Precinct in September of 1918 had requested the support of Harlem's Black leadership to mitigate street speakers' protests against police violence and advocacy of self-defense.[64] Recalling that meeting four years before, Reverend Brown asserted, "Such a course was helpful, not only to the peaceful citizens, but it proved to be a better way in dealing with the criminal."[65] For the safety of the public, including law enforcement, the innocent, and the criminal, Harlemites argued that it was the responsibility of the police to perform its duty in the service of and in concordance with citizens who conferred them with the authority to enforce the law. This way, the innocent and the criminal might trust and feel safe from unlawful police.

After the *New York Age*'s monthlong campaign for an investigation into the killing of Dent, the district attorney Joab H. Banton promised to conduct an inquiry. On June 28, I. E. Dent, Herbert's brother, wrote a letter to Police Commissioner Richard Enright requesting an investigation, and three days later, C. G. Young, Enright's secretary, sent Dent a letter acknowledging the commissioner's receipt of the letter.[66] Then, Fred R. Moore on July 20 wrote individualized letters to District Attorney Banton and John A. Leach, the acting police commissioner, calling for those responsible for Dent's death to be "properly dealt with." Moore also sent a letter to James Weldon Johnson of the National Association for the Advancement of Colored People requesting the organization's advice.[67] The next day, DA Banton declared that he would "gladly make any investigation into the death of Herbert Dent" and had already written Dent's brother and explained that he would do so. Banton then summarized the police officers' testimonies and emphasized that Dent's injuries were the result of "not only resisting arrest" but also "assaulting a police officer." Banton asked Moore for witnesses and invited him to share any evidence with his office. On July 26, Moore, I. E. Dent, and the Black woman who called the precinct to complain about the noise and screams met at the DA's office. As he listened to their testimonies, Banton "expressed strong opposition to brutal methods" and admitted that the third degree made it difficult for him to prosecute criminals. With the DA's office's pledge to inquire into the death of Dent, the *New York Age* hoped that there would be justice for Herbert Dent and the Black community. According to the Black weekly, it was "considered to be a vital necessity that unnecessary and uncalled for brutality and cruelty in the treatment of men and women under arrest, without regard to race, nationality or color, should be entirely eliminated from police methods."[68]

During the investigation, the Dent family retained attorney Herman Hoffman, who served on Boddy's defense team. In spite of his initial agreement to investigate the Dent case, DA Banton neglected to respond to several requests from Moore and Hoffman for a meeting. Hoffman sent a letter dated August 29 to Banton, informing the DA that he would be representing the Dent family. He also proffered his cooperation and requested a transcript of the DA's inquiry. In mid-September, Hoffman once again wrote another letter to Banton insisting that Banton take action.[69] By the end of the month, Banton blamed Hoffman for neglecting to deliver any witnesses to Assistant District Attorney Hennis. In his letter to Hoffman, Banton wrote that Assistant DA Hennis was ready to interview the witnesses but that "nearly two weeks have elapsed and I have not heard from you [Hoffman]." The next day, Hoffman replied and stated that Danton was mistaken, and recounted the multiple times he contacted the DA's office and requested the findings of their investigation. On the matter of the witnesses,

Hoffman refused to provide their names to Hennis and noted that they would only appear in public settings, such as in a hearing, in an open court, or before the grand jury. He stated, "It will serve no useful purpose to have these witnesses exposed to the danger of intimidation by the police in advance of such hearing."[70]

After several months of back and forth between Hoffman and District Attorney Banton, including letters from Hoffman revealing that he had a witness to the beating of Dent, Banton decided not to pursue the case against the NYPD. In early November, the *New York Age* still asked, "Will Joab H. Banton, District Attorney of New York County, keep his promise to conduct an impartial and searching investigation into the death of Herbert Dent . . . ?" By this point, the Black weekly had disclosed that Dent neither had a criminal record nor had been indicted for assault and robbery, as the dailies reported. The *New York Age* also reported that the DA's office was reluctant to hold a meeting with newspaper representatives present and asserted that the DA's office had not anticipated that Hoffman would actually find a witness to the ordeal.[71]

F. Buckley witnessed the detectives' cudgeling of Dent. Buckley and Mr. Flynn, both white Secret Service officers, were in Harlem to visit one of the detectives in the Thirty-Eighth Precinct. At the hearing with Assistant DA Hennis, Buckley recounted his night out with Flynn and detectives McGrath, Gorman, and Shields and explained that they went to "several cafes [and they] returned to the station house about 3 A.M." According to Buckley, intoxicated detectives McGrath and Flynn relentlessly beat Dent with a blackjack. Buckley stated, "Flynn broke his blackjack and then picked up the night stick . . . , struck the man across the side of the head—and then everything was in silence for a moment." The detectives desperately used alcohol to wake Dent out of his stupor. Buckley lamented, "McGrath put his hand under the colored man's shirt. . . . I was crying and McGrath suggested that he give me a drink to straighten me out. They then took the bottle and tried to force some whiskey down the colored man's throat by holding his jaws open." Once they realized that "they could not bring him to," they called an ambulance, and McGrath told Flynn and Buckley to leave. As they departed and the ambulance arrived, Buckley heard his colleague state, "Well, that's one nigger less." Along with his testimony of police ineptitude and violence, Buckley's account made no mention of the presence of Redding. He did mention a uniformed Black patrolman, but Redding was a plainclothes detective. Apparently, the NYPD tried to use Redding's shared race with Dent to stymie any claims of racial discrimination. After the hearing, Hoffman promised to seek redress with the governor if the DA failed to conduct the investigation.[72]

In his letter to Hoffman on December 18, Banton stated that Hennis's investigation found that Dent's death was "not a case of homicide." Banton declared, "After a very careful postmortem examination of the deceased," Dr. Charles Norris, chief medical examiner, concluded that Dent's death "was due entirely to acute alcoholism."[73] After conferring with Norris a month later, Hoffman wrote Banton about the autopsy report's conclusions and explained that Norris admitted that his report "cannot and should not be construed to mean that the death of Herbert Dent was due 'entirely to acute alcoholism' and that he would be obliged to qualify his opinion in that regard."[74] In consideration of this new information, Hoffman requested that DA Banton submit the report to a grand jury or that Hoffman himself bring the case to the Homicide Court. The trail of the New York Age's advocacy for Dent and the campaign against the third degree campaign ended in late January. In spite of his promise to conduct a thorough investigation, Banton disregarded Buckley's testimony, as well as Harlemites' complaints about the brutality of the Thirty-Eighth Precinct. Over the course of time, his promise mitigated the Black community's attention to Dent's death. The dailies in late June and early July had already reported Norris's findings from the report of the autopsy. As the New York Times reported on June 28, Norris stated, "He smelled intensely of alcohol. . . . There was nothing the matter with the brain, no fracture of the skull, and no hemorrhage. If he had not been drinking the beating would not have caused death."[75] Regular readers of the white dailies, the Black press, and Harlemites were aware of the chief medical examiner's report, and indeed, the New York Age initiated its campaign in part as a challenge to Norris's report and the dailies' criminalization of Dent. Thus, Harlem's Black community witnessed the district attorney's inquiry as a protracted artifice of injustice. Though the New York Age's activism against the third degree did not result in any meaningful police accountability or an investigation of the Thirty-Eighth Precinct, it exposed police violence as an unofficial policy of the Thirty-Eighth Precinct and articulated the Black community's conception of law and order. Thus, even while condemning Boddy's killing, Harlemites across the political spectrum argued that he deserved the full protection and safety of the criminal justice system. By the time Harlemites battled the police in late July of 1928 in the aftermath of Clarence Donald attacking Mrs. Zerlena Chavis, they were well acquainted with the third degree and would once again initiate a campaign against police violence.

"Police Terrorism"

As fall arrived in 1928 and the reportage of the July conflagration transitioned from the streets to the court proceedings, Black Harlem read about the abuse of St. William Grant. Grant had witnessed the police pummeling of Donald during the uproar, so the police tried to silence him. The police arrested Grant on August 14 upon the testimony of a white taxicab driver who claimed that Grant robbed him. In a letter to Judge Panger, Grant explained desperately, "They frame me that I Rob a white taximan the Saturday before the Riot in Harlem. Hon Panger I was in Court three times before I was arrested charge for robbing him. He was also there three times, on the 4th time he cause my arrest."[76] The magistrate Hyman Bushel questioned whether it was "probable that he (Grant) would return to court when he knew his own liberty was in danger."[77] It was clear to Bushel that Grant was framed. While in custody, Grant was beaten by Black and white officers. Concerned about the pattern of psychological and physical abuse prisoners endured, Grant's attorney John William Smith requested protection for Grant from the magistrate and explained to him that upon arrest, Grant was unblemished. Detective Webber, the arresting officer, proclaimed that Grant attacked him during the fingerprinting process. "He was yelling 'Murder,' throwing chairs, and he tore all his clothes from him, making it appear that he was beaten by the police and refused to walk," alleged Webber.[78] Webber explained the bruises on Grant's head as the result of his refusal to enter his cell. According to the detective, Grant's battered condition was self-imposed. To sustain his attorney's depiction of the precinct, Webber explained, Grant took off his clothes and banged his head against the walls.

During his first arraignment, while in the lineup, Grant was "hardly recognizable" and could barely stand.[79] His clothes were "in ribbons," nose fractured and skull cut, and he suffered injuries to his ribs and privates. The district attorney Martin attempted to raise Grant's bail to $10,000, stating that "certain colored people upon whose word he could rely" had told him that Grant and Donald belonged to "a vicious organization," the Universal Improvement Association (UNIA).[80] DA Martin foundered on the bail scheme. Grant told the *New York Amsterdam News* about the abuse at the Wadsworth Avenue police station. The police burned him with cigar butts on his hands and legs and threatened him to testify that he stole Ellis's watch and money. Moreover, they promised to drop the charges if Grant testified against Donald, but Grant replied resoundingly, "I will not lie on anybody."[81]

During Grant's second arraignment, he pleaded not guilty. Testimonies by Dermot Bailey and Samuel Grant (St. William's brother) placed Grant at home between 2:00 A.M. and 6:30 A.M. Since Ellis claimed that Grant robbed him at approximately 2:45 A.M., Bailey's and Samuel's testimonies gave St. William an alibi. On December 4, the judge acquitted Grant and stated that he believed Grant was framed. As the Black press had long argued, it was the courts' responsibility to confer punishment—not the police's.[82]

The *New York Amsterdam News* and its readers lambasted the police department and equated its actions toward the Black community with police terrorism. An anonymous respondent of the *New York Amsterdam News* stated, "Our protectors, I think, resort to drastic measures in the treatment of their prisoners, without justifiable reasons."[83] The letter writer insisted, likely expressing a point of view held among many Harlemites, that the police were more oppressive than protective. In another editorial, "Lawless Policemen," quoting from the NYPD's "Police Practice and Procedure," the *New York Amsterdam News* urged "all policemen . . . to commit to memory" that "the power to punish is vested in the judiciary. For instance, if you apprehend a murderer, you must not necessarily strike him. . . . If you do you are usurping the power of the judiciary."[84] In "Police Terrorism," the *New York Amsterdam News* encouraged Harlemites to mobilize and demand police accountability. Police Commissioner Beggans of Jersey City, New Jersey, held a public hearing which 1,500 people attended and the commissioner dismissed the offending officer Lieutenant Dugan, who assaulted a Black woman in the station house. Beggans contended, "Every mother, sister and sweetheart here has every right to walk into a police station and to walk out unmolested." The *New York Amsterdam News* followed with "THE SAME RIGHT belongs to male citizens, whether in Jersey City or Harlem" and asked that the people "get together in Harlem as they did in Jersey City and demand the dismissal of policemen who abuse the privileges of their uniform." To marshal support for a mass-based and political response to widespread police abuse but also to admonish the NYPD, the *New York Amsterdam News* urged Harlemites to raise their own expectations of themselves and gave notice that "they [the people] will soon put a stop to police brutality in Harlem."[85]

· · · · · ·

After the court proceedings ended with Clarence Donald's conviction, Black New Yorkers regularly confronted and complained about police violence in the last year of the decade and the early 1930s. In early March of 1930, thirty-one-year-old Benjamin Chase, just returning from visiting family in North Carolina, was sitting on a doorstep on 121st between Lexington and Park Avenues with his dog when a police officer confronted him. Chase had sat down to recover from a bad mix of whiskey and food. Patrolman Bausbacher, of the East 128th Street Station, commanded him to move, and Chase explained that he could not and felt ill. Bausbacher arrested him for disorderly conduct and took him to the jail. As Chase was plainly ill, the police sent for a doctor from Harlem Hospital, who reported that "nothing was wrong, and that the prisoner was merely intoxicated." The next day, despite repeated exclamations of being too ill, Chase appeared in the Harlem Court before Magistrate Walsh in a "pitiable condition. . . . Blood was clotted about his ears and he was hardly able to stand." According to the *New York Amsterdam News*, Chase could only declare his innocence, since he was too weak to take the oath and testify on his own. The magistrate asked Bausbacher to explain his condition, and the patrolman claimed that he was "faking." Walsh sentenced him to five days in jail and told the patrolman to make sure Chase received medical attention. But upon being dropped off at the prison, Chase fell to the floor, dying before the call for medical support could be made. According to the medical examiner, the autopsy suggested that Chase died of the beating while in custody not alcoholism. A representative of the *New York Age* who viewed the body explained that "there were two bruises on the side of his face and the lower lip was split as though by a blow. Other bruises recently made appear about the legs and lower part of the body." Though his sister believed that the police officer was responsible for killing her sibling, she decided not to pursue the matter any further because she had only recently returned to the city from the funeral of her oldest brother. As she was still in mourning, explained the *New York Age*, "the two deaths had so upset her that she was unable to do anything at this time."[86]

Chase's sister's grief made public the feelings many Black families held as they mourned the death or witnessed the suffering of their loved ones, as victims of police abuse on the streets of Harlem or while under police custody. The experiences of Chase, Grant, Dent, Boddy, and others documented in the Black press paralleled the cases and conclusions found in the Wickersham Commission report *Lawlessness in Law Enforcement*. While Mayor Walker and Police Commissioner McLaughlin failed to rein in police abuse, the Black press exposed the pattern of police violence and interrogated police authority. The Black community articulated its own law-and-order politics that agreed that the police held the authority, as the

Wickersham Commission advanced, "to effect an arrest." Yet Blacks also asserted that police authority was necessarily limited by its assigned role within the law enforcement component of the criminal justice system. Pushing beyond the race-neutral, color-blind language of the Wickersham Commission's report, the Black press interpreted the third degree as an act of punishment, not simply an "unlawful" method of attaining intelligence for crime. Law enforcement responded to crime or prevented it, but, as Harlemites had long argued, "the power to punish is vested in the judiciary." More critically, however, the Black press often understood the third degree in particular and police violence in general as expressions of racial violence—not simply crime-fighting. It was no accident that the *New York Amsterdam News* described the third degree as an act of terrorism and "indoor, lynching or near-lynching." These same issues would remain a constant throughout the remainder of that decade and the next. Months before Governor Roosevelt's Hofstadter Committee set its investigation in motion, the Black community found the judicial system wanting. As they sought justice and accountability for police violence in the courts, Black New Yorkers encountered corruption and obstruction at every turn.[87]

2 A New Deal in Law Enforcement

· ·

In his 1947 posthumously published autobiography, *Night Stick*, Lewis J. Valentine, lauded as one of New York City's most effective police commissioners, wrote, "Criminologists from every nation have come to Headquarters to observe and marvel at our law enforcement machinery, to scrutinize closely our Safety Bureau, the Legal Bureau, the famed Missing Person's Bureau, and our law Library." The reverence the international law enforcement community held for the city's "law enforcement machinery" stemmed from the efforts that Valentine and Fiorello H. La Guardia made to bring an appearance of clean government and professionalism to the New York Police Department. Serving more than four decades in the police department, Valentine retired in 1945, ending his career as the head of police for the majority of Mayor Fiorello H. La Guardia's three terms. Reflecting on his early education on policing in Gotham City, he explained, "The books did not mention political influences, the use of ward politicians or of roving political emissaries who exercised potent influence on the policeman; that promotion of the policeman on the beat depended upon the pecuniary whim of the district political leader." Although there had been previous efforts to reform the New York Police Department, Valentine and La Guardia's agenda coupled with the downfall of Tammany Hall accelerated police professionalism. Throughout the late 1920s and early 1930s, as New York City and other metropolises across the nation debated the "third degree," police discretion, and the use of force, the State of New York was mired in a political battle with Tammany Hall. Because the NYPD's cooperation with the political machine was so instrumental to Tammany's omnipotence, this political clash was about not only the future of electoral politics but also the future of the city's criminal legal system.[1]

Black New Yorkers understood well the consequences of corruption in the city's criminal legal system. As a check on police brutality, they had long understood and promoted "law and order," as the process by which courts, not the police, dispensed punishment through the adjudication of the law. Neither the police nor the court system would protect Black citizens. As the Wickersham Commission had reported, Gotham's criminal legal system was "crooked." In the early 1930s, Franklin Delano Roosevelt, the governor of the State of New York, authorized the Hofstadter Committee, known as the Seabury Investigation, to conduct an inquiry into corruption in New York City's magistrate courts and police department. The Seabury Investigation echoed what many New Yorkers, especially Black victims of police violence and the court system, already knew about their criminal legal system—that it harbored widespread corruption sullying the halls of government.

La Guardia, the former East Harlem congressman born in New York City but raised in the Southwest, was viewed, though not by all, as the savior to Gotham City's debilitating economy and the abiding problem of municipal corruption. Over his three terms, La Guardia brought some semblance of clean government and, as World War II began, with the support of President Franklin D. Roosevelt's New Deal programs, transformed the economy. La Guardia even managed to restrain the violence of the NYPD, at least temporarily. In his first year as mayor, La Guardia challenged police discretion, as he warned police officers not to obstruct and abuse workers on strike or others engaged in civil disobedience. That spring, La Guardia vociferously supported the taxicab drivers' strike and proclaimed public stances that undermined the authority of his chosen police commissioner, John O'Ryan. By banning police use of batons, La Guardia rejected the argument that restraining police discretion contributed to crime, and he reinforced how calls for law and order were often guises to suppress the weak.

In March, the mayor investigated a police riot in Harlem, demonstrating his commitment to not only the working class and labor unions but also Black neighborhoods. The Communist Party held a public meeting for Ada Wright, the mother of two of the Scottsboro Boys, which the NYPD violently broke up, teargassing the crowd and wantonly pummeling bystanders and people fleeing the scene. La Guardia immediately initiated an investigation of the police riot. Then chief inspector Lewis Joseph Valentine found several of the officers culpable. Police Commissioner O'Ryan refused to discipline them, reasoning that he would not ruin their career for minor infractions. O'Ryan later resigned, prompted by La Guardia's suspension of top brass for other transgressions and the investigation of the police officers in Harlem. From law enforcement to the courts, Gotham City's liberal criminal justice system failed to render justice to African Americans. La Guardia undoubtedly brought a semblance of reform to Gotham City, but because he prioritized urban order over racial justice, his liberal gesture of police investigation into the police riot was diminished. This environment persisted when La Guardia appointed Valentine police commissioner in September 1934.

La Guardia's choice of Valentine made political sense. Not only had he served in the police department for over two decades, but he had a long record of fighting police corruption and was a well-known enemy of the Tammany political machine. La Guardia and Valentine believed that the main path to establishing clean government was to extinguish political interference in the policies and practices of the police department. More specifically, Valentine established a standard of police reform and professionalism that rooted out bribery and other forms of lawlessness by the police that stained the legitimacy of the department. Indeed, upon being appointed, he openly warned police officers that politics had no place in policing. With La Guardia as his mayor, Valentine shepherded the NYPD transition from payola to professional police force. Valentine especially warned gangsters that they would be punished—investigated, arrested, and incarcerated. Valentine described this line of police policy as "muss 'em up" policing. Valentine with the public support of La Guardia used police professionalism to sanction this form of punitive policing. Valentine explained that the police, in order to gain political support or monetary benefit, had been in the habit of ignoring criminal behavior. Admitting the NYPD's long tradition of misconduct, the commissioner asserted that police officers had to be reoriented to enforce the law when it came to thugs and gangsters and when necessary, to use coercive force to fulfill the department's duty to ensure the safety and protection of the public. Black New Yorkers immediately saw Valentine's policy as a guise to sanction police brutality. Thus, while the NYPD had formally committed to erasing political influence in policing, it had not committed to the same in the case of anti-Black police violence.

"Unfortunate That Your Son Happened to Stop a Bullet"

On September 9, 1929, a patrolman shot a Black youth in the back on the L train in Brownsville, Brooklyn. Ralph Baker and William Fontaine, students at Lincoln University in Pennsylvania, visiting relatives in Brooklyn, stirred up trouble in a train car on the Fulton Street line at the Grand Avenue Station, explained Patrolman Walter Lowe. The two students tried to force themselves into a seat next to Lowe and his friend, Louise Crocker. Baker asked the woman to move over so he could sit, but she refused. Lowe claimed that Baker "called her a vile name," and the men began arguing. Once the train stopped at the Rockaway Avenue Station, as Baker and Fontaine exited the train, Lowe followed and arrested them. As Lowe walked them to the street, Baker punched Lowe in the face and the students fled. Lowe ordered them to halt, but they continued to run, and he let off four shots, hitting Baker in the back. Lowe apprehended Fontaine, whom he walked back to Baker's prone body and awaited police reinforcements. Lowe then called an ambulance, and with Baker on the way to St. John's Hospital as a prisoner, the patrolman placed Fontaine under arrest. At the police station, the patrolman admitted that he was off duty. Dr. Louis T. Wright, a Black police surgeon, examined Lowe and announced that he was "fit for duty." The two Lincoln students, both from Montclair, New Jersey, were charged with disorderly conduct.[2]

The National Association for the Advancement of Colored People (NAACP) handled the students' case as their legal support and publicized the students' account of the chain of events. From the headlines of the dailies, the storyline upheld the heroic white police officer saving his white woman companion from two philandering Black students. The next afternoon, James Weldon Johnson, the executive secretary of the NAACP, sent a telegram to Police Commissioner Grover Whalen, requesting that the case be thoroughly and exhaustively investigated and that Lowe be suspended because "press reports indicated that shooting was wholly unwarranted." Johnson followed up on the eleventh with a similar telegram to Kings County's district attorney, Charles J. Dodd. Johnson encouraged Dodd to take "prompt action" that would result in the arrest and indictment of Lowe and offered the NAACP's cooperation with the district attorney's office and police authorities in gathering and presenting evidence. Johnson's telegram, in order to demonstrate the NAACP's legitimacy and earnestness, also included the names of revered and notable Black people in the city. As he wrote, the organization "is joined in this protest by alumni of Lincoln University represented by Doctor E. P. Roberts of New York City[,] former member of the Board of Education[,] Doctor George E. Haynes of the Federal Council of Churches of Christ and other white and colored citizens interested in justice." That same day, the New York Times reported that Whalen suspended Lowe pending a departmental investigation.[3]

In addition to contacting the mayor and the district attorney, the NAACP asked for monetary support from Lincoln University's alumni and president, Dr. William Hallock Johnson. On the tenth, Walter F. White, the assistant secretary of the NAACP, initiated the campaign to rally support for Baker. Born in 1893, White was the son of college-educated parents, his father a postal worker and his mother a teacher in Atlanta, Georgia. He graduated from Atlanta University in 1918 and, encouraged by James Weldon Johnson, moved to New York City and joined the NAACP. White could pass as a white person. As he described himself, "I am a Negro. My skin is white, my eyes are blue, my hair is blond." He used his skin color to advocate for his race. As an NAACP investigator, he exposed patterns of racial violence and white supremacy across the South, but in New York City, he confronted a liberal form of racism. White called and eventually wrote Dr. Roberts, a trustee of the university, and detailed the facts of the case and asked him to write a letter to Mayor Whalen. White, explaining the urgency of the alumni's support, wrote, "From all evidence which has come to us up to the time of writing this letter the case is one of cold blooded murderous assault."[4] President Johnson, while writing that the university could not assume financial responsibility for the case, sent the NAACP a personal check of twenty-five dollars and informed the assistant secretary that both students were in arrears and of excellent conduct. White thanked Johnson for the check, updated him on the case, and asked him to testify as a character witness for his students, and the president agreed to unless he had "another imperative engagement."[5] William Pickens, field secretary and attorney for the NAACP, held a meeting on September 19 at the office of Dr. Paul Collins, an alumnus of Lincoln University, to urge the Lincoln Alumni Association to create a defense fund for Baker and Fontaine.[6] Once the NAACP sent out the letter through the alumni association, alumni, current students, and fraternities sent in money to support the students.[7]

After interviewing the students and eyewitnesses, the NAACP learned that the students' story contrasted considerably with Lowe's. On the twelfth, at the Kings County District Attorney's office, officials of the NAACP—Walter White; William T. Andrews, special legal assistant; and Herbert J. Seligmann, director of publicity—met with the assistant district attorney, Hyman Barshay, who took statements from witnesses collected by Andrews. Baker and Fontaine explained that they neither boarded the train car nor had any kind of exchange, verbal or otherwise, with Patrolman Lowe. The students had run up the stairs, and once on the platform, they ran again because they thought the train was departing. As they neared the train, they saw Lowe for the first time. Fontaine, several meters behind Baker, remembered the people getting off the train and that the "people seem[ed] to be terrified." According to Fontaine, Lowe demanded that Baker "come here," so he, in good sense, ran into the train and then out of the car to escape him. In Baker's affidavit, he explained that he thought Lowe was "drunk and half-crazy" and that he ran because "the gun in his hand frightened me."[8] Gladys Brendhagen, a white woman, was on the same train as Lowe. Brendhagen claimed that Lowe, indeed, had a verbal exchange with two boys—but not with Baker and Fontaine. Lowe confronted the youth because he was sing-ing, and, according to Brendhagen, Lowe and his companion "looked an-gry." Once the train arrived at the station, she left the train, and when she reached the end of the car, she heard two shots. She recalled, "I turned around and saw many people running. I saw a colored boy dash past me running and the man following with his gun in the air shooting. The boy kept on running down the stairs. The man kept on after him demanding him to stop. This was as far as the stairs, shooting down at him with the command. The man returned to the train. He did not say 'I am an officer' or 'stop, in the name of the law.' I only remember the word 'stop.'"[9] Brendha-gen also mentioned Baker and Fontaine, as she remembered the "two boys . . . ran by me to catch the train." Enraged with the Black youths' per-ceived arrogance on the train, Lowe had likely projected his animus toward them on Baker and Fontaine.[10]

On October 21, at the Sixth Magistrate's Court, 495 Gates Avenue, Brook-lyn, Magistrate Mark Rudich presided over the hearing on the summons, a complaint issued by the NAACP's William T. Andrews against Patrolman Lowe for shooting Baker. Baker and Fontaine along with their parents and counsel, Andrews and Morris L. Ernst, attended the hearing. Rudich invited all of them into his chambers and expressed that he wanted to avoid the hearing and dismiss all of the charges. He explained that he had heard that Baker's parents "were pressing Lowe for money" and urged them to "take into consideration the earning power of this man who has been suspended from the police force for thirty-two days." Reverend Baker asserted that his family was interested in seeking justice only. As Rudich restated his inten-sions, Baker's mother complained, "Everything you say is in favor of the police officer. . . . Why don't you give us justice[?] You talk of his having had no pay for thirty-two days. How about my poor boy who lay at the point of death? We want justice." Rudich questioned what she meant by "justice." He reasoned, "Even assuming there was a promiscuous use of fire-arms—a careless use of firearms—it is merely unfortunate that your son happened to stop a bullet. I cannot find any malice on the policeman's part and without intent to do harm, I cannot hold him." Ernst encouraged the magistrate to continue the case in court, and "angered[,] Rudich marched out of his chambers, took his place on the bench and called the case." At the end, Rudich decided that no crime had been committed by Lowe and dis-missed all of the charges against the students and patrolman.[11]

A week before the end of the new year, Magistrate Rudich's judicial behavior was under scrutiny because he freed two women shoplifters despite their long criminal records. Chief Magistrate of New York City William McAdoo questioned Rudich's decision-making and his integrity, describing the freeing of the two women with long criminal records as "a miscarriage of justice." On December 30, Mayor Walker declined to reappoint Rudich, whose judicial term ended on the thirty-first, and then on January 4, the mayor requested that James P. Judge, president of the Brooklyn Bar Association, investigate the charges leveled at Rudich by McAdoo and to evaluate his fitness for reappointment.[12] White, following the Brooklyn Bar Association's investigation of Rudich's fitness, then wrote a letter to Chief Magistrate McAdoo on January 11 concerning Rudich's conduct during the Baker-Lowe hearing. White encouraged him to investigate their case as part of the evaluation of the magistrate's appropriateness for reappointment. The NAACP's letter explained the chain of events that brought about the case, Rudich's actions in court, in his chambers, and once again in court, as well as the NAACP's own views of his fitness. Because Rudich initiated, framed, and perpetuated the tenor of the discussion, White argued that the magistrate's behavior "amounted to an attempt to compound a crime."[13]

While the Black weeklies and white dailies reported some of what the letter detailed, White's letter brought forth vital context that was only intimated in the newspapers. The NAACP, for example, believed that Rudich had prior conversations with Lowe and especially the patrolman's father, though the letter made explicit that Rudich had not spoken with Baker's attorneys. The letter pointed out that Lowe's father was a high-level police official, a lieutenant inspector, and that Rudich had encouraged the Bakers to drop the charges. Rudich wanted them to accept a "civil settlement," and he frequently mentioned "the figure . . . five hundred dollars" and how impoverished Lowe was. White also laid bare Rudich's decision to only hear the testimony of one witness, Brendhagen, despite the presence of several witnesses in court who could have spoken on the behalf of the students. Although he dismissed all of the charges, as the newspapers had disclosed, Rudich, according to the NAACP, "placed in the records statements decidedly in favor of the Patrolman." The letter explained that the NAACP had diligently cooperated with the police department and that it had all of the eyewitnesses' testimonies. The NAACP, White admitted, had no confidence in Rudich's fitness and was convinced that he was undoubtedly biased. "To put it mildly," White wrote, "at the conference in his chambers, he acted more in the manner of Patrolman Lowe's advocate than a dispenser of justice or referee."[14]

By the end of January, the grievance committee of the Brooklyn Bar Association submitted its report to Mayor Walker. The grievance committee had come to the decision that there was no evidence to disqualify Rudich from reappointment, but the majority agreed that Rudich "erred in freeing the defendants [shoplifters] . . . and in freeing Lowe," and wrote that Rudich "frankly conceded this." Despite these "errors," the committee, the report concluded, found the "magistrate to be honest, capable and fit to occupy the magistrate Bench." Consequently, the mayor, in accord with the report, promised to follow the recommendation of the committee. Of the seven committee members, only one, Francis L. Archer, dissented and judged the magistrate as incompetent. Archer believed that Rudich's two years of experience on the bench should have prepared him to "identify two habitual criminals with long records of conviction against them and detect the false swearing of a policeman guilty of the crime of assault in the second degree on an innocent citizen by shooting with a pistol and injuring him severely." Rather than judging Rudich's errors as inconsequential, Archer argued that the cases were of "great public importance," especially in the case of shooting an innocent citizen. Rudich, he contended, failed to appreciate the consequences of his decisions "from a public standpoint and therefore he should not be reappointed to this important office affecting so vitally the public at large."[15]

On January 30, White asked Chief Magistrate William McAdoo to order the arrest of Patrolman Walter Lowe. Despite the bar association's judgment of Rudich's fitness, the grievance committee concluded that the magistrate had erred and that Lowe's innocence was deeply suspect. White summarized the case, highlighting the reports of the bar association, the NAACP's continued commitment to support the case, and especially the pain and the aftereffects that Baker continued to endure. As White noted, "Mr. Baker not only lay at the point of death for some time in a hospital but he has been forced to give up completing his college career at Lincoln University because of the shooting and the effect of it upon his health." With the letter from White and the NAACP, the pattern of errors that the bar association pointed out about the magistrate's record, and especially his own suspicion of Rudich's fitness, McAdoo held a hearing, allowing the NAACP to argue its case and witnesses to the incident to testify on Baker's behalf.[16]

On February 4, McAdoo signed and issued a warrant for Patrolman Walter Lowe's arrest on the charge of felonious assault.[17] Lowe's attorney Joseph Solevei disparaged McAdoo for assisting the NAACP in the arrest of a policer officer. The magistrate had overstepped his power, and "his action . . . is a formal notice to gangsters and thugs showing them how a police officer can be kicked around in this way," charged Solevei, touting the police's well-worn discourse of the threat to the police and public's safety.[18] In anticipation of the forthcoming hearing before Magistrate Jacob Eilperin in the Sixth District Magistrate's Court in Brooklyn, White requested notable Black spokespeople, specifically William R. R. Granger, Robert J. Elzy, George E. Haynes, and Dr. Henry Proctor, and other respectable Blacks to attend the hearing. Always concerned about the public presentation of the Black community, White wrote to Haynes, "It would have a fine moral effect upon the Court and the newspapers if well-dressed, intelligent colored people manifested their interest in this case by being present at the trial. Pass the word along, won't you, and by all means be present yourself if you can arrange it." On February 8, White wrote to District Attorney George E. Brower and promised to "volunteer all possible assistance to you in presenting this case to the Grand Jury and in the subsequent trial should the Grand Jury see fit to indict." In a letter to White, acknowledging his letter, Brower replied that the hearing would be held on the thirteenth. On that date, Magistrate Eilperin held the hearing, and after hearing the testimonies of the complainants and the defense, he reserved his decision until March 1.[19]

Throughout the remainder of February, the NAACP diligently tried to convince the DA's office to prioritize its case, but the office's lukewarm commitment to the case constantly frustrated the civil rights organization's efforts. White wrote Brower on February 27 requesting that the DA involve himself directly in the Baker-Lowe case. White was disturbed by the news that the district attorney's office had not received the minutes of the February 13 hearing. He also highlighted the "attitude" of Assistant District Attorney Palmer, who had apparently, without having read the minutes of the hearing, opined that Eilperin should not indict Lowe. Palmer, assigned to write the people's brief by Magistrate Eilperin, had only secondhand knowledge of the testimony from Mr. Pease as presented to Eilperin. White then outlined the details of the case, the investigation of Magistrate Rudich, and the Brooklyn Bar Association's judgment, aggregating his evidence and contrasting his reasoning with the unsupported opinion of Pease. Once again, White implored Brower to "personally take action to the end that vigorous prosecution of this case may be had by your office? The issue involved is much more than the shooting of a Negro. It involves a question as to the safety of any citizen, regardless of race, who might have been shot down by this policeman."[20]

Throughout March, the NAACP continued to question the district attorney office's commitment to presenting Baker's case at the hearing. On March 1, Magistrate Eilperin adjourned the decision until the tenth. On March 5, White once again wrote Brower, reminding him of the previous letter of February 27 and then asking him plainly what the district attorney's office was doing on the matter of the Baker-Lowe case. Magistrate Eilperin, he wrote, postponed the decision because Brower's office had neglected to submit a memorandum of law on the culpability of Lowe. White wanted to know what Brower's office was doing, because the local newspapers had asked the NAACP to issue a statement on the DA's inaction, and while they were in the process of drafting a response, the NAACP was reluctant to do so without giving the DA's office an opportunity to respond to their communication. Brower immediately wrote back to White and requested that he call to see him at once. Because White was out of town, attorney William T. Andrews, special legal assistant for the NAACP, went to Brower's office on White's behalf. Nothing, however, came of the meeting. Andrews and Brower's awkward exchange only created more tension, partly the by-product of Brower's refusal to talk with anyone except for White but also perhaps Brower's own annoyance that Andrews dared to openly express his distaste for being slighted by the district attorney.[21]

On March 10, Magistrate Eilperin decided to hold Lowe before the grand jury.[22] White and Andrews immediately began contacting Baker, Fontaine, and other witnesses. They updated them about the status of the case, informed them that they might be called before the grand jury, and thanked them for their cooperation. White also sent a similar letter, though more upbeat, to Lincoln alumni, recounting the NAACP's efforts from the very beginning, the contributions given by notable alumni, and the considerable financial cost of the case and then ending plainly with, "We need your help." On March 24, the case of *People vs. Walter Lowe* was presented to the grand jury, and after hearing thirteen witnesses, the next day the grand jury returned with no indictment, dismissing the charges against Patrolman Lowe.[23] Despite the NAACP's long legal campaign, Baker's unassailable reputation, and the backing of the university, its alumni, and the Black press, justice for Baker remained elusive. Walter White's ties to the liberal political establishment undoubtedly helped Lowe's case. As a symbol of Black educational potential and academic excellence, Lowe's cultural status as a student at a prestigious Black university garnered widespread support that too few Black victims of police brutality ever received. Yet corruption in the city's criminal justice system won out. The Brooklyn Bar Association conceded Rudich's dereliction of the law. Indeed, upon the arrest of Lowe in early February, Rudich declared, "Show me a petty jury that would convict Lowe or even a grand jury that would indict him."[24] He was right. Beyond DA Brower's idle preparation, Walter White's frustration with the DA's office spoke to its witting disposition to turn a blind eye to police violence. White warned how the court's corruption sanctioned police abuse on its authority and threatened public safety. The costs were quite high. As White contended, the right to be safe from excessive force was vital for "any citizen, regardless of race."

This episode of police and court collusion, however, was not a departure from the customary unlawful actions of the city's criminal legal system. While racism permeated law enforcement, Magistrate Rudich's effort to undermine the NAACP and Mayor Walker's grievance committee and the DA's malfeasance were symptomatic of Tammany Hall's political machine. In 1932, Tammany Hall, spiraling like the nation's debilitative economy, had been under investigation for two years for corruption. By 1933, the city would have a new mayor, Fiorello H. La Guardia, an anti-Tammany politician and former congressman for East Harlem.

"The Best Man in America to Fill the Position"

Fiorello Henry La Guardia was born in 1882 to an Italian father, Achille La Guardia, and a Jewish mother, Irene Luzzatto-Coen. Though born in New York City, he was raised in Arizona, and in 1906, Fiorello returned home to the city with political aspirations and joined the Republican Party. Before becoming the mayor, La Guardia served in Congress twice, for one year in 1918 before becoming the president of the Board of Alderman in New York City, and from 1922 to 1933. Of small stature and openly proud of his Italian heritage, La Guardia was brazenly self-reliant. Since his time as an attorney supporting labor unions and his battles in Congress over immigration legislation, La Guardia put forth an unyielding and outspoken political voice keen to the plight of outsiders and the underrepresented. La Guardia was also committed to and had a record of fairness with African Americans. While in Congress in 1929, when Oscar De Priest, Black Chicago's congressman, encountered disdain among members of the House of Representatives, La Guardia informed the Speaker of the House that he would welcome De Priest as his neighbor. The city's working class especially looked forward to La Guardia as an ally in its battle against capitalism's ills. The 1932 Norris–La Guardia Act had helped to strengthen labor rights, weaken yellow-dog contracts—contracts that forbid employees from joining a union—and protected workers from injunctions.[25]

In 1921, his first campaign for mayor failed when he lost in the primary, but he won the primary in 1928, campaigning as a Republican-Fusion candidate against the incumbent mayor James Walker. Walker beat La Guardia, handily. The incumbent outsmarted the former congressman, and the mayor's wit and style effectively checked La Guardia's remonstrations about many legitimate issues, especially corruption. On November 4, 1928, Arnold Rothstein, banker to the underworld and colluder with Tammany, was shot, and he died two days later. Although the police had spoken to Rothstein before he died and the district attorney had claimed his records, the police found no evidence—no fingerprints, no eyewitnesses, and no weapon to find the killer. But more perplexing was that the police could not find anything in Rothstein's books to indict anyone in his political network and his clients. La Guardia among others believed that the police found nothing because they did not want to find anything, and he charged that Walker had connections to Rothstein.[26] As he asserted in late October 1929, "If Mayor Walker says he didn't know Arnold Rothstein . . . that's untrue," but he later changed his tune. Although he lost this mayoralty race, La Guardia's warning about police deceit, especially the Walker administration's complicity in it, was prescient.[27]

Mayor Walker, ever loyal to the Tammany machine and invested more in enjoying the city's luxuries than in repairing its broken economy, mismanaged the city's budget. Of course, the Great Depression exacerbated these conditions, but the mayor's anemic response to the dire needs of New Yorkers made the need for change more discernible. As the city's tax base dropped, the stubborn mayor refused to slash the city's budget. In the fall of 1931, for example, when Charles W. Berry, the city's comptroller, stated publicly that $14 million could be "cut . . . without injuring the operation of any city department," Walker held a public session of the Board of Estimate to challenge Berry's statement, making the ordeal a public spectacle. Berry and Walker had long clashed over municipal expenditures.[28] While he claimed that he was not against cutting the budget, the mayor complained that the comptroller made errors in his assertions and numbers.[29] In 1932, as Walker begged for funds from the city's bankers to bail out the city, they, too, had "worn the bare path to Washington to beg the federal government to help out with low-interest loans." Walker also failed New Yorkers in need of relief. Citizens faithful to the Tammany machine—even those not in need—received the preponderance of the relief. In Staten Island, for example, Democrats, many of them already employed, were nine out of ten relief recipients. In Manhattan, the borough president's office distributed preapproved relief applications to the district clubs to be distributed to their dutiful membership. Dishonesty in the distribution of relief, however, was only one drop in a sea of municipal corruption.[30]

In 1932, the Seabury Investigation quickened the transformation of the city government, especially its criminal justice system. Judge Samuel Seabury echoed the criticisms that La Guardia leveled at the Walker administration in 1929. Seabury found widespread corruption in the city government. For example, district leaders had collected a half-million dollars on municipal salaries, and a county leader pressured city agencies and employees to purchase cars from his son-in-law's dealership.[31] Seabury found evidence, though circumstantial, that the mayor was not only complicit but also likely profiting from graft, so he set in motion proceedings to remove Walker from office. After a standoff between Seabury and Walker, Governor Roosevelt summoned Walker to Albany to address Seabury's charges. Walker cannily navigated the governor's interrogation but tarnished the Democratic Party's reputation. Al Smith, former governor and Democratic rival of Roosevelt as candidate for the presidency, told Walker that Walker was "through" and that he should "resign for the good of the party." Once Walker resigned, the city's anti-Tammany's politicos deliberated whom they would nominate for the Fusion Party. Now with the support of Seabury, retired congressman La Guardia ably won the mayoral race that November in 1933.[32]

New Yorkers held great expectations for the Little Flower, as he was often called, and for many he did not disappoint. During the mayoral election in 1933, the Black press, including the *New York Age*, once a loyal supporter of Mayor Walker, openly supported La Guardia as a candidate. Black Harlemites, no different from other New Yorkers, wanted clean government. The *New York Age* asserted, "The government needs to be reformed and reorganized from top to bottom. It needs to have its expenditures reduced, its credit restored, its local courts purified and the enforcement of law revitalized."[33] The support of Oscar De Priest, Chicago's first Black congressman, who claimed that La Guardia was "the best man in America to fill the position," solidified La Guardia's push for the Black vote.[34] Once elected, La Guardia created an administration composed of public officials known for their anti-Tammany politics.

He appointed his former opponent for the Fusion nomination, General John F. O'Ryan, as the police commissioner, and the press lauded his choice. At the swearing-in ceremony, La Guardia stated that he chose O'Ryan because he had confidence in him and promised that there would be no interference in the daily affairs of the NYPD and that the department would be professionally run. He warned, "Promotions will be on the basis of merit, and merit alone. There is opportunity for everyone. If you believe otherwise, now is the time to speak up and get out of the Department." Later that day, over the radio station WINS, O'Ryan made, in less direct language, similar comments: "I am sure the people of New York City have generally a high regard for the New York City police. I am sure also that that esteem does not blind them to the fact that there is room for substantial improvement in their efficiency and their dependability."[35] The *Daily News* described O'Ryan among others as one of "Tammany's most relentless inquisitors," and noted that he was against police violence.[36] The general "abhor[ed] the third degree, wanton clubbing and other brutalities by cops," and the daily predicted that "it is a safe bet these practices will be tabooed when the veteran solider takes over his new job."[37] La Guardia's appointment of O'Ryan was crucial to rebuilding and establishing the police department's integrity, as an institution bereft of political corruption and representative of sound, clean government. Indeed, one of La Guardia's first tests as a liberal and an anti-Tammany mayor involved the clash among capital, labor, the political left, and the New York Police Department during the winter and spring of 1934.

On February 3, 1934, between Forty-Second and Fifty-Ninth Streets, more than 1,000 striking taxicab drivers attacked taxi drivers, and their vehicles, who ignored the command to get off the streets before four in the afternoon. The *Daily News* described the strike as "a wake of violence" that "engulfed the midtown section."[38] The taxicab operators blamed the mayor. Throughout the remainder of the month, as the mayor handled other police and labor conflicts, he continued to support the striking taxicab drivers, even as O'Ryan wanted to use more force. On February 14, demonstrators from an array of socialist and Communist organizations, shouting "Bloody Austrian Fascism," "The beast of Fascism," and "Massacre of workers women and children," protested outside of the office of Dr. Freidrich Fischerauer, Austrian consul-general, at 500 Fifth Avenue, near the corner of Forty-Second Street, while a delegation met the Austrian consul. Over the span of several hours from midafternoon to the early evening, the crowd swelled from about 2,000 to 4,000. As the crowd clogged the streets, and speakers atop of the steps of the New York Public Library condemned fascism, about 300 police tried to tame the demonstrators, swinging their nightsticks, hitting men and women indiscriminately. After a complaint from several organizations comparing the NYPD to fascism, La Guardia ordered an investigation.[39]

As police aggression spread across the city and complaints about police misconduct mounted, including in Harlem in mid-March, the mayor's advocacy for the taxicab strikers was steadfast. To mollify complaints of police aggression, La Guardia ordered the police to manage demonstrations without their batons, and the police were utterly overwhelmed. The strikers "pulled doors from cabs, yanked out taxi radio sets, hurled missiles through cab windows and unceremoniously ordered passengers out of cabs."[40] In the mainstream press, La Guardia had become the mayor who endorsed riot behavior. As journalist Fred Pasley opined, the La Guardia "administration, based inherently on a new deal for the common man, has, oddly enough, been marked by an outbreak of riots outstanding for the intensity of mob passions and without parallel in previous administrations." La Guardia disarmed the police force, thereby undermining its authority to use coercive force to control the mob. As Pasley explained, "The police handicapped without their clubs and instructed to 'go easy' were practically helpless."[41] By late March, Assistant District Attorney Dodge opened a grand jury investigation into the mayor's handling of the taxicab workers' violence. During the investigation, the police commissioner told the grand jury, "My background has been military . . . and my training hasn't much to do with liberalism. I don't believe in times of emergency in letting crowds collect."[42] Though uncompromising in his support of the taxicab workers, La Guardia "mobilized extra details" and asserted that the police "have to watch violence on both sides. Both sides are equally to blame."[43]

Despite the apparent conflict between La Guardia and O'Ryan, they respected each other in public and zealously promoted and advocated for police discipline and professionalism. On March 18, following St. Patrick's Day weekend, the mayor and O'Ryan spoke to more than 5,500 police officers regarding recent departmental affairs, especially those shaping the perception of the mayor's office and the reputation of the police department at the annual Communion Mass, sponsored by the Police Holy Name Society of Manhattan at St. Patrick's Cathedral. Commissioner O'Ryan spoke first to citizens' complaints of traffic men, whom the commissioner described as "courteous and considerate under trying conditions." Nonetheless, he acknowledged their fallibility, like any human, yet advised the traffic officers to control their disrespectful behavior toward citizens. La Guardia followed the commissioner but took on a more direct tone regarding police discretion under his administration. He told them they were part of "an experiment in municipal government" and that "the days of privilege and political influence in the Department were over and every man would be judged on his merits." The mayor warned them to respect citizens but commanded them to use force when necessary. He believed that complaints would decline in the future. Regarding the question of use of force, he asserted, "Laws are made to be reasonably interpreted. They can be made instruments of oppression, and the agency of the summons must not be used by the Department for that purpose. On the other hand, there must be no relenting in the prosecution of dangerous criminals."[44] As La Guardia and O'Ryan jointly tried to control negative public attention to police misconduct, the grand jury's presentment exposed internecine strife within the NYPD.

On April 11, the grand jury issued their presentment, criticizing the mayor for mishandling the strike by leaving the police ill-equipped to handle the strikers' violence. Although Chief Inspector Lewis Valentine took full responsibility for the order, the grand jury's report noted that La Guardia "was found to have imposed on the Police Department 'a special obligation of consideration for the striking drivers.'" From police testimony, the grand jury learned from "headquarters that the special police assigned to duty at strategic points could not carry nightsticks."[45] This was an affront to O'Ryan's authority. La Guardia "defend[ed] his course and rebuk[ed] the grand jury for its findings."[46] In the end, while espousing a new era of policing and government, La Guardia blatantly intervened in police affairs, albeit to manage police aggression and expose police misconduct. Despite criticisms from grand juries and taxicab operators and the open objections of O'Ryan, La Guardia consistently and loyally defended the house of labor.

"The Press Has Incited More Lynchings in the South"

Throughout that spring into the fall, Black New Yorkers complained about police charging into their homes and criminalizing and targeting the Black poor. In these occasions of ordinary police violence, La Guardia tended to stay clear from the cases. Police brutality in Harlem and across the city remained a feature of Black life during La Guardia's three mayoral administrations. Police discretion remained unchecked and undeterred by either the mayor or his police commissioners. This was especially true as police corruption and the devaluation of Black life persisted under the guise of crime fighting. On March 10, David Fletcher, president of the Moorish Zion Temple in Brooklyn, heard a knock and then pounding on his apartment door on the third floor, 149 Thatford Avenue, Brooklyn. William Lehr and Louis Tobkes, plainclothes policemen, banged on Bey's door, as part of a policy raid ordered by Commissioner O'Ryan. They followed up on a tip that Bey was operating a policy racket, an illegal lottery. Hours later, Fletcher lay in the prison ward at Kings County Hospital paralyzed, fighting for his life. Lehr had shot him in the spine. At the habeas corpus hearing before Supreme Court justice Lewis L. Fawcett, John E. Field, Fletcher's attorney, charged that the "invasion" was unwarranted and that the officers barged illegally into Fletcher's home. The police claimed that they were admitted and that Fletcher "with the hammer . . . belabored Tobkes over the head and shoulders and with the knife . . . held Lehr at bay." According to Lehr, Tobkes was unconscious, and as his partner slowly rose, Fletcher charged at him. To protect his partner, Lehr shot Fletcher in the back. Fawcett denied the writ, but Field wrote letters to the district attorney and to the grand jury.[47]

During the grand jury hearing on April 5, Field argued that the entire ordeal was unlawful, because the police did not have a warrant. District Attorney W. F. X. Geoghan brought in the detectives but also told the jurors to "get the story from Fletcher's own lips."[48] Lehr and Tobkes stated that as they searched Fletcher's apartment, he became aggressive and attacked them with a hammer and a knife. Because Fletcher could not show up in court, the grand jury went to him. In his hospital room, Fletcher claimed that they charged through him into his apartment as he stood in his doorway. Both wearing caps, with one holding his gun and the other a blackjack, stated Fletcher, they began beating him. Falling to the ground, his hand brushed up against a knife which he grabbed in self-defense, and then Lehr shot him in his right side. Upon their departure, Fletcher's wife found that over $500 of the Moorish Zion Temple's money and her diamond ring were missing. In the Kings County Court, the March grand jury on April 16 handed up a verdict of no indictment to Judge Martin, absolving officers Lehr and Tobkes of the charges. On June 18, Fletcher died in Kings County Hospital of the wounds.[49] Along with unlawful entry and theft, the police, the Black press charged, targeted and criminalized innocent Black men.

From April to November in 1934, the scare of a Black "hammer fiend" who attacked and assaulted white women across the city blazoned the headlines of the white press. By early May, three white women, Mrs. Mary Finan, Mrs. Bertha Smirles, and Mrs. Angelina Barbieri, had been attacked. The police on May 25 apprehended Clyde Allen, a homeless man, whom the police shot in the knee as he tried to escape Patrolman Arthur Wallot, who commanded him to stop. In the house, Wallot found a makeshift bed and an axe. Allen was hurried to Cumberland Hospital. Contending that he was innocent, Allen had been living in the apartment for two months and had run because he thought the patrolman was the owner of the vacant house. Allen encouraged the police to check his axe for blood, and they found none.[50]

The *New York Amsterdam News* doubted Allen was guilty, since his features did not match those of the suspect. Allen was suspected of attacking five women. None of the women identified Allen until Mrs. Mary Dexter, an Indian American woman living at Thirty-Two Ashland Place, did. Detectives William Neubauer and William Kenna of the Poplar Street Station took one of the victims, Angelina Barbieri, to identify Allen. While she thought he might have resembled the predator, she was unable to identify him, yet she stated that the axe resembled the one used on her, though she initially claimed that she was hit by a hammer. None of the other four women identified Allen as the culprit. Three days after the arrest, however, Dexter picked Allen as the man who attacked her. The Black weekly blamed the white dailies and the police, noting, "This time the hunting ground was Brooklyn. Previously it was Central Park. Before that it was downtown Manhattan. But whether it be Brooklyn, the Bronx or the Bowery, these periodic scares are beginning to recur with deadly regularity." The *New York Amsterdam News* compared the city's white dailies and the police to southern lynch mobs. Describing the police's shoddy investigation, the Black weekly complained that the "manhunts" only required the outcries of "some hysterical white woman." The Black weekly urged Black New Yorkers to send their complaints to La Guardia and O'Ryan, since "one should not forget that the press has incited more lynchings in the South than the incidents they allegedly recorded."[51]

The Black press interpreted white dailies' coverage as a racial attack. The *New York Age*, referring to the *Daily Mirror* specifically but indicting the white press in general, wrote, "It seems to be traditional among the majority of editors of daily newspapers in the North, East, South, and West to pay more attention to the fact that a Negro is principal in an act of crime than any other feature of the case, even the crime itself." The Black weekly, however, recognized objective, quality journalism, too. It observed that the *New York Times* did not blast "Negro" across its headline and proffered, "If editors of daily publications are really sincere in wishing to promote better relations between the two races they will emulate the example of the *New York Times*; if they are bent on fomenting racial hatreds and strife, let them continue to needlessly and maliciously use 'Negro' in the headlines."[52] The

Black press clearly understood the cultural power of the white press as an engine of anti-Black violence—what had worked in the South had also worked in La Guardia's New York. Yet while the *New York Times*'s reportage functioned as a model of objective journalism, in the 1940s it would often burrow the path toward "fomenting racial hatreds and strife."[53]

While Allen was in jail, there was another attack on a white woman, Mrs. Pauline Bernstein, fostering more suspicion among the Black press. She later recanted her story, claiming that she "deliberately lied to divert suspicion from the white man." There were other stories of women attacked by a "hammer man," as well as other suspects. Between late May and the trial in October, Allen admitted to attacking one of the women. The trial began on October 10 and lasted six days. During cross examination, Allen recanted his story of guilt, pleading that while he recovered in the hospital, the detectives encouraged him to plead guilty with the hope of leniency. The detectives "told him [that he] had no chance with a jury, but would get a short suspended sentence of a few days in jail if he admitted the attack." On October 16 he was convicted of rape in the first degree and burglary in the second. On the twenty-seventh of November, Judge Alonzo G. McLaughlin sentenced Allen to seventeen to thirty-five years in Sing Sing Prison.[54] Although Black New Yorkers noticed little change in their daily confrontations with the NYPD, the mayor intervened on occasions when police behavior potentially tarnished the reputation of the police department, and thereby, the La Guardia administration. As the mayor drove a wedge between himself and O'Ryan while at the same time aggressively advocating for the taxicab drivers, Black New Yorkers and the Communist Party raised parallel questions about police discretion in Harlem, the so-called Negro Mecca.

"O'Ryan Must Go"

On March 17, 1934, at an open meeting held to honor Mrs. Ada Wright, the mother of Roy and Andy, two of the Scottsboro Boys, sponsored by the Communist Party, the International Labor Defense (ILD), and the League of Struggle for Negro Rights (LSNR), the police department hurled teargas and smoke bombs into a crowd of orderly demonstrators. The Scottsboro Boys were nine teenage Black boys, ranging from thirteen to nineteen years old, falsely accused of raping two white girls in Alabama in March of 1931. The ILD, the legal arm of the Communist Party, represented them and with Wright toured the United States and abroad to spread the news of the trials, build support for their campaign, and demonstrate its commitment to the

FIGURE 2.1 Harlem Blacks protesting against conviction of Haywood Patterson, one of the accused in the Scottsboro case. Bettmann via Getty Images.

civil rights struggle.[55] Before the meeting, holding placards that read "Welcome" and "Welcome Mother Wright," a large crowd marched across Harlem, north from 125th Street and Seventh Avenue to 135th Street, east from 135th Street to Lenox Avenue, and finally to 126th Street and Lenox, the headquarters of the ILD. Growing in size and excitement, the crowd cheered as it waited for Mrs. Wright to appear. The commotion began when two cars filled with detectives drove up to the meeting and one detective walked out and asked Herman Mackawain, of the LSNR, for a permit for the meeting. The detective was told to speak to Samuel Stein, a representative of the ILD. Stein, standing with the honoree on the makeshift speakers' platform, introduced Mrs. Wright and recounted her visit with her sons and all the work she had been doing to liberate them.[56]

While Stein spoke to the crowd, one of the detectives forced his way through the crowd and demanded the permit from Stein, who ignored him as he went along with the speech. Detective Omar Ames demanded, "Show your permit . . . or I'll have to break up the meeting." But Stein smiled, according to the *New York Times*, and continued, unbothered.[57] Suddenly, the police drove a "heavy Cadillac car directly into the crowd in an attempt to overturn the speakers' platform upon Mrs. Wright, who was standing nearby."[58] The demonstrators encircled Wright to protect her and tried to escort her away from the crowd and the police. A detective then threw a tear gas bomb into the crowd. Demonstrators scrambled, and blinded by the gas, they tried to escape. As more police vehicles arrived, the police hurled more tear gas and smoke bombs into the crowd. Solomon Harper and two other women led Wright across Lenox Avenue and up the street. Some of the police cars trailed fleeing demonstrators, while police officers on foot pushed and pummeled demonstrators with their fists. Alarmed by the clamor of screams and thuds from the dazed crowd of demonstrators being beaten upon by the police, Harlemites ran to the scene, and others left whatever they were doing in their home and raced to their windows to see what was going on below. According to the *New York Amsterdam News*, "The police, pushing and slugging, waded into the crowd and continued to strike out indiscriminately." Many of the onlookers defended themselves, and in retaliation "the police invaded the headquarters of the Harlem section of the I.L.D. wrecking the furniture and gassing the premises."[59]

The day after, Mayor La Guardia forwarded the complaints to Inspector Valentine from the ILD and American Civil Liberties Union about flagrant police misconduct and ordered him to conduct an investigation of the police department's response to the Scottsboro meeting. Although Valentine regretted the police's use of tear gas, he explained that the police officers suffered most of the injuries and that he could only know if the police's behavior was warranted once the investigation was completed, reported the *New York Times*.[60] The *Daily Worker* also detailed the brutalities of the NYPD. William Mayers, one of three Black protesters arrested, claimed that Police Officer No. 17073 said that "all niggers should be lynched. The Scottsboro boys have been held too long. They should have been lynched long ago." Six police officers "savagely" attacked Marie Lawrence, a Black woman, as she attempted to save another Black woman, who was knocked down by a police officer. The hearings began on the twentieth but were adjourned until the next day after Henry Lee Moon, a reporter of the *New York Amsterdam News* and a witness, demanded that the press be allowed to attend the hearings. Chief Inspector Valentine "flatly opposed the demand until Moon called upon Joseph Tauber and David Freedman, ILD attorneys, and attorney A.L. Wirin of the American Civil Liberties Union to refuse to participate in the 'star chamber' proceedings," reported the *New York Amsterdam News*.[61]

In his interrogation of Detective Omar Ames, Valentine asked him why he threw the tear gas, and the detective declared that it was "preferable to violence," asserting that the meeting had placed "the lives of policemen and others" in danger. Valentine dismissed the assertion that there was any evidence of disorder, as well as the claim that the meeting had been blocking traffic, another justification offered by Sergeant Maurice E. Savage, who made the initial decision to disperse the crowd. The chief inspector publicly reprimanded Ames and Savage, explaining to them that it was "the policy of this administration . . . to give such meetings the fullest latitude and, even though they interfere temporarily with the rights of others, to give them the fullest liberty." But Valentine also tried to reinforce publicly the police department's commitment to law and order, as well as to solicit sympathy and reverence from the public regarding the police's discipline. After Savage complained about not receiving cooperation from the meeting's leaders, Valentine admonished Savage that his long experience as a policeman should have taught him that he would "get no cooperation . . . [and] be called names but [he] can't get mad."[62] The *Daily Worker* reported that Valentine minimized the police's behavior and that the *New York Times* "cooperated with the police in deliberate lies to whitewash the brutality of the police."[63]

Along with demanding that the press observe the hearing, the *New York Amsterdam News* expected disciplinary action. The police, complained the Black weekly, "acted with vicious, wanton and uncalled-for brutality in dispersing an innocuous gathering." In its March 24 editorial titled "It's Time to Act," the *New York Amsterdam News* agreed that the investigation was necessary but, more imperatively, that "it must be followed by disciplinary action by Police Commissioner O'Ryan and Mayor La Guardia."[64]

On March 26, Valentine submitted the report to the commissioner. The chief inspector effectively documented the grievances of Harlem's Black community and the various organizations representing it, and mostly reflected the *Daily Worker*'s and *New York Amsterdam News*'s depiction of the police riot. Valentine acknowledged the roles of the police that started the "disorder" but principally blamed the crowd members and Blacks from their apartment windows for sustaining it. They "threw . . . miscellaneous assortment of missiles, which consisted of a garbage can cover, one milk can cover, an empty milk bottle and some fruit and vegetables." Valentine reported that disciplinary action was taken against all the police officers mentioned in the report, as well as Acting Sergeant Maurice F. Savage, for "failing to exercise proper supervision." Three days later, O'Ryan sent the report to La Guardia without comment because he would need to adjudicate the cases during their internal trials. It would take another six months before O'Ryan and the NYPD would make a decision about the findings of Valentine's investigation and report.[65]

On May 8, Deputy Commissioner John A. Leach held the public trials to determine the guilt or innocence of Patrolmen Charles Brown and Joseph Pappace. While she was afraid to participate in the hearing in the past, Marie Lawrence, the Black woman assaulted by Brown, testified on her own behalf. William Fitzgerald, an ILD organizer; Clarina Michaelson, a white housewife; journalists Henry Lee Moon and T. R. Poston; and Nathan Solomon all testified that Brown's behavior was unwarranted, that he unnecessarily pulled out his gun, threatened the crowd, and threw a grapefruit at a witness's window. The witness asked that the patrolman's shield number be taken.[66]

Spectators at the trial, witnessing the police officers and their supporters change testimony, believed that justice would not be served. The police officers altered their testimonies since the investigation by Inspector Valentine less than two months before. James T. Richie, a white reporter for the *City News Association* who had initially given damaging testimony against Brown, had "changed his story considerably . . . and gave evidence which tended to exonerate the officer." The *New York Times*'s Irving Stiegel, who described the incident as a "riot" in the daily, testified, from the view of the Black weekly, on the behalf of Brown's defense, confirming the *Daily Worker*'s editorial in March. Police officers testifying at the trial in "machine-like" fashion denied all charges of misconduct. Their collective voice characterized the multiple charges of police brutality as figments of the complainants' imagination. "No officer saw Brown attack Miss Lawrence. No officer saw him pull his gun. No officer saw him hurl the grapefruit. No officer witnessed any attack on Mayers. And no officer saw a single child in the demonstration." Despite the police department's erasure of Brown's assault of Lawrence, Brown's guilt or perhaps his effort to invite sympathy led him to cry at the mention of her name.[67]

Deputy Commissioner Leach submitted the record of the hearing to Commissioner O'Ryan, who was slated to announce his decision in four to six weeks. O'Ryan announced the decision months later and on September 7 rejected charges of unnecessary force leveled at Patrolmen Brown and Pappace.[68] T. R. Poston, city editor of the *New York Amsterdam News*, lambasted O'Ryan's judgement and justification for dismissing the charges of police assault. O'Ryan, to Poston's chagrin, not only sanctioned the patrolmen's and the NYPD's actions but also trivialized the violence that Harlemites, especially Lawrence, suffered at the hands of his officers. He reminded readers of the occasion of the meeting to honor Ada Wright, the smoke and tear gas, the brutality of Brown and Pappace, and Inspector Valentine's investigation and judgment that the police response to the opening meeting was unwarranted. Admitting that Brown lied during both the investigation and the trial, O'Ryan stated flippantly that he was "not going to ruin the record of good men by putting marks against their records on such minor charges" and concluded, as an afterthought, that "if they get in serious trouble . . . [he was] going to sock them plenty."[69]

The *New York Amsterdam News* demanded O'Ryan's dismissal. As the Black daily explained, "We have not allowed ourselves to be swayed in this belief by the oft-raised issue of race prejudice. But at the same time, we have not been able to ignore the fate of the Negro, as a minority group, under your police commissioner." The *New York Amsterdam News* reminded La Guardia that it had questioned O'Ryan's competence months before, mentioning the "slaying of a religious leader [Fletcher] in Brooklyn by two officers, . . . [and] the brutal attack by a uniformed patrolman on an 18-year-old girl in a municipal park and other similar incidents." The Black weekly then told the mayor, "We know that you must realize that your obligation [is] to the people who elected you. . . . We cannot longer remain silent on this vital issue which affects us all."[70]

O'Ryan resigned on September 13, stating as his reason the mayor's "'interference' with police discipline." On that day, the general primary day, as he explained in his statement to the city's press, he and La Guardia had a heated disagreement over the mayor's issuing an order to the chief of staff of the Police Department to station 1,400 policemen and detectives in Harlem. Because of La Guardia's leniency, O'Ryan complained, there were only four arrests on a primary day. The retiring commissioner had no faith in La Guardia's administration to respond prudently and effectively to "serious disorder." According to O'Ryan, La Guardia's interventions—suspension and trial of Inspector Alex Anderson, ban on nightsticks, investigation of the police's reaction to the Scottsboro meeting in Harlem, and other actions— "encouraged the disorderly and criminal class." Furthermore, alleged the former police commissioner, "the rank and file of the police gained the impression that the mayor was in sympathy with the unlawful activities of the demonstrators."[71] O'Ryan's complaints certainly reinforced the inviolability of police discretion and outlined La Guardia's deteriorating relationship with the rank and file. In the mayor's office for less than a year, La Guardia had already broken his promise to remain out of police affairs. He challenged police discretion to protect the taxicab drivers but to a lesser degree the Communists and Blacks in Harlem. Less than a year into his first term, he was already losing the trust of the NYPD.[72]

"Muss 'Em Up"

Lewis J. Valentine, Mayor La Guardia's appointment for the vacant position as the head official of the New York Police Department, represented, somewhat, a departure from O'Ryan's reign of military-style policing. According to the *Daily News*, the appointment of Valentine signaled "a New Deal in law enforcement with leniency as the keynote policy toward the underdog."[73] In representing his style of police administration, Valentine described his approach as conservative. And to ensure a tranquil transition, he claimed that "the General's (O'Ryan's) policy is my policy—enforcing law and rigorously disciplining members of the force." Along with claiming that his policy aligned with O'Ryan's, Valentine was not uncritical of the police force. Valentine opined that 2 percent of them were "potential disgraces or scandals," though the majority, of course, were "decent, hardworking honest men and women who require little supervision." Valentine's criticism of police corruption reflected his long career in the department's Confidential Squad. The antecedent of the department's internal affairs division, committed to "maintaining the integrity" of the NYPD and the uprooting of police corruption, the Confidential Squad was formed by Captain Dan Costigan in 1914. Valentine had joined the Manhattan Police Headquarters in 1903, and as he passed his civil service examinations, he quickly learned that loyalty to Tammany—not merit—determined police officers' destiny. Valentine unwittingly benefited from politicians once and promised that that would be the last time. Before his appointment as commissioner, Valentine and the Confidential Squad were fearless enemies of Tammany Hall. Indeed, the tally of demotions and setbacks that blemished his career symbolized the catalog of corrupt cops he had gotten off the street. As he admitted, "The wearing of the blue uniform was a potent weapon to engage in graft, blackmail, bribery— even connivance at murder."[74] Consequently, as he accepted his new position as the police commissioner, as if a reminder to the patrolmen and detectives that he admonished during his investigation of the teargassed Scottsboro meeting last March, Valentine warned, "We will not tolerate those who bring discredit upon the department, themselves and their families."[75]

The *New York Amsterdam News* graciously thanked the mayor "for his timely announcement of the resignation of Police Commissioner O'Ryan and congratulate[d] him upon the appointment of Chief Inspector Valentine to the post." O'Ryan's resignation was not solely the outcome of the *New York Amsterdam News*'s demands. Nevertheless, it demonstrated the heightened expectations of the Black community and the community's demands for governmental accountability with specific regard to policing.[76] Under Commissioner Valentine's leadership, the NYPD treated labor demonstrations less heavy-handedly. In the police manual, new regulations "recognize[d] the legality of peaceful picketing and of a 'peaceful, orderly strike,' [and] discourage[d] the employment of 'professional bullies and thugs by either side.'" It was not only the beginning of the end of police corruption but also a new deal in policing for the underprotected.[77]

Throughout the fall of 1934 and spring of 1935, the *New York Amsterdam News* reported many cases of police brutality. Despite his promise to bring a semblance of civility to the NYPD, La Guardia's new reform-minded police commissioner Lewis J. Valentine upheld his officers' excessive abuse of criminal offenders and the innocent. Despite his criticism and disdain for police graft, he thought quite differently about the use of coercive force. He disclosed proudly, "When I became a rookie cop I thanked myself for having learned to use my fists well as a boy. Cracking jaws and flattening noses was the only effective means of impressing law and order upon cheap hoodlums."[78] Valentine promoted an aggressive policy of law enforcement that he coined "muss 'em up," to punish hardened criminals, particularly gangsters. In late November, after the commissioner's comments to the men of the department's Detective Division about handling "thugs," the *New York Times*'s front page headlined, "Police Get Orders to Terrorize Thugs," and other metropolitan news outlets followed, including the *New York Daily News*, "'Rough Stuff for Thugs' Valentine Edict to Cops"; the *Brooklyn Daily Eagle*, "Beat Up All Thugs, Police Are Ordered"; and the *New York Herald Tribune*, "Valentine Adds 'Discretion' to 'Muss Up' Order."[79]

In the Christmas issue of *Spring 3100*, the NYPD's magazine, Commissioner Valentine responded to the metropolitan's press coverage of his "muss 'em up" policing. Like O'Ryan and La Guardia before him, Valentine framed police discretion around police professionalism. The confidential conversation between the commissioner and his officers was "not a play of words for publicity purposes." He spoke to responsible members of the police department and knew that his comments "would be gauged from an intelligent viewpoint." Consequently, he insisted, "There was no intention to voice

A New Deal in Law Enforcement   69

a policy of general police brutality. I emphasized and pointed out that decisive action is to be taken in those instances where decisive action is justified." "Muss 'em up" policing was not about police brutality but crimefighting and transforming the NYPD's tradition of collusion and corruption. Police use of coercive force, therefore, reinforced police authority and professionalism. He noted, "Habit, to most of us, is much like a malady—it is not easy to shake off." Valentine had been in the department since 1903, and he well understood the depths of bribery, theft, and various forms of police misconduct. His career had, in fact, suffered because of his long effort to release the police department from the clutches of Tammany Hall. He explained that "for a great number of years many men in the Police Department of the City of New York have come to believe that racketeers, thugs, and criminals," particularly those who "gained them financial and political standing, must, of necessity, be treated with kid gloves." He wrote that it would take more than one "pep talk" to change these habits. The talk was necessary instruction for his men but also "for the protection and safeguarding of the people within this city."[80]

The mayor supported Valentine's approach as an effective and reasonable response to the "crime wave." According to the mayor, "one reason for the widespread wave of crime . . . is the absence throughout the country of a policy which would divide crime into two classes—the first resulting from accident or economic conditions and the second, organized crime, which is directed and sustained by the habitual criminal." He continued, "For treatment of the first class we can be guided by the expert psychologist, social workers, economist and psychiatrist. As to the other class I take the advice of Lewis J. Valentine."[81] "Muss 'em up," then, was Valentine and La Guardia's official crime policy, despite Valentine's claims to the contrary, especially as La Guardia tried to reestablish his commitment to the NYPD. As he expressed at a reception of the Patrolmen's Benevolent Association at Madison Square Garden, "I have attended funeral after funeral of our police." Thus, because of this threat, noted the Daily News, the mayor "expected police to defend themselves against thugs."[82]

As cases of brutality began to pile up, Black leaders rightly cast suspicion on Valentine's promise to protect "the people," especially Black people, from police misconduct. On September 28, only a couple of weeks into Valentine's term as the police commissioner, a white patrolman, O'Neil Hughes, arrested and beat fifteen-year-old William Chase on West 112th Street. Hughes accused Chase of anti-Semitism. The teenager and Mrs. Almira Smith, his mother, claimed that he and others had been watching a scuffle between two Black kids. As the crowd formed, it attracted police officers, and the crowd immediately began to disperse. Chase, following the crowd, fell to the ground, and Patrolman Hughes fell over the boy's body. Embarrassed by the laughter of the crowd, Hughes "snatched the youth from the pavement and . . . struck him brutally in the face." Chase also claimed that Hughes beat him again while in custody after he demanded to see the captain in order to find out what he had been charged with. That same Friday evening, the police released Chase under the custody of his mother. But because of Hughes's testimony that Chase tripped him and that his gang attacked a Jewish boy, Magistrate Brandt returned him to detention until Wednesday, when another boy during his testimony admitted that Chase had only been a spectator. Mrs. Smith intended to "lay the case before Commissioner Valentine" and the mayor. The *New York Amsterdam News* questioned how Valentine would respond to "the first official charge of police brutality since" his appointment as the commissioner.[83]

Though the trail of sources of this story ends here, Ethelred Brown, a longtime critic of police brutality in Harlem, directed his studied attention to Valentine and his "muss 'em up" crime policy. Brown's ethics of safety and law and order defined his critique of Valentine. Evoking the complaints made during the justice for Herbert Dent campaign, Brown, pastor of the Hubert Harrison Memorial Church, concerned with police brutality but also crime, believed that Valentine should be removed from his position. Brown argued that Valentine's brutality and "lust for blood" contributed to more vengeful and violent criminals. "For every gangster we shoot down," he explained, "another rises up to avenge him." But more than provoking more violent crime, Brown also believed that police aggression would be projected upon the innocent, that is, "people who cannot be classed as criminals." For Brown, Valentine's policy was a rejection of law and order, as well as of the basic principles of the American judicial system. According to Brown, "America forgets the maxim that every man arrested is presumed to be innocent until, before a legal tribunal, with legal evidence, he is found guilty. The result is third degree methods that the Wickersham Commission found, and the rooms of torture that are in every police station."[84]

· · · · · ·

In late February 1935, in an editorial titled "Crime and Punishment," the *New York Amsterdam News* detailed a litany of police brutality cases in Harlem since Valentine had become the city's police commissioner. The Black weekly shared with its readers the kinds of police service "Muss 'Em Up"

Valentine valued. The commissioner congratulated Patrolman Isadore Astel for shooting to death Andrew Barnes, a twenty-three-year-old, in a darkened basement in a grocery store. "We want you to know," said the commissioner to his officers, "that we appreciate your work and I want to congratulate you." This recent killing of Barnes by Astel was one link in a chain of killings where minor crimes resulted in the murder of an alleged criminal offender. As the *New York Amsterdam News* lamented, for Blacks "burglary becomes a capital offense—in Harlem."[85] As Black New Yorkers confronted Valentine's era of "muss 'em up" policing, despite La Guardia's and the commissioner's vaguely conciliatory gestures toward reform, the NYPD continued to treat them, to use La Guardia's language, as "habitual criminals."

La Guardia's investigation of the NYPD was a significant expression of racial liberalism and police reform, especially in light of the Wickersham Commission and the Seabury Investigation. Black New Yorkers, like Blacks across the nation, revered Ada Wright's campaign to free her children, so La Guardia's prompt response to the police riot was keen recognition of both the importance of the Scottsboro case to African Americans and Harlemites' violent encounters with the police. The *New York Amsterdam News*'s "O'Ryan Must Go" campaign, along with the ACLU, the Communist Party, and labor, pushed these issues to the fore, especially as O'Ryan protested angrily about the mayor's restraint of police aggression. O'Ryan's complaints echoed police rhetoric that judged any regulation of police restraint as antithetical to law enforcement and a concession to criminals. La Guardia's public challenge to O'Ryan clashed with an entrenched tradition of unbridled police discretion. Yet La Guardia's racial liberalism was limited. Arguably, the mayor went further than district attorneys Banton in 1922 and Brower in 1930. But neither La Guardia nor O'Ryan and Valentine disciplined the police, despite acknowledging the officers' wrongdoing. Valentine even described the police as victims of a crowd of fleeing Harlemites trying to escape flailing police batons and choking tear gas. As a mayor elected to office, in part, to reform the criminal justice system, La Guardia seemed to fulfill this objective except when it came to his Black citizens. As the mayor and Valentine jump-started their own war on crime, throughout the remainder of the decade and the next, Black New Yorkers remained some of the NYPD's prevalent targets and casualties of state-sanctioned violence.[86]

3 Say a Few Nasty Things about the Police

On March 19, 1935, at around four in the afternoon, Lino Rivera, a sixteen-year-old Afro–Puerto Rican, upon leaving the movie theater and heading home, decided to walk through the S. H. Kress dime store on 125th Street because it was a shorter distance to get home. When Rivera entered, there were about 500 patrons, mostly Blacks, in the store. As he passed a counter, he saw a knife that matched his fountain-pen set. Admiring the knife, he admitted, "I wanted it, and so I took it."[1] The manager, Jackson Smith and the two clerks, Charles Hurley and Stephen Urban, chased Rivera and cornered him in the back of the store. Once Hurley and Urban seized him, Rivera bit his captors, who, according to the police, required medical attention. "The customers in the store were thrown into a fever of excitement," according to the *New York Times*, "during which Rivera left."[2] The *Daily News*'s account was different. Kress's employees held Rivera until the arrival of Patrolman Alfred Eldridge of the Crime Prevention Bureau. Eldridge questioned him, jotted down his name and address, and then released him. These inconsistent and conflicting accounts about the apprehension of Rivera contributed to the confusion about the basic facts of the uproar.[3]

The Harlem Riot forced La Guardia to reckon with his administration's failure to reconcile its liberal rhetoric with the Jim Crow conditions that only worsened in the throes of the Great Depression and World War II. The mayor's response was a test of his commitment to interracial democracy and the capacity of his administration to treat all citizens fairly. La Guardia's immediate action, his assembling of a biracial body to investigate the cause of the "disturbance," won the favor of Black leaders, the Black community, and whites committed to racial comity. With E. Franklin Frazier, Howard University professor and sociologist, guiding it as its research director, the commission assembled prominent Black leaders, such as civic leader and dentist Charles Roberts, serving as the chairman of the commission; social worker and attorney Eunice Hunton Carter; poet Countee Cullen; Hubert T. Delany, attorney and public official; socialist and president of the Brotherhood of Sleeping Car Porters Union A. Philip Randolph; John W. Robinson, a minister of the Interdenominational Ministers Alliance; and attorney and

National Association for the Advancement of Colored People (NAACP) board member Charles E. Toney. La Guardia also chose a select group of white civic and religious leaders for his commission, including Morris Ernst and Arthur Garfield Hays of the American Civil Liberties Union; John C. Grimley of the 369th Infantry and a former hospital administrator; Monsignor William McCann of St. Charles Borromeo in Harlem; William Jay Schieffelin, trustee of the Tuskegee Institute; and Oswald Garrison Villard, editor of the *New York Evening Post* and cofounder of the NAACP. Coming a year after the police riot in Harlem in 1934, the mayor's committee signaled a departure from the mayor relying on the New York Police Department to investigate itself. In La Guardia, it seemed Blacks had now found a mayor ready and willing to treat them as first-class citizens. Yet before the work of the commission had begun, La Guardia and other public officials were already convinced that the Communist Party (CP) was to blame. In this version of the riot's story, the Young Liberators stirred racial hysteria and spread the rumor that Kress's management beat Rivera to death, thereby inciting the misled, young Black looters who rampaged Harlem's business district.[4]

Harlem's white entrepreneurial class and liberal Black establishment explained the riot differently. Though they believed the CP hastened the riot, the Harlem Merchants Association and the Uptown Chamber of Commerce complained about crime and the restraint of the police. Some believed that state troopers were needed to do what the NYPD failed to, conspicuously reminding La Guardia and Valentine that the protection of white property was a critical role of the police. Whites' "crime talk" disclosed not only their use of crime as a political tool but also their own insecurities, fears, and preoccupations around race, Blackness, and property. Black liberals and the CP indicted the racism that created the economic and social conditions Black Harlem endured in the city. Undoubtedly, the CP had hastened the spread of the rumors, but the riot was connected to Black Harlem's economic plight and encounters with Jim Crow conditions and police violence. Although the "Don't Buy Where You Can't Work" campaign had imploded, neither Harlemites' pursuit for jobs that gave rise to the movement nor white proprietors' stubborn resistance to hiring Blacks had changed. Many Black leaders therefore believed this smoldered discontent made Kress and white businesses glaring targets of Black outrage.

Black and white New Yorkers, leaders of social reform and civil rights organizations, and educators, among others, wrote letters to La Guardia and his commission in support of the investigation, where they also shared their personal experiences of job loss, racism in the relief programs, and disrespectful and exploitative white proprietors. Many whites, on the other hand, complained about Blacks' attacks upon white property and citizens. Though Harlem's Black population had long claimed the district as its own, some whites remained, and the riot for many of them represented the loss of their respectable neighborhood. Because of Black settlement, they complained, crime thrived, and white life and property were left under siege.

At the hearings, Black witnesses to the aftermath of Rivera's mischief at the Kress store told different stories than the accounts found in the white dailies. Black people seeking information about Rivera's whereabouts received threats from the police. Under interrogation, police officers admitted that they could have handled the Rivera debacle differently. But more than exposing the incompetence of the police, the hearings revealed Black Harlemites' long-standing complaints about police abuse. The hearings were transformative. Held over several months, the hearings were a long overdue public critique of the NYPD and the La Guardia administration. In August, La Guardia released the first subcommittee report on the cause of riot, a damning indictment of the police department and Police Commissioner Lewis Valentine, who failed to cooperate with the commission. The report explained that police violence was institutionalized and that the NYPD suffered from a culture of brutality that predated both the mayor and the commissioner.

One member of the commission, William McCann, condemned the hearings and the report. McCann defended the police and complained that there was "prejudice against law and order." Colonel Leopold Philipp, vice president of the Uptown Chamber of Commerce, agreed, and criticized the report, especially Arthur Garfield Hays, the head of the Police and Crime subcommittee. Philip complained that Hays ran the hearings poorly and lambasted the commission for failing to ask Harlemites about crime. As the subcommittees submitted reports to the mayor, he distributed them to the relevant commissioners of the municipal departments responsible for those areas under investigation. His chief public officials, especially Valentine, gave little merit to the reports.

By late July 1936, as La Guardia publicly undermined his own commission and its recommendations, the *New York Amsterdam News* printed a complete draft of the commission report. While most of the individual subcommittee reports had been published in whole or in part, the complete report, a damning critique of the La Guardia administration, hit the national Black press but was barely mentioned in the white press. The limits of La Guardia's liberal governance had clashed with Black New Yorkers' raised expectations that the mayor would follow through with releasing the report and implementing its recommendations. By September, the mayor still refused to release the report, even as Black liberals tried to create a path for its release without damaging his administration's reputation. A decade after the uprising, Adam Clayton Powell Sr., describing the mayor's committee, complained that it "should have been called the Committee to Delay Action for their report is still in the City Hall."[5]

The battles around the work of the mayor's committee had a powerful impact on Harlem and New York City politics. The hearings especially gave Harlemites, and the Communist Party, an opportunity to air out their grievances to the La Guardia administration. In doing so, Harlemites made a direct connection between their living conditions under the housing and economic crises and La Guardia's New Deal programs and municipal departments. The failures of the police department, therefore, were representative of the La Guardia administration's other departments and agencies. On the other hand, many whites read the mayor's independent investigation of local government, especially its police department, as support of Black Harlem, particularly Black crime. Though the white press did not cover the *New York Amsterdam News*'s publication of the mayor's committee report, it did cover the hearings for most of the spring of 1935 and the fall of 1936. Even though La Guardia refused to formally publish the report, readers of the city's dailies learned about Harlemites' criticisms of the mayor. From the perception of white Harlem, Black Harlemites' criticisms of the NYPD deflected from the threat of Black crime, which they lamented resulted in whites' precarious control of the neighborhood. Nonetheless, white Harlemites, especially property owners, held considerable sway in the city. With Harlem crowded with Blacks as the residential majority, white Harlem called for greater police aggression, in the name of law and order, to protect their businesses and homes.

"Small Groups of Vicious Individuals"

Indignant. The police were violent. Their demeanor irreverent. The police instigated the riot on March 19 that began at the Kress dime store. A patrolman threatened a Black woman with violence for showing concern for and asking about the safety of Rivera. Harlemites' questions went unanswered. During the commotion, a rumor had spread that Rivera was held in the basement and was being beaten. Black patrons, reported the *New York Times*, "went on the rampage, overturning counters, strewing merchandise on the floor and shouting." Once an ambulance arrived across the street, an unidentified woman ran into the street and spread the rumor that Rivera had been killed from the beating. Nearby, Patrolman Timothy Shannon overheard the furor and entered the store and called the 123rd Street police precinct for reinforcements. The police arrived and broke up the angry crowd, and by 5:30 P.M. they had restored "order . . . and the police left."[6] Just before 6:00 P.M., when the Kress store was scheduled to close, a group of two Blacks and two whites of the Young Liberators (YL), a youth faction of the Communist Party, arrived with their picket signs, which read "Brutality Beats Negro Child" and "Kress Brutality Beats and Seriously Injures Negro Child." They marched back and forth in front of the store, and then one of the YL, Daniel Miller, stepped on "a hastily made platform and launched into a harangue." As the crowd swelled, the rumor that the police killed Rivera had now taken on a life of its own. The crowd began throwing bottles and bricks at the store and the squad of police. As several more units of police arrived, the crowd had grown to about 3,000 people. By this time, there were over five radio cars and emergency men, as well as mounted and foot patrolmen. At around 7:00 P.M., as more people arrived, milling at the front and the rear of the store, a hearse parked at a building across from the back of the Kress store. According to the *Afro-American* correspondent, who arrived on 125th Street around 7:15 P.M., the police would not allow reporters into the store and refused to answer the question, "Well, where is the boy?" As uncertainty mixed with anger and frustration, a flock of people congregated across the street. They "talked about mass action, about the beating up of 'the poor little boy,' about 'if this was a white neighborhood and a colored man had hit a white boy, they would have strung him up long ago.'"[7] Then, a Black women yelled, "There's the hearse come to take the boy's body out of the store."[8]

By nine that evening, Deputy Commissioner David J. McAuliffe oversaw about 500 police officers in Harlem. A half an hour later, all available reserves from Manhattan were sent to Harlem and then more from the Bronx and Brooklyn. Upon the arrival of emergency squads, foot and mounted patrolman, and radio cars, they pushed the mass from the store. According to the *New York Herald Tribune*, the police encountered "mobs of Negroes and white sympathizers."[9] Throughout the night and into the morning, throngs of looters and rioters dispersed across the neighborhood down to 120th Street and Fifth Avenue to the east and north to 138th Street and St. Nicholas Avenue to the west, smashing windows, looting, and sounding false fire alarms. The rioters appropriated food, drink, jewelry, and clothing. As the *New York Herald Tribune* detailed, "Their plunder included canned baked beans and bottles of perfume."[10]

Black proprietors, hoping that the rioters would not raid their stores, hung signs with the word "Colored" in their store windows. A Chinese laundry at 367 Lenox Avenue put up a sign that read "Me colored too," and then "someone promptly smashed his window."[11] White storeowners also displayed signs announcing, "This store employs Negro workers."[12] The businesses on Eighth Avenue, between 124th and 130th Streets, the majority owned by whites, were hit the hardest, though Black-owned businesses north of 130th were also looted. Some white proprietors and employees hid in their stores. Bernard Newman, a manager of a jewelry story on 125th Street and Seventh Avenue, recalled that the looters "screamed and tossed bricks, bits of paving, bottles, and anything into stores. The minute the big show case windows went . . . the mob jumped in the windows and scrambled for the jewelry."[13] As streams of people ran into the police, they hurled bricks at and ran from them. The police used their discretion to the fullest—some people were arrested, many were beaten, and several were shot. "Patrolmen roamed the streets from 110th Street to 145th Street swinging their night sticks assaulting every member of the Race that crossed their paths," observed the *Chicago Defender*. Watching the spectacle from their building windows, Harlemites tossed bricks and makeshift weapons at the police, likely seeking retribution for police abuses that many had suffered or witnessed in the past. By two in the morning, when the police finally found Rivera to prove that he was still alive, the riot had subsided but lingered, as occasional outbursts occurred throughout the morning until around 4:00 A.M.[14]

Neither property nor people escaped the furor unscathed. By the end of the night, 697 windows were broken, amounting to about half a million dollars in damages. The police detained more than 100 people, and fifty-seven civilians, mostly Black, and seven police had been injured. One Black man, Lyman Quarterman, thirty-four years old, died in Harlem Hospital, shot in the stomach, presumably during the riot near 121st Street and Seventh Avenue, and two others who were shot lay in the hospital. Over the next couple of weeks, there would be more fatalities. Lloyd Hobbs, sixteen years old, was shot by a patrolman and died of a bullet wound; Edward Laurie, thirty-two years old, died of fractured skull; Andrew Lyons died of internalized injuries; James Thompson was shot by a detective; and August Miller died of a fractured skull. All were Black, except for Miller.[15]

After the disturbance, Mayor La Guardia and other public officials proffered a range of overlapping explanations of the cause of the uproar. Despite slight differences among them, La Guardia and his public officials

FIGURE 3.1 A police officer leads away a man injured in the Harlem Riot of 1935. More than 5,000 police officers, firefighters, and soldiers were sent into Harlem after a night of rioting with four deaths and 195 injuries. Bettmann via Getty Images.

attributed the riot to Black criminals and the Communists. The mayor's response to the unrest was prompt. He sent patrols into Harlem and distributed large circulars, two feet by two and a half feet, appealing to the "law-abiding element" for patience, but also hoped to inform them of the actual chain of events. The rumor that Lino Rivera had been killed by the police had taken on a life of its own in the streets, households, and churches of Harlem. La Guardia's circular described the majority of Harlemites as wholly "decent, law-abiding Americans," but it also assigned guilt to a "small groups of vicious individuals," who perpetuated "malice and viciousness" and had spread rumors. The circular urged Harlemites to carefully inspect any charge or rumor of discrimination and promised that "every agency of the city" would be available to assist in investigating the charges. The circular ended with a statement about his appointing a committee of "representative citizens" to investigate the cause of the uproar and to create a "study of necessary plans to prevent a repetition of the spreading of malicious rumors, racial animosities and the inciting of disorder."[16]

District Attorney William C. Dodge blamed the Communist Party, warning it that it could not come to the United States and "upset our laws."[17] Dodge announced a plan for a citywide grand jury investigation but provided no details. The investigation would target "any persons, no matter what they call themselves, who believe and advocate overthrow of the government." At the grand jury hearing, twenty-six witnesses, mainly uniformed and plainclothes police officers, were heard, with one bearing a folded American flag. Dodge complained that the "reds" had distributed "inflammatory leaflets on the streets" and, he alleged, had been infiltrating American institutions for a long time, but he warned that when they "incite riots it is time to stop them." Police Commissioner Lewis J. Valentine presented a more sober explanation for and assessment of the uproar: Lino Rivera's stealing the pen-knife, "the hysteria of the woman who screamed when she saw store employees searching the boy," the Young Liberators' fallacious circulars and haranguing in front of the Kress store, and the coincidental passing of a hearse. While Valentine agreed that the Communists were culpable, he did not assert, as Dodge had, that they had tried to overthrow the government by "force and violence." Yet, he added, they were always under surveillance and that the police were "always taking steps to suppress them." Harlem's white business establishment, however, questioned the police's vigilance.[18]

Morris Tobin, president of the Harlem Merchants Association, sent a telegram to Governor Lehman asking for military reinforcements to protect

Harlem proprietors. Tobin, a haberdasher, explained that his store, Toby's, at 101 West 125th Street was broken into and the looters stole several thousand dollars' worth of merchandise. Tobin stated, "In the face of the unbridled and open outbreak of violence, riot and plunder of Harlem business establishments, we, the business men and taxpayers of Harlem, demand your personal and immediate intervention. The police officials of New York seem to be inadequately equipped to handle the situation." He explained that he had complained to the police before about the "well-known leaders of outlaws and hoodlums" who stirred racial and religious conflict.[19] Police Commissioner Valentine minimized and rejected Tobin's charge that his officers had lost control. Valentine asserted that the police were "quite competent" and required no assistance from the National Guard.[20] The Uptown Chamber of Commerce's Eugene A. Walsh sent a telegram to La Guardia, commending him on his prudent statement and agreeing with law enforcement's charge of the culpability of the Communists and other radicals. Walsh warned, "Violence will be possible at any time unless immediate and vigorous steps are taken to curb the white agitators . . . who preach violence and disorder and lawlessness." Assuring La Guardia the support and cooperation of the Uptown Chamber of Commerce, Walsh expected the police to protect the "lives and property of decent law-abiding white and Negro citizens."[21]

Black leaders and their allies interpreted the unrest differently. Roy Wilkins, the assistant secretary of the NAACP, asserted that the unrest was precipitated "by discrimination against the Negro in economics, employment, justice and living conditions." Wilkins, a native of St. Louis, Missouri, was born in 1901 and a graduate of the University of Minnesota in 1923. His passion for social justice expressed through his career in journalism led him to move to New York City in 1931, and he joined the NAACP and replaced W. E. B. Du Bois as editor of *The Crisis* in 1934. Wilkins's views were representative of most Black leaders and their white liberal and leftist allies. Jay Schieffelin, chairman of the Citizens Union, stated it was "injustice, exploitation and prejudice." Wilkins, Dr. Robert W. Searle, and others rejected public officials' explanation that the Communists were responsible for instigating the riot. Searle centered the inadequate economic and social conditions that marked the neighborhood. He stated plainly, "We cannot make the Communists the scapegoat for a basic condition which made possible such a hysteric outburst." But what was true was that the CP had advocated on the behalf of Black New Yorkers regarding their civil rights, their economic and housing rights, and their campaigns against police violence.[22]

FIGURE 3.2 March 20: Stores on the corner of Lenox Avenue, between 129th and 130th Streets, after a night of rioting in Harlem. Dick Lewis/New York Daily News Archive via Getty Images.

Rev. William Lloyd Imes, journalist Theophilus Lewis, and Claude McKay viewed the riot through the lens of the "Don't Buy Where You Can't Work" boycott. The campaign began unsuccessfully in 1933 but gained momentum in 1934 before falling apart because of intraracial and anti-Semitic posturing by the end of that year. Emerging out of Harlemites' sense of community rights, Black nationalists, liberals, and secular and religious institutions collectively demanded that stores dependent on Black patronage employ Blacks in white-collar positions. Reverend Imes, of the St. James Presbyterian Church, in a letter to the *New York Amsterdam News*, wrote, "This trouble has its rootage in a very unfair attitude of the 125th Street commercial interests toward the Negro." As a leader of the League of Fair Play, Imes explained that he had evidence of discrimination by white proprietors still reluctant to employ Black people. Lewis and McKay pointed to the dearth of leadership in the movement's campaign that precipitated the internal strife concerning claims of anti-Semitism among Harlem's Black leadership. Lewis, dubbing the leaders of the boycott as "long-distance riot leaders," claimed that street orators repackaged a class problem into a racial conflict that aggravated and eventually fractured the movement. McKay, doubting the anti-Semitism, agreed.[23]

"We Haven't For Got the Five Babys That Was Killed"

Not long after his announcement about his appointed commission, La Guardia and his committee received letters from various organizations and citizens. On March 25, the committee received a letter from two different offices of the International Labor Defense (ILD). In a solicitous letter, the Harlem Section of the ILD suggested that the investigation should be open to everyone and that they should be "given a chance to testify" about the conditions in Harlem, a community in which the ILD had been "closely connected" and therefore had an intimate, "first-hand knowledge" of the conditions there. Mike Walsh, district secretary of the ILD, sent a more direct and confrontational letter, however. Walsh demanded that the ILD be invited to send witnesses and representatives to expose the facts and evidence of the discrimination that Black people were forced to endure, "Jim-crow conditions arising out of . . . segregation . . . in Harlem." Walsh also protested the "slanderous 'red-baiting' drive" employed by District Attorney Dodge, the police department, and the press.[24]

The letter from Henry K. Craft, the executive secretary of the Young Men's Christian Association, lauded La Guardia for appointing a biracial committee to study the unrest in Harlem. Pointing to the work done by the Chicago Commission on Race Relations, Craft encouraged the mayor to use it as a model. He hoped that the study would be used for the good of not only Harlem but also "national life."[25] The commission's report, *The Negro in Chicago: A Study of Race Relations and a Race Riot*, documented the story of the Chicago Race Riot of 1919, the social and economic conditions under which African Americans lived, and their relationships with whites in Chicago. The report was extensive, covering the areas of employment, labor unions, recreation, housing, the Black and white press, and local government. In spite of its appeal to the best sensibilities of Blacks and whites, the commission was unequivocal about the complicity of the police in joining white Chicagoans' brutality toward their fellow Black citizens. It stated in its summary and recommendation chapter that police should "be so distributed as adequately to protect both races . . . and to avoid the gross inequalities of protection which, in the riot of 1919, permitted widespread depredations, including murder, against Negroes in white neighborhoods, and attacks in Negro neighborhoods by invading white hoodlums." Black leaders, including Walter White, had hoped La Guardia's commission might take a similar approach.[26]

White's letter to Eunice Hunton Carter, a member of the committee and its secretary, took an authoritative tone and outlined a set of problems that the committee should investigate and questions the report should answer. White's outline listed areas of inquiry such as relief, employment, crime, housing, health, social agencies, schools, race relations, police, and the immediate causes of the rioting, mirroring the themes and organization that the commission's report would eventually take. In addition to recommending a line of inquiry, White suggested that the committee employ an expert Black lead researcher, such as Ira De A. Reid, Charles Johnson, or E. Franklin Frazier, "who would understand the intangible as well as the tangible factors" that contributed to the unrest. At the end of the letter, White took on a more indulgent tone. Like Craft, White believed that the report would be of great service to New York City and the rest of the nation. Pushing a form of New York exceptionalism—painting the city as a citadel of racial democracy—he wrote that the "liberal attitude on the part of the public" was a model for others to follow. The city, the people, and the press, he applauded, had the "most complete understanding of the economic causes of the disorder of any clash that has occurred within the United States during the last four or five decades." Furthermore, New York City was unlike any other city across the nation, since elsewhere "news of the riot would probably have caused at least talk of the forming of mobs in other parts of the city to go to Harlem to wreak vengeance." The "sound, economic and social approach" of the investigation, undergirded by New York City liberalism, was central to the nation, for it would provide it with an "approach and program" that would "be of untold value to the entire country."[27]

Black citizens also wrote to and shared with La Guardia their experiences of racism and their expectations of the mayor and his committee. On March 23, Mrs. D. J. Williams told him of her family's hardship and struggles to make ends meet. Telling him to "please pay strick [sic] attention to what [she's] going to say," Mrs. Williams challenged the public perception that the Communist Party caused and orchestrated the riot. She refused to allow the CP to be scapegoats and understood that strategy as a way to smear the CP's reputation and, more significantly, erase the experiences of Black people in Harlem. She wrote that Black people were "tired of what [wa]s going on here in Harlem and we are not all dum[b] and radicals as pictured but so much mean and bad treatment will well cause a good watchdog to kill his master."[28] She complained of the city's relief system that "rewarded her with heartac[he]." Told to take her husband to the clinic by a relief investigator, the couple was burdened with expensive medical costs. After being released from relief, they lost their belongings in storage. Bad luck seemed to follow the Williams family everywhere. Writing of her laboring husband, a victim of a racist economy and a corrupt criminal justice system, she explained that her husband had been cut by a Black longshoreman who was freed by a judge "that was paid off by the criminal." She also shared the countless crimes committed against her Black neighbors that were vivid in her own recent memories and likely others:

> And you see we haven't for got the five babys that was killed on 5th Aven near 135th St by a white woman that was drunk and was aloud to go free, and we also havnt for got the man that was killed on lenox Ave for taking one apple because he was hungry also the woman that was kicked in a show repair place and was to become a mother this was done at lenox Ave & 129 St also another woman was kicked a few weeks ago at a bakery shop at 469 lenox Aven and nothing is done about these thing I'm only giving a few outlines of what goes on in harlem out of millions of happening and yet we have no pretiction from the law in being fair with us.[29]

Recounting her experiences with the relief office, the criminal justice system, and the labor market, she wrote, "So you see I have enough to make me go mad and break up Harlem."[30]

Mrs. Williams's encounters with the daily indignities created by state and civilian indifference and racial discrimination mirrored many Harlemites' experiences in New Deal–era New York City. In late March, in a letter to Eunice Hunton Carter, former Harlem resident Helen Mohmed cited an index of problems that plagued the neighborhood, including police brutality, exploitative landlords, and white proprietors who depended on the patronage of Black people but refused to hire them. She argued that Blacks "should have more privileges as . . . American citizen[s]." Calista Turner, writing to the mayor in August, explained that she had gone to the grocery store, "patronized solely by the colored housewives of Harlem," and the storeowner charged sixteen cents for milk. She asked the proprietor when the price of milk had been raised, and "in a very nasty manner he replied, 'how do you think I get ice to keep this milk cold?'" She refused to pay the price, because "the State law did not require" it. Turner, like many Harlemites before her, expected the city to protect "colored housewives[']" economic and consumer rights as central elements of their citizenship. She wrote, "As an American born citizen and a legal resident of the City and State of New York, I demand that this salesman or proprietor of this store be called into question and duly warned if not punished for such atrocious act against these hapless victims."[31]

On April 11, Argyle Stoute, a building engineer–superintendent, wrote to the mayor's committee about losing his job in 1932. Stoute had worked for John J. Hearn of Hotel Winthrop since 1925, but the Depression placed the building into receivership. Once the receivership ended, the Bank of Manhattan Trust Company held the mortgage, which was managed by John Cunehan. The bank asked Cunehan for a report on the building and the employees and in spite of Stoute's receiving an excellent evaluation, he was fired. He asked Cunehan why, and the manager claimed that the bank wanted to replace him with someone else but professed not to know why. Stoute then contacted the bank and spoke with the vice president, who explained that "they had made no such request." According to Stoute, within one month, Cunehan had "systematically eliminated all the Negroes . . . and we were replaced by all whitemen." Stoute had not worked since, and in the interim, had lost his investment in a private home and his savings. Like Mrs. Williams, Stoute framed his plight within the social, economic, and political milieu that he found himself in. Having followed the careers of most of the commissioners, he was hopeful and trusting that the committee would deliver to La Guardia "the true facts and the true cause that forced a few persons to express themselves in the manner that they did." Stoute, rejecting the portrayal of the riot as a criminal act, asked a series of question that exposed the underbelly of New Deal liberalism, the overlapping crises, and racism in New York City: "How can a people eat, clothe and shelter themselves when they are denied jobs and means of supporting their families? Can any people do what is expected of us, under a similar condition?"[32]

Many white New Yorkers viewed the uprising differently. The riot, they asserted, was simply the result of Black criminality. Letters from whites in Harlem often conflated crime with the in-migration and settlement of Harlem. As one anonymous writer claimed, Blacks "ruin[ed] neighborhoods—they move in during the night and in the morning white people are aghast to see the negroes." The unrest from the view of these writers represented Black rage and criminal acts directed at innocent whites. An anonymous writer told La Guardia on March 21 that his public statements "show gross ignorance of the situation." One white letter writer witnessed and others told him that Blacks from every house on their blocks ran out and engaged "in a pitched battle with the white residents, the police and firemen." Harlem, the writer charged, "is one of the most lawless sections in the city." Although he had complained about widespread criminal activity, the police told him that "they [we]re helpless" to fight crime because La Guardia prohibited them from doing so since he "want[ed] the colored vote." The vexed white Harlemite then asked, "If this be true, then I ask you, Mr. Mayor, how much longer you expect to tax the white citizens of this city to support this colored rabble, over 50% of who are on Home Relief?" White New Yorkers had fed, clothed, and housed the "wild, seething, race-mad populace." As a Harlemite since 1914, the district had become worse and Black people were responsible. They believed that Black Harlemites, especially the recent migrants, were criminal and that their virulent racism saturated the district everywhere. As the writer opined, the racism derived "not on the part of the whites but an intense colored hatred for whites." In a letter dated March 20, signed A White Woman with Brothers and Sisters living in that Section, the anonymous letter writer expressed that it was a shame that Blacks got away with the riot in Harlem. They were criminals and whites were unsafe in Harlem, she asserted. Advising La Guardia on how to handle Blacks, especially recent migrants, she charged that the city should "ship them down South where they come from and I bet they would be hung to a tree[.] I don't blame the Southerners for doing it. They got to[o] much lead way."[33]

White New Yorkers' expressions of displacement and the rhetoric of Blacks' abuse of relief and crime shaped interracial relations in Harlem and across the city during and after the commission's investigation. White anger was steeped in decades-long battles over property in Harlem. Indeed, after the turn of the century, as Blacks settled there in large numbers, whites described this movement as a "Negro invasion." As some whites promptly sold their homes for profit, fear and insecurity spread across white Harlem. As the Black community expanded, white Harlem mobilized and engaged in a "border warfare" effort to contain Black mobility and settlement. As whites struggled to maintain residential property in the city, they employed other strategies, including violence.[34] White youth gangs but also adults in Harlem, as they had in other parts of the city, established "deadlines"— boundaries—that Blacks were forbidden to transgress. Bullets Bressan, fondly remembering his tussles with Blacks, explained, "We used to fight the niggers down on San Juan Hill. It was all Black down there. We were up on 69th or 68th, then we come down, beat 'em, threw rocks, plenty of that." Enforcing the artificial racial border, he noted, "They [Blacks] never come up there, we usually went down there. . . . We'd throw rocks, cans, everything. We didn't care if they were ready or not, if they were Blacks, we'd go after 'em."[35] Describing the growth of Black youth gangs in Harlem, one Works Progress Administration writer stated, "The exodus of the downtown Negro to Harlem around 1910 resulted in the formation of gangs." To get to school or to church or to visit relatives, they had to "learn the rudiments of self-protection." As Black gangs claimed areas of Harlem and fought white gangs, often ethnically Irish, white businesses called upon the police to get rid of them. Instead of protecting Black and white youth alike, the police often arrested Black youth and beat them. Consequently, whites' perceptions of Black criminality in Harlem, especially among Black youth, in part stemmed from their efforts to maintain an all-white neighborhood by any means necessary, including turning a blind eye to white youth violence and sanctioning police aggression.[36]

White Harlemites' commentary in the wake of the uproar, therefore, reflected strategies they had long used to defend their neighborhoods and reestablish control that was rapidly slipping from their grasp. Whites' commentary on crime especially challenged Black Harlemites' critique of police violence, white racism, and municipal neglect as contributing causal factors of the riot. By re-centering the criminal behavior of Black rioters and painting Blacks, especially recent southern migrants, as infesting Harlem with crime, whites shifted the responsibility of the riot from La Guardia's "small groups of vicious individuals" to the entire Black community. Many whites believed in the racial fiction, that because of their departure from Harlem the neighborhood devolved into a crime-ridden Black ghetto. The police's claim that La Guardia impeded them from halting Black crime because the mayor "want[ed] the colored vote" reinforced white Harlemites' attitudes about Black crime. When Harlem was white, the police aggressively put Blacks in their place. The appraisal of whites and the police, however, contrasted with the letters from Mrs. D. J. Williams, Argyle Stoute, Mohmed, and Turner, who revealed not only the impact of the slack economy on the Harlemites but also racial discrimination in the management of the city's New Deal bureaucracy. These matters, though, were not limited to city government, as Williams pointed out. The uncivility and violence of white citizens and the exploitation of white proprietors set the stage for Black discontent. These opposing ideas from whites and Blacks would be revealed during the commission's hearings and in the subcommittee reports.[37]

The Subcommittee Hearings

The hearings exposed and aired out in public many of the grievances that Blacks had shared among themselves in their homes and churches and on the streets of Harlem. Operating under the aegis of the La Guardia administration, the hearings legitimated their grievances and gave them hope that their concerns would be heard and their expectations met. On March 30, Arthur Garfield Hays presided over the first hearing held at the Municipal Court, 455 West 151st Street. Investigating the cause of the riot, speakers focused on the long-standing tensions between Harlemites and the police department. Yet the lingering ire from the riot less than two weeks before set the tone. Hays asked Lino Rivera to give an account of his encounter with the police. Rivera testified that the police neither beat him nor threatened to harm him but admitted that Kress's staff threatened him. He remembered, "Two men caught me and one of them said 'come on, I'll take you down to the cellar and beat you up.'" Rivera bit one of them, and after being apprehended, a white policeman, Raymond J. Donahue, escorted him to the basement of the store. Donahue, under questioning from Hays, admitted that if he had shown the Black community that Rivera was unharmed the riot might have been avoided.[38]

The police's recklessness was only one aspect of the first hearing. Verbal battles between the assistant district attorney (ADA) Alexander H. Kaminsky and the CP also took center stage. Hays's decision to invite spectators to question those summoned to testify shifted the power dynamics of hearings and placed the NYPD under scrutiny and on the defensive. Well prepared to defend its actions, the CP took advantage of this opportunity and brought members of the CP, as well as the International Labor Defense (ILD). ADA Kaminsky and Joseph Tauber, an ILD attorney, fought constantly. Kaminsky refused to be questioned by the attorneys, calling them "irresponsible." Hays reprimanded Kaminsky, insisting "that he had no right to call anyone 'irresponsible'" because they held different political views from his. During questioning, Joseph Taylor of the Young Liberators claimed that an unknown person gave out the circulars while he was on the streets trying to verify reports that the boy was killed by the police. The first hearing judged the police singularly responsible for mishandling the situation. Under interrogation by ILD attorneys Tauber and Edward Kuntz, Inspector John De Martino, white, admitted that if he were the patrolman, he would have stopped the rumor by "releas[ing] the boy where all could have seen what he was doing."[39]

FIGURE 3.3 March 19: Lino Rivera with Police Lieutenant Samuel J. Battle and a group of newspaper reporters to whom he is relating the incident that brought on Harlem's race riot. George Rinhart / Corbis via Getty Images.

District Attorney (DA) William C. Dodge's unwillingness to cooperate with the hearings reinforced Harlemites' deep-seated distrust of the police department. During a hearing in early April, Hays read letters into the record that revealed that DA Dodge had requested Police Commissioner Lewis J. Valentine to order his officers not to testify before the mayor's committee. Kuntz argued that "this silencing of the police was extremely unfair." In his letter, Dodge explained that his job as prosecutor was to preserve evidence of crime and refused "to produce the evidence that we had before the grand jury." Hays, agreeing with Kuntz, retorted, "I don't think the attitude of the district attorney is tenable and I think it will be withdrawn."[40] Hays then invited the police officers to testify despite the objections of Lt. Samuel Battle, Harlem's first Black police officer. Hays also asked Harlemites involved in the pending cases to testify, a sharp contrast from the district attorney's reluctance to speak with Harlemites. Patrolman Timothy Shannon, one of the first to arrive at the Kress store, explained that he formed a committee of four citizens, two Black and two white, that he led to the basement to prove that the boy had not been beaten to death. Hays asked Shannon, as he had Donahue the week before, why the police had not shown Rivera to the crowd. The officer explained, "I only did what I was told." Careful not to blame him, Hays expressed that the rumor "could have been stifled at the start if it ha[d] been properly handled by the police."[41] In fact, the rumor stubbornly lingered weeks later. Few doubted that Rivera was present at the store, but others believed that another boy was killed. Others questioned if Rivera had been substituted by either the police or Kress's representatives. Rev. William Lloyd Imes, pastor of St. James Presbyterian Church, announced that while many members of his congregation and other churches believed Rivera was present at the store, they did not believe that he was "the real boy over whom the disturbance started."[42] In spite of their disillusionment regarding the verity of the rumors, the Black community's castigations of the police were vindicated as the hearings exposed the police killing of Lloyd Hobbs.

Russell Hobbs, Lloyd's brother, testified hours before his brother passed away in Harlem Hospital. Returning home from a movie, the brothers stopped to watch the melee near 127th Street and Seventh Avenue. When Patrolman John McInerney yelled "Break it up," the two scattered. While in flight, his brother was shot in the abdomen.[43] Lloyd's mother, Mrs. Lawyer Hobbs, testified that during her last visit to her son in the hospital he "cried out to me: 'mother, a policeman shot me for nothing.'" Four eyewitnesses refuted McInerney's version of the story. Their testimonies contrasted with the police reports, which read that McInerney ordered the boys to stop and that he fired a shot in the air. Howard Mallory and the other eyewitnesses charged that McInerny purposely shot Hobbs. The spectators demanded that McInerney be arrested and held until the outcome of the investigation.[44] In a hearing in mid-April, Mallory explained that there was an attempt to disqualify his testimony before the grand jury because of his criminal record. Mallory's experience raised the question of Blacks' participation on grand juries in the city. No one present could recall of a Black person on the county grand jury, and attorney Louis J. Lavell asserted that he was sure that there had not been more than one in the last thirty years. James W. Ford, the leader of the Harlem section of the Communist Party, exclaimed that "Decatur, Alabama was ahead of New York in that particular."[45]

In mid-April, Patrolman James B. Waterson, the partner of John McInerney, and Detective John J. O'Brien testified. Detective O'Brien, who investigated the shooting of Hobbs, stated that there was no list of goods stolen by Hobbs until three days after the incident and no mention of stolen goods in the first report. "As far as he knew," Hobbs's fingerprints were not recovered from the newfound items alleged to have been stolen, and no witnesses appeared to corroborate the police's account of the shooting.[46] Waterson's testimony invited boos from the audience. He was barely audible and struggled to recount their encounter with Hobbs. According to the *New York Times*, he was "just explaining that he had been forced to hold a crowd with a riot gun." The *Afro-American*, however, claimed that Waterson's details were "not very clear" about what happened before the shooting of Hobbs. The spectators urged him to speak louder, and then someone yelled, "Ask the dog to bark louder."[47] Hays demanded that person to come forward and apologize. Edward Welsh, Black, a leader in the Unemployed Councils, stood up but dismissed the apology. Hays explained that he would not tolerate his witnesses being insulted and threatened to adjourn the meeting unless Welsh left the premises. The crowd "booed and hissed the chairman with unrestrained ardor." Hays adjourned the hearing for ten minutes and threatened to stop the hearing for the remainder of the day if Welsh returned. When the hearing reopened, Welsh refused to leave and then promised to only after Waterson apologized. Defiant, Welsh chose obstinance, "because that officer had insulted all the people of Harlem by getting on the stand and telling lies." L. F. Coles, a journalist well known for his column "Voice of the People" and a friend of Welsh, spoke on his behalf.[48]

During the subcommittee's hearings, other cases of police violence emerged that reinforced the community's allegations of police misconduct. These cases expanded the hearings' attention to not only the cause and causalities of the uprising but also the police's denial of Black Harlemites' constitutional rights. On May 5, Detective Joseph F. Flinter arrested and detained Robert Patterson pending an investigation by the Philadelphia Police Department. Patterson's arrest was based on an anonymous call. After several days, the Philadelphia police disclosed that Patterson had committed no crime. In mid-May, Mr. Hays questioned Flinter about his actions and uncovered that the detective did not know the penal code. Hays described the incident as "disgraceful" and explained the law to the audience and police officers in attendance, emphasizing that the police could not enter a home without a warrant unless they had knowledge that a felony had been committed. The police thought that "'suspicion' of a fellow was enough." He lamented to Samuel Battle, "I think that you, as a high officer in the police department, should charge yourself to see that these things don't happen, especially to your people." Speaking candidly to all of the police officers at the hearing, he surmised that they knew they would not treat a well-known person or someone living on "Park Avenue" that way. Then, he asked the mostly Black crowd in attendance if they had been mistreated similarly like Patterson, and "witness after witness, and a show of hands from the floor, bore witness to the 'general police practice' of searching citizens on the streets and entering their homes" without probable cause or a warrant.[49]

The hearings revealed that police misconduct took other forms. Their flagrant disregard for Harlemites' right to be secure in their persons was matched by their propensity for excessive force. On March 23, less than a week after the unrest, Patrolman Abraham Zakutinsky killed Edward Laurie. Auburn Hill, a counterman at a restaurant at 511 Lenox Avenue, called the police because Laurie appeared intoxicated and threatening. Testifying before the subcommittee in May, Patrolman Zakutinsky, of the 135th Street Station, alleged that Laurie struck him and he retaliated. Zakutinsky's punch felled Laurie, who died in Harlem Hospital from a fractured skull as a result of hitting his head on the sidewalk. Throughout the patrolman's testimony, "the audience arose, booed, and jeered" him.[50] After the hearing, the CP took up the campaign for justice for Laurie in the *Daily Worker*. The daily sent a telegram to DA Dodge demanding that his office investigate the killing of Laurie and to order an autopsy of the body. The *Daily Worker* also disclosed to its readers that the police "speedily exonerated" Zakutinsky, who was still on duty in Harlem.[51] The telegram was followed by a letter from James Ford to the mayor's committee to investigate Laurie's case. Cyril Briggs described the killing of Laurie as an extension of the La Guardia administration's "reign of terror" and reported that, according to eyewitnesses, Laurie was punished because he called the officer "one of them wise coppers." Briggs asserted, "Symptomatic of the terror engendered in Harlem by the La Guardia administration is the evident reluctance with which eyewitnesses of Saturday's police murder related the event to the writer. And not one was willing to have his name used in connection with this statement."[52] After deeper investigation into Zakutinsky's police record, Briggs reported that on September 5 the patrolman killed Santos Fernandez, a Puerto Rican child. At the time, he was assigned to the 123rd Street police station. Zakutinsky found two kids in the backyard of a chain store and accused them of trying to break into a store. Without giving them a chance to explain, he shot Fernandez and aimed his gun at the other kid, who screamed, "Please don't kill me." According to Briggs, his screams incited protests and "saved the intended second child-victim of La Guardia's police thug."[53]

In another case, because of police aggression, Thomas Aikens lost his eye. Aikens, who lived at 760 St. Nicholas and was only recently released from the hospital, testified at the hearing wearing a Black patch over his left eye. Several days before the riot, policemen David Egan and Eugene Cahill dragged him from a breadline at the 169th Regiment Armory. The officers and an armory employee believed that Aikens was a troublemaker trying to skip people on the line. One of the officers, testified Aikens, punched him in the face and another gouged out his eye with a nightstick. Aikens was charged with felonious assault. Buck Brown, an eyewitness, corroborated Aikens's story and testified that the officers beat him and left him on the ground for more than an hour before the ambulance took him to Harlem Hospital. When Egan and Cahill were invited to take the stand to tell their version of the story, they refused, stoking the anger of the audience. The officers claimed that Police Commissioner Valentine and District Attorney Dodge ordered them not to. Charles Romney, executive secretary of the Civil Rights Protective Association, condemned the police department as corrupt, repressive, and disreputable. Police officers, detailed Romney, arrived to work in Harlem "drunk." Romney claimed that the police had taken unemployed Black people, given them alcohol, and used them in courts as witnesses. They had attacked Black men and women without provocation and searched their homes without a warrant. In other cases, they had beaten Black people and, asserted Romney, taken them to Harlem Hospital. According to Romney, they had "never been heard of again." Hays asked him if he could provide a specific case, and Romney mentioned Emory Clay, who lived at the Salvation Army but had not been seen since March 17 after being beaten by the police and taken to Harlem Hospital with a fractured skull. He promised, "The next policeman who interferes with me, my relatives or my witnesses, I am not going to appeal to the law. I am going to take the law into my own hands!" Romney's call for self-protection brought the majority of the audience to cheer him on.[54]

At a hearing on employment in April, Black and white leaders, from liberals to the leftists, testified to the rampant discrimination operating in the city's labor market. Socialist leader Norman Thomas urged the commission to support legislation to ensure equal treatment on all public works or employment funded by government. Thomas also questioned the efficacy of laws and asserted that "perhaps picketing and boycotts are better weapons."

The audience "cheered wildly" for the socialist but booed Paul Blanshard, who defended the La Guardia administration against charges of discrimination by the Public Works Administration (and city contracts). James Hubert, of the New York Urban League, attacked the discriminatory employment practices of stores in Harlem and the city's relief administration. Mrs. Celia C. Saunders, executive secretary of the 137th Street YMCA, explained that educated girls were relegated to working as domestics for room and board and that the few local stores that employed Black women "insisted that the girls be 'fair.'" Frank Crosswaith, organizer of the International Ladies Garment Workers Union, complained that among the 1,000 men working on the federal courthouse, not one was Black, and of the 700 men building a municipal building near the detention complex, only one was hired as a water carrier.[55]

The teachers asked for a closed hearing, fearing reprisal from the Board of Education. Before the hearing, Harold G. Campbell refuted claims that there was racial discrimination and referenced Mrs. Gertrude Ayer, the only Black principal, as an example of the city's commitment to Black educators to disprove the allegation. Campbell admitted that there had not been a school built in Harlem in the last twenty-six years, and that under the new building plan only one had been allotted.[56] Principal Miss Louise E. Tucker was asked whether she could say that no child at P.S. 99, the largest school in Harlem, went hungry, and she lamented, "I cannot. I wish to God I could!" She explained that her school served 700 lunches daily, more than any other school in the city, and she wished there were more. She admitted, "We have children who ask for them, but we cannot supply them."[57]

Public officials, residents, and organizations also debated about housing conditions in Harlem. Leopold Weiss, president of the Upper Harlem Taxpayers Association, claimed that "the housing situation in Harlem is not nearly as bad as it has been pictured," denying that there was much congestion, especially in comparison to the Lower East Side. Will Thomas Williams, an investigator who ran the Housing Authority's survey, testified to some congestion in Harlem.[58] Commissioner Langdon Post testified that Black tenants were charged exorbitant rents by "unscrupulous speculators" and landlords. Agreeing with Post's testimony, the New York Amsterdam News stated the commissioner "verif[ied] what Harlemites have said and written upon hundreds of occasions." The subcommittee made several recommendations, which were presented to the state legislature by the governor.[59]

At the relief hearing, Edward Corsi, director of the Home Relief Bureau, met a wary crowd unpersuaded by his testimony. Corsi offset claims that his division discriminated against Black applicants, citing statistics such as "Out of 3,987 employed for staff work, 765 or 19.8 per cent" were Black and that the Harlem Relief Bureau had the highest expenditure of relief per person. Corsi, indulging the audience, stressed that it was essential to have a relief center in Harlem led by Blacks with intimate knowledge of the neighborhood and sympathetic to the conditions therein. Mildred Gibson, assistant director, responsible for the borough of Manhattan, explained that the bureau was training Black people for administrative positions and that three of the ten students were Black. Victor Suarez, the head of the Twenty-Sixth Relief Bureau Precinct, was the next to testify. Suarez's name had already been invoked when James Ford revealed that Suarez intimidated relief workers and proclaimed that "negroes were inferior workers to white workers." The crowd greeted Suarez with catcalls and boos, wrote Bessye J. Bearden of the *Chicago Defender*. Publicly taking an about-face, he asserted "colored people in every way are equal to the white in the performance of their relief duties."[60] Rejecting Ford's allegation, Suarez claimed that Blacks were more suited to professional positions in the medical, educational, and legal professions than in business. After considering the testimonies, the commission, believing the allegations and concerned about Harlemites' deep distrust of Suarez, recommended that he be removed as director of Precinct Twenty-Six in Harlem. Director Corsi and Suarez reluctantly agreed with the transfer, though mainly because they "realize[d] that it is useless for him to attempt to singly breast the tide that is running so strongly against him."[61]

The twenty-one public and four closed hearings—especially the utterances, the shouts, and the boos—powerfully expressed Harlemites' disgruntlement with Suarez and the La Guardia administration. What Corsi described as the "tide that [wa]s running so strongly" signaled Blacks' long held grievances. Shared privately among family, friends, and their community, these feelings were unleashed out in the open for all to bear witness to. Their collective grievances had the ear and the backing of the mayor.[62] With their political expectations raised, Blacks demanded change. That Corsi transferred Suarez was an indication of the political possibilities of the commission and especially La Guardia's support of the Black community. Yet as the subcommittees completed drafts of the reports and as the mayor sluggishly released them to the public, the Black community, Black leaders, and the commissioners themselves began to question the mayor's commitment to addressing the cause of the riot and his willingness to remedy the conditions that the hearings had publicly shown to all of Harlem.

"A Heritage of Wrong Police Psychology"

Almost three months after the start of the hearing, the subcommittee on police and crime submitted its report to the mayor's office on May 29, 1935, though the mayor would not release it to the public until August 10. The report aimed to explain the cause of the "outbreak." As the hearings revealed, the report stated that while the Communist Party had a role in spreading the rumor, the CP did not cause the outbreak and that it was not a "race riot." Instead, it was the "highly emotional situation among the colored people of Harlem due in large part to the nervous strain of years of unemployment and insecurity." The report framed Harlemites' economic precarity within the circumstances of the Depression, on one hand, and segregated housing, unequal opportunities for employment, inequitable distribution of municipal resources, and police brutality, on the other.[63]

The majority of the report focused on the vexatious relationship between Harlemites and the police. The police, reported the subcommittee, treated the Black community indignantly and repeatedly disregarded their civil and community rights. An eyewitness, a Black woman, recounted her experiences in the Kress store. When the officers congregated in the back of the store, she explained that a small crowd of people grew in the store and followed them. A Black woman demanded to see the manager and the boy. The policemen curtly stated, "It was none of her damn business." Over time, more and more police officers entered the store, but at no point did they explain that Rivera had been released. The police were rude and rough. When the eyewitness asked, "'Can't you tell us what happened?' He said, 'If you know what's good for you you better get home.'"[64]

Beyond exposing the police's disdain for Harlem's Black residents during the unrest, the report argued that the police's behavior was no different from how the NYPD usually treated the Black community—disdainfully and excessively violent. The report recounted the stories of Lloyd Hobbs, Thomas Aikens, Edward Laurie, and Robert Patterson. None of them had received justice since the subcommittee submitted the report in May. By the time the report was made public in August, these stories were well known to Harlemites and the city's Black community. Based on the testimonies of various eyewitnesses, the commission convinced the district attorney to revisit the case against Patrolman John F. McInerney, but for a second time, a grand jury exonerated the police officer. Although McInerney was not indicted, the commission and certainly many Harlemites believed that he murdered Hobbs. When the police claimed that they could not find eyewitnesses, the commission found six to testify, and as the hearing revealed, the first police report did not list any stolen items, which were not produced until eleven days after the shooting. Aikens was not indicted, but neither was David Egan, the officer who punched him in the eye. The report described the police's actions as "indefensibly bad police work when two armed police officers cannot arrest an unarmed man in broad daylight in a public building without beating him up and gouging out an eye." Before the grand jury in June, Albert Dillard and John Cousins, eyewitnesses to Patrolman Zakutinsky's pummeling of Laurie, testified that Zakutinsky and other policemen beat Laurie onto the ground. The policemen assaulted Laurie because he had the audacity to "talk back." Like Egan and McInerney, Zakutinsky was exonerated.[65]

More than detailing individual cases of police brutality, the subcommittee's report offered an argument regarding the basic relationship between the city's Black citizens and law enforcement. Without equivocation, the report concluded that state-sanctioned violence constituted the core character of that relationship. Speaking directly to the mayor, the report stated, "You, as well as the Police Commissioner, have received a heritage of wrong police psychology. . . . The responsibility for a system and psychology which has developed in the course of years, cannot be placed on any individual." The culture of the police force, not simply a smattering of uncivil police officers, was repressive. The report's recounting of Hobbs, Aikens, and Laurie was fundamentally tales of flagrant, excessive police violence. Regarding the shooting of Hobbs, the report stated, "Even granting that the boy was guilty as charged by the policeman, it must be noted that there was no public disorder at the time to call for violent action, life should not have been taken for the offense, and the officer should certainly have fired one shot into the air, if necessary, rather than have shot to kill immediately."[66] The report insisted that the police officers required proper training on the limits of the law and the necessity of restraint. While considering the position that society could not be properly protected if the police adhered strictly to the law and that aggression might result in catching a criminal more easily, the subcommittee prioritized the rights of civilians and rejected resoundingly any grounds for repressive force. The costs of repression were too great. Uninhibited acts by the police might catch a criminal, "Yet the general effect of this attitude is to antagonize a community, to arouse a spirit of resentment and to make people regard the police as enemies rather than as helpful friends."[67]

Centering the safety of Harlem's Black community, the subcommittee advanced four recommendations to remedy the police force's relationship to the city's Black citizenry. First, the subcommittee recommended that the policemen be given thorough instruction in the law. As Hays commented at the hearing, as evidenced by the Robert Patterson case, some of the police officers did not know the law. Second, to build a positive relationship between the police and the community, the subcommittee recommended that the mayor appoint a committee of five to seven residents from Harlem to sift complaints and support the commissioner in an advisory capacity. Highlighting Harlemites' distrust in the local precinct and the department's reporting structure, the report pointed out that "citizens are fearful of making complaints lest there be unpleasant consequences to them. . . . It is contended also that complaints are ordinarily referred back to the precinct where the incident arose and there pigeon-holed."[68] Third, to ensure transparency, the subcommittee recommended that officials charged with violating the law be investigated by not only the police but also the district attorney. The subcommittee contended that it should not be presumed that the police officers were acting in the line of duty and recommended that in every case of a shooting by a police officer an investigation should be made by an officer of the highest rank in the department. Finally, the report recommended that a communication structure be set up in case another disorder erupted. The police department would coordinate with the radio stations and the city's radio station, WNYC.[69] The subcommittee's report prioritized the grievances of the Black community, and though it acknowledged criminal behavior within the community, structural reasons were given to explain the riot rather than Black crime.

On August 15, Priest William R. McCann, a member of the mayor's committee, refused to sign the report and vehemently disagreed with its charge that the police exacerbated the unrest. From the very first meeting, lamented McCann, there was "a definite prejudice against the Police Department," and he objected "to starting the investigation harboring a prejudice against established law and order." McCann questioned the overall tenor of the report as well as the reliability of the commissioners, the spectators, and the people who testified. He described the audience as "mostly communistic" and the first hearing as "nothing more or less than orgies of police-baiting." While remaining committed to the residents of Harlem, as well as solving the social and economic problems that underlay the unrest, McCann opined that "they never will be solved until the committees are manned by those who live and work in Harlem and have the best interest of the people at heart."[70] The Black press and some Black leaders disagreed with McCann's account. James Egert Allen, president of the New York branch of the NAACP, divulged that his office had received countless complaints of police brutality and that his branch had made repeated protests against police aggression to "police commissioners and mayors" over the years. Arthur Reid, president of the African Patriotic League, claimed that the police and the Catholic church "had always been allies," and Ira Kemp, editor of the *Harlem Bulletin*, asserted that McCann led a group of people whom he had little knowledge of. In recent years, McCann's congregation had become majority Black, and they held thoughts, Kemp asserted, that were "entirely contrary to" McCann's. The *Afro-American* interviewed several lawyers who maintained anonymity, and they believed that police officials had made citizens "fearful and ultimately antagonistic," counting Father McCann's "best element" among those who were victims of police harassment.[71]

Once the subcommittee's report went to the public, it was completely rejected by the Uptown Chamber of Commerce (UCC). In a letter to the mayor, sections of which appeared in the press, the UCC's vice president, Colonel Leopold Philipp, questioned the legitimacy of the hearings and report.[72] The UCC, composed of white businessmen in Harlem, received considerable criticism from Harlemites during the hearings on employment, but they were rarely central characters in the hearings on police and crime. The connection between the police and the white business community, however, was the protection white property-owners demanded and received from the police. Indeed, Black Harlem identified both, though in different ways, as oppressive forces in the Black community. The UCC took the subcommittee's report as an affront to law and order. The attendees and testimonies at the hearing, Philipp argued, were not representative of Harlem, and he blamed Commissioner Hays, who presided over the police and crime hearings, for the hearings' unruliness.

Moreover, the hearings smeared the police department and, from Philipp's view, unfairly and unnecessarily interrogated police officers. Describing the poor treatment of the police, Philipp wrote, "When a policeman appears in court to testify against a person charged with committing a crime he has the benefit of counsel—the District Attorney. Before the Harlem investigating body the police, whose sworn duty it was to quell disturbances, were under more severe fire than would be the case if they were under cross-examination by the lowest type of criminal attorney in a Magistrate's Court."[73] He judged Hays as deplorable because he should have praised the police instead of harassing them. Suspicious of the testimonies of "alleged police brutality," Philipp claimed that if these cases were true, they were isolated. Careful to avoid pejorative language, he noted that the majority of Blacks were "decent, respectable, law-abiding citizens," but the "criminal element were desperate." More significantly, the subcommittee should have praised the police for fighting crime in Harlem. Philipp contended Harlem "has more crime per capita than any other section of the city." Harlemites were victims of crime, not victims of police brutality. He "condemn[ed], in language as strong as that used by the committee, unwarranted police attacks upon innocent members of any race, but we resent the impression created by the committee, on the basis of what we believe to be flimsy evidence, that every innocent colored man stands in constant fear of being assaulted by an officer."[74]

Harlem had a crime problem, and all of Harlem knew it. Philipp wrote, "It seems inconceivable that Mr. Hayes . . . [could] have been conducting outside investigations . . . without learning that major crimes in some sections of Harlem are as frequent as traffic violations in other parts of the city." He asked why the police commissioner Valentine did not interview Black and white victims of crime. The subcommittee's recommendation, or argument, about the need for restraint threatened the security of the entire neighborhood by weakening the police's ability to protect Harlem citizens. Philipp wrote, "To force the police to handle murderers and thugs with kid gloves—a policy that committee seems to favor by inference—would provoke unjustified attacks upon officers and result in an outburst of crime in Harlem that would shock the city." Philipp contended that "the most significant feature of the report" was the absence of any condemnation directed toward those culpable for triggering the riot. Instead, they were "let off by the committee without so much as a slap on the wrist." Philipp warned that restraint would handicap the police and contribute to not only more petty crime but also another disorder. The discretion of the police officers, according to Philipp, must remain unchallenged. He wrote, "If the police must face charges of brutality and discrimination . . . the Police Commissioner might as well withdraw his men from this section and leave citizens to the mercy of the criminal element. A policeman afraid to take the measure he believes necessary to the proper discharge of his duties is worse than no policeman at all."[75]

St. Clair Bourne, a journalist for the *New York Age,* lambasted Philipp and questioned the veracity of his support of law enforcement and his commitment to all of Harlem. Bourne saw through Philipp's incongruous commentary on crime in Harlem, asserting that Philipp's letter was "nothing more or less than a downright insult to the average resident of Harlem. By direct inference, the missive characterizes the community as one in which the criminal element far exceeds the law-abiding citizenry." Philipp's sentiment of Black Harlem as mainly "decent, respectable, law-abiding" was a pretense. The double-speak, from Bourne's view, masked Philipp's true feelings of Black people. Bourne vehemently disagreed with Philipp's commentary on police discretion and contended that the·UCC's vice president supported indiscriminate punishment of Black Harlemites. Describing the business leader's letter, Bourne noted, "He openly advocates free use of gun and club, declaring that to prevent the police from using them would be tantamount to removing all restraint in the section. In short, Negroes, like any wild animals must be kept in terrified subjection." Bourne rejected Philipp's views on crime and policing for several reasons. He pointed to Philipp's silence on "prejudice and discrimination practiced against Negroes," and his disbelief of verified cases of police brutality undermined the integrity of Philipp's letter. Bourne contended that Philipp's disposition and people of his ilk were responsible for the riot. As he asserted, Philipp's "letter fairly reeks with the prejudice and contempt for Negroes which is the main cause of the community's present state of unrest." Bourne encouraged Philipp to investigate the actions of white proprietors, who "discharg[ed] the colored help which they hastily hired immediately after the rioting."[76]

In spite of the Black community's defense of the subcommittee's report, whites' concentration on Black crime was a constant. Like whites' complaints in the immediate aftermath of the riot, Philipp and McCann reinforced the need for and the legitimacy of lethal force. In his response to Arthur G. Hays's letter of the twenty-fifth of September, Police Commissioner Valentine sustained this line of argument. Valentine's letter dismissed all of the subcommittee's recommendations, describing them as either unwarranted or unfeasible. Valentine's comments left no room for discussion of police reform or even the possibility that police officers or the police department had done any wrongdoing. The suggestion for an impartial committee that included civilians from Harlem was "unnecessary and impracticable" because "this Department draws no line as to race, color or creed, and every complaint regardless of its source, whether the writer is anonymous or identifiable, against civilians or members of our Department for alleged misconduct is thoroughly investigated and appropriate action is always taken." Police officers, regardless of rank, received no special privileges and were treated like any person charged with committing a crime.[77]

Commissioner Valentine wholly rejected the subcommittee's report. The New York Police Department's nondiscriminatory policy and the unbiased investigation of police officers, as articulated by the commissioner, pre-cluded any discrimination. Valentine's emphasis on the department's unbi-ased investigations was a signature articulation of liberal "law and order," and an effective discursive act of evasion and dissemblance. Promulgating the department's color-blind policies and police procedure, he rebutted the commission's findings, including the testimonies of Black eyewitnesses to the actions of police officers on the day of riot, as well as Black Harlemites' overall feelings toward the police department.[78] Without directly mention-ing McCann and Philipp, operating almost like a political bloc, Valentine reinforced their general sentiments. Crime was the problem, and more pun-ishment was the answer.

"Too Hot, Too Caustic, Too Critical"

As the Black community campaigned for the release of the subcommittee reports, the commission drafted several versions of the full report. In early January of 1936, Frazier submitted a draft of *The Negro in Harlem: A Report on Social and Economic Conditions Responsible for the Outbreak of March 19, 1935* to the commissioners. The commission, believing that the report was too controversial, too left leaning, never shared Frazier's report with La Guardia. The commission immediately revised Frazier's draft and sent it to the mayor in March, a year after the riot. La Guardia then sent the reports to the heads of the departments under investigation, and while some agreed with the report, others nearly rejected the report entirely. In early May, Edmond B. Butler, secretary of Emergency Relief Bureau, replying to La Guardia's request for his appraisal of the commission's report, argued that the report was written from the "viewpoint of the 'Negro" and that while he had no problem with that, if any improvement would be made, "the re-port should have been factual." For Butler, "facts" were evidenced by a sta-tistical analysis and, likely, a report produced singularly by whites. For example, because Blacks constituted approximately 4.8 percent of the city's population but represented 8.6 percent of the bureau's Works Divisions Staff and 8.4 percent of the Temporary Emergency Relief Administration staff, Butler claimed that it was not a fact that numerically "there has been any discrimination against the Negro race." For much of the twentieth century, white liberals and conservatives employed statistics as inherently objective evidence to explain racial inequality. La Guardia's white liberal public officials—confronted by damning evidence—used them to argue for racial equality. At the same time, in his memo to the mayor, he recounted instances of discrimination and admitted, "I haven't any doubt that this happened," but explained it away as "but one instance."[79]

Police Commissioner Valentine took a similar approach, claiming that he would refute the report based on "facts." If Butler relied on statistics, Valentine aimed to disprove the reports based on his department's official reports. Valentine's comments were a mix of sociological analysis and proceduralism. Appearing to summarize "facts," because of his neutral language, the commissioner used statistics to attest to the criminality of Black people—not just those in Harlem. He stated, "Adult delinquency is high among the negro population of the United States as a whole, . . . which figures would indicate the environment of Harlem would not be the sole cause of adult delinquency and criminal behavior. This would also indicate that the police of Harlem have a special problem which does not exist in areas populated by whites." Offering a racial explanation while effectively marginalizing the political and economic environment that the La Guardia administration helped to foster, Valentine vindicated the NYPD's behavior in Harlem during the uproar and the ongoing investigation of it. As he noted, "this condition imposes the necessity of greater activity on the part of the police which, in turn, creates unjustifiable resentment on the part of the criminally inclined, who are the objects of police activity." Valentine then explained away each case of police abuse that Harlemites disclosed during the hearings. Commenting on citizens' complaints about police behavior, he stated that in police procedure, "investigations are made strictly within the meaning of law, and any infractions of law or the rules and regulations of the Police Department are immediately taken cognizance of by this Department."[80]

For example, in the case of Robert Patterson, Patterson "consented and accompanied" the police to the precinct, though the report asserted that the police searched Patterson's place without a warrant and unlawfully held him for several days. And in the case of Lloyd Hobbs, he wrote that McInerney fatally shot Hobbs in the act of committing a crime. By stating that his patrolmen followed police procedure, the commissioner reestablished that the NYPD executed the rule of law. Valentine concluded that the report "erred in stating that the population of Harlem bears resentment toward the police." After the riot, according to the commissioner, the police department received "many letters of commendation." He asserted that Harlem letter writers, without identifying any particular race, would have testified at the hearings to support the police, but they were afraid of being "ridiculed by the audience, comprised of irresponsible persons, so termed, by

Assistant District Attorney Kaminsky."[81] Black letter writers, in fact, had complained to the mayor about crime, including vice activity and youth crime, but this was well publicized in the Black press long before the uproar. Valentine's comments not only absolved the NYPD of any responsibility but also put forth a veiled attack on the Communist Party, and more significantly for the mayor, exonerated the La Guardia administration of any wrongdoing. The police were simply doing their job, that is, directing their attention to the "criminally inclined, who are the objects of police activity." Police aggression was a legitimate act of force, since the police "conformed to clearly defined laws, administrative protocol, and due process."[82]

As La Guardia reviewed and weighed his departmental heads' responses to the commission's report, his administration publicized the ongoing work it had accomplished for the nation's most celebrated Black community. In mid-March, Stanley Howe, the mayor's secretary, made a plea for patience at the Salem M. E. Church in Harlem. Speaking in the place of the mayor at the Interdenominational Preachers Meeting of Greater New York and Vicinity and the Baptist Ministers' Conference, Howe explained that Harlem held a special place for the mayor and while the mayor knew that his administration's efforts "were insufficient for community's needs," some progress had been made. La Guardia had allocated funding for two new school buildings, created a women's pavilion at Harlem Hospital, and, claimed Howe, brought about "a possible decrease in police brutality as indications of better times." Rev. O. Clay Maxwell, of Mount Olivet Baptist Church, reminded Howe of Harlem's political interest. He noted the "unjust proportion" of Blacks in jobs across the city, including City Hall. He stated, "If Negroes will register and vote, they can help Mayor La Guardia if Mayor La Guardia will help us."[83] Black Harlemites, as Maxwell asserted, expected political accountability and economic investment. Yet more pressing, Howe's and Valentine's commentary on police brutality contradicted not only Black sentiment at the hearings but also, as the next chapter will demonstrate, citywide Black protests against police brutality during and after the commission's investigation.

The delay in releasing the reports as well as public officials' disregard for them once they were released heightened the tensions between the La Guardia administration and Black Harlem. The subcommittee on health and hospitals' report published by the *Daily Worker* in early April charged Harlem Hospital with rampant discrimination, inadequate facilities, and administrative laxity. Since La Guardia had the report since December, some Black weeklies asserted that the mayor tried to suppress it. The report claimed that the hospital's medical board managed the hospital with "autocratic authority" and that Black physicians and nurses were treated with disdain. The report also exposed the unequal and "Jim Crow" training that Black medical professionals received. According to the report, "Discrimination exists so far in the training of Negro nurses that the authorities are willing to give them the regular nurses certificate, although they have not had the prescribed courses." It explicitly singled out the obstruction of Dr. S. S. Goldwater, La Guardia's commissioner of hospitals, who "'flatly refused' to testify." The subcommittee report concluded, "By that act Dr. Goldwater has shown a flagrant disregard for the sentiment and opinion of Harlem citizens."[84]

On April 22, the *Survey Graphic*'s editor Paul Kellogg asked La Guardia if he would allow Alain Locke to read the commission's report, hoping to "carry a full length interpretation of the findings of the Commission." The mayor agreed and requested that Kellogg give the article "his personal attention." As part of their arrangement, Locke submitted the article to the mayor for revision before publication. In a letter dated June 12, Locke wrote La Guardia, proposing strategies and recommendations on how the mayor might proceed. Locke "strongly urge[d] the speedy publication" of the report, and at the same time outlined ways for the mayor to circumvent potential criticisms. Locke's letter, a summary of his considerably more subdued article published four months later, urged the mayor to release the official report and warned that not to do so would "further undermine public morale in Harlem and provide a festering source for racial unrest and social agitation." He explained it would have been strategic to publish the report and to have "placed the blame" for the current conditions on the "civic neglect under previous city administrations." He advised La Guardia to avoid the "quibbling" of his department heads about certain facts, many of which were true when the report was made, and explained that the public would view the recent improvements and promises made as a way to forestall the report. He questioned the integrity of Commissioners Goldwater, Valentine, and Butler in particular because none of them cooperated with the commission's investigation. In Locke's view, "the only program that will restore public confidence . . . will be the announcement of further improvements which will makes these recent moves seem the beginning of a new program rather than concessions."[85]

In late June, at the pile-driving ceremony for the new Central Harlem Health Center, La Guardia refuted many of the charges of his own commission while at the same time, observed the *New York Amsterdam News*, he asserted that "his administration [wa]s way ahead of the recommendations of the commission." Claiming that he anticipated the needs of the Black community, he explained that he made plans about public housing a year ago and asked the audience rhetorically, "What have I been going to Washington all these months for?" La Guardia made promises about schools, recreation, housing, and hospitals, but he avoided the commission's assessment of police repression.[86]

By midsummer, frustrated by the La Guardia administration's shenanigans, the *New York Amsterdam News* published what it called *The Complete Report of Mayor La Guardia's Commission on the Harlem Riot of March 19, 1935* in July. The report exposed not only racism among white civilians but also, and most controversially, the general negligence of city government to serve its Black citizenry. According to the *Pittsburgh Courier,* "The report . . . holds Mayor La Guardia personally responsible for the jim crow conditions in the city."[87] As expected, the report revealed the discriminatory hiring practices of the public utility companies and the city's large stores, as well as the exclusionary practices and the selective membership policies of labor unions. While acknowledging that public utilities and private businesses were not controlled by the city, the commission reported that the Independent City-Owned Transit Railroad, which was operated by the city, "attempted to restrict the Negro to employment in those positions which have been traditionally regarded as Negro jobs. . . . It appears that it was the established practice to refuse to give Negroes application blanks for positions but that of porter."[88] The committee's investigation of the city's relief bureaucracies was damning, particularly in the area of work relief. The report stated, "While there may be some question about discrimination against Negroes in home relief, it is an incontrovertible fact that systematic discrimination has been carried on against the Negro in work relief."[89]

The commission reported that "next to the problem of securing a livelihood," finding affordable, healthy, and safer housing was "the most serious problem of the Harlem Negro."[90] Black New Yorkers had long searched for better housing to escape exorbitant rents and negligent landlords. The Depression only worsened these conditions. Black grassroots activism against poor housing conditions had long been a tradition in Harlem. So, while the commission's findings were not unexpected, they disclosed a decades-long pattern across multiple mayoral administrations. The problem had always been landlords' capacity to exploit Black tenants because residential segregation limited them to a restricted housing market. Consequently, while Black and white tenants lived in comparably poor housing, the nexus between racial discrimination in the housing and labor market made Black neighborhoods more congested and rents significantly higher. As Richard B. Moore, a member of the Communist Party and leader of the Harlem Tenants League, explained in 1928, "Negro workers are set upon at the point of consumption by rent hogs and landlord sharks who take advantage of their segregated situation."[91] This remained the case in the mid-1930s. The report stated that white property-owners and residents had restricted Black settlement between 135th Street and 168th Street west of Convent Avenue. Residential segregation had forced Blacks into a seemingly fixed cycle, where they moved into housing abandoned by whites. Whether the Black family was poor or middle class, as they moved into available housing, the rents were higher than for the departing white families. As the commission observed, "The same fate has overtaken the better-situated Negro families that have sought improved living quarters in the northern section of Harlem."[92]

Although the *Complete Report* was "considered too hot, too caustic, too critical, too unfavorable by the Mayor," in comparison to the subcommittees' report, its critique was measured. The chapter "Crime and the Police," for example, was a restrained version of the subcommittee's report made public the previous August. The subcommittee's language and tone openly condemned the police department. Nonetheless, the language in the Black weekly's *Complete Report* was less forgiving than the unpublished draft, *The Negro in Harlem*, submitted to the mayor. For example, the latter states, "Police aggressions and brutalities more than any other factor weld the people together against those responsible for their ills," while the former states, "Police aggressions and brutalities more than any other factor weld the people together for *mass action*." While both emphasized Harlemites' deep resentment regarding police violence, the *New York Amsterdam News*' draft articulated their resentment as the impetus for political action.[93] *The Negro in Harlem* also omitted the accusatory language that undergirded the subcommittee's report and the *Complete Report*. Gone was language such as "the citizens are fearful of making complaints," which potentially jeopardized the possibility of building amicable relationships between the Black community and police. In the last chapter of the report, "Conclusions and Recommendations of Commission," the commission provided a set of recommendations for six of its topical chapters. For "Crime and the Police," the *Complete Report* included five recommendations, but only four were in *The Negro in Harlem*. The latter omitted the recommendation to close nightspots that catered to whites' carnal pursuits and any entertainment that excluded Blacks as patrons. The commission, undoubtedly, felt it needed to make those conciliatory revisions in language for the report to be accepted by La Guardia.[94]

The Negro in Harlem was nonetheless explicit about the pattern of police aggression Blacks encountered as well as their conviction that police officials failed to hold police officers accountable for misconduct and flagrant violence. The report argued that the New York Police Department—not just individual officers—was implicated in illegal and repressive actions. When the police condone or "hide behind such subterfuge as the exoneration given by grand juries . . . , then the Police Department as a whole must accept the onus of these charges." The report pointed to Commissioner Valentine as both the head of the police department and representative of its culpability. Referencing the letter Hays received from the commissioner, the report condemned the behavior of Valentine and argued that his behavior was endemic in the Black community's relationship with the NYPD. Valentine maintained that there was no need to discipline the actions of police officers, neglected to engage the individual cases of the grand juries, and "justified the action of the police in the Patterson case."[95] As Black Harlem and Black America discussed the report in the Black press, Alain Locke's article appeared in the *Survey Graphic* that August.

Published a month after the *Complete Report*, Locke's "Harlem: Dark Weather-Vane" adroitly advocated for the publication of the commission's report while advancing the agenda of the La Guardia administration. Situating the neighborhood of Harlem in its past cultural glory, Locke characterized the Harlem uprising as a response to the Depression as well as to the long-standing neglect of municipal public officials. But Locke was careful to blame past city administrations, as he urged La Guardia to do in the confidential letter. "Harlem: Dark Weather-Vane" was, in some ways, partly a corrective to La Guardia's minimizing of his commission's report. As Locke writes, "The Commission in complaining of present conditions is careful to make plain that the present city administration has inherited most of them and that, therefore, they are not to be laid at its door." Locke was being generous. Certainly, the report pinpointed past administrations' inattention to the neighborhood's needs, yet the composite of the hearings, the subcommittee reports, and multiple revisions of the full report represented a theme of continuity rather than change regarding the La Guardia administration's treatment of Black Harlem.[96]

Locke's defense of La Guardia was matched by his advocacy of Harlem. Though he openly exalts La Guardia, his criticisms of the mayor's

high-ranking officials are acute. In a muted criticism, likely directed at Butler, Locke makes plain the necessity of employing Blacks in positions that
shape public policy, differentiating positions of influence from mere positions in municipal government. He writes, "One of the fatal gaps between
good intentions and good performance is in this matter of local administra-
tors, where often an executive policy officially promulgated gets short cir-
cuited into discrimination at the point of practical application." This critique
undermined arguments that the absence of outright discrimination in public
policy necessarily results in equality, and it questioned the claim that hiring
Blacks at statistical rates proportional to their demographic representation
in the population had any bearing on the indignities Blacks' encountered
in an unwelcoming labor market. More significantly, Locke's emphasis on
"practical application" exposed the artifice of racial liberalism. La Guardia's
head officials, Butler and Valentine, used color-blind policies and statistical
measures to disqualify Blacks' complaints of racism and police lawlessness.
Harlemites, Locke explained, were not anti–white police officers. Instead,
they held as much animosity for "Negro police as toward white police,"
including Police Lieutenant Samuel Battle. Again, while not mentioning
Commissioner Valentine, who claimed an external committee was unnecessary, Locke claimed that the biracial Citizens' Public Safety Committee was
fundamental to "restor[ing] confidence" in law enforcement, and without it,
"Harlem's wound will not heal."[97]

At the tail end of September, Oswald Garrison Villard, cofounder of the
NAACP, representing the commission, asked La Guardia to officially publish the report or else it would be forced to do so. The commission, he explained, had received "widespread attacks" because of allegations that the
commission had been abandoned and that the mayor was afraid or did not
want to publish the report. Villard asserted that the commission was "less
affected" but more concerned about the timeliness of the report and warned
"respectfully . . . that if it had been intended to nullify [the] report no better course could have been followed." La Guardia's telegram to Villard, dated
September 29, slighted Villard and claimed that because of his "sojourn in
the country . . . apparently you have not kept informed about all that has
been done in the Harlem situation." The mayor said that the report had been
available for ten weeks and that reports had been previously printed in the
Daily Worker and the *New York Post*. Commenting on Villard's absence from
the city, La Guardia expressed regret that Villard missed the last meeting
of the committee and hope to see him upon his return. Villard responded
the next day. He explained, despite his reprieve at his country home, he had

kept in touch with the committee. He was "astonished to have your assurance" that the report had been published, since the *Herald-Tribune* had pestered him about the report and other members of the committee, namely, Mrs. Carter, Arthur Hays, and Dr. Roberts at the last meeting he attended, had believed that the report had not been released to the press. Accepting the mayor's telegram at face value, Villard pledged to inform the *Herald-Tribune* and other newspapers that the mayor had released the report. Upon his next meeting with the mayor, Villard stated that he hoped to express his gratitude with the progress the mayor had made with voters and, he concluded, "will take that opportunity to say a few nasty things about the police!"[98]

• • • • • •

Villard's distaste for the police was shared across Black New York. The report and even Alain Locke, the mayor's Black liberal ally, were explicit about the police department's failure to work with the commission. While the *New York Amsterdam News* and *Daily Worker* managed to get subcommittee reports and drafts of the full report, La Guardia never officially released his own commission's report, despite his claims otherwise to Villard. The mayor's dismissal of the commission's recommendations was a lost opportunity for Black New Yorkers, the La Guardia administration, and democracy in the city. Black Harlem's airing out of their grievances exposed patterns of excessive violence by the NYPD, and the report, building on this, put forth an argument about the pathology of the NYPD. The hearings for Black Harlem were transformative. This consensus among community members, civil rights leaders, Communists, and social reform leaders about the brutality of the police openly challenged police authority and legitimacy. Not since the Wickersham Commission and the Seabury Investigation had the NYPD and law enforcement been under sustained scrutiny. Although Harlemites had always fought against police brutality, the composite of the riot, the hearings, news reportage, and the commission report had made it a pivotal issue of Black mobilization and racial polarization in New York City politics.

The length that it took for La Guardia to release the subcommittee reports, the commission's efforts to accommodate the mayor, the obstructive efforts of law enforcement and other city agencies, and the mayor's public undermining of his commission's recommendations steadily diluted the impact and urgency of the report. By the summer of 1936, the mayor's public pronouncements of good faith to Black Harlem did not match the actions of his administration. Indeed, even as the mayor publicly acknowledged that the uproar was partly a response to economic conditions, he keenly evaded criticisms that his administration was partly culpable. As he had after the police riot in Harlem in 1934, La Guardia's public and prompt decision to investigate the riot ushered forth the promises of racial liberalism. The riot offered the mayor the opportunity to assemble an interracial commission, which immediately enhanced his reputation as a liberal and as a reformer. Yet again, like the aftermath of then–police inspector Valentine's investigation in 1934, the NYPD eluded discipline and accountability. Whatever his reasons for not releasing it, as Locke forewarned, the commission's report continued to "provide a festering source for racial unrest and social agitation."

Indeed, the only robust policy initiative La Guardia would make would be stationing a contingent of patrolmen, detectives, and mounted policemen stationed in Harlem, where they remained for over a year. Despite the unrelenting outcries of police brutality from a politically awakened Black community, the same outcries detailed in the report, La Guardia sided with the NYPD and white Harlemites, such as McCann, the Uptown Chamber of Commerce, and the Harlem Merchants Association, who blamed the uproar on unchecked Black crime activity. Indelibly awakened to the pattern of police unaccountability, Blacks in Harlem, Bedford-Stuyvesant, and elsewhere across the city mobilized to protest police violence.[99]

Withdrawal of the Police Army of Occupation in Harlem

· ·

In April 1936, Tommy Aikens wrote a letter to Adam Clayton Powell Jr., who published it in "The Soapbox," a column Powell wrote for the *New York Amsterdam News*. Aikens, an unemployed theatrical producer, was the victim of police brutality a week before the Harlem uprising of 1935. Aikens's story of how he was beaten and lost his eye became part of Harlem lore after he shared it at the commission's open hearings, and it was incorporated as evidence of police aggression in the commission's report. But pain, trauma, and the unanticipated consequences of police brutality for Aikens and many others outlasted the initial moment of violence, and like many Black New Yorkers, Aikens continued to hold expectations for the city's liberal mayor. Describing his experience over the last year, he wrote, "I have been made to suffer beyond the knowledge of my friends, and have been denied work on account of my injuries." In the midst of the Depression, finding work was difficult, especially for a Black man with use of only one eye. The damage suit against Police Officer David S. Egan was still underway. Aikens "fe[lt] that if you will talk to Mayor LaGuardia on this matter he may get the city to make me an appropriation to compensate me for my injuries, inasmuch as the police are representatives of the law enforcing body of the City of New York." Powell responded, "No, Tommy. 'Little Flower La Guardia' won't do anything for you. . . . I know that while you lay on the sidewalk unconscious, they kicked your left eyeball out of its socket and today you are blind in one eye. I know they then dragged you, twisting in pain, to the prison ward and ARRESTED YOU for disorderly conduct. But the Little Flower doesn't care. He's mayor, and you're just a brown boy."[1]

In many ways, Aikens's expectations for La Guardia mirrored Black Harlemites' anticipation of municipal reform led by the mayor in the aftermath of the uprising. The mayor wittingly thwarted his commission's capacity to investigate the uproar which sent a message to Black citizens about his commitment to them. Throughout the spring of 1936, his administration minimized the subcommittees' report findings, and La Guardia's refusal to release the full report sullied his reputation among Black New Yorkers. La

Guardia's actions recast them as second-class citizens and reinforced the conclusions detailed in the report that spotlighted the pattern of police violence and municipal neglect. Certainly, Powell's claim that the mayor would do nothing was an overstatement. It did reflect, nonetheless, Black New Yorkers' well-founded suspicion that the mayor would do little to make the New York Police Department accountable for its actions. In public La Guardia condemned police brutality, yet in private the mayor sanctioned police violence against Black men, women, and children. The city's police force under the leadership of Police Commissioner Lewis J. Valentine continued to inflict punishment on Black people. Like Aikens and the others documented in the Mayor's Commission report, they would rarely receive justice.

More than a year after the Harlem uprising, Black leaders described the police presence in the neighborhood as an "army of occupation" and called on Commissioner Valentine and La Guardia to reduce the police contingent. This same demand was admitted and expressed cogently by the commission in its conclusion: "Today, extra police stand guard on the corners and mounted patrolmen ride through the streets of Harlem." The commission, correctly speaking for Harlemites, continued, "To the citizens of Harlem they symbolize the answer of the city authorities to their protest of March 19th. To Harlem this show of force simply signifies that property will be protected at any cost."[2] The "show of force" demonstrated La Guardia's commitment to the safety of white Harlem and white property-owner organizations, such as the Uptown Chamber of Commerce. With occupation came violence, and for Black New Yorkers it was ubiquitous. They unsurprisingly complained about police brutality during and after the commission's hearings and investigation of the riot. By the summer of 1936, Black leaders had three interrelated demands: the reduction of the "police army of occupation," the public release of the commission's report, and the implementation of the report's recommendations. Black Harlem wanted action. Black leaders and their allies across the political spectrum argued that La Guardia intentionally buried the report to avoid exposing his administration's role in underserving Harlem as detailed in the report. Instead of substantive support for hospitals, schools, and relief, La Guardia and Valentine sent the police.

Throughout the late 1930s and early 1940s, Blacks faced police violence in their homes, on the streets, and sometimes at their workplace. Nowhere were they safe from, unaware of, or at some point not a witness to police brutality. Police violence in the city was promiscuous, stretching out to other boroughs, especially in emerging Black neighborhoods in Brooklyn and in Long Island. While police brutality for Blacks was always a problem in Brooklyn's Bedford-Stuyvesant, it appeared to worsen throughout the 1930s. Joining forces with a mobilized white community, the police department, as it had decades before in Harlem before World War I, tried to contain the expansion of Brooklyn's growing Black population. If Blacks had not experienced it, they read about it. In the pages of the Black press, they found stories about Black victims of fatal shootings, aggressive arrests, and beatings in police precincts. The police also reported cases of Black suicides that raised the suspicions of their families, friends, and the community. Throughout the spring of 1936, they also read about their mayor disparaging the report that had powerfully shone a light on the NYPD's complicity in fomenting the riot. To redress the ongoing problem of policing, the Black community had to rely on themselves—on their family, community institutions, the Black press, the NAACP, and other protest organizations, including the Communist Party. Black New Yorkers held meetings, sought justice in court, and wrote letters to the mayor calling on him to fulfill his promise to protect them from police aggression.

Concurrent with Blacks' clashes with and opposition to police violence, the commission hearings were pivotal to raising Black New Yorkers' political consciousness around policing. The convergence of the NYPD's yearlong occupation of Harlem, the commission hearings, and Black protest across the city transformed police brutality into a central issue of Black protest. Indeed, the confluences of Blacks' experiences of municipal indifference and neglect fostered Black mobilization not only among the already organized but also at the grassroots level. As the *New York Amsterdam News* noted in August 1935, Mrs. Chaney, former director of the South Side House and chairwoman of the Committee for Equal Opportunity, charged the "Negro ministry" with "indifference, cowardice and selfishness and cited an almost total lack of co-operation by the clergymen in the movements for slum abatement, against police brutality and discrimination, and for economic security for the race."[3] These multiple ways of engaging and confronting police violence often included self-defense, long a tactic for Blacks to defend themselves. Despite varying forms of resistance, Black New Yorkers found collusion in the courts and obstruction in the police departments. Thus, while Blacks could not escape police violence and fought doggedly to contain—if not stop—it completely, La Guardia's criminal legal system offered them no avenue for true police accountability or safety.[4]

"Police Are Too Free with the Use of Their Clubs"

On March 29, only ten days after a now-quieted furor, the *New York Amsterdam News* observed, "Riot squads and scores of 'borrowed' patrolmen, afoot and mounted, were still on duty in Harlem."[5] As the city's departments were under investigation, despite outcries from the Black community to La Guardia and Valentine and appeals that the police detail in the neighborhood be reduced, the police remained at the ready to halt any trouble. Public outrage at the NYPD's behavior during the uprising as well as the criticisms of the department's pattern of misconduct changed little. In fact, police brutality thrived across the city. Hearing a commotion on the street in mid-June, Vivian Darden ventured out to her friend's apartment, 1743 Fulton Street in Brooklyn, to see what was going on. A couple of buildings down, in front of 1747 Fulton Street, James Shannon, a patrolman of the Eighty-First Precinct, attempted to take control over the commotion and saw Miss Darden. He pushed her for "not moving fast enough," and she complained, "Don't push me. I am not well." He then pushed her again, and as she stumbled, she brushed against him. He then "pinioned her arms behind her back and pushed her in the direction of a waiting taxicab," and as they drove to the police station, he kicked and beat her. Several eyewitnesses verified Miss Darden's story, and Magistrate David Hirshfield dismissed the charges against Darden. Through the joint efforts of Rev. Joseph N. Carrington of the Mount Carmel Baptist Church and George E. Wibecan of the Crispus Attucks Community Council, Darden received a modicum of justice after Shannon apologized for his behavior.[6]

In July, in front of 1884 Dean Street, three white plainclothes police officers accused Milton Fletcher of playing dice on the sidewalk in Brooklyn. Fletcher, unaware that the three white men were officers, "struck the first one that seized him." Angry about the spate of police brutality cases in Brooklyn and across the city, the *New York Amsterdam News* reported, the crowd of Black onlookers surrounded the police and demanded that they release the boy, who, they explained, was not among the youth playing dice on the sidewalk. When one officer, it was alleged, yelled, "Get away from here, you niggers," the fighting began. "Women and children rushed from houses carrying missiles and others threw sticks and stones from windows and rooftops," reported the Black weekly. Whites nearby also joined the fray, banding together with the police officers. As the melee grew, Fletcher escaped from the clutches of the police. Despite being outnumbered and overwhelmed, the police officers somehow fought through the crowd to a doorway, where they drew their guns and fired into the air. Rousing the crowd and the onlookers from the surrounding buildings, the crowd retaliated with a barrage of makeshift weapons. Someone called the police headquarters, and once the reinforcements arrived, the police began cudgeling through the crowd. As the crowd rebounded and encircled the police, Elvin Sullinger, a Black veteran and commander of the National War Veterans Association (NWVA), at 486 Ralph Avenue, commanded the people to stop and ordered the police to "leave the situation to me, I will take care of it." The police put away their weapons, and as the crowd dispersed, Fletcher and Henry Urguhart, thirty-eight years old, of 489 Cumberland Street, were arrested and charged with felonious assault.[7]

Later that afternoon, another rumpus arose when siblings Joseph Harrison, seventeen, and his sister, Loretta, thirteen, came upon a white man dragging a Black boy near Howard Avenue and Bergen Street. When plainclothes police officer Samuel Letowsky found Joan, his six-year-old daughter, crying in the street after a tussle with a little Black boy, he mauled the boy, dragging him across the street. Joseph heard the boy's outcry and, without knowledge that he was speaking with law enforcement, told Letowsky to unhand the boy. Joseph crossed the street and grabbed the boy by the hand, attempting to pull him away. Letowsky punched him in the mouth, "knocking the lad down to the sidewalk." Watching her brother being beaten, Loretta threw a shoe at Letowsky, hitting him on the back. Black and white eyewitnesses joined the fray siding with their own racial group and battling until the police arrived and managed to subdue the crowd. Sullinger complained to the *New York Amsterdam News* that "the police are too free with the use of their clubs" and that "Negroes are tired of being beaten up." He recommended that Black police officers be assigned to the district but also railed against Captain McCowan of the Seventy-Seventh Precinct and Captain Heddon of the Seventy-Ninth Precinct. According to Sullinger, "To the insulting attitude of these men may be traced much of the trouble in the Negro districts."[8] Sullinger argued that "the white patrolmen in the precinct reflected their captain's attitude," and as a result of his protest, McGowan was transferred to another precinct.[9]

In the throes of the Mayor's Commission hearings, Blacks in Brooklyn confronted what seemed like a barrage of police attacks. As readers of reoccurring cases of police brutality but also as victims of and witnesses to this violence, as Sullinger declared, "Negroes [we]re tired of being beaten up." Their fatigue reiterated the statements and testimonies that had been expressed at the hearings in late March and April. Indeed, because of the ubiquity of police violence, Blacks tied these residential and neighborhood spaces to their individual and collective experiences and memory of police brutality. As the crowds that defended the Harrisons, Fletcher, and Darden suggest, the memory and knowledge of past violence likely precipitated their physical and political actions to resist the police. As the *New York Amsterdam News* wrote, "Negro residents of Brooklyn have long been incensed over police brutality. Last year, Fletcher Bey, a Moorish leader, was shot to death in his apartment by officers. In February, Audrey Knight, 23, fell victim to police bullets. Prior to this, a young girl had been severely beaten in a park by a white officer, and just a few weeks ago, another young girl was beaten and arrested by a policeman."[10] The interracial clashes between Blacks and white civilians defending white police officers illuminate the impact of shifting demographical changes occurring across the city. As the police deployed larger contingents across the borough of Brooklyn, it tried to contain the expansion of Black communities in Bedford-Stuyvesant and Brownsville. Community and grassroots leaders such as Sullinger, Carrington, and Wibecan were critical to creating political spaces to discuss these issues, informing Blacks of their rights, and mobilizing the community when necessary to effect police accountability.

Not yet six months after the Harlem uprising in July, the *New York Amsterdam News* published an editorial titled "Memo to Mr. Valentine" and demanded that the wave of police violence in Brooklyn cease. The police had no compunction about accosting Black women, and the paper cautioned that Black people in Brooklyn would not accept this mistreatment. The Black weekly further warned that widespread racial discrimination and unemployment, as well as poor housing compounded by police brutality, might incite another "lawless outbreak." The *New York Amsterdam News* cautioned, "We don't want a repetition of what happened in Harlem." The NYPD recognized no boundaries to violating the dignity of Black people. Not even Black girls could avoid the threat of police violence.[11]

In early March 1936, white patrolman John Kenney slapped Virginia Perry Brown, a sixteen-year-old student, twice because she ignored the traffic stop sign and walked across the street at 119th Street and Third Avenue in East Harlem. The assault loosened her teeth and caused her mouth to bleed. Fifteen-year-old Anna Nash, an eyewitness and Brown's classmate, confirmed her testimony and revealed that she had problems with a police officer at the same precinct, Patrolman Hirsh. She "had been forced to bite Patrolman Hirsh . . . during a similar assault on Thanksgiving Eve." Brown's story and Nash's testimony of her own confrontations with police violence, much like Blacks' testimonies at the Mayor's Commission hearings, reveal the ways the impact of police violence lingered within the Black community, including among the youngest and most vulnerable.[12]

On the twenty-eighth of March, a patrolman clubbed into unconsciousness John McNeil, a twenty-six-year-old cabinet maker, on Lenox Avenue near 127th Street in Harlem. According to the police report, Patrolman Charles Brown tried to arrest McNeil for disorderly conduct. As Brown placed him in the cab to take him to the police station, McNeil lunged for Brown's baton. During the tussle, McNeil fell out of the car and "under the wheels of the other taxi." George Lewis, an eyewitness, however, explained that Brown had no grounds for beating McNeil. Brown was the sole aggressor, kicking him "with all his might." Lewis explained that throughout the ordeal, Brown "was waving his gun and club . . . [and] he acted like a maniac, a fanatic." Admitting that McNeil was intoxicated, the witnesses stated that Brown had incessantly beaten McNeil even as the patrolman placed McNeil in the cab. They also explained that the force of the blows—not McNeil's resisting arrest—propelled him out of one cab and beneath another. Under arrest, as he lay recovering from the beating in Bellevue Hospital, Mrs. McNeil, his wife, acquired the legal support of Harlem's civil rights leadership. A delegation named the Provisional Committee for the Defense of Civil Rights in Harlem (PCDCRH) spoke to Police Inspector De Martino of the Twenty-Third Precinct. In addition to Mrs. McNeil, the delegation included Charles Hamilton Houston of the NAACP; Frank Spector of the District International Labor Defense; Benjamin Davis, the reporter for the *Daily Worker* and future councilman; Jimmie Green of the Harlem ILD; Mike Walsh, ILD leader; Victor Gettner of the American Civil Liberties Union; George Lewis, John Harris, and Leroy Hudson, eyewitnesses to the beating; and I. Lawlor from the Joint Committee against Discriminatory Practices.[13] Brown's bellicosity was familiar to the delegation. The Black patrolman's fury was on full display two years prior in March at the Scottsboro meeting detailed in chapter 2 sponsored by the ILD to greet Mrs. Ada Wright, the mother of two of the Scottsboro boys. At the gathering, Brown was charged with beating a Black woman, brandishing a revolver, and throwing a grapefruit at a man in a second-story window who encouraged the crowd to take Brown's shield number. Despite apologies from police officials regarding Brown's behavior, former police commissioner O'Ryan dismissed the charges against him. Once again, the committee wanted police accountability. But while initially claiming that "he had no power to recommend Brown's dismissal," De Martino admitted that he indeed had the authority to take

Brown's badge "if he so desired . . . [and] that this was just another of 150 cases of complaints filed against policemen."[14]

Because of De Martino's casual dismissal of the complaint against Brown and civilian complaints in general, the delegation went to the court and obtained a summons. Osmond K. Fraenkel, the renowned attorney who argued the appeal of the Scottsboro case before the U.S. Supreme Court, led the group of lawyers organized to prosecute Brown.[15] The *Daily Worker* reported that a police officer attempted to intimidate George Lewis by calling him at home. The court hearing was scheduled for April 9 but then postponed for the twenty-first. On the twenty-first, as people assembled into the Fifth District Court, East 121st Street, near Lexington Avenue, they noticed that the courthouse was "surrounded by an extra heavy guard of policemen." There, Magistrate Stern rescheduled the hearing for Friday the twenty-fourth. Friday morning, the Magistrate Overton Harris presided over the hearing held at the Fifth District Court. As the hearing continued the next day, "a tall, well-dressed, brown-skinned" unnamed Black woman, who "refused to be bullied by city corporation, Brown's attorney, . . . stuck staunchly to her story that the policeman had brutally assaulted John McNeil."[16] The court set the continuation of the hearing for the twenty-eighth but once again rescheduled it for May 4. Attorney Fraenkel complained about this pattern of postponements, and spectators charged that Harris attempted "to discourage and inconvenience McNeil's witnesses," who often had to miss work to testify at the hearings.[17]

Throughout May, the committee held several meetings and a conference at the Renaissance Casino on May 23. On the fourth, after a preliminary hearing, Magistrate Overton Harris decided that Brown would stand trial in Special Sessions in June. At the conference on the twenty-third, the invited speakers were Frank D. Griffin and Rev. John W. Robinson, a member of the Mayor's Commission. Griffin encouraged associational unity and singled out the work of the provisional committee as evidence of the progress that might be made through solidarity and organizational cooperation. Reverend Robinson supported the federated committee and averred that the mounted police, radio police cars, and the riot truck on Lenox Avenue "invite[d] a higher rate of disorders and police clashes."[18] In the midst of the postponed hearings and conferences, the police shot another Black youth, Leonard Brown. Patrolmen John Barret and George Rouse and Detective Francis Childs found the thirteen-year-old and his friend, Joseph Arnold, twelve years old, on a rooftop at 258 West 117th Street, apparently skipping school. Afraid that they would get caught, Brown and Arnold ran, and the police officers fired several shots, with one hitting Brown in his right temple. On May 13, the PCDCRH met with Police Inspector J. J. De Martino to request an investigation of the policemen and learned that Patrolman Charles Brown was still allowed to work the beat. They charged that it was "criminal" for the police department to allow Brown, whom they described as "a menace to the Negro people of Harlem," back on the streets.[19] On the twenty-sixth, the United Civil Rights Committee of Harlem (UCRCH), formerly the PCDHCR, met with Valentine about reprimanding Brown, and the police commissioner stated that he would not be suspended and that he was already being "persecuted" by public scrutiny. In response to calls for police accountability regarding the shooting of Leonard Brown, Valentine "said it was an unfortunate accident" but also described the boy as a "truant."[20]

On June 16, Judges Noonan, Pearlman, and Solomon at the Special Sessions Court at Thirty-Two Franklin Street acquitted Patrolman Charles Brown. The judges, opined the *Daily Worker*, "dipped their brushes into a pail of whitewash and wiped out a perfect case of simple assault against Brown." In spite of the dozen witnesses the UCRCH had produced in defense of John McNeil, Assistant District Attorney Maurice Spaulter brought only three witnesses. Instead of advocating for McNeil, Spaulter "browbeat eyewitnesses called to testify against Brown." Spaulter limited his interrogation of Brown to asking him if he was intoxicated when he attacked McNeil. McNeil's legal team, Osmond K. Fraenkel and ILD attorney Samuel Chassy, never got the opportunity to interrogate Brown. The district attorney's office refused to allow them to participate in the court proceedings. Brown again escaped any form of legal recourse from Gotham City's criminal justice system, despite his documented pattern of police misconduct. Frank D. Griffin, secretary of the UCRCH, charged, "This outrageous acquittal of Policeman Brown, who is notorious for police brutality in Harlem, must be made the beginning of a powerful campaign not only for the removal of Brown . . . but also to put a stop to the rapidly increasing police attacks against the people of Harlem."[21]

During the case against Patrolman Brown, Black leaders had once again called attention to the extra police patrols in Harlem. During that meeting on May 26, the UCRCH asked Commissioner Valentine when he would remove the police force in Harlem and if the presence of the police represented a greater crime problem in the neighborhood than elsewhere.[22] Valentine answered, "No . . . , but there is a great deal of tension in Harlem and a large force is needed."[23] As an example, the police commissioner cited a public

FIGURE 4.1 July 11: Scene outside the offices in Harlem of the Pan-African Reconstruction Association, as some of Harlem's male population study the banners and posters before signing up for the possible war service in Abyssinia (Ethiopia). Bettmann via Getty Images.

meeting organized by Ira Kemp held at the corner of 133rd Street and Lenox Avenue on May 19 over the Italo-Ethiopian War that quickly turned into another police riot. As approximately 400 people listened to the speakers, riot trucks, squad cars, detectives, and about sixty mounted policemen bumrushed the crowd. Patrolman Michael Ronan shot Lee Cornish, a Black man, in the ankle as Cornish defended himself from James A. Showers, another police officer.[24] Black New Yorkers—but also people of African descent across the United States and the—world were angered by and mobilized against fascist Italy's invasion of Ethiopia. Since October 1935, Benito Mussolini's army brutalized Ethiopia, which was the beacon of African independence on the continent and across the Diasporic world.[25]

Valentine also explained that the "better elements" of Harlem were in accord with the police presence. While the police commissioner surely viewed Blacks as part of the so-called better element, he was probably referring to the white Harlemites, residents and businesses, who argued that Harlem was crime infested. Responding to the commission's subcommittee on Crime and Policing's report, Valentine stated that "the present force would be maintained for some time to come and that the report . . . was 'mainly false and dishonest.'" Valentine admitted, "If I had enough money to recruit more police, I would send them to Harlem." The *New York Amsterdam News* pithily described that meeting and the commissioner's sentiments: "Harlem needs police most, commissioner tells delegation." Florina Lasker, chairwoman of the New York City Civil Liberties Committee, stated that Valentine's attitude "goes far to explain the existence of the present tension in Harlem" and that his "casual dismissal . . . indicates that prompt action by the mayor is necessary."[26]

In an editorial a week later titled "Time to Reconsider," the *New York Amsterdam News* again urged Commissioner Lewis to reevaluate UCRCH's recommendation to curtail the detail of police in Harlem. Acknowledging Valentine's point of view about the recent disturbances regarding the Italo-Ethiopian war, the Black weekly still questioned his judgment and countered that it was the heavy police presence that inflamed and flagrantly abused Harlemites that intensified the situation in the district—not Black street speakers and public protests of imperialism and fascism. According to the Black weekly, "Shootings of citizens guilty of slight wrongs or imaginary ones are frequent these days. Insult by policemen is not infrequent." Recounting the experience of one Black journalist who mistakenly ran a red light because a truck had cut off his view, the *New York Amsterdam News* claimed that the police scolded the newspaper man and threatened, "I ought to shoot you full of holes!" The Black weekly warned of another melee and complained that the police commissioner's failure to discipline the police had only emboldened police misconduct. "Most Harlemites," the Black weekly explained, "desire to, and do, live quietly, shunning disorder." But "concentration of policemen who feel free to be both judge and officer cannot contribute toward peace. An armed camp is almost certain to become a battleground." Throughout the rest of the summer, Black civilians and protest organizations across the ideological spectrum continued to fight police brutality.[27]

Before the inquiry on officer Brown was completed, Alton Dunn of 438 Jefferson Avenue, in Brooklyn, was arrested for a hit-and-run accident and interrogated at the Seventy-Seventh Precinct on June 6. According to Dunn, Officer Charles Keegan repetitively pounded him with the nightstick when he protested his innocence. In the presence of the desk sergeant, as Dunn tried to protect himself from an onslaught of the officer's blows, four officers held him down as Keegan whaled on him, busting his head open. Not until the next day would he receive treatment when he was taken to jail. By the end, the police dropped the hit-and-run charges after the culpable person was found but, nonetheless, charged Dunn with disorderly conduct. The Brooklyn Council of the National Negro Congress pressed civil and criminal charges against Patrolman Keegan to exact justice and to fine police officers who harassed and beat citizens. The council requested that community and civic-minded organizations send letters to Valentine to stave off "the wave of police brutality now existing in Harlem." Valentine and La Guardia promised an investigation.[28]

As the campaign for justice for Dunn unwound, the *New York Amsterdam News* once again called for the removal of extra police in Harlem. An editorial titled "Police Occupation" cited the work of the Harlem Committee for Independent Political Action; asserted that La Guardia, Valentine, and Inspector De Martino condoned police brutality; and enumerated several cases, including the killing of Edward Laurie and the beating of Lloyd Hobbs. In the column, "Letters from Readers to the Editor," Dr. Charles Augustin Petioni, businessman and editor, criticized the Mayor's Commission for not responding to the police commission's assessment of the report as "m[ain]ly false and dishonest."[29] The commission's nonresponse, he warned, meant that not "much could be expected from them," complaining that "they seem to be willing not only to allow their report to remain unpublished but to submit to direct accusations against their integrity." Petioni called for a community response, a protest against Valentine's "provocative statements, in addition to the presence of what can be called a police army of occupation for which I can see no real necessity." The *New York Age*'s Ebenezer Ray tied more explicitly than Petioni the relationship between policing and the catalog of racial inequities that the commission's report revealed: "The placing of an unusual number of police officers in Harlem is Commissioner Valentine's solution of the Harlem problem, probably because he can do a better job of heading New York's police department than he can trying to readjust a badly adjusted social and economic system."[30] On the seventeenth, the United Civil Rights Committee of Harlem sent individualized letters to Governor Herbert Lehman, District Attorney Dodge, and the Board of Aldermen regarding the disregard and dereliction of duty by public officials, namely, District Attorney Spaulter and Inspector De Martino. In the letter to the governor, the UCRCH stated, "We feel that . . . when the lives of men, women, and children are taken with the only explanation from the law-enforcement agencies 'accidentally shot' while the officers were performing their duties, it is time that you, as Governor of the State of New York take action when said city authorities and law enforcement agencies refuse to give the citizens adequate explanation of their actions."[31] Later that month, the *New York Amsterdam News* asked, "How long can Mayor La-Guardia expect us to remain a patient, suffering people?" The Black weekly expected police accountability. Valentine had fired more than 100 men from the police force as commissioner. One had been let go because he allowed a child to steal from him his gun and handcuffs. Pointing out Valentine's low value for Black life, the Black weekly lamented, "When a policeman loses his gun, that deserves the severest punishment in the commissioner's opinion. If a citizen in Harlem loses his life or is slugged by a disdainful policeman, that's the Harlemite's ill-fortune."[32]

"The Recall of the Heavy Extra Detail of Patrolmen in the Area"

As the summer months transitioned to the fall and winter, the Black press, Black citizens, and Black leaders and their allies persistently called for La Guardia to officially release the report and commit to the recommendations as laid out in the report. Yet along with discussions of the commission's report, Harlemites vociferously outlined the imbalance between the presence of the police and the mayor's lackluster response to Blacks' economic and social conditions. La Guardia met with commission members for a two-hour meeting on June 30 to discuss the commission's chapter on police and crime and individual cases of police abuse. The mayor claimed that Harlemites' complaints of police brutality would "be properly and thoroughly investigated" and that the police were in Harlem to prevent crime and arrest criminals, "but no police officer will be permitted to abuse any citizen in Harlem more than anywhere else."[33] On July 22, three days after the *New York Amsterdam News* published the report, a committee of twenty-seven leaders of the community met the mayor at the Summer City Hall in Pelham Bay Park. Dr. Petioni, representing the committee, criticized the mayor for not releasing the report, as well as the "jim-crowing of high school students" and segregated conditions in hospitals and other areas of local government across the city. The committee demanded a permanent commission on Harlem with a secretary paid by the city. The mayor, however, offered Harlem's leadership little as far as implementing the report's recommendations. He acknowledged the social and economic plight of Harlemites but explained that he was "as helpless as the League of Nations was in the Italo-Ethiopian War and that he expected the heartiest cooperation from the people of Harlem." After this initial meeting, La Guardia requested the committee to form a delegation of five that he would meet with periodically to further discuss the report's recommendations.[34]

By that meeting in late July, the Black community had been demanding the removal of the large police presence in Harlem for more than a year. The committee demanded "the immediate and unconditional removal of all mounted police in Harlem, the recall of the heavy extra detail of patrolmen in the area, [and] the transfer of Inspector John Di Martini." La Guardia's claims of intolerance to police violence were mitigated by his public advocacy of Police Commissioner Valentine, whom he described as "a responsible commissioner." La Guardia's public challenges to former commissioner O'Ryan two years before undermined his claim that he could not intervene in police affairs. Instead, the mayor rationalized police violence, asserting that "our police are attacked in Harlem and certainly they must defend themselves."[35] Thus, despite public acknowledgment of police violence, La Guardia's ambivalence toward Black victims of police brutality legitimated police occupation of Harlem and the repression of its Black denizens. In July, the Citizens Democratic Club of 204 Lenox Avenue adopted a comparatively modest resolution, which called for the replacement of 50 percent of the night patrolmen with Black patrolmen. These criticisms against the NYPD had been made in the context of the fatal killing of Valance Brynoe, a seven-year-old Black boy of 167 West 126th Street; the near-death shooting of Leonard Brown; and the acquittal of Patrolman Brown.[36] In August, only three weeks after the meeting with the mayor about releasing his report, the Committee of Five, like other groups since May, once again demanded the "withdrawal of the 'police army of occupation in Harlem.'"[37]

In mid-August, the Stuyvesant Heights Branch of the Communist Party wrote a letter to La Guardia and Police Commissioner Valentine, listing multiple cases of police misconduct and aggression in Brooklyn and making several demands. The cases of police aggression represented a pattern of police misconduct. The preponderance of police in Harlem, the CP asserted, was a reference point for the brutality occurring in Brooklyn. Describing police presence in Harlem, the letter complained that "an army of policemen sent by Commissioner Valentine represents a permanent provocation to a peaceful people." Among the five demands, the CP called for the immediate end to police brutality, immediate publication of the "suppressed report of the Mayor's Committee on Conditions in Harlem," immediate suspension of the police officers implicated in the cases, immediate dismissal of charges against Dunn and Mrs. Moore, and open hearings in cases of police brutality. By November, Dunn still had not received justice, though the Brooklyn Council of the National Negro Congress continued to demand justice, questioning the relationship between the NYPD and the district attorney's office.[38]

This wave of police violence overlapped with Harlemites' demands for aggressive political action. Over the course of the year, the Black community understood that the La Guardia administration prioritized policing over addressing the economic, political, and racial crises that the commission's report detailed. Since the spring of 1935, the commission's public hearings had made clear that the La Guardia administration had underserved Harlem's Black community, and no doubt Black New Yorkers in general. In August 1936, the conservative *New York Age* asked, "How about Some Action?" In assessing his meeting with Petioni and the committee in late July, the Black weekly admitted that La Guardia had "done many commendable things" but asserted that his recent actions were "unaccountable and without precedent." The *New York Age* wanted him to release the commission's report, and while acknowledging that it was made "public"—because it could be found in "one Harlem newspaper," its competitor, the *New York Amsterdam News*—it should have been released to all the newspapers. The *New York Age* characterized the mayor's behavior as a political tactic, an attempt to "bury the report." Knowing the *New York Amsterdam News's* reach within the color line, the *New York Age* argued that "had it [the report] been given simultaneously to all the papers of the city and published or commented on generally by them it would have reached the attention of the state and national leaders in politics and economics." More significantly, the *New York Age* lamented, "Only one paper published the report and the people who read it already knew the conditions."[39]

Even before the Mayor's Commission started the hearings, Claude McKay and others had made the connection between the uprising and the "Don't Buy Where You Can't Work" campaign. The hearings had pointed out local governmental inattention and confirmed the economic and racial basis of the uproar, which La Guardia admitted during his meeting with the committee in late July. He stated, "Of course, the basic trouble in Harlem is the economic situation—we are all agreed on that and there can no question about it." The mayor, however, was being disingenuous when he explained that "the same condition prevails in other parts of the city as well as through-out the country." La Guardia nimbly shifted the blame to the Great Depression, while at the same time he evaded his own administration's racism—as the hearings and the report he refused to release disclosed—that contributed to Harlem's "economic situation."[40]

That winter, the *New York Amsterdam News*, like the *New York Age*, lambasted La Guardia's dubious treatment of his commission's report and his duplicitous response to demands from the Black community. In early October, in an editorial titled "La Guardia's Long, Hard Road," the Black weekly stated that the mayor "adopted a policy of denial on a great number of the accusations" and singled out two heads of departments—Dr. S. S. Goldwater, commissioner of hospitals, and Lewis J. Valentine, police commissioner, who were investigated in the report—who rejected the merit and soundness of the report. Questioning Valentine's claim that "his policemen are enjoying the confidence of the law-abiding element," the Black weekly asked, "What about the repeated shootings of citizens and the bandaged heads?" Understanding the city's long neglect of its Black citizens, the *New York Amsterdam News* acknowledged that La Guardia inherited many of these problems. That fact made La Guardia's denial, from the perspective of the Black weekly, unnecessary. Instead, he engaged in political theater: "He waits until a few corrective steps have been taken and then yells that nothing is wrong." Months later, the Black weekly asked him, "State Your Intentions, Mr. La Guardia" and questioned if he would fulfill his promise to meet with the Committee of Five, which he had met with only once since July. The Black weekly delineated La Guardia's pattern of wily excuses, "indirect repudiation of his own proposals and failure to publish the 'Riot' report," and no action. The paper asked for transparency and proclaimed, "If the mayor does not intend to recognize or respect the committee, then he should say so in plain words. . . . No one appreciates dodging."[41]

Thus, despite these public appeals, La Guardia was politically remiss. If anything, as the hearings and the report made plain, law enforcement was the principal "public good" that the city had long delivered to the Black community. Yet instead of public safety, it daily served indignant treatment and brutality to Black people. It was apt, then, that the Black community and the CP portrayed law enforcement's presence as a "police army of occupation." In the context of the Italo-Ethiopian War, anticipating Black activists in the 1960s and 1970s who dubbed "Negro ghettoes" as "internal colonies," the Black press and Black leaders saw the NYPD as a political instrument of racial repression. That these police units were manned by mainly white officers to control a Black neighborhood brought to public notice that their presence represented more than an effort to stop a "disorder"—it was a political strategy. As Valentine emphasized in late May, if not for budgetary constraints, he would have augmented the police contingent in Harlem. Dr. Charles Augustin Petioni and especially Ebenezer Ray had also made this connection clear—that La Guardia's principal policy response to the uprising and the commission's report that investigated it would be police occupation. Throughout the remainder of the 1930s and early 1940s, in Harlem, Queens, Brooklyn, and wherever else Black people settled in the city and its metropolitan area, they confronted police aggression. Whether in the streets or in their homes, if Black people committed actual crimes or just happened to be walking too slowly or perhaps in the wrong direction, cops cursed, arrested, bludgeoned, detained, and killed them—men, women, and children. Any expression of dignity and expectation of respect by Blacks, the police often interpreted as an affront to their authority. Consequently, police violence often occurred without any legal justification—arrests were unnecessary. In other cases, police used an array of charges from disorderly conduct and vagrancy to felonious assault to sanction police intimidation and excessive force.[42]

· · · · · ·

Just before New Year's Eve, on December 30, 1936, Theophilus Johnson, a postal worker, went to the roof in his building on 537 West 133rd Street in Harlem to repair the radio antenna around 11:00 P.M. A white neighbor several doors down from Johnson's called the police, complaining that someone was "prowling on the roof." Patrolman Williams, responding to the call, appeared on the roof and without asking any questions attacked Johnson. Williams struck him with a billy club several times, "cutting a deep gash under [his] left eye." Johnson had to receive stitches and lost a week of work. On New Year's Eve, the officer charged him with disorderly conduct. Johnson remained in police custody until January 3, when he was tried at the City Magistrate Court, Twelfth District Manhattan. After hearing the testimony, the magistrate dismissed the charges against him.[43] In a similar case, on March 27, 1937, William Dunne was confronted by three police officers in front of 450 Herkimer Street in Bedford-Stuyvesant, Brooklyn. When they ordered him to open his suitcase, he refused, but invited them to open it themselves. Because he defied their authority, the cops attacked him, slugging him across his head and face and charging him with vagrancy. Three women witnessed the beating, and according to the *New York Amsterdam News* were mainly responsible for the detaining of the police officers. Like Johnson, the charge against Dunne was dismissed.[44]

In mid-August 1937, near 4:30 A.M., as Cecil Ross and his friend walked home, they encountered the tail end of a commotion near their apartment building. As they tried to walk to their building, a police officer told them to "get away." Cecil tried to explain that he lived in the building on 113th Street in Harlem, and as he walked in the direction of his building, the officer pushed Cecil, beat him with a nightstick, and then punched him. Later that morning, Cecil and his brother went to the police station on 123rd Street to complain about the assault and were told to return at 8:00 A.M. for a lineup. Upon their return to the station, they pointed out the officer, but the inspector "tried to make them say that [he] was not the cop [and that] they could have been mistaken." The police also refused to give them the name and badge number of the officer. The officer, they alleged, even claimed that he was at a hospital with another cop when the incident occurred. Although bruised and unable to receive justice, Cecil escaped an arrest and criminal charges.[45]

Police officers' harassment of Black people, including women and children in their own homes, prompted protest and grassroots organization. In a letter to the NAACP, James St. John, chairman of the Citizens' Committee in Brooklyn, invited civil rights leader to attend a meeting about the flood of police attacks in Brooklyn and Long Island on June 30 at the Grenadian Recreational Center. St. John explained, "This is not a political issue, and as such, we seek no party lines, but as Negroes, we are interested in the Negro first." He delineated three topics that would be discussed: the illegal imprisonment of "our people," the illegal search of their homes, and the "creation of much unnecessary expenses to our group." Listing five cases, three involved searching Brooklynites' homes and two threatening women and children. In one case, the police "invaded [a home] . . . without [a] warrant . . . [and] rushed into the bedroom where this man's wife and children were sleeping, pulled the covers of the bed, etc. These people protested but was answered by the officer: 'SHUT UP, YOU BLACK SON OF A B——, OR I'LL SHOOT YOU.'" St. John also noted that these were respectable people. The police raided a woman's reception and though the "people were orderly and dignified, nevertheless, they were subjected to arrest and illegal imprisonment overnight."[46] The utter disrespect, the brutality, the incarceration, the expenses paid, and the wages lost were all reasons, he argued, that Blacks needed to organize according to race regardless of political affiliation.[47]

On September 24, 1937, two detectives broke into the apartment of Mrs. Louisa McLeod, 322 Thatford Avenue in Brooklyn. They ransacked the apartment, where McLeod and her two sick children lay in fear. When she questioned what they wanted, one of them said, "Keep you d——Black mouth shut or I will kick you in your d——mouth." She obtained their shield numbers, Nos. 13356 and 18332, and departed for the Seventy-Third Precinct police station, where she recognized them and made a complaint to the desk sergeant and requested that her door be repaired. The police gave her ten dollars to fix the door and lock, and the sergeant "admitted the men were in the wrong when they broke into her home and had made a mistake, but they would catch h—for it."[48] In November, two Black women would not get off as easily. As Mrs. Vera Sanders was putting her children, Bernard, three, and Reginald, fifteen months, to bed, she heard a knock on her door and opened it for two police officers. One of them asked for Miss Roberta Lewis, and she explained that she was at a show and asked if she could take a message. One of the officers said, "Hell, no," and they pushed their way in. They refused to show their badges. One officer knocked down Sanders, and the other punched her sister, Roberta Thomas, in the face. As the children watched in fear, the officers pummeled both women. One of the officers even drew his gun and told them, "Shut up . . . or I'll blow your brains out." They searched the apartment, but, as Sanders explained from the beginning, Ms. Lewis was not at the premises.[49]

The police beat the two women in their own home and charged them with felonious assault. Adam Clayton Powell Jr., the future councilman and congressman, defended the honor of the Black women. Born in 1908, Powell was raised in New Haven, Connecticut, and graduated from Colgate University in 1930 and followed his father, Adam Clayton Powell Sr., as the pastor of Abyssinian Baptist Church. Powell pointed out the irony of two Black women assaulting two policemen, six feet in height, and asserted in his column "Soapbox" that it was "important that the police department of New York City realize that this community wants those women freed and the real guilty ones—the detectives—tried." The women were scheduled to appear in Special Sessions Court on December 13. The conclusion of the case is unclear. Yet the violence these women endured at the hands of police officers was unmistakable, at least from the perspective of Black New Yorkers. Many Black women feared the police, who violated their bodies and their homes in front of their children. With seemingly unbridled power to feign victimhood, the police, as Powell pointed out, criminalized Sanders and Thomas as aggressors. Even when Black women were not the "real guilty ones," they were treated as such.[50] Powell's criticism of the police echoed the sentiments of other victims and communities organizing against police brutality in Brooklyn. Whether police searched, arrested, or detained them, Blacks in Brooklyn and across the city interpreted cops' actions as "illegal." As Powell made explicit regarding the patrolmen's treatment of Sanders and Thomas, Blacks knew their own innocence and asserted it by pointing out that criminal behavior permeated law enforcement. Though Sanders and Thomas may have walked away from this violent ordeal with the police, many Black New Yorkers and their families were not so fortunate. Their encounters with the NYPD were fatal.

Nine days before Christmas in 1937, seventeen-year-old William Shepard of 589 Gates Avenue was fatally shot by police officers from the Fulton Street Station on Reid Avenue in Brooklyn. The police officers were so convinced that Shepard had committed a crime and were so indifferent to the feelings of his mother, they neglected to tell her that he died until the end of the investigation and then lied to her about shooting him. The police officers exclaimed that Shepard, carrying a package, looked "suspicious." Patrolman Albert Meyers and another officer found two watches and a couple of pawn tickets in his pocket. According to Shepard's mother, he was delivering a package of clothing to his aunt, Lucille Franklin, who had recently given birth. Mrs. Shepard also complained that they charged into her home and "tore up pillows." They took her to the police station and told her that Shepard had stolen goods. She told them about the bundle, and then one police officer brought it out, and as she explained to the reporter, "It was just exactly as I said it was." They abruptly escorted her first to Shepard's grandmother's apartment and finally to William's brother, Walter Shepard. The "police turned [Walter's] apartment upside down and refused to answer questions" and claimed that William said that he and Walter robbed a house at 312 Herkimer Street. After Walter denied participation in the robbery, the police took Mrs. Shepard to the morgue. She said that they told her that they found Shepard's body "on Fulton Street and Albany Avenue 'when they knew very well they shot him at Fulton and Reid.'"[51] Shepard died in St. Mary's Hospital. The Citizens' Civic Affairs Committee, headed by Reverend George Frazier Miller, launched an investigation aiming to take up the case with La Guardia and Police Commissioner Valentine. While the trail of this case ends here, the Shepard case glaringly demonstrates how police violence entangled the victims and their families. By abridging the Shepards' Fourth Amendment rights, the police extended their violence beyond the reach of their initial victim, compounding the pain and grief that undoubtedly outlasted the fatal shooting and police harassment.[52] While some Blacks died from conspicuous police aggression, others died under more complicated and suspicious conditions.

In the late spring and early summer of 1937, the police alleged that two Black men under police custody had committed suicide. After fighting with an unnamed man on April 17, Albert Swette-Moore, known as Sandy among his family and friends, sent his opponent to the hospital with a cut eye. Three days later, the police arrested Albert for felonious assault while he was playing ball with some friends. Within hours of the arrest and being taken into custody, he was found dead in the cell in the Gates and Throop Avenue police station in Brooklyn. Charles Moore, Albert's brother, questioned the police's story, believing instead that the police killed Albert while he was in their custody. District Attorney Frank Madden and Detective James Kale immediately asserted that it was suicide, not "police third degree." The police claimed Albert hung himself by the seam of his shirt in the jail cell. Before his arrest, he did not have marks on his body. Charles became suspicious when his half-brother told him that he saw a three-inch bruise on Albert's forehead and other abrasions on the body lying in the funeral parlor. Mary Jane Ealy, a friend of Albert, claimed that the police officer threatened him the day before. "You better be careful. The next time we get you we'll kill you" and upon his initial arrest, the police refused to explain what he was arrested for.[53]

Charles wanted his brother's body exhumed and examined. He obtained a show cause order from the court and signed a petition and supporting affidavits explaining his suspicion. In early June, a mass meeting, which the *New York Amsterdam News* described as "tumultuous," was held at Evening Star Baptist Church at 534 Gates Avenue in Brooklyn. Moore's attorney, Oscar J. Albert, and Rev. Miller, pastor of St. Augustine Protestant Episcopal Church, headed the Citizens Civic Affairs Committee, the same grassroots organization that mobilized around the killing of William Shepard. Albert reported that Moore's medical report showed a bruised heart and head and death by strangulation. Yet once Moore's body was disinterred, the investigation could not determine the exact cause of the death. The examination raised other questions. Moore's brain was now missing, yet the first autopsy reported that Moore had a mark on his head. By the end of the month, Moore's cause of death still remained a mystery, and more questions remained unanswered. Attorney Albert continued to ask a series of questions: "Why did the District Attorney tell me that the shirt with which the boy allegedly strangled himself was lost when all the time it was in the hands of the property clerk's office? Why did Dr. Nidish testify at the morgue that he saw no marks on the boy's body after having told a reporter on May 19 that he had noticed a mark on the boy's head, but attributed it to a pressure mark?"[54] Albert's questions went unanswered.

Months later in November, the police alleged that John Brown, another Black man in Brooklyn, committed suicide in jail. On November 26, Brown pleaded not guilty before County Judge John J. Fitzgerald. He was awaiting trial for assaulting a woman, Virginia Lundy, as well as police officer Arthur J. DeMarrais. Black Brooklynites demanded a state investigation of police activities in their borough. According to the police, Brown created a noose from his bedsheet and hung himself from the upper bunk of his cell at the Raymond Street Jail. John Kennedy, the jail's keeper, found the body as he was delivering breakfast to the prisoners. Lundy, Brown's ex-girlfriend, had called the police on November 7 and complained to DeMarrais that Brown had molested her. After his arrest, Brown "savagely" bit DeMarrais on his face, neck, nose, and hand. As Brown endeavored to escape, DeMarrais shot, subdued, and arrested him. That evening, DeMarrais was taken to the hospital, and while awaiting treatment, the officer died of strangulation, caused by food eaten before he arrested Brown. Although Brown was initially charged with homicide, DeMarrais's medical report and the district attorney's office confirmed that undigested food caused his death, clearing Brown of the initial charge. *Spring 3100*, the police department's journal, depicted DeMarrais as a hero who saved a Black woman and died at the hands of Brown. Both alleged suicides occurred in the context of probable police retribution. Brown's perceived guilt by the police, at least before the medical report, as well as the police's propensity for excessive force against Black people might have created the conditions for the police to manufacture the suicide. Moore's long criminal record and likely hostile relationship with law enforcement plausibly explain why his friend Ealy noted that the police officer promised to kill Moore the next time they saw him.[55]

Just east of the borough of Queens, Blacks in both Nassau and Suffolk Counties on Long Island organized to fight against police violence. In 1937, Blacks in Bay Shore founded their own political club, the Progressive Democratic Club of Bay Shore, led by Harry Van Hoesen. The club aimed to change the political landscape and mobilize a political bloc to vote out the Republican establishment. The political club published its own newspaper, the *Afro-American Echo*. In the first issue on October 25, 1937, it explained why the newspaper was titled *Echo*. "Echo is a repetition and the lives of Colored people are full of repetitions, such as unjust arrests, unjust court decisions and unjust punishments, over and over again, like an echo." It covered a story in North Amityville of a Black man, Frank Borges, who was fatally shot in the back by Officer Walter W. Weeks, who claimed that he shot Borges in self-defense. Weeks stated that Borges "made a motion as if to reach for a gun" and the officer fired one fatal shot. The police found no gun on Borges, who died before the arrival of a doctor.[56] The *Echo* wrote, "NOTE: Cases like the above are of common occurrence where Colored people are concerned" and urged Blacks to vote for the Democratic ticket because Republicans refused to bring them justice. Likely in response to the murder of Borges, along with other cases of police aggression, a group of Black civic-minded citizens from North Amityville created the Citizens Defense Committee of North Amityville, held two meetings throughout the month of November, and sought help from the NAACP to establish a local chapter.[57]

"It Makes Me Very Nervous to Know They Could Get Away with What They Did to Me"

Most victims of police violence, for various reasons, were unable to secure legal support, yet for those who did, public officials in the criminal legal system still managed to stifle their efforts. In early February of 1937, several months before the killing of Borges in North Amityville, NAACP special counsel Charles Hamilton Houston wrote Martin W. Littleton, the district attorney of Nassau County, regarding the assault of Mattie Holsey, a Black woman living in Inwood, Long Island, by Patrolman Bates of the Nassau County Police Department. In late October 1936, Bates beat Holsey for asking him why he charged into her home and grabbed and beat Landous Irving. Because she could not get Inwood's law enforcement to take her complaint seriously, she sought the legal support of the NAACP. Houston inquired about Littleton's letter to attorney Jane Bolin in mid-November, in which the DA claimed that high-ranking police officials had tried to speak with eyewitnesses in the Holsey case but they found no one willing to cooperate with the investigation. Littleton also claimed that he encouraged Holsey to go before a justice of the peace for a warrant if she had "a sound complaint." Bolin, whom Mayor La Guardia two years later appointed to the bench as the nation's first African American woman judge, represented Irving and requested leave from Judge Ekenberg to withdraw Irving's plea of guilty, which he granted. The jury, nonetheless, found Irving guilty. Following up with the case now as Holsey's counsel, Houston questioned the sincerity of Nassau's police department and informed the DA that he, in fact, held five copies of affidavits in his possession. The eyewitnesses included Jeff Holsey, Mrs. Holsey's son; Martha Moore, a friend who was sitting in Holsey's home; Pauline Blanchard, Holsey's neighbor living right across the street; McKinley McClurin, who called the police to squash an argument in his restaurant; and Rosa Smith, who lived across the street from the restaurant.[58]

McClurin, according to his affidavit, called the police because Landous Irving had been arguing in his restaurant, but by the time Patrolmen Bates and Francis arrived, Irving had already departed. Since Irving was gone, McClurin told the cops that they might be able to find Irving's whereabouts from his friend John Stewart, whom McClurin had seen in the street.[59] Rosa Smith stated that she overheard the exchange between McClurin and the police. She claimed that "as long as he [Irving] had gone, he [McClurin] did not want anything done to him."[60] Pauline Blanchard, who lived across the street from Holsey, explained that she heard Bates threatening Stewart with his nightstick raised. Bates had guided Stewart by his collar, cursing him, "You Black son of a bitch, you show me the house where he lives or I'll beat you up."[61] Stewart, according to Jeff Holsey, knocked on the door and asked for "a fellow who had just come in there, saying he did not know his name," but Irving did not see the "policeman on the stoop with him." When Mr. Holsey, who was catnapping, approached and called out to Stewart, Bates rushed into the house and asked Stewart to point him out, and he did, and Bates grabbed Irving, cursing, "You're the son of a b—h I want." Bates yanked Irving out of the chair and began beating him, as Patrolman Frances pulled him outside.[62]

Martha Moore, who had been sitting with Mr. Holsey and Irving when Bates burst into the house, stated that Mrs. Holsey confronted Bates outside her home and asked what Irving had done and if Bates had a warrant, but Bates pushed her and continued onto the street.[63] Mr. Holsey, who had been in the house fetching his coat, then followed the cops to Wanser Avenue, where he saw a crowd in front of Mac's Restaurant. "Bates was swinging his night club at everybody and cursing at them and yelling at them to get across the street," observed Mr. Holsey. He asked the cops to show him a warrant, and Bates cursed, threatened, and chased him across the street. His mother then came out, after phoning the police, and the mother and son walked across the street.[64] Moore witnessed Mrs. Holsey asking the cops if they had a warrant, and Mr. Holsey began writing Bates's badge number. Then Bates seized him and raised the baton to beat him. Mrs. Holsey also began writing his badge number and asked the officer not to hit him since he had not committed a crime. Bates questioned what she had to do with Mr. Holsey, she explained that he was her son, and Bates once again swore at her. He complained that she was trying to be "so damn smart" and shoved her. When Mrs. Holsey commanded him not to push her, he replied, "'G—d—you, I'll give you some of it' and jabbed his night stick in her stomach, almost pushing her over backward," stated Moore. She fell back against the wall of the restaurant and held onto Bates's baton. Bates demanded that she let it go and yanked it away. Blanchard then stepped in and told Bates not to hit Mrs. Holsey again. Bates and Frances pushed Irving and Mr. Holsey in the police car and drove to the precinct. According to all who witnessed the beatings, neither Irving nor Mr. Holsey ever tried to retaliate or resist arrest in any way.[65]

The affidavits undermined DA Littleton's claim that police met resistance from eyewitnesses. They also put into suspicion his suggestion that Mrs. Holsey should ask Judge Ekenberg to issue a warrant for Bates's arrest. As Houston noted, referring to McClurin's affidavit, "Judge Ekenberg . . . tried to coerce him into giving a statement which would have exonerated the patrolman of breach of discipline."[66] In his letter dated February 15, Littleton bypassed Houston's comments, undercutting his claim that the police endeavored to investigate Mrs. Holsey's complaint, and instead focused his comments on defending Ekenberg's legal integrity and reputation. He then cast uncertainly on the affidavits. "I must point out to you, however, that which I should have presumed you to know, that if such affidavits could in and of themselves disqualify the judges in our criminal courts from acting in given cases, it would be the inauguration of a precedent which soon would preclude any judge from sitting in a criminal case where an affidavit of alleged prejudice was presented," and then he continued to explain the basics of criminal procedure. The exchange between Littleton and Houston ends there. Littleton responded to Houston's inquiry, which might be read as an invitation to Littleton to push forward Mrs. Holsey's case, with a patently condescending letter that suggested coordinated machinations across Nassau County's criminal justice system. Black youth thrust into the city's criminal justice system encountered similar roadblocks.[67]

Two years later in Brooklyn, a Black family confronted a judge who tried to vindicate police violence. In some cases, Black victims of police brutality often pleaded guilty of crime because of police intimidation, embarrassment, and even self-prescribed guilt. But judges, more likely to accept the statements of the arresting officer, sometimes used their power to browbeat defendants and even their parents into internalizing parental delinquency. In early June 1939, James Samuel, a nineteen-year-old high school student, of 763 Cleveland Avenue, Brooklyn, had an altercation with three police officers, William Hufnagel, William Booze, and William Arnato.[68] This confrontation occurred in the street, where Samuel witnessed a car collision in East New York involving his friend Jack Pierce. At the court hearing, the arresting police officer William Hufnagel offered to reduce the initial charge from simple assault upon a police officer to disorderly conduct. Asked to describe his interaction with Samuel by Judge Jacob Eilperin, Hufnagel explained that he told Samuel to "move away and he refused to move away." Samuel, according to the officer, struck him. During the preliminary discussion of the charges, the Samuels willingly accepted the charge of disorderly conduct. Eilperin even encouraged the Samuels to accept guilt on behalf of their son.[69]

But their willingness was temporary. While acknowledging that there was no "legal warrant for it," Eilperin asked the parents, "Do you plead guilty along with your boy?" and both mother and father pleaded guilty on behalf of their son. The judge asked Hufnagel if James Samuel should be sent to jail, and the officer said no and that the suspension of the sentence was enough. The judge then asked James to apologize. Eilperin commanded him to "turn to the officer and say to him, 'I am sorry, and never again will I raise a hand in the direction of a policeman." James stated, "No." Once again, Eilperin pushed him to admit his wrongdoing: "Here, do you think it was a nice thing, and decent, and American-like, to raise your fist in the direction of a police officer; in violently taking him by the left arm and making use of your fist?" The judge, losing patience, asked once again, "Do you not think that an apology is in order?" James said, "No, I won't apologize." The judge explained, "You don't have to" and fined him ten dollars and warned that if he defaulted on the payment, he would spend two days in jail.[70]

Upon James's refusal and his father's heartfelt request for time to speak with his son, the judge suspended the session. Eilperin spoke with the father and encouraged him to persuade James to apologize. Yet knowing that he "didn't do anything to apologize for," James refused, and Eilperin restored the initial charge of simple assault, a misdemeanor. Then James and his parents contacted the NAACP, and attorney William Pickens argued his case. On the streets of Brooklyn, James endured both the ordeal of physical and verbal punishment in the street and in court—the judge tried to force guilt upon not only the youth but also his parents. The Samuels, therefore, were criminalized thrice. James, despite this, avoided criminal charges and was able to go free. Much like other Blacks, James defended his innocence and refused to accept the criminal justice system's effort to define him as a criminal. At the Special Sessions of King's County Court, Justices MacDonald, Kozieke, and Hoffman unanimously acquitted him of the charge. Though Blacks sometimes found a measure of accountability especially with the support of counsel in the court system, they found their search for redress in the NYPD's bureaucracy elusive.[71]

While Black victims seeking justice often ran up against judicial collusion that stifled any effort to investigate the police, others barely cracked open the door to initiate internal investigations of the police in Commissioner Valentine's police department where bureaucratic obstruction prevailed. In mid-August of 1937, Marian McDonell attended a show in Times Square around 9:30 in the evening, and after midnight, she walked to Forty-Second Street and Fifth Avenue in mid-Manhattan to catch a bus to go home. After waiting for some time with no bus in sight, McDonell walked two blocks north along Fifth Avenue and stood at the edge of the sidewalk. As she waited, several white men accosted her and, as she explained in the affidavit, they "tried to get me to get in their cars." The last car stopped, the door opened, and two men exited, flanking each side of the car. They forced her into the vehicle, bruising her ankle and leg. In fear for her life and believing that she was being kidnapped, she begged them to release her so she could go home to her little dog. She offered to give them her rent money and pleaded with them to let her go. Then the man on her right, whom she later found out to be Detective James Tedesco, revealed that they were police officers searching for a pickpocket suspect. She told them that she was an honest working woman and gave them her business card. They detained her nonetheless and roughly escorted her to the Seventeenth Precinct. They took her to the backroom, where she cried, still unaware of why she was being arrested. Annoyed by her behavior, one of the officers threatened to intern her in Bellevue Hospital. She demanded that they tell her why she was detained, but "they wouldn't answer." She then asked one of the arresting officers his name and shield number and he smugly quipped, "Tedesco, shield number 9161, you had better play that number tomorrow."[72]

The police then took her into the patrol wagon and drove to the Fifty-Third Street Station, where she lay in a "bad smelling cell until 8:30 A.M." Thereafter, she was taken to the court on Fifty-Seventh Street, stuck in another cell without food until Detective Tedesco showed up at 12:00 noon, and then he had her arraigned. Tedesco arrested her for disorderly conduct, alleging that she had asked men to take her home and that she tried to bribe the officers. She pleaded not guilty and explained to the judge that she was a working woman, and she gave him her business card and invited him to "investigate my life where I live and work." The judge told her to bring them in, adjourned the case, and set her bail at $200. McDonell was finally able to use the phone, and she called her employer, Mrs. Bertha Harris. From the courthouse, she was taken to a detention home where she showered, was given a physical examination, and was placed in another cell at about 8:00 P.M. Several hours later, Mrs. Harris arrived with Mrs. Lottie Fraser at the detention home. They could not get her out on bail until the next day. Thursday morning, she was taken to another cell, where she was accosted by her cellmates. She remembered, "The girls laughed at me, threw off on me terribly bad." At around 2:00 P.M., she was released, and Mrs. Harris and another woman came and took her home.[73]

Mrs. McDonell contacted the NAACP to represent her in the court case, as well as to counsel her as she sought redress from the police department. Thurgood Marshall and William Pickens worked on her behalf. Marshall corresponded mainly with officials of the police department, and Pickens represented her in court and at the hearings. McDonell, Marshall, and Pickens constantly ran up against bureaucratic roadblocks. Marshall wrote Commissioner Valentine three times, asking him to give the case his "personal attention." In the August 25 letter to Valentine, Marshall summarized the circumstances of McDonell's arrest from her perspective, her grievances with the two police officers, and the overall ill-treatment she endured while in custody. In the second letter dated September 7, Marshall requested a different inspector to oversee the hearing and investigation. That same morning, Inspector Charles Neidig heard the testimony of several police officers, including Tedesco, and an eyewitness, the white man who drove the car. Neidig called Marshall to inform him that McDonell neglected to appear at the hearing and asked him to come to the precinct to speak with the witness, because he did not want to inconvenience the witness with another meeting. When Marshall arrived at the precinct, the eyewitness had already testified, but he retold what he said in his testimony. Marshall explained to Neidig that the witness's testimony was different from McDonell's testimony. He requested that McDonell have the opportunity to come to the hearing at a future date to bring witnesses and tell her side of the story. Neidig told him that "he did not care to hear her." Marshall commented that he understood departmental policy but objected to the adjudication of a "hearing" based on only one side of the question. Neidig told Marshall that he could not care less about McDonell's testimony—that "it made no difference to him what type of person Mrs. McDonell was; it made no difference to him what her reputation or character might be, her testimony could have no weight with him; that he had the facts in the case and that was all that mattered."[74]

Near two o'clock that same afternoon, McDonell called and notified Marshall that she had only received the notice the morning of the hearing and that it was delivered to her by a sergeant. McDonell's explanation was verified by Neidig's office. Since she did not have an opportunity to testify and because of Neidig's refusal to hear testimony, Marshall requested that the hearing be headed by another inspector. From Marshall's perspective, Neidig had "clearly disqualified himself to hold an impartial hearing." Marshall asked Valentine to request that Neidig give Marshall an account of the manner that he held the hearing and to "be given an opportunity to confront him" in Valentine's presence. Despite Marshall's concerns, Neidig held the second hearing on September 15, and the inspector behaved the same way. In his final letter to Valentine, Marshall lamented, "Instead of assuming the attitude of an unbiased finder of fact, Inspector Neidig assumed the attitude of protector of the particular policemen and constantly took the attitude that Mrs. McDonell was telling deliberate falsehoods and that testimony of the witness for the policemen was absolute fact."[75]

Marshall's third letter questioned the impartiality of the hearing and charged that the police department failed to protect Black women. He reminded Valentine that at the court proceedings where McDonell's case had been dismissed, the police did not present a witness and asserted that the police were unwilling to have a witness testify when "the question was up as to the enforcement of the laws of the city of New York." Marshall argued that the case was important not only to clear the name of McDonell but also to expose the police department's pattern of mistreatment of Black women. He noted that McDonell lost two days of work and suffered "mental anguish by being incarcerated." The NAACP, he wrote, had received many complaints from Black women about the mistreatment they received at the hands of white motorists and the NYPD. He wrote, "Instead of protecting Negro women against being harassed by white motorists constantly driving up beside them, making insulting remarks and molesting them, these policemen arrest a woman and charge her with disorderly conduct." In the particular case of McDonell, he noted, while two people were arrested and deemed guilty of a crime, only the Black woman was jailed and charged with disorderly conduct. The police's white witness, who pleaded guilty to his charge, however, was fined and released. Marshall stated that it was regrettable that "the policemen in the city of New York are making a practice of carrying on a campaign to protect motorists yet are doing nothing to protect Negro women who are being molested by many of these motorists."[76]

On September 24, Marshall sent the mayor a letter, along with his correspondences to Valentine, outlining McDonell's case and his concerns about Neidig's intolerance and Valentine's complicity in the ongoing investigation of the police officers. La Guardia might have intervened, because Inspector Michael A. Wall, of the Manhattan borough office, contacted Marshall in late October and explained that the case was to be reopened. There were likely two additional meetings in November and December. By the end of the first week of December, La Guardia wrote to Marshall disclosing that the police department's report confirmed the innocence of the officers and cleared them of any misconduct.[77]

Four days before Christmas, McDonell wrote Marshall, thanking him and the NAACP for their support and "effort [on her] behalf." She was sorry that they lost and speculated that the officers must have jointly practiced their testimonies to ensure that their statements aligned. In spite of avoiding the charge of disorderly conduct, McDonell remained concerned about her welfare. She asked Marshall, "Do you think those police officers will try and get me some way? I do now. It makes me very nervous to know they could get away with what they did to me." Marshall believed that she could "rest assured that those two particular detectives will not do this again." He wrote, "I am certain they will stay as far away from you as possible."[78] Although Marshall tried to assuage McDonell's concerns about police retaliation, she had good reason to fear the NYPD. In spite of his certainty, in his letter to La Guardia, even he charged that there was a clear pattern of the police department actively protecting white men who had preyed upon Black women. Marshall and McDonell's concerns about police retaliation echoed the Mayor's Commission report and underlined the same fears that Black New Yorkers had long protested about. Indeed, as he had with his commission report, La Guardia ignored the pleas of the Black community, despite Marshall's letters exposing the duplicity of Inspector Neidig. Though he availed himself to the NAACP about police abuse, the mayor, like Commissioner Valentine, routinely sided with the police officers. As an expression of liberal law and order, the mayor did respond to Marshall's pleas for investigation. La Guardia undoubtedly conceded by assigning Inspector Wall to McDonell's case, but ultimately the mayor was reluctant to question the veracity of the NYPD. In his letter to Marshall, he explained, "In the report submitted to me by the Police Department it does not appear that the officers involved were guilty of any misconduct." But his concluding comment to

Marshall, an appraisal singularly directed toward this particular case, sheds much light on La Guardia's unofficial policy toward the issue of police violence and Black people. As he wrote to Marshall, "The facts seem to be the same as in all cases of this character."[79]

· · · · · ·

The battle against police brutality in Harlem, Bedford-Stuyvesant, and metropolitan New York remained a fixture of Black resistance and politics throughout La Guardia's three terms as mayor. The Harlem uprising of 1935 and the occupation of Harlem and other Black neighborhoods, especially Bedford-Stuyvesant, that were occupied to contain Black settlement set off a critical period of Black political activism around policing. No longer would Blacks rely on political journalism and Black ministers to lobby the precinct police captain, the police commissioner, or the mayor. While these forms of protest continued, they overlapped with grassroots organizing, mass meetings, and litigation in cooperation with the NAACP, Black public officials, and the Communist Party. The mayor's promise that he "would not tolerate police brutality in Harlem nor in any other section of Manhattan" was merely rhetoric. La Guardia's and Valentine's urban policy of criminalizing and policing the crisis in the face of Black leaders' demands for political action jump-started Black New York's first anti–police brutality movement and made police brutality along with housing, jobs, and education a central issue of New York City politics.

Though the mayor failed to protect Black citizens from police brutality, he availed himself, though inconsistently, to Black leaders. While his administration demonstrated a measure of interracial cooperation, La Guardia's racial liberalism delivered mainly more punishment. Only a year before the uprising, La Guardia intervened in police affairs and aggressively advocated in favor of striking taxi drivers. White leaders and business owners' outcries of crime, however, called forth a greater political response than Black Harlem's demands for equitable government support. The mayor and Commissioner Valentine stationed a police contingent in Harlem, which Harlem's Black leadership complained about for well over a year. Instead of operating as conduits for police accountability throughout the remainder of the decade, the courts and police officials bolstered police violence, just as they had done before La Guardia became the mayor. Whether Black New Yorkers read about police aggression in the pages of the Black weeklies or if they witnessed it in the streets, the threat of police violence was unavoidable.

Part II

5 As Opposed to Police Brutality as We Are to Lawlessness

. . . .

In the first two weeks of 1939, the *New York Age* lamented that Harlem's New Year's holiday had been "marred" by the brutal killing "of one of its most promising youths." Robert "Bobby" Forbes, a nineteen-year-old Lincoln University student, was the son of Mr. Frank Forbes, an athletic director, and Mrs. Whitlock Forbes, a public-school teacher. Wally Paige killed Forbes after a "slight scuffle." Forbes's death shocked Harlem. Though this kind of crime was not unfamiliar to Harlemites, Forbes's "passing causes us to pause and reflect as to what can be done to stop this homicidal wave which has engulfed both youth and old." For several years, Harlemites had been demanding better policing, even as they fought against police brutality. This murder was different, however, because the victim *and* the convicted represented the promise and future of Black Harlem. "Wally" Paige was no thug. He was a group leader at the Harlem branch of the YMCA and carried letters of reference from the "Y." The fact that Harlem youth of this caliber were entrapped in crime was a clarion call to the community. As the *New York Age* asserted, "There can be no excusing the slaying on the ground that it was done in an impulsive moment. Nor can it be said that the slayer was underprivileged, unschooled and unaware of what was right or wrong." The Black weekly "condemned" the police for permitting the sale of knives, the courts for being too lenient with juvenile offenders, and the State of New York for providing no corrective institutions for "young Negro boys and girls." The *New York Age* "particularly condemn[ed] Police Commissioner Valentine and his subordinates who transfer inferior white policemen and men under charges to Harlem as punishment thereby placing an unfair stigma on those upright and courageous Harlem policemen who have been here for years, who are respected and who respect Harlem's ideals."[1]

The *New York Age* espoused a politics of law and order but one shaped by the values, experiences, and plight of the Black community. The Black weekly's sentiments generally matched the Black community's views on Black crime and the criminal justice system. When the jury convicted Paige of first-degree murder and sentenced him to be electrocuted, few publicly disagreed with the decision. As Forbes's father stated, "Sending him to the chair won't bring Bobby back, but it ought to certainly help in curtailing crime here in Harlem."[2] Crime and intraracial violence appeared in Black neighborhoods in every borough of the city, and Black New Yorkers, not unlike others, expected safety from crime. Black youth crime but also New York State's criminal justice system and "particularly . . . Police Commissioner Valentine" were to blame for Bobby's death. During the late 1930s, Black New Yorkers, especially in Harlem and Bedford-Stuyvesant, expanded their efforts for equitable policing and police accountability, demanding justice as victims of crime and calling for and expecting police protection. Overpolicing and underprotection violently coexisted, exposing the failure of the La Guardia administration to protect Black citizens. Black New Yorkers' demands for equitable police protection, much like their protests against police brutality, were a seminal aspect of their politics of safety, and anti-crime activism was a community affair. As Blacks organized among themselves to fight crime in general, juvenile crime gradually became the center of their attention. The Black press, civil rights organizations, and reform and civic associations played key roles in keeping the community aware of crime activity, while promoting anti-crime efforts among Blacks as an integral aspect of community responsibility.

Black anti-crime efforts across the city overlapped with white New Yorkers' outcries about Black street crime in Harlem and Brooklyn. Throughout the late 1930s, crime in Harlem, not the district's cultural renaissance, persistently made the headlines in the mainstream press. As the Black press demanded equitable policing in Black neighborhoods, it also challenged misrepresentations of crime in Harlem in the white press, distinguishing legitimate concerns about crime from those deriving from anti-Black impulses. In Bedford-Stuyvesant, in addition to correcting race-laden crime news, Blacks organized to protect themselves from the threat of white violence and police aggression. During the 1920s but especially the late 1930s, as the Black population grew, white civic, religious, and real estate associations mobilized to stem Black settlement in Bedford-Stuyvesant, and when that did not work, they tried to contain it. Led by Sumner Sirtl, a white attorney, and his organization, the Midtown Civic League (MCL), this well-organized tide against the "Negro invasion"—as it had in Harlem decades before—fused its battle against Black property ownership with a campaign against Black crime. Thus, as Sirtl argued that Blacks lowered property values, he also called upon the La Guardia administration and Police Commissioner Valentine to increase the police force in the neighborhood. Although his efforts to halt Black movement in Bedford-Stuyvesant failed, Sirtl's campaign to expand the police presence prevailed. Like Commissioner Valentine in Harlem in 1936, Sirtl framed his campaign around not only the need for white safety but also the need to expand the city's police force. The MCL's anti-Black campaign built upon the rhetoric of white Harlemites who asserted that Black crime caused the 1935 uprising and upon the long tradition of white New Yorkers using police and white civilian violence to maintain all-white neighborhoods. While Blacks' campaign against police brutality and demands for police protection represented an expression of the politics of safety, whites' activism to expand the police presence in Brooklyn represented a racist movement in defense of all-white neighborhoods by any means necessary.

"The Vigilantes 'Ride' Again—This Time in the Bedford-Stuyvesant Section of Brooklyn"

During the late 1930s, southern and Afro-Caribbean migrants as well as Black New Yorkers moved to Brooklyn, namely, the Bedford-Stuyvesant section, to find affordable and less congested living space. Between 1930 and the 1950, Brooklyn's Black population tripled. Bedford-Stuyvesant's Black community and the characterization of it as crime-ridden increased so significantly that the white press began to dub it "Brooklyn's Harlem."[3] Although there had been Blacks in the Bedford and Stuyvesant sections since the colonial era, the Black community began to expand in the 1920s. Because of declining housing and the development of modern housing and public transportation to other areas, such as Bay Ridge, Coney Island, and Flatbush, Bedford-Stuyvesant housing was more affordable.[4]

In the 1920s and 1930s, whites formed property-owners associations to keep Black settlement at bay. The Gates Avenue Association and the Bedford Avenue Property Owners Association, for example, endorsed urban development projects, such as the construction of the Fulton Street subway, but rejected others, such as the creation of a playground. While they believed that the subway would increase the neighborhoods' property values, which might make it too expensive for most Blacks to rent or purchase property, whites in 1929 purported to oppose the playground in Rusurban Park because it would worsen the already poor traffic conditions. The *New York Amsterdam News* doubted the sincerity of their rationale. The Black weekly quoted a daily that printed a letter from Charles E. Wissner, of the Wissner Piano Company, who warned of the threat to white women. He lamented the playground "would not be safe for woman who are obliged to pass this neighborhood at night, as they would undoubtedly be subjected to insults and possible bodily harm." Attuned to whites' color-blind racism, the Black weekly opined, "While he did not mention Negroes in his letter, a number of persons are of the opinion he meant them because so many are in the district."[5] Racial, anti-Black animosity reared its head in the church.[6] On September 15, Rev. William Blackshear, rector of St. Matthew's Protestant Episcopal Church, from his pulpit reading from the church bulletin announced that the church "did not want Negroes' money nor Negro membership." Emeline Munt, a Black woman attending church that day, relayed that "one young Negro woman in the congregation got up and went out, wiping her eyes with a handkerchief. I talked to another of the Negro women after the service ended and she felt as badly about the matter as I did." As Blacks no longer obliged to attend white churches, they purchased more property, including near-empty churches as white flight accelerated and interracial conflict worsened.[7]

In June of 1937, the Bethel African Methodist Episcopal Church (AME) tried to purchase the "white debt-ridden" Grace Congregational Church, at Stuyvesant and Jefferson Avenues. Sumner Sirtl and Mrs. E. O. Boiling, founder and vice president of the Hancock-Halsey Neighborhood Association, protested the settlement of Blacks in that section as well as Bethel AME's attempts to purchase the white-owned church. In late June, they charged that the sale of the church would lower the realty values and "the general quality of the neighborhood."[8] As president of the Midtown Civic League, Sirtl promised to assist "residents who wish to sell or rent their property [to] desirable tenants or purchasers" and infused his rhetoric about property values with a color-blind discourse of anti-Blackness.[9] By "residents," he meant white residents, a political constituency with which he aimed to build his campaign. Yet despite Sirtl's neutral language, Bedford-Stuyvesant's Black community called out the MCL's racism. Alexander Clayborn, a member of the Citizens Civic Affairs Committee (CCAC), stated bluntly that the MCL "fan[ned] the fires of race hatred and prejudice" and assured that his committee was "deeply interested in preserving peace and tranquility in the community, especially among the various racial groups."[10]

Sirtl rejected Clayborn's accusations of racism. Representing 900 members of the MCL, Sirtl explained that they were interested in the civic betterment and the desirability of their community and the preservation of its dignity. The "racial hysteria" assigned to the MCL by the Black press and Clayborn was "only in the mind of Mr. Clayborn," he said.[11] The next week,

Sirtl made his views of Blacks as property-owners and renters clear. They were simply negligent. Sirtl admitted that "certain white realtors have the habit of renting houses to colored people without making any repairs thereby depreciating the value of property." Denying racism, he charged that Blacks neglected to request repairs to their homes. "Now, white people demand repairs on the houses they rent from realtors. As a rule, colored families don't. Therefore, the houses run down. Slum conditions start. Whites move out. All because the colored people don't demand their repairs. They should!" Sirtl's explanation that Blacks depreciated property was a well-worn tactic to justify segregation, founded on presumed and naturalized racial differences. Though unsuccessful at containing Black settlement, Sirtl's mobilization of the white community did gain some ground in its efforts to criminalize Bedford-Stuyvesant's growing Black community.[12]

In mid-January, the MCL circulated a petition with more than 2,000 signatures requesting additional police for the section. At the YMCA on Bedford Avenue and Monroe Street, Sirtl proclaimed that "these petitions will be circulated until every person living in the district signs it."[13] Once the petition attained 10,000 signatures, Sirtl promised to submit it to La Guardia and Police Commissioner Valentine. The petition read,

> Whereas the Police Department of New York City is far below its regular quota of members, and Whereas the Bedford section of Brooklyn has had two recent slayings during holdups, a notorious attack case, and far too many recent robberies; and Whereas the women and children of the Bedford section of Brooklyn do not feel safe to venture out on the streets alone at night:
>
> Therefore we the undersigned, hereby petition you to not only increase the number of patrolmen to its full quota, but to also specifically increase the number of patrolmen in the Seventy-Seventh (Atlantic Ave.), Seventy-Ninth (Gates Ave.) and Eighth (Grand Ave.) Precincts. We furthermore feel that should the present wave of crime continue in this section then you are to blame for not heeding our petition.[14]

The petition was not only a request but also a warning to public officials. At a meeting at the Bedford YMCA in late January, the MCL's secretary Joseph Kirby complained that Brooklyn's police quota was short by 1,200 men.[15] In February, Sirtl sent a telegram to Raymond Ingersoll, the Brooklyn Borough president, requesting a meeting because Ingersoll, complained Sirtl, ignored a letter dated February 4 asking for additional police. The MCL along with the Hancock-Halsey Neighborhood Association then wrote to La

Guardia and Valentine. By mid-February with more than 5,000 signatures, the MCL's support for police expanded to other groups, such as Mothers' Club of Our Lady of Victory, Mothers' Clubs of Public School 44, and the Taxpayers' Union of the Bedford-Crown Heights. By March, fed up with La Guardia's silence, Sirtl protested the shortage of police officers in the department, blaming it on the mayor because he was responsible for the police budget. Sirtl reasoned that while the department years before had been 19,000 men, the current police quota of 17,000 was unacceptable especially since the city's population had increased to over half a million.[16]

By the fall, Sirtl, the MCL, and the white community directed their campaign for more police toward the district's growing Black community. In mid-September, Sirtl complained that there were six robberies in the last ten days and that women in the neighborhood were afraid to go out at night. In late October, he urged the fourth deputy police commissioner David McAuliffe to assign more patrolmen to the area because the radio cars' loud sirens warned the would-be criminals. Sirtl suggested that members of his league be granted gun permits, but McAuliffe rejected this idea.[17] By November, the *Brooklyn Daily Eagle* had described the spate of crimes as an outbreak. The victims were white women and elderly men. According to the police, the "complaints have been numerous and in most cases the victims described their assailants as Negroes." The police detailed twenty Black patrolmen to the district, and Sirtl claimed that 200 businessmen and homeowners had agreed to apply for gun permits and to distribute police whistles.[18] Angered by whites' complaints of inadequate police protection, fifty policemen from four precincts offered their own time and created a volunteer patrol to halt crime in the area. In addition to the volunteers, the police detail had been increased by eighteen detectives.[19]

Clayborn of the CCAC saw this new patrol as a paramilitary operation. Sirtl and heads of four precincts, alleged the *New York Amsterdam News*, "concocted this new patrol" of fifty Black and white police officers. The Black press interpreted the MCL's requests for gun permits as a veritable license to organize a vigilante committee. The *New York Amsterdam News* queried, "Will we see an example of the Ku Klux Klan workings in Brooklyn, many borough residents are questioning." The Black weekly tied the crime scare to Black settlement and especially bouts over property: "Sirtl is the 'emotional agitator' of the white group which vehemently protested" Blacks' attempt to purchase Grace Presbyterian.[20] Clayborn rightly feared the mobilization of Brooklyn's white community, for it had effectively leveraged its power to expand the police presence in the neighborhood. As both the Black weekly and the *Brooklyn Daily Eagle* admitted, upper-level police officials, such as Inspector John J. O'Sullivan, commanding the Brooklyn uniformed division; Acting Deputy Chief Inspector John Gallagher; Captains Paul J. Byrne, Arthur D. Downs, and Bernard A. Ditsch; and Lieutenant Williams Ahearne, joined Sirtl's call for police protection. Clayborn believed that Sirtl's campaign represented a "spirit of terror and mob violence," and the CCAC set up a meeting with the NYPD for December 2 and encouraged "every Negro . . . with any race conscience to be present at the gigantic mass meeting" that would be held at the former Bethel AME Church.[21]

Rev. Horace E. Clute, the white rector of St. George's Episcopal Church, claimed that there was no "racial antipathy on the part of [his] church" but applauded the "heroic spirit" of white Bedford-Stuyvesant's campaign against lawlessness. Clute expressed that his church and the Bedford Ministers' Association had tried to help Black churches in the area. Nonetheless, he asserted, "We have the right to ask the city, Mayor La Guardia and his Police Commissioner for protection of property and of life and limb, which have been seriously injured and are now constantly threatened."[22] Throughout the remainder of December, Sirtl and the Consolidated Civic League, composed of fifty-nine organizations in the borough, continued to hold meetings and demand that La Guardia and Valentine expand the police presence in their neighborhood.[23]

"The vigilantes 'ride' again—this time in the Bedford-Stuyvesant section of Brooklyn," charged the *New York Amsterdam News* on December 11. The Black weekly claimed that some of the MCL's members had already begun practicing at a shooting range at the 106th Armory. Brooklyn's Black leadership understood Sirtl's efforts as a sinister attempt to thwart Blacks' efforts to rent and purchase property in the neighborhood. Various labor, civil rights, and civic organizations, such as the NAACP, the Workers' Alliance, the American Labor Party, the Communist Party, the Citizens Civic Affairs Committee, and others held a "public 'trial'" at the Howard Studio and found the MCL "guilty of inciting race hatred."[24] This was not hyperbole. In late December, at the Girls High School at Halsey Street and Nostrand Avenue, the MCL sponsored a mass meeting featuring John L. Belford, rector of the Church of the Nativity, known in the Black community as an "arch-enemy of the Negro race." Blaming Blacks for the neighborhood's deterioration, Belford stated, "We know the people who are the cause of it. . . . Conditions are so bad in this community that my church has been forced to discontinue its night meetings on Sunday because the women are afraid to walk the streets." The rector called Blacks "irresponsible baboons" whom "God made . . . , but they made themselves what they are." The solution Belford proposed was punishment. He asserted, "I am in favor of giving the police, not one, but two nightsticks and teaching them how to use them. The only language this type of people understand, and God knows where they come from, is the language of pain. I'm in favor of giving the police the power of mussing 'em up."[25]

The *New York Amsterdam News* compared the Midtown Civic League's tactics to white supremacist organizations, such as the Ku Klux Klan and fascists in Europe, asserting in 1938 that "the spirit of fascism [had] reared its ugly head in Brooklyn, in the guise of the Midtown Civic Association in the Bedford-Stuyvesant section." By the end of that year, Sirtl had called for 1,000 more policemen to "guard Brooklyn and check holdups" in anticipation of the World's Fair in 1939.[26] The *New York Age* also attacked Sirtl's and Belford's "crime wave" rhetoric and the expansion of the district's police force. Journalist Alfred A. Duckett not only identified the racist motives of Sirtl and Belford but also pointed out an inventory of crimes committed by whites in the neighborhood. Duckett also included white criminals' national and religious backgrounds. "A Jewish youth was held in felony court on a charge of assault and robbery. . . . Two Italians were arrested in Brooklyn for faking money orders." In consideration of this trail of crimes committed by whites, he questioned whether or not "Negroes have any monopoly on crime."[27]

Whites' attacks upon Bedford-Stuyvesant's emerging Black community echoed complaints whites made about Black crime in Harlem, especially in the aftermath of the uproar in 1935. Crime talk among whites in both neighborhoods intertwined with actual crime, exaggerated stories of victimhood, and rumor but also with their concerns around property and housing and their defense of all-white neighborhoods. White New Yorkers organizing against "crime" were implicated in and shaped by an uncertainty that fed on the fear of violence and racial discourses of Black crime. White Harlem's castigations of crime reflected not only actual acts of crime but also the sense of loss Harlem's dwindling white community felt when its numbers thinned as people were pushed out to Washington Heights and outer borough areas of the city. As whites in Brooklyn witnessed Blacks purchase Grace Congregational Church, they viewed it as a "Negro invasion" and mobilized "for the protection of property and life and limb." Though Sirtl emerged as the leader, he had the backing of Belford, the business community, women's associations, and law enforcement. Blacks in Bedford-Stuyvesant and the Black press understood what they saw as a movement motivated by racial hatred. Thus, in recalling Harlem's out-migration of whites and its 1935 uprising, white Bedford-Stuyvesant saw signs of their future, one it had endeavored to avoid.[28]

"Notorious 'City of Negroes'"

Though Black New Yorkers and their allies rejected Sirtl's calls for crime prevention, interpreting it as a scheme to criminalize, punish, and contain the Black community, they never denied the occurrence of crime. Blacks viewed crime as a social, economic, and political problem—not a racial one. Harlemites' push for Mayor La Guardia to follow up with the commission's recommendations in 1936 was recognition that poverty and the lack of municipal resources partly drove criminal behavior. But Blacks also understood that socioeconomic solutions alone could not effectively curtail illicit activity, for crime in general and youth crime in particular were getting out of hand. Black women across the city, especially in Brooklyn and Harlem, were often prey to robbery and other forms of crime. As Blacks weathered the attacks of whites in Bedford-Stuyvesant, they also tried to establish community discipline and promote lawful behavior to counteract the mainstream press's and public officials' use of crime to blemish their neighborhoods' reputation. For decades, Black New Yorkers had battled intraracial crime, as they endeavored to condemn characterizations of their neighborhoods as crime-laden ghettos, and this remained true throughout the La Guardia era. The Black working class and poor often moved across the city and to other neighborhoods to avoid crime and moral threats to the family's stability.[29] During the Prohibition era especially, Black residents spoke out against loud parties, fighting, and especially prostitution in apartment buildings. Black journalists and Black reformers often blamed "slumming" whites and white-owned nightspots for the spread of vice activity in Harlem. In 1926, the *New York Amsterdam News*'s Edgar M. Grey lamented that whites partied in Harlem, in part because they could participate in behaviors "which they would not attempt in their own communities." But whites enjoyed Harlem principally because the police turned a blind eye to their misdeeds. In 1928, the Committee of Fourteen, an anti-vice organization, reported that "colored areas of Harlem seem to be inadequately policed, and its dancehalls . . . [were] practically unsupervised."[30]

Working-class Harlemites writing to the mayor's committee in 1935 made similar complaints about prostitution. A taxicab driver, who preferred to not sign his name, complained to Rev. William Lloyd Imes of the St. James

Presbyterian Church, "No white men are able to pass by their without them stopping them nor a well-dressed colored man." He felt powerless and charged "there must be something done." He asked Imes to leverage his power to pressure the police to do their duty, but admitted, "True the Police are brutes, but you can not handle those people with silk gloves." While Harlemites had long demanded police protection in their neighborhoods, they also understood that crime thrived in their community in part because the police allowed it to, and that white New Yorkers were complicit. One of the Mayor's Commission's recommendations to reduce crime in the aftermath of the Harlem uproar made this point, urging "that the police close up the dives and pleasure dens that cater to the vices and disreputable pleasures of white patrons." Because the Black community was concerned about the reduction of harm and its right to safety, it acknowledged the responsibility of members of its community and racial group. Consequently, while protesting police corruption and slumming whites' complicity, Black New Yorkers expected unimpeded access to the services of the police department, especially when it came to fighting juvenile delinquency.[31]

In March 1936, as Harlem awaited the release of the commission's report, Police Commissioner Valentine promoted a Black police officer, Sergeant Lewis Chisholm, to lead Unit No. 3 of the Juvenile Aid Bureau (JAB). In the late 1920s, religious, civic, and social reform leaders across the city concerned about the ever-mounting issue of juvenile crime requested and demanded municipal support. In 1930, the city created the Crime Prevention Bureau, renamed the Juvenile Aid Bureau, in 1934, and in 1932 set up the Police Athletic League (PAL).[32] At a conference sponsored by the JAB in February 1936, S. Mindlin, a Harlem realtor, suggested that the NYPD create a junior police force. Mindlin believed it would "prevent minor fights between the children . . . and would also instill in them a respect for property rights."[33] Coming less than a year after the uproar, Mindlin's recommendation unsurprisingly aligned with the Black district's property-owners. The JP might have been modeled on the Juvenile Park Protective League formed by the National Urban League and the NYPD in 1914. By July, Unit Three announced that it would establish a local club of the Junior Police of the City of New York for boys from ten to sixteen years old. Membership to the club would be free, and the program included instruction in courtesy, drilling, first aid, hygiene, traffic regulation, and athletics.[34]

Despite these efforts, crime among Black youth persisted throughout the 1930s, stirring community action. At a talk in early February 1937 titled "Youth and Crime" at St. Jude's Community Forum, Nineteen West

FIGURE 5.1 1930s: Policeman chatting with Harlem kids. Gamma-Keystone via Getty Images.

Ninety-Ninth Street, Lieutenant Chisolm stated, "We cannot stop crime; we can only suppress the elements which create crime." In November, Patrolman Charles F. Jones, of the Crime Prevention Bureau, predicted to an audience at the Harlem YMCA that a decline in juvenile delinquency would occur because of the assiduous work of the bureau. With the aid of and coordination with social and welfare reform associations, the bureau's efforts would be considerably improved, Jones asserted.[35] Black journalists joined the campaign to prevent crime. The *New York Amsterdam News's* Thelma Berlack-Boozer authored editorials informing readers about the services of the JAB. In "Aids Delinquent: Bureau Helps Wayward Ones," Berlack-Boozer wrote about the preventive work of the bureau, especially its efforts to turn youth away from the court. In another article in October, Berlack-Boozer discussed the fragility of families and how the "broken-home" factored into influencing criminal activity among youth.[36]

FIGURE 5.2 November 29: Police Lieutenant Samuel J. Battle *(left)* watches his young guests having their Thanksgiving dinners at Mother Zion Church in Harlem, at 151 West 136th Street. Chef James Glen is holding a couple of mince pies. Dick Lewis / New York Daily News Archive via Getty Images.

Black New Yorkers tied their broader concerns about crime to their demands for police protection for the most vulnerable. In November 1937, assaults on Black women in Brooklyn stirred the community's discontent. While walking along Macon Street between Lewis and Stuyvesant Avenues, Maria C. Lawson, a seventy-three-year-old community leader, was attacked by three unidentified Black boys. The assailants threw her to the ground and snatched her pocketbook. Gladys Clark, secretary of the Siloam Progressive Club, sent Police Commissioner Lewis J. Valentine a letter protesting the assaults against her neighbors. Acknowledging the presence of Black police officers on well-lit Fulton Street, she complained, "They serve no purpose in adequately policing" other streets and adjacent avenues, such as Bainbridge, Decatur, Hancock, Macon, and Halsey. She also called for more support directed at youth crime, noting, "The Juvenile Aid Bureau is not carrying on any sort of intensive program in this area where there exists an exceedingly high rate of juvenile delinquency."[37]

In January 1938, Black tenants at 121 West 144th Street in Harlem complained about robberies along their street. On their return home from work, they found that their clothes, radios, and any item salable or that could be pawned had been stolen. The *New York Amsterdam News* described the block as a "contender of being Harlem's 'most-robbed block.'" The residents believed that a youth gang had been committing the robberies. Some of them felt that the police had neglected to protect them. As the Black weekly noted, "Although, according to one occupant of the building at 121, each robbery is immediately reported to police, to date the series of losses goes on merrily." As Harlemites demanded police attention and sought the services of the juvenile bureau, they also tried to encourage neighborhood discipline, civic engagement, and responsible lawful behavior to protect the community *and* defend Harlem's reputation.[38]

On June 23 at Yankee Stadium, Joe Louis knocked out Max Schmeling. Louis felled the German three times in the first round. In the one-round victory, Louis symbolically beat Adolf Hitler and all that he represented. Blacks in the city and across the nation celebrated the win, as if they had been in the ring with Louis and defeated Schmeling and Hitler themselves. Only two years before, Schmeling beat Louis in Yankee Stadium, and while Louis represented the United States, many white Americans rooted for the German. Dr. Herman Warner, a Harlemite, remembered attending the first fight, and when the whites applauded, he asked, "What the hell is wrong with these people?"[39] Black Harlem remembered this, so the victory filled them with joy and merriment but also race pride. Police Commissioner Valentine acknowledged this. Commenting on the Black masses swelling Harlem streets, he stated, "This is their night—let them be happy." After leaving the fight, he visited the West 135th Street police station and ordered the police to redirect traffic between 125th and 145th Streets on Seventh Avenue. The *Afro-American* wrote that on 129th Street, a group carried a cardboard that read, "Louis for President."[40]

The mainstream press saw the celebration differently. The dailies reported that Edward Grout, a mounted patrolman, was hit by an ash can, and another patrolman, Albert Stier, "suffered a wrenched shoulder." In the white press, Harlem descended from revelry to unrest. The *New York Times*'s headline read, "Harlem Celebrants Tossed Varied Missiles," and the *New York Herald Tribune*'s drophead read, "Extra Police Keep Crowds in Check after Idol Scores Quick Knockout of Foe."[41] The *New York Age*'s editorial, titled "Too Much

FIGURE 5.3 Max Schmeling (1905–2005) the former champion (1930) is floored by Joe Louis (1914–1981) during their World Heavyweight bout on June 22, 1938, at Yankee Stadium in the Bronx. Referee Arthur Donovan holds back Schmeling's cornerman Max Machon after the fight. Hulton Archive via Getty Images.

Enthusiasm," condemned the unlawful behavior, especially among the "youngsters in their teens," complaining that they "mar[red] the cleancut victory scored by Joe Louis and add[ed] to the bad name of Harlem." According to the *New York Age*, "Many whites have gained the impression that we, who live in Harlem, are savages and when we lose control of ourselves as many did on Wednesday night, we give some basis for this impression." Instead, the editorial urged Harlem Blacks to take greater pride in their race and neighborhood and to follow Louis's "example in self-control." In the three years after the uprising and two years since the neighborhood was occupied by the police, discernible crime sullied Harlem's reputation, giving credence to white Harlem's bromides about the district being crime-ridden.[42]

In a September editorial titled "Local Lawlessness," the *New York Amsterdam News* denounced wrongdoing but also reported that the police were

FIGURE 5.4 Harlem crowds celebrate Joe Louis's victory over Max Schmeling. Bettmann via Getty Images.

reluctant to fight crime in Harlem, "complain[ing] that they are afraid of precipitating another riot." The NYPD's claim about "precipitating another riot" was a rhetorical sleight of hand that would be used to explain both the cause of the 1935 uproar and the prevalence of Black crime throughout the remainder of La Guardia's second and third terms. Black crime incited the riot—not police brutality among other municipal shortfalls. According to this logic, the police were simply enforcing the law. Consequently, Blacks' protests against police mistreatment, from the NYPD's point of view, were principally lawbreakers' tacit complaints about effective law enforcement. The police's allegation downplayed its culpability in instigating the riot and justified its brutal behavior because of it. The *New York Amsterdam News* keenly understood this as a ploy to malign legitimate objections to police brutality. Underscoring the Black community's right to safety, the Black weekly asserted, "We are just as opposed to police brutality as we are to lawlessness. It is not brutal, however, to enforce the law impartially for all of the citizens of the city regardless of color." Articulating a politics of color-blind liberal law and order, as well as a defense of Harlem's reputation, the Black weekly argued, "It is up to the citizens of Harlem and the cops to see that the law is enforced so that Harlem will not continue to be known as a notorious 'city of Negroes.'" The police employed this crime discourse as a political weapon to combat the groundswell of Black agitation against police brutality after the riot. This pattern of underprotection forced the Black community to strengthen its efforts to prevent and fight crime.[43]

"Face the Facts about Crime and Then Do Something about It"

By 1939, the *New York Amsterdam News* had begun to aggressively challenge Black ministers, civic leaders, educators, and especially Black parents to halt crime. The Black press's anti-crime activism aimed to not only reduce crime but also check the labeling of the race as inherently criminal. The riot in 1935, increased police patrols, the episodes of violence after Louis's victory, and Councilman Joseph Clark Baldwin's allegations about crime brought unwelcome attention to Harlem, initiating debate and action in the community. As Archie Seale, a columnist for the *New York Amsterdam News*, asserted, "So many of our leading citizens will throw the blame on our present economic problem, which in reality is just an 'OUT' for them. . . . The youth of Harlem have too much freedom."[44] While the weekly had always covered crime stories, the Forbes murder transformed its format. The *New York Amsterdam News*'s readers promptly responded to the new format. Many of them complained about the emphasis on crime news and the "morbid pictures." In its January 21 editorial, "A Perennial Problem," the Black weekly informed its readership that it studied the public's demands for its product and acknowledged that its aim, like that of any other business, was to sell papers by "giv[ing] the public what it wants." Nonetheless, while admitting its profit motives, the *New York Amsterdam News* argued that neither it nor the Black community could ignore the problem of crime and refused to cast it aside. The weekly asserted that "Harlem cannot afford, we think, to consign the sordid crime conditions to the limbo of the unspeakables, but it must face the facts about crime and then do something about it." Foregrounding crime news was an expression of activism. Crime was a fact of life for the Black community, and as long as it remained, so it was the weekly's "duty to print it as news."[45]

In late January 1939, in the editorial "Crime in Harlem," the *New York Amsterdam News* recited the explanations of various public officials, including Councilman Baldwin and Police Commissioner Valentine, and lamented that while "everybody, in fact, is talking about crime in Harlem . . . no one is doing anything about it."[46] Baldwin asserted that Harlem experienced a crime per day in 1938, which Valentine and other police officials denied.[47] The editorial recalled the Mayor's Commission and how La Guardia "politely pigeoned-holed the report," reminding its readers that along with municipal reform and investment, Blacks needed protection. According to one detective, crime conditions in the neighborhood had improved, and the detective admitted that in the recent past, "the cops used to throw up their hands and say, whenever one Negro killed or otherwise assaulted another: 'just a nigger case. It aint worth getting in a sweat about.'" Though the *New York Amsterdam News* expected public officials to serve the Black community dutifully, it insisted that the people of Harlem must play a role in policing themselves. The editorial questioned the reliability of public officials and complained that they had treated crime in their neighborhood "like weather—they talk and do nothing." The Black weekly warned, however, that crime "isn't the weather. Unless, like a hurricane, it destroys everything in its path. Morally, physically and in every other way. Now is the time to act to control it." The *New York Age*'s Ebenezer Ray minimized Baldwin's characterization of Harlem as likely overstated, but he welcomed responsible law enforcement and acknowledged the long-term need for improved social and economic resources, which "no one can honestly deny." He prioritized the urgency of Black safety—from crime and police violence, warning, "Put away the smoke-screen defense that Harlem is no worse than other sections. Let the powers that be give us better police supervision. Not engaged police officers bent on brutality which only provokes resentment; but officers capable of enforcing the law as it stands."[48]

The weekly's crime news also took on a sensational tone, prompting support and criticisms from their readership. The *New York Amsterdam News* headlined lurid stories such as "6 in 4 Days—Murder Record!" detailing descriptions of killings, and sweeping editorials on the danger of switchblades, such as "Switchblade Knife—A Familiar Story!"[49] In late February, one letter writer, signing as Disgusted Reader, described the weekly's crime reportage as the "most common piece of trash in circulation today." The reader was ashamed to read the weekly in public, since it misrepresented Harlem as "a hell hole and all its people are dangerous criminals." The reader concluded that if the *New York Amsterdam News* had to advertise murder, it should do it on the back and "give your readers at least one interesting, elevating cover sheet." The *New York Age* also criticized the *New York Amsterdam News*'s crime reportage and complained that whites used the *New York Amsterdam News*'s crime news as an excuse to boycott Black businesses in Harlem. In *The New York Age*'s "Letter to the Editor" column, Harold Austin invited the Black weekly to "aid me in a campaign" against sensationalism in crime news, pointing to the *New York Amsterdam News* as the target of his criticism. While not denying criminal activity, Austin believed that sensational journalism was partly responsible for crime among youth, who, he claimed, were more susceptible to sensationalism "than to the worthwhile happenings of the day." Austin was particularly incensed because had the white dailies "play[ed] up crime," the same editors of the *New York Amsterdam News* would have renounced them. Austin's solution was to urge "decent people of Harlem [to] boycott" the Black weekly if it refused to "change its tactics," and he ended his letter promising to encourage his friends to read "*The New York Age* whose policy is more constructive."[50]

Other than the sensational headlines, the *New York Amsterdam News* and Harlem's Black leadership waged a campaign to regulate the sale of switchblades. From January to April, the Black weekly reported on the hazards of switchblades from various angles and perspectives. Describing the fact of gang life in the streets of Harlem, as well as the absence of youth recreation and adult supervision, the Black weekly noted that Black youth claimed that they carried knives for their own protection. While there might be "a germ of truth in this," teachers, policemen, and others nonetheless had "frisked Harlem children and taken murderous looking switchblades from them." The problem was simple. Harlem's children could walk into any hardware store, drugstore, or pawn shop and purchase a switchblade. The *New York Amsterdam News*, therefore, supported government reform and regulation. The Black weekly asserted, "It is the duty of the people of the State or city to see that the legislators pass a law to abolish the sale of switchblade knives which have snuffed out the lives of more persons in Harlem than any other weapon."[51]

Harlemites held two conferences within days of each other. The first, organized by Acting Lieutenant Lewis Chisholm of the Juvenile Aid Bureau, was held at 250 West 135th Street on February 9. Magistrate Myles A. Paige; Deputy Chief Inspector John J. De Martino; Gertrude E. Ayer, principal of Public School 24; Assemblyman Daniel L. Burrows; Councilman William A. Carroll; and other community members were in attendance. All agreed that the sale of knives might be controlled by speaking with store owners in the neighborhood as well as by media advocacy. They aimed to use the Black press, posters, movie trailers, and the radio to inform the Black community about the dangers of switchblades.[52] The conferees encouraged Parent-Teacher Associations, United Parents Associations, and other forms of parent-led groups to warn their children about the hazards of carrying knives. The attendees, however, were not only committed to crime prevention through the media and parental and community reform. Surveillance and law enforcement were also essential instruments. The attendees agreed to use school teachers and principals, as well as members of the Juvenile Aid Bureau and other members of the police force, to confiscate knives and other weapons from children. At the community level, they would "encourage the communication of this fact to the parents of the individual children . . . with accompanying warnings to the parents against the dangers of knife-carrying." They also encouraged judges of the Children's Court to "be more severe in the handling of youth who ha[d] long previous histories of knife-carrying or knife-use and to encourage them to be as severe in treatment as possible with the so-called 'bully' leaders that come before the Court." Attending police officers, especially members of the JAB, pledged to support these efforts and to meet again to consider implementing these recommendations. The next afternoon, the *New York Amsterdam News* organized a meeting held at 3:00 P.M. at Captain Pritchard's office in the West 123rd Street police station. Many of the same public officials, civil rights, and social reform organizations attended this meeting and agreed with the strategies and legislative goals discussed days before. Through these collaborative efforts at both the state and municipal levels, the Black community and public officials pursued legislative action against the sale and possession of switchblades.[53]

As the *New York Amsterdam News* waged its campaign against switchblades, it directed its attention once again to the underprotection of Black women. An anonymous letter writer stated in early March 1939, "The streets of Harlem are getting more and more unsafe for our women." Highlighting the contradiction between overpolicing and underprotection in Harlem, the writer lamented, "This is a terrible state of affairs when you consider that we have so many police and they cannot protect us." Only a week later, the Black weekly reported a similar story of a Black woman being preyed upon in Brooklyn. "I ought to kill you!" spewed Mrs. John Miller's assailant, a tall and thin Black man, marked "with a scar on his right cheek." Mrs. Miller, forty-one-years-old, of 531 Madison Street, lived, noted the *New York Amsterdam News*, "in the heart of the respectable section where 200 extra police are patrolling the streets." Arthur Holmes, arrested in April, violated Mrs. Miller on the first of March 1939. The perpetrator, armed with a switchblade, broke into her apartment, robbed her of some money, and forced her to the roof of the building. The "maniac," described the Black weekly, tied her up and brutally raped her on the rooftop of the building at 525 Madison Street. Noting both Mrs. Miller's beauty and vulnerability, the Black weekly chastised the New York Police Department for failing to protect Black women in particular and Black people in general from criminals.[54] The Black weekly, along with denizens of the neighborhood, wanted to know the status of the police investigation, but the police "told Mrs. Miller's family that they could 'work better' if no mention of the case reached the press." Thus, concluded the weekly, rather than pursuing the culprit, "the police have been doing all in their power to keep the affair quiet."[55]

Mrs. Miller and concerned Black neighbors complained about police inaction. Many of the residents, noted the Black weekly, asserted "The idea that had a white woman been raped by a Negro every man answering the general description of the rapist would have been placed under arrest within twenty-four hours. But they felt, since it was a case which concerned Negroes only, police were indifferent." Throughout the remainder of March and April, the New York Amsterdam News, the Millers, and "incensed" Black Brooklynites persistently pinpointed the contradiction between the expansion of the police presence in Bedford-Stuyvesant, induced by Sumner Sirtl and the MCL, and the lackluster efforts of the police to find the rapist. They demanded "adequate policing," protested police neglect, and spotlighted how Black intracommunity crime rendered Black women invisible in the eyes of law enforcement.[56]

In the face of an acknowledged crime problem and police unaccountability, the New York Amsterdam News featured a series titled "The Truth about Harlem Crime" written by St. Clair Bourne and Marvel Cooke during the spring months of March and April. The series framed Harlem as a respectable community weathering a season of crime. In the opening editorial, Bourne and Cooke wrote that they had canvassed the spectrum of Harlem's Black community. "The average Harlemite, the hard-working good citizen . . . and the vicious, innately depraved being, . . . have been inspected," along with interviews with public officials and leaders in social, welfare, and juvenile agencies. After sketching a picture of criminal activity from the statistical data from 1930, they acknowledged the inarguable prevalence of crime. Overall, though, crime in Harlem reflected the "presence of economic rather than innately vicious or criminal factor as the main element of responsibility." The *New York Amsterdam News* published six additional stories to complete the "Truth about Harlem Crime" series. Each story detailed a distinct aspect of crime. In an editorial, subtitled "Life of Prostitute in Harlem Bared by Reporters in Crime Crusade Survey," Bourne and Cooke described the plight of sex workers in Harlem and pointed to the dearth of employment opportunities to explain why the institution of prostitution thrived in the Black neighborhood. But poverty was not the sole reason. Although District Attorney Thomas Dewey promised to eradicate prostitution from the city's streets, especially Harlem's, according to Bourne and Cooke, his anti-vice campaign mainly resulted in relocating it from Lower Harlem to its Sugar Hill section.[57]

In another editorial, Bourne and Cooke made it clear that Harlemites rarely engaged in sex crimes. Though rape was "rare" among adults, the majority of these cases occurred among minors. Cooke and Bourne explained these cases as the product of overcrowding and limited space for parental supervision. In their discussion of minors, they highlighted the vital work that Lieutenant Chisholm and the Juvenile Aid Bureau were doing for the neighborhood's children. Cases that had been initially referred to the Children's Court had been directed to the JAB, which cooperated with neighborhood social agencies and the Works Progress Administration. Loiterers preying on young Black girls were especially a problem in Harlem. According to Bourne and Cooke, "In most instances the man has been white and in only of three probation reports examined by the *Amsterdam News*, was the man meted out just punishment." They noted further, "As far as adults are concerned, Harlemites are of the opinion that the Police Department is lax over reported sex violations in the area and it is a direct challenge to the department that few arrests are made when it is reported that Negro women have been criminally assaulted." Recalling the Miller case, the journalists wrote, "A typical case is that in which a well-known Brooklyn woman who lives in a heavily policed district, was recently atrociously assaulted and, to date, despite the fact that she has given the police department a minute description of the rapist, not one single suspect has been arrested to date."[58]

The *New York Amsterdam News*'s alarm about criminal activity in Harlem was mainly directed at the killings and violent property crimes that had colored its front pages over the last several months. Referencing the murders of Bobby Forbes and Myles Milligan, Bourne and Cooke explained that the majority of the homicides were spontaneous and often precipitated by "innocent little quarrels."[59] Half of the homicides, according to police reports, were accidental, and most of the time, the victims were slain by a knife, usually switchblades. The pattern of homicides and property crimes, especially by Black male youth, loomed large across the series. "Harlem kids are not out and out bad—but they can be and are awfully pesky," the journalists admitted. Harlem's rates of child delinquency led the city, however. By parsing out different kinds of crime, they explained that those that reflect "criminal tendencies" are "no greater on average" in the Black district than they were elsewhere in the city. Though organized crime was not characteristic of criminal activity among Blacks in Harlem, many Black youth belonged to gangs and brandished switchblades. One public official, reinforcing racial tropes, admitted to the journalists, "We're very much surprised when we find one kid without a knife." The propensity for Black youth to wield the knife was an expression of masculine power, "an excess of bravado by the knowledge that a knife is in his pocket within easy reach." Property crimes made up the majority of juvenile crime, and youth gangs robbed other children, salespersons, and people serving the community in various capacities.[60]

The series discussed various types of property crimes, including purse-snatching, car robberies, and housebreaking, among others. But Bourne and Cooke singled out "mugging, . . . one of the commonest occurrences." Mugging was described as the "type of holdup . . . favored by criminals because no weapons are necessary, thus minimizing the punishment if they happened to be caught. Practiced by groups of three or more generally, it is a very simple job whose chief drawback is that the returns are seldom very large." Muggers generally chose dimly lit streets and hallways in tenement buildings, offering them opportune circumstances in which to hide and surprise potential targets. One assailant attacked and held the victim from behind while the others searched the victim's person and liberated his or her possessions. In the majority of the cases, the thieves felled the victim so that they could escape into the dark before any attention could be raised.[61]

At the end of year, the *New York Amsterdam News* featured another series by Leon E. DeKalb, a probation officer in the Adolescents Court in Brooklyn, on juvenile delinquency. DeKalb asked, "Are you, as a parent, letting economic worries make you disagreeable and quarrelsome at home? Are you such of a nagging disposition that your children, as well as your wife or husband, are glad to see you leave the house? Are you interested in the boy across the street whose father is dead, whose mother is forced to work all day in order to support him, while he roams the streets at will? Are you doing your bit to secure more play streets, recreation centers, and parks? Are you willing to fight for the clearance of slum areas?" Like Bourne and Cooke, he acknowledged the impact of the economy on youth crime, writing, "No one will deny that economic insecurity . . . is responsible for a large portion of the Juvenile Delinquency." Yet, as his line of queries indicate, juvenile delinquency was also about civic, parental, and community responsibility.[62]

DeKalb told stories of two Black families to illustrate this perspective. Foregrounding the theme of the broken home, DeKalb "sketch[ed] briefly the history of the Jenkins family to show what effect a lack of proper parental supervision can have upon a child." DeKalb's narrative of the family outlined the family's migration from a small town in South Carolina, low-wage employment, and eventually job loss and alcoholism. The Jenkinses had two sons, Harold, sixteen years old, and Charles, fourteen; both were eventually arrested for burglary and robbery, respectively. The second case, the Carters, a family of seven, was a sad story of family breakdown, child institutionalization, and youth crime. Mr. Carter "never supported his family," and because Mrs. Carter worked, the five children were often home alone. Because of the complaints about child neglect, the children were placed in an orphan asylum. Thereafter, the story turned to Mrs. Carter's petitioning to take care of her own children. She was denied because she lived with another man, and her two older boys, James and Herbert, "boarded out" to live with another family. Eventually Mrs. Carter married Mr. Johnston, and all five of the children lived with the new couple. Yet "from the beginning," DeKalb writes, the children clashed with Mr. Johnston. He eventually left, and then James and Herbert were arrested for burglary.[63]

The Black community's anti-crime campaign was fought on multiple fronts and shaped by issues predating the Great Depression. As DeKalb and others laid out, the Black community often tied criminal behavior to the instability of the Black family and its household.

The intertwined dynamics of crime and poverty had long been perceived to be connected to the actions, or inactions, of the Black family. Scholars, white and Black, had long asserted that Blacks' work ethic or cultural practices explained their economic station in life, yet the Black community also talked about these issues among themselves. Much like the probation officer's editorials, the Black press, social workers, and religious leaders unduly pointed to the behavior of Black women. Blacks perceived the home and Black women's management of the household as a contested site of racial uplift and respectability.[64] At best, social scientists, journalists, and social reformers blamed juvenile crime on the breakdown of the Black family, especially the alleged listlessness or even the death of the Black man. And yet, somehow, Black women were too often deemed responsible. As DeKalb put it, the youth had walked the streets because his "mother is forced to work all day in order to support him." At worse, Black women were blamed for parental neglect or criticized for the kinds of leisure activities they enjoyed in their own homes. This intraracial community policing around crime, gender, and domesticity played out especially in the apartment buildings. Black tenants called the police to complain about noise, violence, and crime in their apartment buildings. Black parents themselves, often the subject of social reformers' criticism, also accepted responsibility. Some parents moved to other neighborhoods in search of more respectable and safer places for their families, while others even called the police and anti-vice associations on their own children to protect them from themselves and to avoid a life of crime.[65]

· · · · · ·

In its 1941 July issue, *The Crisis* reported that Dr. John A. Singleton, the president of the Jamaica, Long Island, branch of the NAACP, had "long fought against the poorly-li[t] streets, narrow roads, lack of supervised playgrounds, and juvenile delinquency." This "long fight waged," as the civil rights magazine described it, represented Black New Yorkers' vision of "law and order." It included recreation *and* improvements in the neighborhood's built environment. Singleton also "requested that more Negro police be assigned there," and Police Commissioner Valentine promised "additional police protection in the South Jamaica area."[66] Black New Yorkers understood police protection as an extension of their civil rights and their citizenship, and this was expressed across the class spectrum and the associational and organizational life of the Black community. Crime prevention and crime-fighting, though officially the work of law enforcement, were fundamentally a community affair for Black New Yorkers, and both Harlemites and Brooklynites understood law and order as the responsibility and respectability of the broader Black community. Because of the neglect of the NYPD and other public officials, including La Guardia, to ensure the safety of the Black community, Black citizens and leaders and the Black press argued that "now is the time to act to control" crime. The role of the Black press was essential here—not only as a source of news but also as an archive of the sundry viewpoints Black people held on crime. As the exchanges among the *New York Amsterdam News*, the *New York Age*, and the readers' letters demonstrate, intracommunity crime was always contested and debated. Yet in spite of this range of views and debate, Blacks understood crime first and foremost from the lens of Black safety, neighborhood responsibility, and law enforcement.

Concerned not only with its reputation, Harlemites prioritized safety in the Black district. Law enforcement, therefore, was instrumental to community stability, and the efforts of the JAB were deeply needed and welcomed. Yet as an extension of law enforcement, the JAB placed Black youth under surveillance and operated as a mechanism of social control. Many in the community, as the attendees at the conference expressed, supported punishment, including judges incarcerating Black youth. Yet while Black New York was committed to law and order, police protection of the Black community was elusive. As Blacks across the city complained, the police failed to protect them and even to respond to their complaints about crime. Public officials, the *New York Amsterdam News* reported, "talk and do nothing." Blacks described law enforcement as inadequate, nonresponsive, and unaccountably harmful, especially to Black women and children. In Bedford-Stuyvesant, while Blacks galvanized their community for safety from crime, they also witnessed the influence of their white counterparts to employ the NYPD for their own objectives, displaying not only the separate and unequal protection the police rendered Black Brooklynites but also how white Brooklynites determined how the Black community was policed.

Of course, while these overlapping issues of police underprotection were discussed in Black cultural and institutional life, they were often hidden from and ignored by whites. Either not deemed newsworthy or of public concern for white newsreaders, these stories of Black crime, community politics, and policing were absent in the white press. That this occurred while police violence thrived in Harlem, in Bedford-Stuyvesant, and across the city undermined the NYPD's claim that it was reluctant to fight crime out of fear of inciting a riot. Several months after Valentine pledged to send "police protection . . . [to] South Jamaica," white New Yorkers' fears, insecurities, and demands for police protection illuminated these tensions, as Black crime in Harlem across the color line took center stage in the white press and city politics.

6 When a Mayor Thought More of Law and Order and Human Decency Than of Votes

On November 1, 1941, James O'Connell, a white fifteen-year-old, of 1518 Madison Avenue, was stabbed fatally by one of three Black youths near Central Park. Two days later, the *New York Times* ran a headline that read, "Hoodlums Hunted in Fatal Stabbing" and four days after that, "Crime Outbreak in Harlem Spurs Drive by Police." Less than a week later, on the sixth, Joseph Keelan, a thirty-two-year-old laundry worker, was found dead on a footpath in Morningside Park. According to the police, Keelan was probably "mugged." The *New York Times*'s definition of a mugging typically involved a group attack on an unsuspecting individual, when "one member of a gang 'mugs' the victim by stealing up behind him, throwing an arm around his neck and holding a knee in his back. As the helpless man is choked and bent backward, other members of the gang turn his pockets inside out and sometimes steal his clothing as well."[1] This definition was not very different, though certainly more descriptive and visual, from the one given by the *New York Amsterdam News* two years before. Journalists St. Clair Bourne and Marvel Cooke described it as a "type of holdup [that] is favored by criminals because no weapons are necessary, . . . Practiced by groups of three or more generally, it is a very simple job whose chief drawback is that the returns are seldom very large."[2]

But although the term had been used in the past by the Black press, the *New York Times* had now attached it to a particular group and neighborhood. Muggings, the paper noted, were a "favorite way of throttling a victim in Harlem." Both Morningside Park and Central Park bordered Harlem's predominantly Black neighborhood. These areas, therefore, were locally understood and policed as racially distinct and contested white neighborhoods. As various newspapers, both Black and white, reported, the stabbing of O'Connell occurred only ten blocks from La Guardia's apartment building on Central Park East.[3] The killing of two white people angered white New York not only because of the loss of life but fundamentally because whites and especially mainstream dailies perceived them as criminal acts against their neighborhoods and their race, by extension. White New Yorkers felt that they and white-identified areas were under siege. Noting the peculiarity of muggings, white dailies constructed them as criminal acts with both racial and spatial consequences for the safety of white people in Harlem and across the city.[4] White property, too, was threatened, including white-owned businesses. As the *New York Times* explained, "Milk and insurance companies have curtailed their business in Harlem because of the repeated robberies of their collectors."[5]

The killing of O'Connell by Black youth in Central Park triggered a crime scare. White New Yorkers sent a succession of angry letters about Black crime to La Guardia and Valentine. White dailies' crime-laden narratives about citizens' fears of crime drove the NYPD's war against "lawlessness" and led to the surveillance of Black neighborhoods in Harlem and Bedford-Stuyvesant and the punishment of Black people. White New Yorkers and the white dailies not only constructed Blacks as hyper-criminals but also leveraged their political power to punish Black citizens as threats to whites' security. Whether Blacks actually committed a crime or it was just a figment of whites' imaginations, newspapers' stories about crime contributed to the "regularity and frequency" of images of Black deviance. At the same time, the rhetoric and actions of the NYPD reinforced the idea that Black citizens were not worthy of protection but were worthy of regular repression.[6]

Black crimes against whites provided the NYPD an opportunity to exploit the situation to its advantage. Building on whites' complaints about Black crime in the aftermath of the 1935 uproar in Harlem and in the late 1930s in Bedford-Stuyvesant, the NYPD proffered several explanations for Black crime, all pointing to La Guardia's professed political ties to the Black community.[7] O'Connell's death occurred in the midst of the mayoral campaign and La Guardia's eventual victory. The police told victims of crime, white and Black, as well as the press that they could not adequately stop Black crime because the mayor restricted their discretion to use coercive force to prevent another riot. The police discourse had transformed patrolmen into victims of La Guardia's political machine that cravenly complied with criminals who used police brutality as an excuse to offset legitimate police work. Using the white and Black press to broadcast its rhetoric, the NYPD had effectively manipulated legitimate Black protests against police brutality. In this context, the NYPD framed calls for police accountability and justice for Black victims of police violence as justification for the prevalence of Black crime. With the power to define and explain crime and mark, detain, and punish would-be criminals, the NYPD's discourse of discretionary constraint contributed to the fear of white New Yorkers. As these explanations were published in the white press, Black neighborhoods and La Guardia became the pivotal targets of irate white New Yorkers.[8]

But the white press did more than simply report crime news. Roy Wilkins, writing in *The Crisis*, charged, "Led by the *New York Times*, the daily press of New York has manufactured a 'crime wave' in Harlem, and by persistent distortion and misrepresentation has branded the 200,000 residents of that section as criminals."[9] By singling out and publicizing crimes committed by Blacks on whites, as well as emphasizing the vulnerability and innocence of white women and children, white news media manufactured a racial scare. The NYPD weaponized the crime wave of 1941. The crime wave gave the police an opportunity to spread a political fiction to combat Blacks' protests against police brutality. Concomitantly, citywide discussions of policing among New Yorkers, as articulated through and debated within and between the Black and white press, began to shift from Blacks as victims of police brutality to whites as victims of Black crime. Because of the sheer cultural predominance of the white press, these stories splashing across the front pages of metropolitan newspapers rendered invisible Black citizens and their demands for equitable police protection since the late 1930s. These exaggerated media-driven narratives, depicting Black areas as crime zones, triggered a letter-writing campaign by white New Yorkers, who demanded on the basis of their rights as citizens and taxpayers that La Guardia protect them from "negro thugs."[10] While the letter writers used crime as the impetus for writing the mayor, others insisted that La Guardia, who actively sought out the Black vote, favored Blacks because they helped him win the mayoralty. They believed that La Guardia delivered his favoritism in the form of lax policing of Black crime. Set in motion by the fusion of Black street crimes, the fiction of police discretionary restraint, the white dailies' crime narratives, and white civilians' complaints, Police Commissioner Valentine assigned more patrolmen to targeted areas of the city to protect white people. The convergence of the race-laden crime wave and white demands for safety and punishment led to the occupation of Black neighborhoods, once again. Under the guise of law and order and fighting crime waves, the NYPD singled out and harassed Black people in Harlem and across the city.[11]

Aghast at the mayor's instant protection of white citizens, the Black community mobilized to expose the color-conscious policing practices of the NYPD and the media-manufactured "crime wave" and pointed out police neglect, underlining how the NYPD prioritized the protection of whites. By demanding their right to safety and explaining crime and juvenile delinquency as symptoms of poverty, racial discrimination, and un-equal access to municipal resources, Black leaders framed Valentine's law-and-order campaign as a proxy for La Guardia's failure to follow through on the recommendations detailed in his own commission's report on the causes of the Harlem Race Riot of 1935. Concerned about Valentine's aug-mentation of the police presence in Harlem, Black and white civil rights, social welfare, and criminal justice leaders in December of 1941 created the City-Wide Citizens' Committee on Harlem (CWCCH) to address the grow-ing problem of juvenile crime. Like the Mayor's Commission on the Harlem Riot of 1935, the CWCCH rooted Black crime in the multiple crises of the economy, housing, and the criminal justice system.[12]

"Gangs of Nigger Thugs Who Molest White People"

Mayor La Guardia and Commissioner Valentine promptly responded to the news of the killings of O'Connell and Keelan and maintained that the po-lice had already been investigating crime around Central Park. Mothers and neighbors of O'Connell picketed a block away from La Guardia's apartment building and complained that the police failed to respond to instances of harassment and robbery in and around Central Park. The mayor explained, "The matter has received attention for some time. The fact that arrests were made indicates that. The situation is indeed a bad one. What makes it all the more difficult is that the crimes are committed by young hoodlums in their teens, from twelve to sixteen years." By acknowledging the assailants' youth, noting that they were "mere youngsters," La Guardia suggested that the allegation of a "crime wave" was exaggerated and that he had control over the situation. He claimed that he "personally took charge of one case," ordered "strong reinforcements of police in that locality," and affirmed that the problem would be resolved. In addition to speaking to the concerns of the public, the mayor also wrote to the Board of Estimate. La Guardia ex-pressed that juvenile delinquency was partly the result of a dearth of "proper housing and recreational facilities" and promised additional resources, in-cluding acquiring land to build a school and a neighborhood playground in East Harlem, around 114th Street and Lexington Avenue. The mayor ex-plained that his administration had already anticipated the needs of Cen-tral Harlem and that he would request that the Board of Estimate acquire a title for a proposed public park near 143rd and 145th Streets and Lenox Ave-nue as well as another by Harlem River Drive, between West 143rd and 145th Streets.[13]

In contrast to La Guardia's color-blind approach, Commissioner Valentine mentioned the race of the perpetrators and described the violent crimes of the adults. Valentine admitted that the NYPD was undermanned and explained that he intended to ask for more police officers after January 1. He employed the mainstream press to argue for additional police reserves, using the protection of white people from Black predators as his rationale. Highlighting the work already done, he revealed, "Only last week two men were arrested for raping and assaulting a white woman in Central Park, and, as you know three Negro boys were apprehended in the murder of the O'Connell boy."[14] In response to the white dailies and citizens' outcries, Police Commissioner Valentine assigned 250 additional police in Harlem "to stamp out [the] crime wave" and doubled patrols near Central Park, including male police officers disguised in women's clothes to trigger attackers. Valentine described Harlem as a war zone.[15] According to the commissioner, "Up in Harlem even my own men are not safe. You remember some time ago two policemen were attacked by two hold-up men in Harlem and one of the policemen had his clothing slashed, although they finally shot and killed the men who attacked them."[16] The police department, Mayor La Guardia, and white dailies directed their attention, resources, and police patrols to Harlem, though solely to protect white neighborhoods bordering Black areas. Over the weekend of November 8 and 9, the police arrested two Black boys for assaulting a white youth, a Puerto Rican man, charged with possession of a double-bladed knife, and four Black men "loitering" on East 109th Street, who were identified by a man from New Jersey as the men who robbed him a week before.[17]

Valentine, like others before, raised the question of safety. Under his leadership, the NYPD demonstrated its capacity to obtain justice for white women, in particular, echoing the sentiments of Sumner Sirtl and the Midtown Civic League years before. In addition to protecting white citizens, the commissioner noted that "up in Harlem even my own men are not safe," comments that La Guardia made in 1936, as Black leaders and their white allies complained about the yearlong police occupation of Harlem. To the readers of the *New York Times*, the commissioner made it clear that Harlem criminals would be stamped out with force. No longer would public officials like Councilman Joseph Clark Baldwin question Valentine's commitment to law and order in Harlem. Thus, with his forceful language and authority, the commissioner provided white New Yorkers a rationale for their demand for "muss 'em up" policing and the augmentation of the police. As the white dailies published more and more stories of crimes committed by Blacks on whites, white New Yorkers aggressively questioned La Guardia's commitment to their safety.

The *New York Times*'s and other white-owned dailies' editorials sparked a "moral panic" among many white New Yorkers in the early 1940s.[18] Of course, some of the crime reportage addressed the social and economic issues blighting Black neighborhoods. In an editorial "Policing Is Not Enough," the *New York Herald Tribune* acknowledged the "inadequate policing" in Central Park but asserted that "it would be a tragedy if the 'crime wave' in Harlem were considered as simply that—a sporadic outbreak of lawlessness to be cured by the temporary application of increased police protection." But despite its appeal to the living conditions in Harlem, prejudice, and intolerance, that daily still published articles that reinforced tropes of Black criminality.[19] Outraged by the murder of a white youth but also by what seemed like a torrent of crime committed by Blacks upon whites, white New Yorkers wrote letters to La Guardia, demanding that he and the police protect white people from Black "thugs."

Though the so-called crime wave in Harlem held much in common with Sirtl's campaign in Bedford-Stuyvesant in the late 1930s, there were some key differences. Then the Black press, Bedford-Stuyvesant's mobilized Black community, and Black activists from various organizations across the city checked the rhetoric and actions of the Midtown Civic League and Sirtl and framed them as the expressions and practices of segregationists and white supremacists. Though Sirtl and Belford articulated their racist ideas through racializing crime, the impetus of their crime discourse erupted ostensibly out of their endeavors to keep their neighborhoods all-white. Both "crime waves," nonetheless, articulated a defense of all-white neighborhoods, and whether their defense was predicated on property rights or safety, it ultimately criminalized Black people.

The crime waves of 1941 and the early 1940s, however, emerged apparently from criminal acts against whites and white media–generated tales of Black criminality. The police's complaints about their discretion and especially the white press reinforced and expanded white New Yorkers' crime talk. These early World War II–era crime waves, more so than those in Brooklyn, homed in on white innocence, Black criminality, and the failure of the police to protect whites. Whites living in the Central Park area appeared less concerned about the in-migration of Blacks and their purchasing property as they were in Brooklyn in the late 1930s and Harlem before World War I. Whites' complaints derived from, in part, the decades-long battles over Harlem, but this episode was about containment, controlling Black youth mobility and their occupation of white-identified public space, and punishment. The 1940s crime waves, building on the rhetoric of whites in Brooklyn, directed its animus toward the La Guardia administration under the allegation that it constrained police authority and sanctioned Black crime. The police reiterated the narrative that the mayor constrained police authority for votes, the same rationale it gave to whites in the aftermath of the Harlem uprising in 1935. Because La Guardia neglected to check Black criminal activity, many white New Yorkers believed that no white person was safe. The mayor's public rhetoric about checking police brutality in Harlem in 1936 publicized in the white press, despite the lethal pattern of police brutality since then documented in the Black press, gave credence to the police's defense of itself as unsafe in the mid-1930s but especially in the 1940s.[20]

The O'Connell killing enraged whites and presented them with an opportunity to share their own encounters with juvenile crime to public officials with greater authority than their local police precinct. Anne Kolodney, a woman from the Bronx, explained that a gang of "hoodlums" robbed her nine-year-old nephew "of a brand new football." Kolodney had even interviewed some of the kids in the neighborhood, who told her the name of the gang and that they "take delight in frightening the children and have been known to threaten them with an open penknife." She informed the mayor that she had made complaints to her local precinct, but they had done nothing. Disappointed, she queried, "Must we wait until a child is killed before the police will take action?" Gertrude Blanchard of Riverside Drive in Manhattan observed that juvenile crime had been a problem for the "past few years." She explained that she had a fifteen-year-old son who reported these incidents to her, but she had done nothing but warned him not to be out after dark. The "ruffians," she noted, "in this neighborhood were not colored," and she urged the police to encourage the principals to instruct their students to reports the incidents. Blanchard's letter was telling for a couple of reasons. By bringing to light that the boys "were not colored," she revealed not only the white press's exaggerated focus on Black juvenile crime but also how effectively the white press had been in linking "hoodlumism" and "ruffianism" to Black youth. Another letter signed by a group of mothers asked for an increase of the police presence, particularly of uniformed officers, near Central Park West in the upper sixties and, like Blanchard, noted, "Many of the assaults and thefts have been committed by white persons." Another letter writer, George Belmont from Yonkers, explained to the mayor that he was assaulted on 117th Street near Seventh Avenue in Harlem in August. Belmont believed that "the technique employed by my assailants was exactly the same as that used on the late Joseph Keelan except that they probably were scared away before [they] finish[ed] me up by the presence a hundred yards away of two unsuspecting police officers." Belmont identified the race of the assailants, noting that he was "the victim on the part of a gang of young Negroes." Without using the word "mugging," as defined by the *New York Times*, he used its description to conclude that "Keelan's murderer may also be responsible for my hold-up." But despite his reporting of the assault in August and again in October, he "received no reply."[21]

Beyond reporting their experiences of crime and the negligence of their police precinct, other letter writers made more explicit connections between juvenile crime, race, and punishment. In a letter to Mayor La Guardia dated November 7, Thomas Curtin, a white New Yorker, claimed that "life among the Negroes [wa]s cheap." Consequently, the perpetuation of crime—regardless of the kind—was likely to result in violence, because "whether or not the potential victim's life has to be taken in order to obtain the loot, is not considered." The letter writers also believed that crimes committed by Blacks against whites was a citywide problem. As Curtin noted, "Not only has Harlem been affected by these hoodlums, but also colored sections in Brooklyn and Queens. The negroes travel in cliques of three or four and pounce on their prey who is usually alone."[22] Many of the letter writers, like Curtin, described Blacks not as individuals but as part of a violent mob. This crime discourse reflected white New Yorkers' real and imagined encounters with crime committed by Blacks and their internalization of stereotypes of Blacks as inherently or culturally criminal, ideas perpetuated both in southern and northern news outlets, popular culture, and social science scholarship.[23]

Despite La Guardia's shelving of the report on the riot of 1935, he overwhelmingly secured the Black vote in the mayoral election only days before. The temper of whites' ire to the murder of O'Connell in Central Park, therefore, was also, in part, a reflection of the perceived political power that Harlemites and Black New Yorkers had gained in the aftermath of the election. The city's public officials often parroted the idea that Black Harlemites, particularly recent migrants from the South, abused the city's relief system. Magistrate William E. Ringel claimed that Black southerners had come to the city because of the "laxity" of home relief laws. Ringel warned that home relief officials did not investigate applicants "thoroughly enough to determine whether they were lawbreakers, disorderly and immoral persons." According to Ringel, many of the cases over which he presided included Black southerner "home relief recipients who were engaged in the bootleg and policy rackets."[24] In a letter to the mayor dated November 10, an anonymous letter writer claimed, "On the eve before election you went up to Harlem to tell the niggers what fine people they are and that you of course expected them to vote for you for favors received, such as relief etc. All of this has made the niggers unmeasureably bold."[25] Other letter writers agreed. Because he won the election with the support of the Black vote, according to this logic, La Guardia somehow sanctioned their criminal activity. As one letter writer, with the pseudonym "The Real American," wrote, "Every nigger in Harlem has the Mayors telephone in case the Police interferes in any way with this business whether lawful or otherwise, a nice state of affairs, in my humble opinion this should be brought to the attention of the Grand Jury."[26]

Thus, for many white letter writers, La Guardia impeded the police from fighting crime and, more urgently, protecting white citizens to cement his political aspirations. Some letter writers demanded police protection based on their right as respectable citizens. Edwin Fadiman, who lived at 101st Street and Fifth Avenue, expressed his disappointment for the lack of police protection he received and reminded the mayor that his apartment was located "not too far from your own." While appreciating "the tremendous problem you [La Guardia] have to deal with in connection with the negro and Porto Rican population," Fadiman asserted that there must be an intelligible way to combat this "problem." Describing himself as a "respectable, law-abiding, tax-paying citizen of New York City," concerned about his family, his neighborhood, and the city, he appealed to La Guardia for police action. Otherwise, each occasion of violence, he opined, strengthened the convictions of the "lawless elements . . . to consider themselves little Black Hitlers."[27]

Letter writers demanded police protection and punishment, tethering white safety to deterrence and violence. As one wrote, "The present crime wave in Harlem would never have arisen if you had let the police take the measures[,] which were necessary long ago. But you asked the police to go easy for fear there might be another riot."[28] Police officers, summarized the *New York Times*, confirmed this: "Individual policemen assigned to Harlem have often complained to newspaper men in a district that they were hampered in doing their work by Mayor La Guardia's repeated invitations to the population to report any instances of police oppression directly to City Hall."[29] In the *New York Daily News*, a letter writer, signed "Police Reporter," asserted that the "Harlem 'crime wave' is nothing new." Police Reporter lamented this new era of policing and blamed La Guardia for interfering in police affairs. The letter writer reminisced of an idyllic time of policing: "When a cop did not face a tongue-lashing from a magistrate before whom he brought an offending person; when a policeman was permitted to carry his night stick on a Harlem beat." The letter writer condemned the mayor for condoning Black crime through his administration's inaction. Again by juxtaposing La Guardia's police department with those of past administrations, Police Reporter nostalgically remembered "when a cop's uniform was something to be respected in Harlem instead of spit upon; and when a mayor thought more of law and order and human decency than of votes."[30] For one anonymous letter writer, the La Guardia administration and the NYPD behaved "cowardly," adding, "If the niggers cannot behave and leave the White people alone they will have to be treated as they are down south." Similarly, another letter writer warned La Guardia and Black leaders in Harlem that "their race . . . will have to reform or take the consequences."[31]

Fadiman's demands for police protection spoke to not only a call for law and order but also the question of liberal governance. Fadiman and other letter writers undermined the mayor's promise to protect Black people from police violence by pivoting to whites' right to safety. Whites spelled out not only their concerns about crime but also their perception of Black political power. The mayor's professed appeals to Blacks' right to safety and protection in 1936 and his alleged solicitation of the Black vote in the recent election became fodder for the cops' claims that the mayor compromised their autonomous police discretion. The tales of police violence against Blacks, though well documented in the Black press and well known among Blacks, the mayor, and the NYPD, were generally missing in the white press. There, white readers learned about the threat of Black migration and Black criminality and that the mayor impeded the police from protecting whites to avoid a race riot. White New Yorkers interpreted this alleged laxity, whatever its origins, through the lens of their own political and spatial insecurities as well as their racist views of Black people. The nefarious terms "hoodlum" and "thug" and "mugging" had now taken on lives of their own. These racist tropes of Black crime were not unfamiliar. Nonetheless, the contradictions between whites' perception of Black electoral power, abuse of relief, and widespread Black crime in the context of white precarity shaped the elements of this formulation. Consequently, because Black crime had crossed the color line, it was now a crime problem for white people, so they summoned the mayor and Valentine to correct it. Otherwise, whites threatened, extralegal means would be necessary.

"Blitzkrieg on Harlem"

On November 7, James H. Hubert, the New York Urban League's (NYUL) executive director, wrote a letter to the mayor. Hubert acknowledged the problem of crime among Black youth, but his letter, while foregrounding the need for social and economic remedy, also questioned the police's commitment to protecting the Black community. Hubert explained that the league had been called about youth gangs near Central Park and Colonial Park. "In fact," he wrote, "for a long time many Harlem women have been accosted and, as a result, would not run the risk of crossing the park after sunset." While recognizing the juvenile crime, Hubert also revealed the actions Black women took for self-protection, but these individuated acts for safety were not solely in response to Black gangs. He wrote, "We had brought this to the attention of the police department on more than one occasion without results and I am very happy to note that you are assigning additional police to patrol these parks." As executive director of the NYUL, Black New Yorkers' most trusted social reformer organization, Hubert had considerable knowledge about and experiences with the concerns of Harlemites, especially its working class. Hubert's letter unearthed the varied perspectives of Black New Yorkers regarding the so-called crime wave, as it spoke to the disparate dimensions of Harlemites' encounters with law enforcement in La Guardia's New York. The letter effectively described Black New Yorkers' past complaints to the mayor about crime and anticipated the contours of the debate among Blacks throughout the remainder of the La Guardia era. As he opined, Black youth crime derived from social and economic conditions, especially in the area of employment, where Blacks were paid low wages or excluded from the labor market. Thus, Hubert's politics of safety included not only demands for police protection but also policy-oriented responses to the various crises that harmed Harlem. While Hubert applauded the mayor's expansion of the police, he asserted, "Until these conditions are met, scarcely no amount of police protection will be able to cope with the situation. It will be only a shot in the arm, temporarily easing the pain but not removing the cause."[32]

Although Blacks expressed a variety of opinions on the significance of O'Connell's death, Harlem was united in denouncing the allegation that there was, in fact, a "crime wave." Although the language of the "crime wave" was found in the Black press in the late 1930s and early 1940s, Black journalists knew their readership and constituency and took for granted the humanity of Black people. Black protests against the white press's crime news, and implicitly whites' crime talk, exposed how Black New Yorkers framed their internal discussions of crime and policing through the lens of Black self-determination and safety.[33] The NYPD's response to the uproar in 1935 made it clear that whites' preoccupation with Black crime and calls for punishment, as evidenced in the police occupation of Harlem and Bedford-Stuyvesant, resulted in anti-Black police violence.[34] The police occupation of Harlem over the duration of the La Guardia Commission's more than yearlong investigation of the riot and years later in Bedford-Stuyvesant were dangerous precedents that Black New Yorkers saw no need to relive. But the death of a white youth, with the aid of the white press and the police, had now set another racial crime scare in motion.

Black Harlem believed that white dailies, particularly the *New York Times*, misnamed the killings and unfairly targeted Harlem as a war zone. One editorial in the *New York Amsterdam News* described white reportage of the so-called crime wave as a "Blitzkrieg on Harlem."[35] As the editorial explained, continuing with military metaphors, "This isn't the first time the daily press has let loose its big guns, firing adverse publicity at Harlem and its people. But this time some of them, the *Times* particularly, have opened up both barrels, which has set many alert persons in this community to thinking about the motive behind their action."[36] Roy Wilkins, in his weekly column "The Watchtower" in the *New York Amsterdam News*, interrogated the plausibility of labeling the slaying of two white youths a crime wave. Wilkins asserted, "The *New York Times*, the *Daily News*, and the *World-Telegram*, not to mention the *Sun*, have manufactured a 'crime wave' in a city of seven million people out of two murders." He doubted that there would be a series of stories on the front pages of the white dailies, especially the "august *Times*," "if the victim of the little Black hoodlums had been Black." The *New York Amsterdam News*'s editor C. B. Powell also penned an editorial, which condemned the white press for manufacturing a crime wave derived from "some juvenile delinquents" near Central Park. Describing the white moral panic as a cohort of "usual cranks and psychic publicity-seekers," Powell questioned the verity of their stories and recounted one tale of a white woman who lived in La Guardia's apartment building and alleged that a Black man robbed her of a $300 watch (she later remembered that she lost it a while before) and thereafter $10 from her drawer. Powell, recalling previous efforts of the white press to "deliver a black eye to Harlem and its citizens" during the World's Fair in 1939, believed that the white press tried to deter white visitors from shopping in Harlem to satisfy their advertisers, such as restaurants, hotels, and clubs.[37]

The NAACP, like the *New York Amsterdam News*, criticized the white press, especially the *New York Times*, and called for a conference, requesting the attendance of Mayor La Guardia, Police Commissioner Valentine, judges of the Children's Court, other public officials, and civil rights and welfare organizations to explore what triggered the recent string of crimes. In a statement by its board of directors, the NAACP warned New Yorkers not to jump "to hasty conclusions" about juvenile crime around Central Park, asserting that the white dailies' reportage constituted "shameless racial slander and incitement to hatred and distrust between the races." Condemning Black juvenile delinquency as well as "the evil of which these crimes are the inevitable product," the board asserted that "New York needs to wake up to the conditions that bring such gangs into being." Racial discrimination caused poverty, which begat crime. Warning of the riot of 1935, the board referenced Mayor La Guardia's report of 1936 and the New York Temporary Commission on the Conditions of the Colored Urban Population of 1939. The board urged that the mayor's report be revisited and that the recommendations be put into action. Defense and private industry had "slammed the door of employment in the face of Negroes." The board painted a devastating picture of the dire consequences of economic racism and the impact it had on the Black family. The absence of parental supervision, necessitated by the need for both parents to work in menial positions to pay for the high cost of living—exorbitant rents and goods—produced "door key children." Police failure to combat vice activity in Harlem as well as the exclusion of Black children from Protestant-run welfare agencies left them especially vulnerable to "crime breeding places." On account of these disparate reasons, few of which were under the control of the Black community, Black children, lamented the board, "are being made by society into desperate Bigger Thomases."[38]

Not all of Harlem, or Black New York for that matter, agreed that greater resources would adequately halt juvenile crime. The *New York Amsterdam News*'s Carl Lawrence agreed with the need for more police and admitted that various factors precipitated Black crime, such as racial prejudice, "prostitution and too many taverns." But for Lawrence, the dearth of "colored cops heads the list of reasons as to why our crime-rate is so high."[39] Ebenezer Ray and Ludlow W. Werner, columnists at the *New York Age*, directed their attention at the Black community. Werner, in his column, "Across the Desk," agreed that the Black community needed better-paying jobs, but he believed that Black parents were negligent. He even went so far as to assert that corporal punishment was necessary to discipline children.[40] In his column, "About People and Things," Ray stated plainly that crime among Blacks in Harlem was a major a problem. He wrote, "We might as well be frank about it. Lawlessness in Harlem is reaching an unbearable point and nobody is doing anything about it." Ray directed his criticisms at adult and juvenile crime. He especially censured the offensive language that Black men and boys used around women and girls in public. According to Ray, a man "can rarely take his wife, his mother, his sister, or his daughter on the streets of Harlem without a volley of indecent language offending her ears." Arguably, Ray's mention of Black women and girls became a way to focus on Black men, for he seemed particularly concerned about how the usage of "indecent language" around Black women reinforced disreputable masculinity. Consequently, he judged Black men's use of indecent language as a criminal act and encouraged "Commissioner Valentine . . . [to] add more police officers to Harlem armed with their night sticks, to crack the skulls of these older men with their foul tongues." So, while he sincerely wanted to halt criminal activity in Harlem, especially against Black people, crime fighting for Ray was also an act of erasing problematic public representations of Black manhood.[41]

Black New Yorkers' letters to La Guardia reflected the complaints of Black leadership. Dorothy Simons, of 849 Saint Nicholas Avenue in Harlem, expressed her sympathy for the parents of O'Connell but admitted she felt sorry for the parents of the children responsible for his death. Simons's racial and class position as a working-class mother keenly informed the tone of the letter. Simons wrote, "Those boys' parents are in the same shoes that I am and that is being on the relief." She stated plainly, "I definitely know your Honor that we colored people on relief don't get what your people get even though we may have the same no. of people in our family." She was sent to a course on waitressing by the relief office, but once she completed it she was told that she had to take a job regardless of the pay. She charged, "I spoke up and said that unless a job paid me enough that I in return could pay some one to look after my children I would not accept it because I didn't intend to throw my children in the streets." Simons asserted that while her thirteen-year-old son was raised to know "right from wrong," without childcare and a livable wage, he might be just like the kids who killed O'Connell. Poor children, she asserted, were no different from other children, for their economic station in life did not preclude them "from wanting things that other children want." Simons believed that the boys should be "given their just punishment," and she urged La Guardia to investigate their living conditions.

She opined, "Who knows what might have caused them to want, that made them act in the first place. They could have been half hungry as we often have to be. When I say we I mean colored people on relief." Simons's letter spoke for many Black people, especially Black working women confronting unequal access to relief across the nation. Simons's letter was a contrast to Magistrate Ringel's characterization of the criminal, unscrupulous Black relief recipient. Instead of focusing on white recipients, she matter-of-factly identified those partly to blame for Black poverty. When she wrote "your people," Simons directed her criticism at the unfairness of local government, and, by extension, Mayor La Guardia, a white public official who gave more to white citizens than to Black ones. While sympathetic to the victim's and the perpetrators' parents, she underlined the nexus between the expectations of Black youth and the gendered responsibilities and pressures Black women endured to prioritize the parenting of their children. Simons, like the NAACP's statement, urged La Guardia to consider the impact of economic precarity on the Black family and the roles of local government in contributing to the conditions that often fomented crime.[42]

While some focused on the economic plight of Black people, others criticized the white dailies' smear campaign, as well as La Guardia's failure to combat crime in Harlem. Adele Wist wrote to the mayor, "I read, with much disgust and humiliation, that statement Commissioner Valentine made in *The News* to reporters, that colored boys are found to be perpetrators of all the crime thus far com[mi]tted in that section. I think the statement to be unjust and would like very much to have him retract it." Another concerned Black citizen, H. Wigden, described the *New York Times* reportage as "hysterical" and like Mrs. Wist argued that "there is no crime wave in Harlem and [there] never was."[43] Yet Harlem's collective denunciation of the white dailies' smear campaign and the police department's criminalization of Black youth did not silence the community's criticisms of crime among Blacks in Harlem. Black citizens, news outlets, civil rights organizations, and Black leaders had consistently called on the New York Police Department to hire more Black police officers and assign more police to their neighborhood. As recently as February 1941, nine months before the O'Connell incident, the *New York Amsterdam News* had "urg[ed] some kind of New Deal at the Thirtieth Precinct, located on Amsterdam Avenue near 150th Street, and responsible for policing practically all the so-called Sugar Hill district. The immediate cause of our campaign was the mysterious death of two women in one week, both having been killed by falling from windows."[44]

Harlemites knew that they had a crime problem, but they described it as a problem of crime, child delinquency, economic inequality, and policing—not their race.

On October 2, a month before the so-called crime wave, a letter writer describing herself as "A Negro Residen[t] of Harlem" sent a letter to the mayor complaining about the neighborhood's crime problem. She stated that crime thrived throughout Harlem, especially between 110th Street and 130th, and described that area as "deplo[r]able." She complained that girls shared the streets with prostitutes, gamblers, and drug dealers. The letter writer was especially concerned about the restaurants and nightspots that housed "pimps and prostitutes" and that vice activity prevailed around Wadleigh High School on 115th Street and Seventh Avenue. But along with mentioning the existence of crime, she pointed out the complicity of the NYPD. Referencing the Twenty-Third Precinct, she asserted, "It's my belief that the officers are aware of these conditions but do nothing about it[;] they all neglected their duty."[45] Mrs. Wist and Mr. Wigden's criticisms of the police for neither fighting crime nor protecting Blacks in Harlem were consistent with the letter from "A Negro Residen[t] of Harlem." As Wigden, recalling a conversation with a friend, explained, "A man I know at 2434 Eighth Avenue went out to report to the police suspicious actions indicating one of the roof-top robberies that are prevalent in Harlem, and could not find one, of course. That is my contention—the police are paid, but they don't care what happens to the colored people." For many Harlemites, police negligence was the problem, not Black people. Yet like their white counterparts, Blacks also viewed police behavior as a reflection of the NYPD's racial politics. So when Wigden claimed that the police "don't care what happens to the colored people," he spoke to his own and many Harlemites' conviction that the NYPD only valued and protected the lives of white people. As Mrs. Wist indignantly interrogated, "Do you think that because the white people of the 99th Street section and thereabouts have received protection ample enough for their needs that since colored (?) boys are doing all the killing, robbing, etc., that the colored people of Harlem condone it and need no protection?"[46]

Wist and the Dunbar Housewives League (DHL), a Black women–led civic association, concentrated on the welfare of Black women and the broader Black community. As Wist noted, "We need protection from these groups of boys, who grab pocketbooks, waylay and molest women (colored women) brandish and use their knives all too freely!!!" By stressing "colored women," Mrs. Wist suggested, as the Black community in Bedford-Stuyvesant had in 1939, that Black women were ignored, unlike white women, whom the police protected. Anna L. Moore, the president of the DHL, bluntly stated, "Attacks have been made upon our women; assaults and robberies, against our men. Our boys and girls have been forced to use roundabout ways to and from school, in order to avoid the possibilities of these criminal attacks." Moore asserted their rights as "upright Americans" and questioned if they should be "deprived of proper Police protection which is our due." On behalf of the DHL, as taxpaying and law-abiding citizens, Moore demanded immediate police protection in her Sugar Hill neighborhood and around the Colonial Park area. Mrs. Wist and Moore pinpointed not only the occurrence of crime but also, and more significantly, the consequences of crime and Jim Crow policing. Both focused on the impact crime had on the community, especially Black women and children. The consequence of underprotection meant that Black citizens, especially the most vulnerable and often invisible, were targets of crime precisely because predators knew that cops would not protect them. For Black letter writers, this policy of the NYPD flagrantly protecting only white areas brought into high relief the observation that Commissioner Valentine and La Guardia were singularly concerned about the welfare, the rights, and the safety of their white citizens.[47]

Describing white dailies' characterization of crime and policing in the *New York Amsterdam News*, Lawrence D. Reddick wrote that the NYPD "confused 'adequate policing' with 'police brutality.'" Reddick believed "the majority of residents in Harlem, as elsewhere, insist upon law and order." Yet, he wrote, Harlemites were "equally insistent" that this situation should not be taken advantage of as a reason to instigate "a reign of terror by the clubs and firearms of the police." According to Reddick, the lack of municipal resources to improve the economic situation of the Black community was the relevant issue. He asked, "What are the conditions which produce these mostly teen age 'muggers,' purse-snatchers and pilferers? Many of the answers to this question are found to be in the report of the Mayor's Commission on the 'Harlem Riot' of 1935. This report still is unpublished."[48] Five years after the completion of the report, the Black community, despite its political support of the mayor, still found him and the police unaccountable for conditions that his administration had wrought.

The City-Wide Citizens' Committee on Harlem

By the latter part of November, Harlem's leadership, public officials, and social reformers held several meetings and exchanged private correspondences about how to respond to the incidents of crime as well as the white press's "crime wave" reportage. Writing Roy Wilkins in mid-November, Margaret C. Byrne, principal of Wadleigh High School in Harlem, described the "recent publicity" about Black youth crime as problems that "those working in the community have long recognized as critical." But she was concerned about and disagreed with the mayor's handling of it. She wrote, "Their solution [to Black youth crime], which is essential to the best social and economic development of the city as a whole, cannot be found, however, solely in increased police protection and punitive measures." Instead of punishment, Byrne prioritized "planning and executing" by the city leadership that would create a program to "eliminate the weaknesses in the areas of health, recreation, employment, education and character development." Byrne's concern led her and her faculty to organize a meeting at the school for November 24, where she shared that parallel conversations had been underway among other civic-minded citizens in Harlem and across the city.[49]

During the initial adjudication of the O'Connell case, Magistrate Anna M. Kross, the presiding judge, defended the white press's reporting, claiming that it tried to protect the public. Morris Levy, the attorney for one of the boys, Norman Davis, believed that the case had attracted too much publicity. Kross, however, "hope[d] . . . that this case [would] bring it to the attention of the general public so that steps can be taken to try to solve this problem."[50] On November 19, Robert W. Searle, executive director of the Social Service Bureau, held a conference at the courthouse. The conference was well attended, representing a diverse swath of the city's civic, reform, and religious leaders: "more than 200 persons, Negro and white . . . jammed [into the] Harlem Court." While the attendees broached a range of topics, including education, home relief, and housing, as well as the ubiquitous problems of racial prejudice and poverty, juvenile delinquency and crime-prevention garnered the attendees' main concern. Searle shifted the conversation from the cause of crime to formulating ways to inform the public about the "basic nature of the problem" and how resources might be mobilized to address it. Like many of the other attendees, Searle disapproved of the white media's characterization of crime in Harlem, especially "the impression that the problem was chiefly one for the police to handle." By the end of the conference, they voted that Searle would select a few members from those in attendance and form a subcommittee that would report to the larger group.[51]

On December 3, Dr. Algernon Black, of the Ethical Culture Society, called a meeting of twenty-five social reformers, civil rights and labor leaders, and public officials, and they assembled at Two West Sixty-Fourth Street. The conferees formed the City-Wide Citizens' Committee on Harlem. The CWCCH rejected the white press's allegation that Harlem was saddled with a "crime wave" and asserted that discrimination "against colored workers by labor unions, public utilities, private industry and public institutions; and the lack of adequate housing and recreational facilities were responsible for the sordid social conditions" in Harlem.[52] The committee was composed of 300 members and led by an executive board of thirty members. The executive board consisted of many of Harlem's civil rights, labor, and welfare leaders and politicians, including William T. Andrews, Frank R. Crosswaith, Lester Granger, Hulan Jack, Benjamin McLaurin, Fred Moore, A. Philip Randolph, Adam Clayton Powell Jr., Adam Clayton Powell Sr., and Walter White. The executive board created subcommittees for housing, health and hospitals, education and recreation, employment, and crime and delinquency. Each subcommittee was interracial and led by specialists in the relevant fields.[53] The CWCCH framed its origins in the socioeconomic conditions, especially the housing and employment crises that hit Harlem during the early Depression years, declaring that these conditions mixed with "disillusionment with democracy . . . [and] resulted in a social explosion—a riot." The CWCCH criticized the mayor for his support of police occupation, noting that La Guardia "assigned mounted police to keep law and order along 125th Street in Harlem." Like the NAACP, and others since 1936, the CWCCH pointed out that La Guardia failed to release his own report, which disclosed "evidence of neglect by city departments," and observed that "the mounted police still patrol 125th Street and serve as silent reminders of the riot."[54]

By the spring of 1942, the subcommittees completed their reports and presented them at the inaugural Citywide Harlem Week during the week of May 24. Throughout that week, the CWCCH sponsored entertainment, information sessions, and panels featuring civil rights leaders, public officials, and heads of the district's and city's civic, welfare, and religious organizations. At the first meeting, the Housing, Employment, Education, and Health subcommittees presented their findings. Collectively, the reports recommended changes in government and nongovernment agencies, new legislation, and strengthening existing facilities. Much like La Guardia's unreleased commission report in 1936, as well as other reports since the late 1930s, the CWCCH's reports documented that Black New Yorkers were underserved in all areas of local government. The speakers articulated the needs of Black New Yorkers within the context of local, state, and federal government, as well as the importance of community engagement. The CWCCH encouraged "extensive development of community relationship[s]. This involves parent-teacher groups, after-school programs and activities."[55]

The *Report of the Sub-committee on Housing of the City-Wide Citizens' Committee on Harlem*, echoed previous studies on housing in Harlem before and during the La Guardia administration.[56] The *Second Report of the New York State Temporary Commission on the Condition of the Colored Urban Population* in 1939 stated, "Residential segregation in the State of New York is a social development unauthorized by law and dependent entirely upon public attitudes for its continuance." That commission stated that the State's Black communities had been constructed from the outside. Unwilling to "discuss the ethical question," the commission used neutral language, and stated there existed "a determination on the part of [the] surrounding community that the Negro district shall not expand." Despite this color-blind approach to highlighting the efforts of white communities that produced residential segregation across the state, the commission stated that the "socially irresponsible groups and individuals" resulted in the "exploitation of Negroes."[57] These conditions were well known among New Yorkers, especially among realtor associations that actively participated in segregating and exploiting Black people. The commission, without disclosing his name, quoted "a prominent New York City realtor" writing to members of the Real Estate Board: "I believe a logical section of Negro expansion in Manhattan is East Harlem." The realtor's suggestion exposed his and the board's power to determine residential options of the city's Black community, as well as the realtor's intention to extract exorbitant rents on the basis of the residential segregation of Black people. The realtor admitted, "An influx of Negroes into East Harlem would not work a hardship to the present population (Italian Americans) of the area, because its present residents could move to any other section without the attendant racial discrimination which the Negro would encounter if he endeavored to locate in other districts." Not much had changed three years later.[58]

The subcommittee's report submitted by its chair, Charles Abrams, asserted that residential segregation, high rents, congestion, and unhealthy living conditions continued to characterize the housing situation that Black New Yorkers confronted in the early 1940s. Like the state commission, the subcommittee used neutral language, though it made clear that whites exploited Black Harlem. "There is considerable absentee ownership. There is some ownership by Negroes of property in Harlem and elsewhere but in general equities are thin and ownership tenuous."[59] White landlords' exploitation of Black tenants and what the committee described as the "physically sound structure" of Harlem's apartment buildings made purchasing property by the city or state costly.[60] The subcommittee, while centering Harlem, framed the city's housing crisis as a national problem and recommended that the housing crisis be addressed through the coordination of federal, state, and local government. It argued, "Harlem can become a socially solvent community only if the Negro problem is solved nationally. Long range planning, therefore, demands . . . building housing in all communities, by planning post-war employment opportunities." The subcommittee recommended that the housing authority purchase as much available land as possible, prioritize housing for "the lowest income Negro," enact special taxes for public housing and rent control legislation, and enforce housing violations laws.[61]

The subcommittee on Crime and Delinquency's report centered the dearth of resources in the city's public and private crime prevention programs and agencies, as well as educational and welfare institutions. The subcommittee observed that "there is a striking correlation between the slums and juvenile delinquency" and that in "practically every study of juvenile delinquency in New York City" it was revealed that crime and delinquency endured "chiefly in the crowded and poverty-stricken sections of the city." Describing the rhetoric of the "crime wave" as misleading, the report nonetheless pointed out that the rates of crime and delinquency among Black adults and youth were higher than those of whites in regard to their proportion of the city's population. None of this information was new. The report noted and explained that Blacks faced "racial prejudice" in their encounters with the police during arrests and in court and in all probability that increased their arrest and imprisonment rates. As the report explained, "While the five to one of Negro to white imprisonment in New York City seems very high, it is no higher than in some other cities." Racial exclusion and neglect explained the racial differences between Black and white juvenile crime rates. The Black press, Black social reformers, and others had long documented the exclusionary practices of the city's probationary resources and foster homes, as well as the limited support allotted to preventive programs in schools. The report wavered on whether the police department discriminated against the Black community "systematically or deliberately." Admitting the occasional incompetence or "race bias" among individual officers, it asserted that their misconduct and racism "should not be attributed to all police officials."[62]

By the end of the year, the CWCCH had made some advances in the area of jobs and social welfare. During the summer, members of the Subcommittee on Employment met with representatives from several department stores to hire Blacks for white-collar jobs. By October, that committee reported that Macy's, Bloomingdale's, Lord and Taylor, McCreery, and McCutcheon had hired Blacks in clerical positions in stock and other areas of white-collar work. During that spring, the Subcommittee on Crime and Delinquency pushed for legislation that would withhold municipal funds to private organizations that refused to accept Black children. On April 20, the committee proposed the Race Discrimination Amendment to the city's budgetary legislative committee. Paul Blanshard, Judge Jane Bolin of the Domestic Relations Court, and Dr. Robert W. Searle, members of the subcommittee on Crime and Delinquency, presented the recommendation to the Board of Estimate of New York City. The Board of Estimate deferred the adoption of the amendment for future appropriations beginning October 1, which would impact $1,000,000 of the city funds that went to Protestant and secular institutions, some of which excluded Black children. Thereafter, in order to receive municipal funds, the institutions would have to prove to the city's commissioner of welfare that they accepted a "'reasonable proportion' of every racial group in the community which needs the services of the institutions." Blanshard exclaimed that the amendment was "a significant victory for racial justice" and believed that William Hodson, the commissioner of welfare, could "be counted upon to administer it fairly."[63]

CWCCH won an important victory for Black New Yorkers and racial liberalism, but some childcare associations refused to comply. At the October meetings of the steering committee and executive board, the Crime and Delinquency Committee reported that five childcare agencies had refused to comply with the new law, and they passed a motion to take up this issue with the Department of Welfare. In November, Commissioner Hodson found five orphanages that refused to admit Black children: American Female Guardian Society and Home for the Friendless, Bronx; Orpheum Asylum Society of the City of New York; Orpheum Asylum Society of Brooklyn; Saint Mary's in the Field, Valhalla, New York; and the Society for Relief of Half-Orphan and Destitute Children. Spokesmen of the five institutions, noted Commissioner Hodson, stated that "it was not practical nor a wise policy to have Negro and white children in the same home and that it was 'too difficult' to try and solve the problem." The CWCCH encountered similar obstacles in other areas, yet despite these setbacks, it had done significant work in just a single year.[64]

· · · · · ·

The barriers Hodson encountered with the city's juvenile reform institutions paralleled Black New Yorkers' experiences in other areas of the city's private and public sectors, especially public safety. The right to safety—a public good all New Yorkers expected—remained unmet for Gotham City's Black population. Throughout the late 1930s and early 1940s, Black New Yorkers complained about intracommunity crime, held forums and conferences on juvenile crime, and worked with and supported the city's Juvenile Aid Bureau. Black anti-crime efforts also included calls for community responsibility and self-policing. Blacks' demands for safety were an expression of self-determination. Consequently, Black churches, civic associations, and especially parental accountability were also elements of Black New Yorkers' law-and-order politics. All these institutions, along with Blacks' individual and collective experiences as victims and witnesses to police violence, shaped Blacks' crime talk, which influenced the ever-evolving ideational basis of their politics of safety.

The "crime wave" during the winter of 1941 brought citywide and national attention to New York's so-called "negro crime problem." But whites planted the seeds for the crime wave in the aftermath of the Harlem uproar in 1935 and the anti-Black campaign in Bedford-Stuyvesant in the late 1930s. The killing of O'Connell especially turned the spotlight on the mayor's crime policy and whites' angst about Black crime. Whites' demands for police protection were tethered to their own insecurities about Black migration, settlement, and especially Blacks' growing access to local government and New Deal programs. As street crime persisted and stories of white victims hit the front pages of the dailies, whites believed that Blacks leveraged their vote for La Guardia to protect Black criminals. The white press's coverage of these crimes reinforced these fictions and validated whites' perceptions of themselves as victims and Blacks as predators. By fusing the dailies' crime reportage with their own experiences with street crimes, as well as the rumors and stories they told and shared among themselves, whites created their own complex, contradictory narratives of Black crime. Because of the configuration of street crimes, they fused Blackness and public space to produce a nimble crime discourse that conflated Black youth with "hoodlums," "thugs," and gangs. The NYPD's fiction of discretionary constraint simultaneously justified whites' feelings of insecurity and gave life and purpose to their criticisms of La Guardia's failure to protect them.

With Black neighborhoods occupied by the police, the Black community checked the white press's crime news coverage. Even though they were angered by the exaggerated stories of crime, Blacks strengthened their demands for police protection and shone a light on the NYPD's failure to keep them safe in their own neighborhoods. As Blacks called for "adequate policing," they contended that Black crime was inextricably tied to multiple crises in the economy, housing, and municipal government. Reddick's, the NAACP's, and others' return to La Guardia's "still unpublished" report reflected the Black community's long memory of police violence and government neglect. Along with the CWCCH, the Black community's anti-crime, anti-smear campaign in the early 1940s echoed complaints Black Harlem made in 1936 after the *New York Amsterdam News* published the mayor's report. At the same time, this local movement tried to set forth a policy agenda rooted in research that might challenge "the impression that the problem was chiefly one for the police to handle." The CWCCH's subcommittee reports especially illustrated how little changed since the Mayor's Commission completed its report in 1936. Years later, Black kids were still excluded from many juvenile justice institutions, and the city's responses to Black New Yorkers' economic and housing needs remained inadequate. By rooting their critique in the wanton behavior of the NYPD and racial discrimination in local government, the CWCCH, the NAACP, and Black citizens exposed Valentine's law-and-order campaign as a policy of policing the crisis.

Nonetheless, the so-called crime wave of 1941 and the moral panic that it triggered shifted public discussion of policing from Blacks as victims of police brutality to whites as victims of Black crime. Anti-Black crime discourse, of course, was not new. As chapter 3 demonstrates, many whites in Harlem argued that widespread Black criminal behavior, not police brutality and socioeconomic factors, precipitated the Harlem uprising. In both Harlem and Bedford-Stuyvesant in the mid- to late 1930s, whites' criticisms and protests of Black crime often arose from, and were led by, white property and business owners. As Sumner Sirtl's offensive had in Bedford-Stuyvesant in the late 1930s, the 1941 citywide campaign for more police and punishment attracted not only white citizens but also the white press and public officials. In 1941 and throughout the 1940s, the NYPD's political fiction became more prominent than ever, masking the veiled racism of Sirtl and the overt venom of Belford in the late 1930s that continued throughout the 1940s. Rather than the aggressors, the police had refashioned themselves into victims of La Guardia's socially engineered riot-prevention policy that let loose Black criminals on innocent white women and children. The early 1940s, therefore, not only represented a critical transformation in the public debate on policing, crime, and race but also forced the Black struggle for safety to mobilize itself to challenge the white press's manufactured crime stories and an open policy of state-sanctioned "muss 'em up" policing. Taken together, these counterattacks by the white press and the NYPD exposed the intertwined dilemma of underprotection and overpolicing. Along with the fight for safety, Black people now had to engage in the political work of destigmatizing Black crime.

Making the Word "Negro"
Synonymous with Mugger

. . . .

During the spring of 1943, R. H. Macy and Company advertised a "mugging night stick" for women. The "mugging sticks," ranging from size ten to nineteen, were modeled after a police baton but adorned with silk-tasseled wrist bands. They were advertised with gloves and handbags, and the sign below them read, "Spring Tonic for Your Suit . . . Carry a Billy Stick and Feel Safe at Night." Benjamin J. Davis and an interracial committee, including the support of the Congress of Industrial Organizations's union at the store, convinced the department store to discontinue the sale of the weapons. Along with pointing out that the sale of the nightsticks was illegal, Davis asserted, "Daily newspapers have made the term 'mugging' synonymous with Negroes and that the sticks therefore represented incitement against Negroes" and "that any white woman who possessed one of the weapons could attack any Negro whose looks she did not like and later plead defense against possible 'mugging.'"[1] While Davis's efforts symbolized a victory, they also signaled the cultural, racial, economic, and political power of the white press. Criminalizing Black poverty not only sold papers but also legitimated punishment—civilian and state sanctioned.

The so-called crime wave of 1941 redirected citywide and even national attention to street crime committed by Blacks and kick-started the white press's remaking of Black criminality in Gotham City. Certainly, Blacks had already been criminalized, and the white press had always played a signature role. The white press's rearticulation of robbery as "mugging," however, occurred in the context of Black activism against police violence and the criticism of police discretion as articulated in the Mayor's Commission's report. Moreover, it coincided with the New York Police Department's backlash against the Black community's and their allies' aggressive challenge to police authority. Since the *New York Amsterdam News* printed the report in July 1936, Black leaders and their allies had demanded that La Guardia officially release it. The mayor's report—but also the City-Wide Citizens' Committee on Harlem's reports—painted a picture of institutionalized racism in the private and public sectors. Along with the various campaigns waged by Black labor, social reform, and civil rights leadership, Blacks across the city, especially in Harlem and Bedford-Stuyvesant, fought for safety from crime and against police violence. Building on its demands for safety in the fall of 1941, the Black community challenged white dailies' reportage that linked Blackness with street crime. But along with its anti-smear campaign, the Black community reinforced its own ethics around law and order. As the previous chapters demonstrated, law and order for Black New Yorkers meant not only preventing and fighting crime, regardless of the racial and ethnic identity of perpetrator, but also demanding equitable police protection. This demand for "adequate policing" pointed out the failure of the police to respond to the Black community's calls for protection, as well as the propensity of the police to invariably punish Black people. In the spring of 1942, the Black press, Black public officials, and the Black community led by Adam Clayton Powell Jr. and *The People's Voice* raised the issue of police brutality once again, as it protested the beating and fatal shooting of Wallace Armstrong.

During the spring of 1943, Blacks organized committees to fight crime and to challenge the dailies' use of mugging to criminalize Black youth and racialize crime. In January, Walter White questioned Magistrate Abner C. Surpless's characterization of La Guardia, whom he blamed for Black crime in his court. Months later in April, the NAACP's White and Roy Wilkins—with an interracial coalition of leaders in civil rights, criminal justice, and social reform—led a campaign against the white dailies, particularly the *New York Times*, to change how it reported its crime news. While there was often pushback from the dailies, Police Commissioner Lewis J. Valentine's claim that "mugging" was not a term used by the NYPD helped to validate the Black community's charges against the white press. The efforts overlapped with a crime conference in February, where conferees supported juvenile institutional reform, responsible parenting, and punishment. Overall, Black politics around safety reflected an endeavor to "deracialize" crime, that is, to dissociate Black youth from "mugging" and to spotlight occurrences of crime, regardless of the person's race. Beyond misrepresenting crime news and singling out Black people, the coalition asserted that the dailies incited interracial conflict and the disproportionate arrest of Black youth. Black criticisms of crime but also requests for fair policing signaled Blacks' framing of law and order around municipal government intervention and cooperation between law enforcement and Black institutions. This community-oriented approach to law and order reflected Black New Yorkers' tenuous relationship to the NYPD, as well as their effort to democratize law enforcement from the bottom up. While many of these stories were reported consistently in the Black press, these multilayered forms of activism against inequality, as well as Blacks' various views of and efforts to fight crime, were mainly absent from the white press. Consequently, despite this activism, as Davis curtly explained, the dailies had "made the term 'mugging' synonymous with Negroes." The unequivocal cultural power of the white dailies reinforced the fabricated narrative of the police department, while at the same time undermining Black activism against harm.[2]

The Black Press and the "Myth of the So-Called Harlem Crime Wave"

Throughout 1942, the Black press proffered counternarratives to the crime wave and mugging narratives publicized by the white press. While acknowledging that Blacks committed crimes, the Black press questioned the sincerity and motivations of the white media. The white press's reportage was mainly a ploy to tether crime to Black people and neighborhoods and to augment their circulations. The Black press, therefore, exposed white dailies' machinations and championed Black efforts to reduce crime. For example, during the 1941 crime wave scare on November 9, the police arrested Charles Reaves, twenty-three years old, of 55 West 110th Street, for robbing Celia Moskowitz of twenty-seven dollars at 1274 Fifth Avenue. She allegedly screamed bloody murder as she was being accosted. Compounding the hysteria of the crime wave, the robbery story was plastered in the dailies because Moskowitz lived directly across the hall from the mayor. The police picked up Reaves along with thirty-one suspects, fifteen of whom were Black and the remainder likely Puerto Ricans. Reaves was held on bail for $7,500 and defended by Black attorney Harrison S. Jackson. In late January of 1942, the Black press publicized that white dailies had possibly manufactured the crime. The *New York Age* claimed that the case became the cause célèbre for white dailies, and the *New York Amsterdam News* dubbed Reaves a "crime wave martyr." Jackson cross-examined the police officer, Mrs. Moskowitz, and John Thomas, the elevator operator. Moskowitz admitted that she did not make an outcry, that Thomas and Reaves had not ridden in the elevator, and "that not much of a report of any kind was made." The police officers were unsure if there was a robbery at Moskowitz's apartment at all. At the end, Judge Saul S. Streit stated that "the evidence didn't warrant an indictment in this case." Attorney Jackson told reporters, "This case . . . exploded the myth of the so-called Harlem crime wave" and said that he believed that "we should give the white press the same sort of medicine that Harlem has been getting."[3]

The *New York Amsterdam News* relentlessly interrogated white dailies' reportage that conflated Black neighborhoods and people with criminality. In early May 1942, Murray Davis, of the *New York World-Telegraph*, wrote about the problem of the numbers racket in Harlem. In "NY Telegram Begins New Smear Series," the *New York Amsterdam News*'s Inez Cavanaugh singled out Davis, reminding him that "numbers . . . is exclusively in the hands of whites, [and] many of whom don't live in Harlem, nor intend to." Formulating crime in the city as primarily a white-controlled enterprise, Cavanaugh suggested, "Perhaps the *World-Telegraph* program . . . is to direct attention to any other phase of underworld activities not controlled by whites and to browbeat colored operators out of the picture so that the *World-Telegraph* may summarily get the credit for gaining another point for whites." Cavanaugh described Davis's story as an oppressive and racist license to punish the Black poor in Harlem. She explained that anti-crime efforts by the police pushed crime to Harlem: "A survey has revealed that criminal elements from all parts of the city are shunted into Harlem by the police with the knowledge of all who should be in the know." Harlemites played the numbers, so that they might "buy food or to help out on the high rent [Cavanaugh argued] is the most important" issue. Tellingly, she noted, "Yet the most insignificant link in the whole messy business" was "the little guy in Harlem who pushes his dime across the counter and crosses his finger for a hit." Cavanaugh's editorial was a tale of the conundrum of the Black poor and the informal economy. The story of the "little guy in Harlem," who engaged in illicit activity to supplement his meager wages, received undue attention. Instead of the *New York World-Telegraph* exposing the racial and economic roots of the numbers racket, it reinforced tropes of Black criminality and masked the fact that whites controlled the illegal operation and that the police facilitated it.[4]

The Black press's anti-smear activism also foregrounded crimes committed by whites, especially the types of crimes white dailies associated with Black people. The *New York Amsterdam News*'s Tommy Watkins asserted, "While the daily press was busy painting a mythical 'crime wave' for Harlem, they failed to print the story of a fifty-three-old white man who lured a nine-year-old girl into the basement . . . and criminally assaulted her." The pedophile, John Gunyer, offered the girl an ice cream cone and dinner and she told him that she had already eaten dinner and was not hungry. Upon arrest, he claimed that he had been drinking and "didn't know what he was doing." The NAACP's Roy Wilkins, in his *New York Amsterdam News* editorial section, "The Watchtower," in late September also wrote a story about white crime. As he stated, "This is another one of those essays written not in the gloating, but just for the record." In this case, Wilkins wrote about white dailies' reportage on the case of Edward Haight, a white seventeen-year-old who murdered two young white girls, one seven years old and the other eight. According to Wilkins, most Blacks knew that Haight was "not Black." Noting that rape is the "sort of crime white people are fond of declaring only Negroes commit," Wilkins, citing the research of Harvard University's Earnest Albert Hooton's book *Crime and the Man*, explained that "Negroes more often commit petty burglaries." Haight, Wilkins noted, showed no remorse for the murders. He drove a station wagon and gave the young girls a ride, raped and killed them, and dropped one off into a brook and the other into a reservoir. Wilkins questioned the white dailies and white America's commitment to crime fighting. Crime fighting, from Wilkins's perspective, was a double-edged sword when it came to Black people, since the offense of one Black person was projected upon the entire race. "No one, as yet, has yelled 'Lynch him!' Plenty of persons are thinking Haight ought to be lynched, but the mob has not formed. If he had been Black . . ." Instead, he observed, "When a seventeen-year-old white boy commits a fiendish murder, people declare he must be insane." The white dailies had not treated Joseph Spell, the Black man accused of raping a white woman in her Greenwich home two years earlier, with the same level of grace. On the contrary, "the *Daily News* assumed Spell was guilty and used all its skill in headlines and feature stories to convict him before he ever came before a jury." Admitting that the stories were not "pretty" and that his commentary did not reflect "a 'holier-than-thou' attitude, but only for the record," Wilkins's reportage exposed the hypocrisy of both the white dailies and white America's customary response to crime. He concluded, "We cannot judge millions of sober, law-abiding white people by Haight or Bailey[Robert Taylor Bailey, white, raped and murdered two social workers, Neil Pietrangeli and Dorothy Baun from Kenosha, Wisconsin, in early September]. They should not judge the millions of Negroes by an occasional horrible crime committed by a Black man."[5]

"I'm for Law and Order, First, Second, Last and Always"

Despite their outcries about the "anti-Negro" smear campaign, Black New Yorkers did not lose sight of the problem of crime in the city. And the Black press, while interrogating the integrity of white dailies' manufactured, race-laden crime reportage, continued to advocate for the safety of the Black community, especially Black women and children. Black New Yorkers used the Black press to express their anger at crime in Black neighborhoods. Mrs. Lucille Grant, a Black woman, in her letter to the editor titled "Crime in Harlem?" in the *New York Amsterdam News* in late August, criticized the anti-smear campaign. Grant explained that a white man was not safe to walk the streets of Harlem, and rather than shout that there was no crime wave, the editor should tell the truth. Grant complained, "Instead of shouting 'liar,' why not admit the truth and try to do something about these outrages." These crimes against whites but also Black people were, she suggested, well known and widespread. She admitted, "Yes, I am a colored American, and I, too, am afraid to walk the street after dark. I know several people, poor people, who were robbed and beaten if they didn't have money to give or be taken by these muggers."[6]

A week later, the *New York Amsterdam News* featured a four-part series titled "Crime in Harlem" from mid-September to early October, and Carl Lawrence's column "Harlem Roundup" featured his views on crime, safety, and the Black community's roles and responsibility in the anti-crime campaign. Crime prevention and fighting often overlapped, from the Black weekly's and Lawrence's perspectives, with responsible parenting, equitable policing, and the Double V campaign. Black women especially received the Black press's condemnation. In the September 12, 1942 editorial, the first of the "Crime in Harlem" series, the Black weekly opened with the question, "The most serious and pertinent question outside of how can we help win this war, is: Are hoodlums to rule Harlem?" While acknowledging the problem of Black-on-white crime and the misconduct of Black youth, the *New York Amsterdam News* argued that the problem of crime was primarily the result of the "breakdown of domestic standards and a demoralization of values among our parents who are showing so increased inability to control their own offspring." Focus on the Black family, however, became a path to direct misplaced censure on Black women. The editorial admitted the need for affordable and modern housing, juvenile recreation, job security, and "properly . . . regretted" the flood of bars and grills. Yet none of those reasons were legitimate excuses for negligent parents. Black women had lost their moral core: "It is an indication that that sturdy, God-fearing capable type of Negro womanhood, which has stood guard over our progress not only here but throughout the nation, is disappearing and in its stead is appearing a younger and more modern type of womanhood which believes it can indulge itself in its own pleasurable pursuits and at the same time successfully rear law-abiding, self-respecting children."[7] Lawrence had similar concerns but directed them at the institution of prostitution and saving Black womanhood. Muggings and robberies, he believed, were connected to prostitution. Hoodlums and pimps exploited sex workers, who also operated as their lookouts. These parasitic men, Lawrence explained, taught them to abuse alcohol and drugs, and the pimps specifically "told [them] not to bother about work because work isn't 'actually necessary.'" Black women, therefore, "need our help and protection and, if we put pimps and hoodlums in their place, we'll be striking a real blow at the vicious system which has slaved out women (by the thousands) in recent years."[8]

Crime and "hoodlumism" were not the sole product of disreputable, secular Black womanhood and manhood, however. The *New York Amsterdam News* extended this characterization to the "glamour of New York City," where "overindulgence in questionable pleasure" might engulf all "in a wave of immorality." Crime in Harlem was especially deleterious, the *New York Amsterdam News* lamented, for it impeded the struggle for equal rights in the city and across the country. "The rise of hoodlumism in Harlem," the Black weekly lamented, "comes at a difficult period." Hoodlumism "slap[ped] the community in the face when it would press home points for advantage in the continuous war of oppression that is being waged against us here all over America and which threatens to defeat the Negro in New York, where he enjoys a measure of social freedom that is foreign to the Negro in other larger northern metropolitan centers." The Black weekly recommended a vigilance group patterned after the Chicago Committee of Fifteen or the Chicago Crime Commission. The group would have no affiliation with any political party, but its single purpose would be "tackling the problem of hoodlums in Harlem" and to support the police department and relevant law-enforcement agencies.[9]

Beyond the problem of hoodlumism, the *New York Amsterdam News* also zeroed in on the necessity of policing. Like the "Crime in Harlem" series, Lawrence, in more forceful language, rejected socioeconomic inequality and racial discrimination as excuses for juvenile delinquency, stating, "That's where I differ with the social service brigade." He expressed contempt for Black criminal behavior and demanded law and order. Lawrence advanced punishment as a legitimate response to crime. He wrote, "Let's damn all this alleged police brutality business. Leave the cops alone, let 'em finish their scrap with the bums, first." Lawrence stated emphatically, "I'm for law and order, first, second, last and always; afterwards we'll take up the question of what caused it all. Otherwise, the filthy scum of the gutter will be ruling those of us who believe in living up to certain codes and standards."[10] Yet while Lawrence and many Harlemites supported law and order, the police too often neglected to protect Black citizens. In "Crime in Harlem II," the *New York Amsterdam News* pointed out that Blacks living near 150th and Eighth Avenue complained about purse snatching, robberies, assaults, open gambling, and even murder, yet very little was done. On September 12, a Black gang attempted to rob a Black youth, who escaped and fled into a building on 150th Street. The gang threatened the elevator operator for refusing to tell them where the boy ran and severely beat the superintendent who asked them to leave the building. An hour later, "the young thugs" threw stones at the windows of the apartment building. According to the *New York Amsterdam News*, "The police, citizens claim, have been called several times, but *none* showed up." The NYPD failed to protect Black citizens, knowing, the Black weekly emphasized, that Blacks had complained about the crime and where the crime was located. "Police cars patrol the neighborhood regularly during these daylight hours and MUST or SHOULD know what is going on." The Black weekly judged, "The police show an amazing ineptitude in doing their duty. More emphasis is laid on protecting big business establishments than the lives and persons of our citizens."[11] Police protection and crime fighting were never something Black New Yorkers could take for granted. Frustrated with inequitable policing, Harlemites believed that underprotection made parenting more difficult for Black families. The Black weekly concluded, "Harlemites are tired of taking a rap that properly belongs to the Police Department. They know the law, but they don't enforce it. We in Harlem do not condone candy stores that are headquarters for 'nickel and dime' gambling where our children go in and out, see and hear things that cannot but help catch on in their minds."[12]

Many Harlemites agreed with the *New York Amsterdam News*'s series and Lewis's column devoted to crime fighting. An anonymous letter writer congratulated the weekly on the "Crime in Harlem" series and expressed shame about the Black community allowing "a handful of hoodlums to wreck the whole community with vice and crime." The writer urged the Black community to cooperate with the police and erase "fear from their minds."[13] Harlemites wanted an immediate end to crime in their community and believed that the issue of crime required everyone's attention and needed to be discussed among family members, in churches, and in all areas of Black institutional, cultural, and social life. As Walter L. Thomas wrote, "It behooves as many members of the community as possible to awaken to the threat these people, and many of our own, have hung above our heads. This is truly a job for the community. Neighboring parents . . . must be enlisted in this regenerative moment: sometimes subtly and again, even forcibly with the aid of the proper authorities."[14] Crime fighting, safety, and protection were expectations, Thomas averred, that the community required of itself. Law and order would be achieved through reform or, if necessary, punishment. Thomas drew a clear line between the law-abiding and those involved in criminal behavior. As he ended his letter, "And woe unto a future in which hoodlums of today will be the citizens of our communities. On with the Vigilantes!"[15]

Letter writers, while agreeing that crime and hoodlums demanded immediate attention, also questioned the quality of the policing they received. One writer, signed as "A Harlem Mother," responding to Lawrence's "Harlem Roundup," explained that her seventeen-year-old son was arrested for robbery and stabbing a man, though he was at the movies when the crime was committed. Complaining about the $3,000 bail she's struggling to pay, she queried, "Some justice, don't you think Mr. Lawrence?" Similarly, Earl A. Ballard appreciated Lawrence's position on crime fighting but questioned the police department's commitment to ensuring Blacks' safety, in regard to both police brutality and crime prevention. Only white businesses, Ballard averred, received the protection of the police department. Accordingly, he writes, "We are . . . desirous of having GUILTY PERSONS not the innocent pay for their crimes. We want as much protection for the colored residents as we've been getting for the white business men who after all are making a living as a result of our patronage."[16] Thus while the NYPD remained a presence in Harlem, it was not there to protect Black people. Harlemites, in other words, were clear that the presence of the police was a form of occupation rather than protection. As another letter writer, signed BREWSTER, wrote, "Nowhere have I seen patrolmen exercise such laziness and indifference to their duties as we have here in Harlem, except where they feel it expedient to shoot down one or two for an impression."[17] As Blacks demanded a more rigorous response to crime from the police, their campaign against crime often included the appointment of more Black police officers. In the column "We Ask the Question," the Black weekly asked five people along West 125th Street, would you advocate an increased Negro personnel in the police department as a means of combating the so-called crime conditions in Harlem? All stated yes. Ruth Pointdexter stated, "I most certainly do. There is a feeling of resentment toward the attitude of white policemen in Harlem by most residents. The Negro officers would get more cooperation and support from the public in general because they are not only interested in their jobs but in the welfare of the community and its economic problems."[18]

Pointdexter and others' support and desire for more Black police officers raised questions about the meaning of "law and order" in New York City. The push for Black cops was about crime fighting *and* fighting police violence, though Black leaders and citizens had long learned that Black patrolmen, such as Patrolman Charles Brown, were also prone to take part in police misconduct. At the same time, despite the presence of the police, as the *New York Amsterdam News* and Earl A. Ballard lamented, cops mainly served white businesses. The issue of law and order, therefore, was a paradox for the Black community. Their long-standing demands for Black police underlined the broader problem of law enforcement and policing, on the one hand, and systemic racism, on the other.

· · · · · ·

Black New Yorkers also complained about incessant police repression in spite of the police's allegation that La Guardia commanded them to go easy on Blacks to prevent another riot. Throughout 1941, the Black press continued to complain about police brutality. In late July, Alfred A. Duckett, the *New York Age*'s Brooklyn editor, wrote to Valentine in late July to complain about police abuse by a rookie in the Eighty-First Precinct. He charged, "We are decent citizens in the main and we do not need a Gestapo to keep us in line." In response, Valentine augmented the police detail, and Duckett questioned whether if this was done to "protect the police or the rookie."[19] By the end of August, Valentine promised to "straighten" the officer out after being ordered by La Guardia to contact the newspaper to request more information about the occasions of police harassment detailed in the letter.

Though the *New York Age* applauded the mayor's intervention, the Black weekly wrote to La Guardia and Valentine that they were "not talking through [thei]r hat" about police violence. They were at the ready to call upon community leaders in Brooklyn and Harlem to compile all of their information into a report and present it to public officials. The *New York Age* believed the police did not believe they could "back up [thei]r allegations," but stated, "That feeling, if it exists, is without foundation." Duckett mentioned the activism of Lewis S. Flagg Jr., the chief council for the local NAACP, and his campaign against police harassment of children in Brooklyn; Elvin Sullinger, commander of the National War Veterans Association; and Dorothy Funn, the "energetic" vice president of the Brooklyn branch of the National Negro Congress (NNC).[20] In February 1941, police officers shot Lindsey Weaver, a Black man working as a junkyard helper. As Weaver walked home carrying three tires, officers Barney Shannon and William Long asked

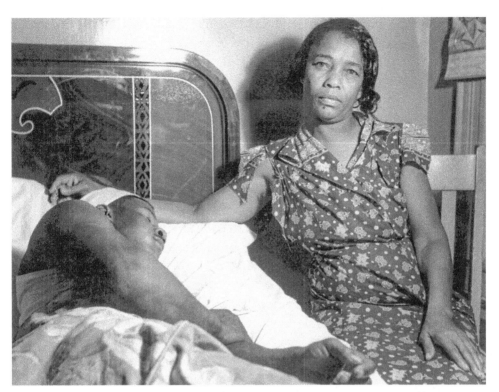

FIGURE 7.1 A woman sits next to the bed of an African American man injured by police brutality in Bedford-Stuyvesant, Brooklyn, 1940s. Joseph Schwartz / Corbis via Getty Images.

Weaver where he got the tires. He explained that a garage man had left them on the street. Officers Shannon and Long took him to the garage man, who verified his story. Nonetheless they "dragged Weaver away . . . whereupon . . . they began beating him mercilessly with their nightsticks." When Weaver tried to escape, the police shot him twice in the right shoulder and right thigh. Once he fell to the ground, the "officers lunged upon him and beat him severely."[21] Funn and the NNC held several meetings at the Mount Carmel Baptist Church to support Weaver and discuss police brutality in the borough. At the meeting, the predominate messages were "Free Lindsey Weaver" and "bring to justice and convict" officers who assaulted Weaver and other "Negro young men." By mid-April, Weaver was convicted of simple assault.[22]

Throughout the year, Blacks' complaints about police violence were constant. Police threatened Black women, children, and men. In July, police sergeant Dennis King slapped both Mrs. Susie Haskins, a "prominent Bronx clubwoman," and her daughter, Beryl. Over 200 people attended the meeting to support the Haskinses.[23] In August, Patrolman Morris Kluger ordered four Black women to stop talking, and they refused. Kluger pushed Marie Bakry, twenty-six years old of Seventy-Three West 118th Street in Harlem, "jabbing" her with his nightstick. Once she escaped, she and her friends tried to run down the subway steps, but Kluger caught up to them. During the scuffle, the patrolman was stabbed three times. Upon their arrest, Kluger blamed Bakry for the assault and claimed that Kathleen Odom, eighteen years old; Maude Watson, twenty-five years old; and Virginia Moore, thirty-seven years old, assisted Bakry.[24] In a mid-October editorial titled "On Police Brutality," the New York Amsterdam News criticized the NYPD for the absence of transparency, asserting, "Much too often we have been forced to report instances of police brutality inflicted upon ordinary citizens of Harlem. And far too often we have waited in vain for the opportunity to report that the victim has secure redress."[25] In December, only weeks after the incident in Central Park, Harvey McLaughlin, a white police officer, shot fourteen-year-old William Jackson. According to McLaughlin, he surprised Jackson as Jackson tried to break into a store. The Black press doubted this story, because it thought the officer should be capable of handling a teenager without firing a gun.[26] The Black community questioned his competence upon learning that McLaughlin had been transferred to Harlem after a police department trial charged him with negligence. As Maurice Dancer of the Chicago Defender reported, "The shooting might have passed without creating more than ordinary interest had it not come at a time when all Harlem is indignant over its designation as a 'crime capital,' responsible for more than its share of the city's lawlessness."[27]

In May 1942, police harassed Black women and girls in Brooklyn and Queens. At the Brooklyn Regent Theater, the manager asked two Black women, Mamie Cephos and Laura Brown, to leave the movie theater because they were "making unnecessary noise." When they refused, Patrolman Dooley escorted them out of the theater and refunded them their money. Another officer, Patrolman Leo Murphy, "lambasted" Brown "to such an extent that she was unable to appear in the Pennsylvania Ave. Court on Monday morning."[28] Weeks later in Queens, a committee of the United Negro League held a special hearing at Ozone Park to protest the way "detectives swooped upon a beauty parlor at 109-03 Union Hall Street, Jamaica and manhandled the proprietress, Mrs. India Stepp." Police officer Oscar Wiesner, who led the raid, apparently was given incorrect information. A concerned resident, Mr. Benowitz, had given the police the address to the beauty parlor because he worried that gambling, "crap" games, would jeopardize the businesses in the neighborhood, though no one was gambling. Indeed, Mrs. Stepp complained that "the raid [negatively] affected her business."[29]

On May 9, Assemblyman Hulan E. Jack wrote a letter to Mayor La Guardia requesting that La Guardia provide more municipal resources to remedy the economic plight of the Black community. While acknowledging Police Commissioner Valentine's efforts to rid Harlem of "vice and crime," Jack described the arrests as "sensational," questioning the efficacy of this approach. Explaining flatly that while he supported "law and order," he was "unalterably opposed to any attempt to indict all of the citizens of Harlem and newspapers printing columns of articles that are degrading. Crime prevails in every underprivileged and poverty stricken community." Crime, in other words, was mainly a symptom of the deeper problem of poverty and racism in Harlem and across the city, and punishing the Black community was no way to remedy the situation. The "vicious claws of discrimination in employment lashing out against Negroes and Puerto Ricans," he asserted, caused poverty. Schools provided inadequate facilities and were overcrowded and understaffed. Six months after the police occupied Harlem again, Jack made arguments that Harlemites had been making since the *New York Amsterdam News* published the La Guardia commission's report in July of 1936. He believed that La Guardia had not gone far enough to provide Blacks with adequate services and reminded the mayor of his "shelving of the 1936 report of the Mayor's Commission of Harlem on the riot of 1935" as evidence that the city's executive had the opportunity to get at the root of the problem. But La Guardia, he complained, had not "dared to." Harlem, however, was "impatient." Now was the time for the mayor to act. If he neglected to, Jack warned, "the oppression of the exploiters" would destroy the morals of the community.[30]

"Shot Down like a Dog by the Police"

Just three days after the assemblyman's letter to the mayor, police officer Harold Reidman fatally shot Wallace Armstrong, a mentally ill Black man. According to the *New York Amsterdam News*, "2000 angry Harlemites swarm[ed] around Harlem Hospital." The killing of Armstrong reignited the movement against police brutality. Although short-lived, the justice campaign for Wallace Armstrong symbolized the dilemma Black New Yorkers encountered as they fought for safety from violence—criminal activity and police brutality—in their neighborhoods. The NYPD and the Black press reported competing versions of the chain of events regarding the death of Armstrong. The only element they shared in common was that Lindsay Armstrong, father of Wallace Armstrong, called the ambulance to escort his son to Bellevue Hospital. According to the NYPD, Armstrong first ignored the police officer's command and then "struck Ptl. Reidman twice with his cl[e]nched fists," threw him to the ground, and drew his knife. Reidman pushed him off and got to his feet, and then Armstrong "lashed at his neck . . . cutting the collar of his Winter Blouse." Then Reidman drew his service revolver. As they walked westward, they encountered Patrolman Patrick Smith. When Armstrong placed the knife in his pocket, Smith tried to take it from him. Armstrong drew his knife again and thrust it to stab Smith, who avoided the attack but fell to the ground. As Armstrong approached Smith, Reidman shot him once in the body, and then Armstrong moved to attack Reidman, who then fired another shot.[31]

While the police justified Reidman's shooting, the Black press, particularly the *People's Voice*, depicted Patrolman Reidman and the other police officers as the aggressors. Police Officer Reidman asked Armstrong where he was going, and Armstrong explained that he was going to the laundry around the corner. Reidman "caught him by the arm, spoke roughly, [and Reidman] was answered by a powerful blow in the face when he persisted in handling Wallace roughly." They fought, with "the officer getting the worse of it," and then Armstrong pushed him down on the street. The police officer tumbled to the ground and began hitting him with his nightstick "freely, dazing Wallace, who drew a knife." The *People's Voice* reported that as the crowd grew, it followed the combatants throughout the ordeal. Indeed, according to eyewitnesses, Reidman threatened to shoot, but he was "afraid of the crowd which followed despite his continuous orders for them to stay away." As they reached Eighth Avenue, Officer Smith appeared and struck Armstrong on his hand that held the knife, and Smith, Reidman, and another officer began beating Armstrong on the head, according to the *People's Voice*. A mounted officer began threatening the crowd with his drawn gun, which he swung in a semicircle, and the police officers continued to beat Wallace, "who had ceased trying to resist [; he] was only trying dazedly to escape further beating."[32] Armstrong did not resist. He only endeavored to "wrench away," and his "blood began to ooze more freely from the brutal beatings as he knocked one of the officer's cap from his head."[33] The crowd hurled curses—from their windows and from the streets—at the police officers, while others begged the officers not to shoot Armstrong. Armstrong staggered, almost on his knees, with his back to the curb, as the three police officers continued to pummel him with their nightsticks. According to the *People's Voice* and the *New York Amsterdam News*, Reidman shouted he would "like to shoot this fellow," and another cop answered, "Go ahead and do it." Reidman, standing near the center of the street, only a few steps from Armstrong, "with deliberation which infuriated the crowd, . . . fired a shot into Wallace's dazed body, sending him reeling back, staggering, then fired again." By this time, a legion of police officers had arrived, some on foot, others mounted on horses, and they began dispersing the crowd and threatening to shoot those who did not leave the premises.[34]

The news of the killing of Armstrong spread swiftly across Harlem and New York City. Harlem citizens, the Black press, and the NAACP called for a thorough investigation of Officer Reidman. Lionel C. Barrow, the president of the New York Branch of the NAACP, and Walter White highlighted that the considerable contrast between the police version and the eyewitnesses accounts contributed to "widespread indignation in the Harlem area and reiterated charges of brutality and cold-blooded murder." White sent Mayor La Guardia an affidavit of Ms. Elizabeth Ingram, who stated that Armstrong was shot twice in the back by a second police officer. La Guardia, replying to White and referring to Ms. Ingram's account, noted that according to the medical examiner's report, there were not two bullet holes in Armstrong's back.[35]

Harlem citizens also wrote La Guardia, requesting that Reidman be investigated and that justice be brought to Armstrong and the Black community. Yet more than demanding justice, Black letter writers also framed this case of alleged police brutality in the context of police and white racism and violence. Edwin Washington, who described himself as 100 percent for the U.S.A and 100 percent American Negro, asked, "Did the police have to pull on him because he was colored and he probabl[y] doesn't like n—
—s is what the white people call colored people." Black letter writers understood police violence as antidemocratic and characteristically American. Washington wrote, "I hear you talk about I am an American, with liberty and justice for all. That [the killing of Armstrong] certainly was an act of Americanism. That is just as bad as Hitlerism or worst." Another letter writer, Ernest N. Barringer, described the police as a "gestapo" and made similar comparisons. Barringer asked La Guardia, what he was going to do about the police killing of Armstrong and answered his own question, stating, "Nothing." Barringer believed that the mayor was worse than Hitler if he failed to "act at once on th[e] brutal slaying."[36]

Councilman Adam Clayton Powell Jr. wired La Guardia and Police Commissioner Valentine and planned a mass meeting at the Golden Gate

Ballroom, 142nd Street and Lenox Avenue, for Sunday, May 17, at 5:00 P.M. The circular that announced the meeting blazoned "One More Negro Brutally Beaten and Killed! Shot Down like a Dog by the Police." La Guardia did not contact Powell, but through his secretary, Lester Stone, the mayor warned that the mass meeting threatened law and order. La Guardia's consternation about the meeting was likely influenced by the letter from Valentine. Framing Powell as a troublemaker, Valentine opined that "Powell knows . . . that this type of rabble rousing is dangerous and might result in serious disorders."[37] Consequently, he urged the mayor to advise Powell to "cancel the proposed Mass Meeting in the public interest and await the action and decision of the New York County Grand Jury." Stone dutifully relayed this message to Powell. As he stated, the mayor "told me to call you and convey to you the information in the letter . . . was a dangerous situation" and warned, "If it produced any difficulties you would be held responsible." Powell exclaimed that he was more concerned about the well-being of his community, reminding Stone that he contacted the mayor and Valentine but neither responded, promptly. He acknowledged that he received a letter from the commissioner "forty-eight hours after the wire was sent. That was pretty slow timing." Situating himself as an accountable politician, he explained, "After all, I am responsible to the people up here." And yet Stone, speaking for the mayor's office, unrelentingly focused on the circular, which he called "inflammatory." The exchange between Powell and Stone exemplified the differing concerns of the mayor and Harlem's Black councilman and, as significantly, gives reason for Powell's distrust of the city's criminal justice system. After telling Stone that he had spoken with the district attorney, Powell explained that he refused to give the DA the names of the eyewitnesses because, in the past, "some of them have been beaten."[38]

The mass meeting at Golden Gate was well attended. Powell had organized a People's Committee of political leaders, representing the spectrum of the city's Black leadership. The committee included Congressman Joseph Gavagan; Harold Brightman, Odell Clark, and Charles Farrell of the American Labor Party; Assemblyman Danny Burrows; Roy Jones, Democrat, Twenty-Second Congressional District; attorney Louise Streat; Assemblyman Hulan Jack; James Pendelton, basketball player and YMCA worker; Assemblyman William T. Andrews; and Herbert L. Bruce, Democrat, Twenty-First Alderman District. Powell opened the meeting recounting the killing of Wallace Armstrong by Police Officer Harold Reidman. He also made public his conversation about the meeting with La Guardia's secretary, Lester Stone. He stated, "Mr. Lester Stone, being advised about this matter, had called me frequently to have this meeting called off, because the Mayor feels that such meeting would be an incitement to riot" and that he waited twenty-four hours before announcing the meeting. Powell asserted that the meeting was one of unity and that it would have been unnecessary if the "mayor would have acknowledged our wire."[39]

While Congressman Gavagan, the lone white speaker, explained that it was the duty of the District Attorney to investigate the "procedure of law," the Black speakers, rightly suspicious of Gavagan's procedural justice, vehemently renounced the pattern of police brutality that tormented Black New Yorkers throughout the city. Brightman, Clark, and Jones were particularly critical of the string of cases of police violence. Jones admitted that he might have been biased, because he "had some bad experiences with them." The Black speakers encouraged witnesses to come forth to support the Armstrong family, warning that any one of them might be a future victim of police brutality. As Loise Streat stated bluntly, "There are 6000 people here and there are plenty of witnesses. You must say to yourself that justice will be done. You must do this because you may be next." Beyond the local matter of police brutality, many of the Black speakers framed safety from state violence as a political right and an extension of the Double V campaign, an African American-led social movement that asserted that the war abroad was intrinsically tethered to their freedom and safety at home. Odell Clark asserted that democracy was more than equal access to the subway and the bus station or "sitting in the same section with the white man." Democracy meant being treated with dignity and receiving the protection of the state, even if the criminal was a police officer.[40]

Commentary on the killing of Armstrong from the Black press was critical of the white press and the police. The white dailies, asserted the *People's Voice*, tried to "whitewash the story." The *New York Times* described Officer Reidman's killing of Armstrong in a sympathetic fashion, explaining that he "tried his best to avoid using the pistol." In general, the white newspapers characterized Wallace as the aggressor, as either a "knife-wielding Negro" or a derivation, "blade-wielding Negro."[41] The *People's Voice* also took up Police Commissioner Valentine's allegation that the meeting and the circular would incite a riot. In "Harlem's Police Expected Trouble," journalist W. Thomas Watson noted that there were approximately 100 uniformed and plainclothes police officers stationed in strategic places at the meeting, but the police officers at the Thirty-Second Precinct, at least 200 officers "awaited the call that didn't come." Placing the blame on the police instead of the Black community, Watson asserted, "It all goes to prove that Harlemites don't cause riots, they are forced upon them."[42]

In his weekly column, "The Watchtower," Roy Wilkins questioned the police's account of the story. According to Wilkins, "The police version does not sound convincing; the eye-witness stories have more of a ring of truth although they, naturally, are larded with group sympathy and told under emotional stress." Recounting the story from the perspective of the police and white dailies, Wilkins argued that if Armstrong had slashed Reidman and if he had shot Armstrong in self-defense, Reidman should have shot him well before they reached Eighth Avenue, before Officer Smith arrived, and before the three cops pummeled Armstrong to the pavement. Wilkins doubted Reidman's story of self-defense. Reidman's life was not in danger, particularly after Armstrong, dazed and deflated, had dropped the knife. Wilkins stated emphatically, "Everyone knows cops do not take chances with an armed man. They do not take chances with a mental case, and especially if the mental case is armed. But all the stories here seem to indicate clearly that the killing took place AFTER the man had been rendered helpless and harmless. That smells like murder and the city officials ought to act promptly. If they don't they are going to have something of a situation on their hands in Harlem."[43] Wilkins then recalled recent occurrences of Blacks battling police misconduct in Miami, Florida; Kansas City, Missouri; and Baltimore, Maryland. He encouraged Harlemites to seek redress from the governor, as they had in Kansas City and Baltimore. But Wilkins also found it necessary to defend Harlem's integrity as a law-abiding neighborhood. He wrote, "We don't say everyone in Harlem is an angel but we know all Harlemites are not crooks to be kicked around, beaten and shot by any policeman who happens along." Harlemites were no different than other citizens. They wanted safety from crime and "bad characters, men and women, taken into custody." Commitment to law and order, from this vantage point, was not only a strategy to expose police brutality but also a critique of the police department's withholding protection.

Following the meeting at Golden Gate, Harlem citizens and their elected officials, according to the *People's Voice*, "confronted District Attorney Hogan," demanding a thorough investigation of Officer Harold Reidman. Distrustful of grand juries because of the pattern of not indicting police officers, Powell's People's Committee wanted a public inquiry. "The Harlem group, pointing out that past records gave little basis for expecting grand jury hearings . . . insisted that the policeman be brought before open court," stated the *People's Voice*. When told that the grand jury hearing was the best procedure, the killing of James J. Marrow in early March by Patrolman Michael Curley was brought up. As expected in mid-July, the grand jury decided unanimously that Officer Reidman did not shoot Armstrong "with any criminal intent."[44]

"The Mugging Problem Becomes, in Its Essentials, a Problem of Negro Crime"

By early 1943, Walter White and other Black leaders juggled multiple problems regarding the so-called crime wave. Police Commissioner Valentine's law-and-order campaign persisted without restraint, in spite of the questionable conditions under which Wallace Armstrong was killed. The Black press and Black citizens, while challenging the "crime wave" narrative propagated by the white press, continued to demand adequate police protection. After more than a year of the term "mugging" featured in the white press's headlines, it had become tethered to street crimes committed by Blacks, especially Black youth. On January 17, the *New York Times* printed a story on Magistrate Abner C. Surpless's criticism of La Guardia's alleged policy of undermining law enforcement in Black neighborhoods. Weeks before, Surpless had told Mrs. Alice Thompson that "she had done her race a disservice."[45] Surpless was dismayed by an alleged mugging by William Brown, a twenty-year-old. Brown, according to the patrolman, had "lifted" $4.55 from someone at Herkimer Street and Ralph Avenue in Brooklyn. Since the witness had disappeared, Surpless could only sentence Brown to ten days in jail for disorderly conduct. After listening to the case, Surpless stated, "I am tired and sick of these muggings and assaults on city streets night and day." Neither the *New York Times* nor the magistrate mentioned the racial identity of Brown, however. But if the term "mugging" did not explicitly indicate Brown's race, Surpless's broadsides against La Guardia indicated that he was referring to the Black community. He stated, "Some day we'll have a Mayor who won't be so solicitous of different groups that make up our population, who think only of the people as a whole. Then the police will be able to carry night sticks and follow out the policy of the late Mayor Gaynor: that it is a police duty to make the streets safe for all people day or night."[46]

Walter White wanted the judge to state explicitly what group he was referring to in the *New York Times* article. On January 19, White wrote Surpless and asked, "Would you care to tell us what particular groups in the city's population you are referring to . . ." and quoted the *New York Times* article.[47]

Three days later, Surpless responded with the question, "What in the world induced you to write me?" Convinced that La Guardia had requested White to write him, Surpless told him, "You have my permission to tell him he needs no intermediary," and noted, "Incidentally, there has been no denial by him of any statement made by me. Until there is such denial, I suggest that you rest on your oars."[48] White wrote the magistrate another letter dated February 1, wherein he denounced the claim that La Guardia asked him to intervene and declared he wrote the magistrate with only honest intensions and made it clear that he was not "interested in either being approved or repudiated by the Mayor, since I am not seeking any political jobs." Nonetheless, since Surpless mentioned La Guardia, White told him that the mayor would be informed of their conversation. He explained that he was concerned with "all matters which may appear to affect Negroes and, in a larger sense, Americans generally." White then made his intentions more explicit and explained the white press's practice of identifying the race of perpetrators or alleged criminals when a Black person was involved. That practice, according to White, was "giving rise to the opinion by many people that the Negro is more criminal than any other racial group." And then White rephrased his question, asking Surpless if he was referring to "the Negro in your cryptic statement," and concluded with a final question, "May I have a yes or no answer to this question?"[49]

Surpless, in his letter of February 6, avoiding White's question, told him to speak with the white press, since his "grievance" was with them, and intimated that he did not have the time, despite his urge to thoroughly answer White's question. But he ended where he began: "Now that you . . . have placed the matter in the lap of Mayor La Guardia, where it belongs, will you rest on yours oars."[50] White, responding in kind, stated that he too had a lot of work to do, but reminded Surpless that he asked him a simple question and, if Surpless answered it, "this entire correspondence could be terminated by your answering that question directly and without superfluous phraseology."[51]

Two weeks later, following the exchange between White and Surpless, state senator John J. Dunnigan, Democrat and minority leader, blamed La Guardia for the crime waves. Touting rhetoric akin to that of Surpless, Dunnigan complained, "The Mayor instituted a new policy, a policy of mollycoddling—until today the entire city of New York is living in dread and suffering for it." Accordingly, Dunnigan supported the Ostertag-Hammond bill to expand the police and fire departments with temporary appointees and limit the number of appointments to the number of police officers called into the armed services.[52] While the bill was initially proposed to address over 1,500 vacancies in the police department, white civic leaders such as Brooklyn's Sumner Sirtl in the past and Dunnigan had strategically used Black youth crime as the pretext for their own political objectives. "The Mayor stands guilty of all of this," Dunnigan charged, but the senator "hope[d] that the when the new men joined the force, that they will have the support of the administration. They are more important to the residents of our city than the agitators who stand behind the muggers." On March 5, Governor Dewey signed the bill.[53]

Throughout the spring, in the midst of resistance against police violence, Black New Yorkers, the NAACP, and the Black press continued to challenge white dailies' reportage of Black street crime. During the months of March and early April, white dailies, especially the *New York Times*, published a series of articles featuring some derivation of "mugging" as part of the headline. Black letter writers not only used the Black press to broadcast their thoughts about the "crime waves" but also took their grievances directly to the dailies. On March 18, John Morsell penned a letter to Edwin L. James, the managing editor of the *New York Times*. Morsell questioned the veracity of the *New York Times*'s reportage of street crimes involving Black perpetrators, claiming that it elevated and overemphasized the phenomenon of "muggings." While acknowledging that it was "as reprehensible as any other type of felonious assault," mugging was "no more so." Attentive to the nuances of the overlapping discourses of race and criminality, Morsell was clear that the *New York Times* and other dailies exaggerated, misrepresented, and magnified the degree and the significance of the crimes and unreasonably targeted the Black community. Morsell believed that white dailies made "mugging" newsworthy because it had "become a matter of concern . . . [when] whites became victims of it." He interrogated the nexus of the daily's racial and spatial reportage and argued that the label "mugging" had become a convenient means to criminalize Black people in general and the neighborhood of Harlem in particular. According to Morsell, "As time has passed, however, we have seen the term applied, first, to any and every kind of assault or holdup taking place in Harlem; and, finally, to any crime of violence occurring anywhere in the city in which a Negro is involved, or alleged to be involved."[54]

James flatly rejected Morsell's allegations. While there might have been "an isolated case or two" for the misuse of the word "mugging," the *New York Times* had accurately identified those most responsible for committing the crimes. James noted, countering Morsell's claims of racial exaggeration and motivation, that they were "so frequent and widespread that they constitute quite a problem for the police and law-abiding elements of the city." More significantly, "Since the police records show beyond question that most of the 'muggings' are done by Negroes, it seems to me it is a pertinent part of the reports of these crimes to mention that fact." Thus, if there was indeed a problem, it was the mugging perpetuated by Black youth that "effect[ed] an unfavorable racial attitude." James redirected Morsell's attention to the civic responsibility of Harlem's Black community. He averred that if law-abiding citizens like Morsell would invest in efforts to stop the muggings, then "the results might be advantageous." The *New York Times* and the other dailies, in other words, were solely reporting the facts, and, indeed, informed their readership of the true culprits of crime—"negroes." Rather than inciting a moral panic and reinforcing the connection between "mugging" and Black people, James perceived the *New York Times*'s reportage as a gesture of its civic duty.[55]

A week later, echoing Morsell's critique, Roy Wilkins also wrote the managing editor of the *New York Times*, charging the paper with intentionally criminalizing Black people, exaggerating the spate of muggings across the city, and attaching them all to Black perpetrators. He censured the *New York Times* for sullying its own reputation, as "revealed in the treatment of these stories—not necessarily the facts—is what might be expected of a sensational tabloid, but not the *Times*." According to Wilkins, "There seem[ed] to be an effort, a deliberate and calculated effort, on the part of the daily newspapers of the city of New York, led by the *Times*, to spread these routine police blotter cases into not only a 'crime wave' but into a blanket indictment of one racial group in the city, namely the Negro citizens." There was no explanation for the *New York Times*'s exaggerated reportage, he believed. The NAACP had long been a "careful reader of the *Times*," and could not recall a time when minor crimes were "ballooned to the proportions created by the *Times* in the present alleged 'wave' and that of the fall of 1941." The *New York Times*'s racially motivated reportage singled out crimes committed by Blacks. Zeroing in on the daily's racial politics, Wilkins rejected the *New York Times*'s and other white dailies' claims that their agenda was principally to expose the crime problem. These stories were newsworthy solely because "most of these suspects are alleged to be Negroes and many of the victims are alleged to be white people."[56]

To make his case, Wilkins showcased several articles that he believed represented the *New York Times*'s agenda to criminalize Black people and the neighborhood of Harlem. He described the daily's coverage of the attack

upon Frederick W. Teichmann Jr., the fifteen-year-old son of Reverend Teichmann of Christ Evangelical Lutheran Church, as particularly egregious. In
the March 15 article "Pastor's Son Stabbed by 'Muggers' as He Protects Girls
against Gang," the *New York Times* tailored and contrived a story that reinforced stereotypes of Black men and exploited white America's insecurities
around interracial sexuality. Wilkins writes, "This story was a vicious attempt to stir up an emotional response in the public by combining two
'touchy' aspects of the interracial relations, namely, (a) an attack by a gang
of Negroes armed with knives on a white boy and (b) an attack by a gang of
Negroes to harm white girls." Wilkins also criticized the *New York Times*'s
follow-up story to the Teichmann attack from the day before, titled "Two
More Muggings in Harlem Spur Police to Added Precautions." While the
headline continued with the string of "muggings" across the city, particularly an attempted robbery and stabbing of a white woman, Katherine
McConville, the story now disclosed "that the attack on the Teichmann boy
was not a mugging" and that the boy was neither alone nor attacked by a
gang. Along with highlighting the incongruity between the story and the
headline, Wilkins questioned where the reporter got "his weird and inflammatory story displayed so gleefully and so vengefully" and if the daily
understood its duty as the leading metropolitan newspaper of New York
City. Since the city is composed of "many racial groups," it was the *New York
Times*'s responsibility to accurately and fairly report the news. Considering
that the story was published on the front page, the daily should have taken
"the utmost care . . . in checking the facts and in writing the story."[57]

Wilkins asserted that "it seems to us that the conclusion is inescapable
that" the *New York Times* "was attempting to pillory and brand Negroes and
the Negro community by its treatment of this story" and that it was more
committed to "such pillorying than it was in the wiping out of street holdups." A March 23 editorial, "Wave of Crime in Harlem Denied: Conference of
Ministers and Police Says Situation Is 'a Social Condition,'" Wilkins believed,
also made clear the *New York Times*'s intention to weave a racist narrative of
Black criminality. The article's content diverged from the substance of the
title. The spin begins with the lead reading, "While a trial date was set yesterday in Bronx County Court for a Negro charged with mugging, . . . four
clergymen, representing parishes in Harlem and Washington Heights, met
with police officials of the two districts and reached the conclusion, based on
police statistics, that 'there is no crime wave in Harlem.'" The sentence referred to the trial date for William Austin, whom the police arrested for
attacking a woman in the Bronx. According to the *New York Times*, "The

'conference' resulted from current reports of 'muggings' and 'racial' disturbances in both Harlem and Washington Heights." Wilkins charged that the daily discounted the significance of the meeting by placing the word "conference" in quotations marks and framed the conference as racial, "including the word racial in quotation marks." Rather than reporting that the ministers met with police officials as civic-minded New Yorkers to discuss crime as a problem of the city, charged Wilkins, the *New York Times*'s rhetorical and framing choices had made the meeting a conference about Black New Yorkers and muggings as a racial problem.[58]

Wilkins observed that the *New York Times*'s narrative buried the point that the "police statistics prove[d] that there is no crime wave in Harlem" and misrepresented the spirit of the meeting. He questioned why the daily had not "consulted or used" the police statistics, since their statistics had been available to the *New York Times*. He proposed, "If a condition in a city the size of New York is deemed to be serious enough for Page 1 treatment by *The Times* one would imagine that the paper would attempt to sustain its reputation for accuracy, fairness, and lack of sensationalism." In order to ascertain an accurate portrait of the situation in the city, he wrote that it would be interesting if the *Times* used the police blotter to assess "these minor crimes" across the entire city and determine what proportion of the crimes were committed by Blacks and whether the crimes reported in and nearby Harlem represent an increase over the usual crime rate in the area. Wilkins regretted that the NAACP had come to the conclusion that the *New York Times* was not only dishonest but also "petty in treating this news; that it has deliberately branded the Negro community unfairly; that it has been false to its trust as a respectable recorder and interpreter of the news; and that it has been guilty in this instance of the particularly reprehensible practice, considering the times in which we live, of spreading suspicion, hatred, and discord among the racial groups of our population at a time when unity and mutual respect are the needs of the day."[59]

James responded to Wilkins in much the same manner as he had to Morsell the week before. He acknowledged that "in . . . the haste with which a daily newspaper must be prepared there are bound to occur from time to time minor errors and discrepancies." Nonetheless, the *New York Times* had not exaggerated the import of the crimes but rather that the daily was doing a service to the public. He flat out disagreed with Wilkins's characterization of the newspaper's reportage, particularly that it aimed to "cast aspersions on the Negro race." Muggings, he argued, were a citywide problem, acknowledged and articulated by all branches of city government. If the muggings were only minor crimes, "then the Mayor of our city who has declared publicly that the muggings must be stopped, then the judges of our city who have said the same thing, then our Commissioner of Police who sent five-hundred extra men to Harlem to deal with the matter, are all wrong," he opined. James added that muggings involving knives had often caused death and therefore are major crimes, and the police records, he claimed, evidenced that muggings are primarily committed by Black youths "and, therefore, the mugging problem becomes, in its essentials, a problem of Negro crime." Thus, rather than the *New York Times*'s unfairly tethering mugging to Black youth and broadly Black people, it pointed its readership and generally public opinion in the right direction and placed the crimes "in their proper perspective."[60]

Anticipating James's response, Wilkins corrected the *New York Times*'s managing editor about the purpose and content of his and the NAACP's criticism of the recent reportage of the daily. Reminding James of the police statistics, Wilkins flatly rejected the editor's claim that the police "record [would] show that most of the muggings [we]re committed by Negro youths," declaring that it was "an old defensive excuse" of white people to urge Blacks from complaining about prejudicial reportage and to "do something" about it themselves. But more directly to James's assessment of his criticism, Wilkins wrote, "The point of the letter was not an objection to the reporting of these crimes by the newspapers of the city of New York: almost the entire letter was an objection to the *method* of reporting these crimes." For Wilkins, however, the *New York Times*'s "method" and the editorial choices the daily made from one article to the next established a flagrant narrative that equated Black people with muggings. That dangerous narrative—not the reportage of facts—wove a much larger tale: binding Blackness with criminality foregrounded the substance of the NAACP's activism. Accordingly, Wilkins wrote, "I submit that the record of the *Times* from day to day over the last ten or twelve days in reporting these crimes of muggings demonstrates clearly that the paper had shaded, colored, manipulated, twisted and exaggerated these crimes with the intent, deliberate or unconscious, of branding the Negro community and making the word 'Negro' synonymous with the word 'mugger.'"[61]

The way that the police, the mayor, and other public officials responded to the alleged crime wave, Wilkins asserted, reflected the typical way that the nation responded to "racial crises." Wilkins then made the connection between the white newspapers' discursive practices, white New Yorkers' demands for safety, and police occupation in Harlem. He noted, "The hysterical dispatching of 500 police to Harlem may be only the response to the public clamor created, not by the muggings, but by such journalism exemplified in the Teichmann case." He argued that crime was the problem of the city, not a particular ethnic or racial group, and noted that the New York Times asked neither that the "Little Italys" address the criminal acts by "persons of Italian descent" nor that the Jews "should do something about anti-Semitic speeches and actions and Nazi activities right under our nose." According to Wilkins, this was the work to be done by the city's agencies in consultation with various racial and ethnic groups and the neighborhoods involved. Returning to the daily's "Wave of Crime in Harlem Denied," he asserted that the substance of the crimes was "social conditions" and that the city had yet to render its resources and services equally to the Black community. Wilkins reminded him that this was an old story, one "outlined elaborately, accurately and in great detail in the Mayor's report of 1935, which has been suppressed. It was revealed in several studies made by the City-Wide Citizens' Committee on Harlem." But "despite this, it appears that the only action that has been forthcoming is a brutal and unintelligent slugging of the whole community by the daily press in New York."[62] While Wilkins's assessment was correct, so was James's. Wilkins rightly pointed out and criticized the New York Times for its two-year-old pattern of weaving a series of stories into an overarching narrative of Black criminality. At the same time, La Guardia and other criminal justice officials' support of punishment as demonstrated visibly and spatially by Valentine's deployment of police to Harlem and other Black neighborhoods—despite the police commissioner's statements to the contrary—validated James's point. This did not mean, however, that street crimes were essentially a "problem of Negro crime," but that the criminal justice system believed and behaved like it was. Wilkins, nonetheless, refocused the issue of crime on the larger problems of the city and not Black people, and returned the discussion, as others had done before and continued to do, to the Mayor's Commission.[63]

In the midst of Wilkins's exchange with James, a committee of Black and white leaders on April 8 met with editors of the city's major dailies. The committee was an interracial body of leaders in various fields, including criminal justice: Samuel Battle, parole commissioner of the City of New York; judges Jane Bolin, Justice Wise Polier, and Hubert T. Delany; civil rights and protest organizations; Walter White, secretary of the NAACP; Max Yergan, executive director of the Council on African Affairs; and multiple board members of the YMCA. Before the meeting, the committee sent a memorandum that outlined their concerns about the dailies' crime news, specifically, how it tied Black people to "mugging." It stated plainly, "It is to be noted that almost invariably when a crime is committed by a Negro the fact that it was a Negro who committed the crime is so reported that the Negro and crime are tied together to the extent that whenever people think of one they think of the other." From the committee's perspective, the dailies' crime news set in motion a chain of events that simultaneously stigmatized Blacks as a racial group and indiscriminately punished Black youth. The crime news unfairly singled out Blacks, incited "racial friction" between Black and white youth, and led to the arrest of Black youth "without warrant while permitting white youth engaged in a similar fracas to escape arrest." The memorandum noted that the crime news "demoralize[ed]" Blacks fighting in the armed service abroad and warned that it fostered the conditions for another riot. The memorandum pointed out the apparent unfairness and asked them to "consider the howl that would go up over the land if the press were to report 'Mike O'Connor, Irish Catholic Killer' or 'Jake Enstine, Jew Killer' or 'Joe Thomas, Episcopalian Killer.' In juxtaposition to the word killer any one of those sectarian designations would become an imprecation. As it is now, only the Negro is singled out in this manner."[64]

On April 9, Walter White wrote letters to Police Commissioner Lewis Valentine and Arthur Hays Sulzberger, the president of the *New York Times*. White's letter to Valentine referenced the meeting of April 8 with the dailies' editors, particularly the comments of Lee B. Wood, managing editor of the *New York World Telegram*, about what White described as the "excessive use of the word 'mugging.'" Wood, he explained, stated that since the dailies were without a staff to search out the facts, they relied singly on the police. More controversially, the editor stated that "all crime news is received from the police and that the newspapers accept the statements and the terminology of the police." White reminded Valentine of the responsibility of the NYPD to report the news accurately, especially in light of the commissioner's recent report about "the utter falsity of the story told by Mary Mazzitelli," a white woman, alias Sally Bruno, alias Mary Ritchie, who claimed that "two Negroes" mugged her. He then thanked the commissioner and the NYPD for their "careful investigation" and for making that news public. White also noted how white southerners used news stories in New York, more recently the Teichmann case, as evidence to sanction the "virtual" enslavement of African Americans in the South.[65]

In his letter to Sulzberger, White complained about the *New York Times*'s story on Mary Ritchie and pointed out Valentine's disclosure of the white woman's criminal past and true identity. White asked, "If the Times considered it journalistically necessary to feature the word 'Negroes' in the story of the attack which was later proved to be false, why did it not in publication of the truth include that circumstance?"[66] As Wilkins had asserted to Edwin James, White argued that identifying the race of the criminal or alleged criminal triggered "bitter" feelings against the race of the assailant and warned that pre-Nazi Germany had engaged in similar practices. By accurately documenting that Mazzitelli had falsely accused Blacks, the story might have remedied its error in the first story. Instead, it simply read, "the story that Mary Ritchie, 28 years-old, told the police early last Monday morning of being mugged by four men at Lexington Avenue and 102nd Street was revealed yesterday to be fiction." He ended, "We are certain that the *Times* would not wittingly be a party to the dangerous whipping up of divisive hatreds and prejudices . . . but, wittingly or unwittingly, that is precisely what the *Times* is doing."[67]

On the tenth, in a brief letter, Commissioner Valentine responded directly to White's inquiry about the "mugging" terminology. Valentine explained that the NYPD provided a summary of the cases handled at headquarters and that the dailies copied the facts and prepared their own news stories. In response to Wood's claim that dailies lacked the staff to conduct thorough investigations, he reminded White to the contrary that newspapers employed reporters to investigate stories and write articles "for which the Police Department cannot be held responsible." To the issue of the police's terminology, the police commissioner wrote, "This Department does not use, nor did it invent the term 'mugging.' We use the term 'assault and robbery' which appears in the penal law and means the taking of personal property by the use of force from the person."[68] Upon receipt of the commissioners' letter, White immediately shared it with other members of the committee who met with the editors on April 8 and used it as a basis to challenge white dailies' use of the term "muggers." Throughout that spring and summer, the NAACP reached out to and persuaded the Associated Press and the American Newspapers Publishers Association to resist using race in crime stories committed by Blacks.[69]

Upon receiving White's letter, Sulzberger shared it with James and asked for his advice on the matter. James wrote that White's letter filled him "with some chagrin." James's dislike for White, however, did not prevent him from agreeing with him. He had to admit that White was right that the "second story should have told that the woman falsely accused Negroes." He wrote, "As difficult as it is to agree with Walter White, who perhaps more than any man in the country is responsible for unwise agitation at this time among the Negroes, I am obliged to say that I agree with him on this particular story." Nonetheless, he asked Sulzberger if he could talk with him further before he made any promises to White. Showing his distaste for the NAACP official, he opined, "Walter White . . . [wa]s certainly not the person to preach diminution of racial prejudice. He ma[d]e his living doing the contrary."[70] James was not fully convinced of the NAACP's criticisms of the *New York Times*'s crime news. Nonetheless, Sulzberger responded apologetically four days later, explaining that it was a "regrettable" mistake and conveniently admitted that since the daily was making "a studied effort . . . to avoid the use of the word 'Negro' in crime stories it was omitted where it should have appeared."[71] But he assured White that there was no intention of being unfair or biased.[72]

James then asked the daily's revered columnist and author Meyer Berger to write a story on mugging in the city. Berger's draft detailed the history of "mugging." He wrote that the "term [wa]s ancient, . . . and so [wa]s the practice." He placed its origins in India and followed its usage in England and the United States. Throughout the ages, Berger noted that muggers came from all racial groups but in the early 1940s, Black youth in Harlem and Bedford-Stuyvesant were primarily responsible for the crime in the city. Berger defined muggings as "approaching a victim from behind, digging a knee into his back and shutting off his wind at the throat by forearm pressure while a confederate or confederates take his valuables." According to "an important figure on the force," Commissioner Valentine, who asked to remain anonymous, "without the current Negro problem there would be virtually no crime problem in New York today." Berger's story fluctuated, from the police framing the popular usage of mugging as exaggerated to, at the same time, establishing that it was a citywide problem.[73]

The police admitted that "mugging" was not a legal term and that "the number of robberies by mugging is not so great as is popularly believed," yet they warned of a "newer robbery technique." This "new" technique was "the use of either a single-bladed or double-sided spring knife." Using police statistics, the number of robberies had decreased over time. The total number of reported robberies in the city was 1,182 in 1942; 1,261 in 1941; 1,392 in 1940; and 1,427 in 1939. Berger also reported that on March 19, Police Commissioner Valentine started a new detail in Harlem and Bedford-Stuyvesant. The commissioner took men from their desk duties, other precincts, detective bureaus, and the new rookie class, which gave them an extra patrol of 150 patrolmen and detectives. They worked alternating nights from eight in the evening to two o'clock in the morning. This effort was effective. The police stated, "Since March 19, as a result of this maneuver, the robberies have dropped sharply in the worst areas." Nonetheless, according to one official, the police were "'sitting on a dynamite keg' so far as the city's Negro population is concerned. If the police do not add the Harlem patrol the cry goes up that the district is not properly patrolled. When more men were added, the cry was 'persecution,' the official said." The police stated that the shortage had worsened the situation, which was the result of the federal government's call on men of eligible age for military service.[74]

After submitting the draft to Sulzberger, Berger admitted in a letter to the daily's president that it was rough and needed to be considerably edited but that it held merit, especially because of its history of mugging. He also trusted his sources. He wrote, "Commissioner Valentine, his top aides, gave most of the information and I have every reasons to believe the picture is accurate." James also wrote Sulzberger but was not sure if the editorial should be published. James was "at a loss as to whether this sort of story would do good or harm." He thought it might "offend the Negroes even more than the occasional mention we made of Negro 'muggings.'" Like Berger, he noted that the draft "represents largely Valentine's point of view, and he ought to be something of an authority." Considering that Valentine had recently written to Walter White that the police department had no influence on crime news, it is no surprise that the commissioner did not want his name attached to the story. Berger's story remained unpublished. Charles Merz, *New York Times* editor, discouraged Sulzberger from publishing it but believed that "it should be shown to any group of people who are concerned about the problem of the Negro in New York." Accepted as the authority on crime, Valentine and the NYPD shaped crime news. Despite admitting that the stories were exaggerated and that "mugging" was not racial, the NYPD portrayed Black youth as predators principally responsible for the "crime problem in New York."[75]

· · · · · ·

The NAACP's exchanges with the white press overlapped with the Black community's public critiques of the white dailies' characterizations of Black street crime. Recalling the Black ministers' meeting in March at the West 123rd Street police station, the *New York Amsterdam News* pointed out that the police rejected the dailies' stereotypes and their exaggerated use of the "mugging" term. Because the police were reluctant to publicly affirm the white dailies' allegations, the Black weekly asserted, "Representatives of the *New York Times*, the *Herald-Tribune*, the *Daily News*, the *Mirror*, the *Associated Press*, and the *Chicago Tribune* walked out in a huff." The white dailies' departure exposed their efforts to race-bait and paint Harlem as a crime-ridden neighborhood. The white press's "vicious program of working up the city to the verge of interracial discord" cast a negative shadow on the Black population and harmed Black citizens.[76] In the weekly column "The People Speak," T. H. Hernandez, a letter writer, claimed that "the customary distortion of the facts make it appear that whites alone are the victims." These distortions Hernandez described triggered whites to insult Black people in public. Referencing one instance, Hernandez told of a white woman "admonish[ing]" a young Black man on the subject of mugging, yet "he had never before in his life seen her."[77]

For many Black New Yorkers, as well as Black public officials, the white dailies' "smear" campaign represented an effort to sabotage Blacks' Double V campaign, the fight for democracy and against racism at home and abroad. Describing the dailies' reportage as a military tactic to sully the fearless service of Black soldiers, Hernandez stated, "Hitler and his gang of Nazi medicine men gained power in Germany by the same methods. They made it a sin to be nice to Jews by the same stench bomb tactics now being brazenly employed here against Negroes."[78] Deftly channeling W. E. B. Du Bois's 1918 clarion call for interracial unity during World War I, in a letter to the *New York Amsterdam News*, Frank Griffin in early April proclaimed, "We must close ranks . . . [as] a counter offensive for freedom and democracy against this new campaign of slime." Griffin claimed, "It is . . . obvious that this 'crime wave' is whipped up at a time when American Negroes throughout the country are making a valiant protest against Jim-Crow and segregation in industry and in the armed forces which are geared for an all-out fight against fascism abroad."[79] The dailies tried to sabotage the valor that Black soldiers had demonstrated in the war, particularly the "ever-growing section of public opinion towards equality of Negroes" in the war effort. Griffin believed that the smear campaign had the support of the entire police department, including Police Commissioner Valentine. He averred, "The dead bodies of Negro soldiers murdered in the South and the humiliation which they are forced to undergo is a case of 'mugging' far more serious and far more outrageous than the spurious newspaper crime wave in New York." Stories of police misconduct, contrived stories of fake victims, and criticism from the legal profession brought greater attention to the white dailies' problematic reportage. For example, in April, Magistrate J. Roland Sala criticized the police officers, newspapers, and other judges for their overuse of the "mugging" term. After reducing two defendants' bail of $10,000, he asserted that the "exaggerated severity of punishment serves no purpose. It doesn't stop crime." He then explained that the label "mugging" was a misnomer and that it was "just plain robbery." Sala was especially offended by the judges who scolded prisoners by claiming that they "are not a credit to their race" and charged that he would "enjoin any newspaper or news agency from identifying a defendant according to race, creed or color unless the identification is as essential part of the story or the crime charged."[80]

Beyond criticizing white dailies, Black New Yorkers expanded their attention to crime fighting, yet crime fighting was always articulated through the lens of an anti-racist politics around community rights, civil rights, and economics. Although La Guardia never held a conference to discuss the problem of juvenile crime as Walter White and the NAACP suggested in November 1941, Harlem's Black leadership, forced by a pattern of intraracial crime, organized a meeting to figure out a way to address the safety of its community. On February 20, the NAACP held a crime conference at the YMCA in Harlem. Leaders from the various reform and protest organizations attended, as well as religious leaders and politicians. While all agreed that something must be done about youth crime in Harlem, there was no agreement on a singular approach. Several of the attendees concentrated on the dearth of viable options for Black youth in reform institutions and schools. Dr. George H. Sims, for example, explained that the city underserved Black youth delinquents and that, besides Warwick, they were excluded from preventive institutions. He, therefore, suggested that Harlem build such a center for its children. Crime was not racial, stated Edward Lewis, and he suggested that the conferees consider the juvenile delinquency work being done across the country, such as the Hill City Project in Pittsburgh, Pennsylvania, the Coordinating Council of California, and the Friendly Service Bureau in Columbus, Ohio. Assemblyman Hulan Jack spoke about the problems in the city's educational system, such as the bribe system. To convince teachers to work in Harlem schools, the board of education offered them "ten free periods a week, and the opportunity to transfer within three years."[81]

The roles of parents especially received the conferees' attention. Rev. Dr. Imes shared that a cooperative plan had been created among the churches to formulate an effective approach to halting juvenile delinquency. The problem, stated Imes, was a lack of parental control. Assemblyman William Andrews, believing that because of the war, state and municipal agencies would intervene on behalf of the city's youth, urged that the NAACP, the Urban League, and the West Harlem Social Agency establish a joint committee that would coordinate with the churches, social groups, and the parents of delinquent children. Lionel Barrow and Mrs. Lillian Alexander agreed with the necessity of working with parents. Mrs. Alexander, however, lamented that she, through her sorority, Delta Sigma Theta, attempted to "solve the delinquency problem" by contacting the parents of delinquent children but that it was unsuccessful. In her work at the Young Men's Vocational Foundation, she also tried to inculcate strong values regarding their "personal behavior, approach to jobs, etc." in young men before they graduated from school. The conversation about the roles of the church, schools, and reform agencies brought up the issues of crime, discipline, and law enforcement.[82]

Several of the attendees, such as Mrs. Alexander, Miss Amanda Kemp, and Ludlow Werner, promoted the need for discipline in the schools. Miss Kemp, a teacher in a Harlem school, complained about rules prohibiting teachers from "touch[ing] the children to reprimand them." Students took advantage of this, so she recommended that teachers be authorized to "make students behave." Mrs. Alexander also supported corporal punishment. Along with his support for students' being disciplined, Werner asserted that delinquency was a serious problem in Harlem and that the community "should stop making excuses for it." Elmer Carter, who missed the conference but sent a statement in his stead, stated that "a number of policemen have told me that they can clean this situation up within seventy-two hours." But that Blacks' complaints of police brutality protected "criminals . . . against whom it is sometimes difficult to prove a specific crime, take refuge in the knowledge that any police aggressiveness will be severely condemned." Carter favored "giving the police the green light to rid Harlem of its criminals and of throwing the fear of God and nightstick into that group of young men to whom no appeal can be made on the basis of decency, of pride, or anything else."[83] Though no one else followed Carter's lead in endorsing police aggression, they affirmed the necessity of law and order. Judge Charles Toney, however, focused on the "psychology behind the entire crime situation." He believed that discrimination and mistreatment had made Black people "hostile to police discipline," and because of this, Black criminals did not hold the same stigma with Blacks as with other people. He urged the ministers as they closed their sermon to call attention to the problem of crime in their midst and to civic pride.[84]

Although some of the conferees supported discipline and punishment, reform of juvenile institutions, and parental engagement, all agreed that community institutions, not singularly the police, were central to bringing about the safety of the Black community. In an editorial, "The Dailies vs. Harlem," the *New York Amsterdam News* questioned the city's efforts to halt crime in Harlem. Citing widespread municipal neglect, "cheap politicians," and "the employers who refuse to hire Negro labor" as causes of the crime, the Black weekly also questioned the city's deployment of police officers. According to the Black weekly, "The sending of 1,000 police on special assignment to Harlem and into the Negro districts of Brooklyn solves nothing unless they are to be kept permanently on duty on these areas. We had just as well as face facts and realize the cruel truth." The problem of crime, then, was often the failure of the NYPD to prevent and stop crime. The police's undervaluing of Blacks' safety resulted in both negligence and the targeting of Black people. As the *New York Amsterdam News* asserted strongly, "It is one thing for a policeman to know that a tavern, a candy store, a fried fish restaurant is a hangout of known pickpockets, muggers, hoodlums, etc., and it is another thing for that policeman to go in and take action to have the place closed." Along with centering the wrongdoing of the police, the Black weekly also shined a light on the district's white visitors, observing that "muggings" were often the outcome of white men "prowling Harlem streets after midnight in search of Negro girls." By shifting the narrative from Black street crime to white criminal behavior, the *New York Amsterdam News* charged that "mugging would soon be a thing of the past" if the courts prosecuted the white Johns and if they received the "same publicity the daily papers are giving the Negro muggers."[85]

In a mid-April editorial, "Solving Harlem's Problems," the *New York Amsterdam News* argued that it was time for Blacks to rely on themselves. Protesting city neglect, poverty, and biased news stories "won't do any good." Appeals to fairness and civic responsibility would not work with dailies, because "only Negroes are injured by such stories and they don't matter much at least in the eyes of those who own and manage the vehicles of information and propaganda." Because of unyielding racism in the labor market and the La Guardia administration's selective and uneven support, the Black community had to manage its own problems, judged the Black weekly. Gauging the array of social, political, and economic problems maligning Harlem, the *New York Amsterdam News* questioned the historic neighborhood's civic pride and duty. Acknowledging that "Harlem has also always been ignored and ill-treated by the city officials," Harlemites had to devote the majority of their "time to the grim task of trying to make a living and survive." Harlemites had to take control of their own destiny. "Harlem

[had] to forget their excuses though justifiable, and assert themselves about their community until they are both heard and felt." Harlemites could depend upon neither the city nor white dailies to treat them fairly. The index of problems social reformers and others delineated in the Black press, such as juvenile delinquency, unwed mothers, and homeless children, were the result of economics, poor housing and health, and underresourced schools. Doubting the city's sincere commitment to protecting the rights of Harlemites, the Black weekly reminded its readers of the city's longtime neglect: "Remember Mayor La Guardia investigated us in 1935 at a cost of about $100,000 of the taxpayers' money? Whatever became of the report about us duly made to him? What's been done about what the report recommended? The only way to get anything done about Harlem is for Harlemites to do it themselves. And let the chips fall where they may."[86]

Rev. Ethelred Brown, unyielding in his fight for social justice, directed his criticism at the New York Police Department. Writing to the *New York Amsterdam News*, Brown acknowledged the problem of crime and mugging, but he posed the long-standing tension between Black street crime and police misconduct as a problem of law and order. Brown charged that police brutality was "a serious menace and call[ed] for drastic treatment." Speaking to the fundamental contradiction between the duty of the police and police abuse, Brown asked, "What can we expect in any community when officers of the law imprudently and arrogantly and brutally defy the law they have sworn to defend and support?" Reverend Brown signaled the essential problem that Black New Yorkers had been arguing for decades, that unlawful and violent behavior were characteristic of policing in Black neighborhoods. Brown observed, more significantly, that police officers' immunity from punishment encouraged their imprudent and arrogant behavior. Brown recalled the recent abuse of Black customers at the Rhythm Club along with the killing and beating of Black people in Harlem and around the city. Brown claimed that police too often had no reason for their belligerent treatment of Black people. He asked and proclaimed, "What justification is there for a responsible police officer to walk in to the Rhythm Club and insult all present with his impertinent and vulgar address: 'What do you bums do when a white man is around?' That question was a criminal provocation to commit breach of the peace."[87]

He recalled several cases of police violence from the past, including the killing of Wallace Armstrong and a young Black woman, whom the police slapped and locked in the men's room in the subway. Brown charged, "All these violators of law are policemen and not one was arrested or even suspended. Herein is their license to continue to insult, to beat and to kill."[88] His criticisms of the police coincided with the Black community's long-held views of the NYPD. Letter writer Frank D. Griffin believed that Police Commissioner Valentine and the entire police department supported the white dailies' smear campaign. Framing police misconduct in imperialist terms, Griffin asserted that Blacks and their allies needed to write letters and telegrams, and organize against "the colonialistic policing of our neighborhoods."[89] The *New York Amsterdam News*, echoing arguments that it, the *New York Age*, and the *Daily Worker* made in 1936, asserted that the mayor's anti-poverty policy was policing. City officials, according to the *New York Amsterdam News*, were "more willing to bludgeon Harlemites into submission than to assist them to become a more integral and useful part of the city."[90]

· · · · · ·

In early June, Walter White and the NAACP created the Public Relations Committee to challenge problematic crime reportage in the white press. Since the winter of 1941, the white press had effectively fabricated tales of crime in the city into a "negro problem." Certainly, as the Black community admitted, Black youth and adults had committed crimes across the city, especially crimes within Black neighborhoods, yet the sum of these did not constitute a "crime wave." The white press nonetheless had managed to tether crime reportage, especially in cases of street robberies, known colloquially as "mugging," with Black people. Secretary White, the Black press, and Black New Yorkers were clear about the roles of white media in shaping the nation's perceptions of crime and race. In New York City, the image of Richard Wright's "Bigger Thomas" competed with, if not replaced, the stereotype of the Italian gangster that frequented the daily newspapers and Hollywood films, as the proverbial image of the "hoodlum" or "thug."

By the spring of 1943, actual crimes against whites with the aid of white dailies had once again transformed Black neighborhoods into occupied territories. Blacks' efforts to challenge the white press's stories had limited impact. Still, the anti-crime, anti-smear campaign waged by the Black press and the NAACP helped to deracialize crime. By exposing how the white press covered stories of crimes committed by whites, as well as the fact that whites committed the same crimes as Blacks, the *New York Amsterdam News* had advanced, at least to its Black readership, that criminal behavior was not racial. The exchange between Wilkins and the *New York Times*'s managing editor, Edwin James, revealed some troubling truisms. While Valentine admitted that the white press had created "mugging," the police commissioner, as James pointed out, also detailed several police units to Harlem. Some of the city's judges, such as Surpless, also weighed in. But so did the Black community. While some supported releasing the cops on Black criminals, others were weary of appeals to punishment because they had witnessed police violence, not crimefighting. While the Black community had a memory of the Harlem uprisings in 1935, multiple cases of police brutality since, especially the killing of Wallace Armstrong in May 1942, laid bare the lie in the police's rhetoric. La Guardia, Police Commissioner Valentine, and especially the NYPD had placed Black New Yorkers in a terribly untenable position of having to choose between what Lawrence Reddick described as the difference between "adequate policing" and "police brutality." This choice, of course, was dangerously unfair, since there was really no choice at all. For the NYPD they were one and the same.

Beyond the dilemma of Harlemites' political struggle for safety, La Guardia's commitment to Harlem and Black New York was tested in other ways. In late 1942, despite protest from Black Harlem, La Guardia permitted the Women's Reserve of the United States Naval Reserve (WAVES), which excluded Black women from service, to use Hunter College as a training facility. In May 1943, the city closed Harlem's famous Savoy Ballroom for vice activity, and the district's Black leadership, namely, Walter White and Adam Clayton Powell Jr., took the closing as a political effort to besmirch and further criminalize the Black community. Roy Wilkins believed the city was trying to police racial mixing and questioned why other establishments, such as the Waldorf Astoria, where prostitution thrived, had not been closed.[91] The NYPD's attack upon the Savoy was an intensification of the anti-vice campaign waged in Harlem to protect white soldiers a year before. And while it exposed the unfairness of Valentine's anti-vice campaign, it also represented another case of La Guardia and the NYPD protecting white people and ignoring the pleas of Black citizens, who had long complained about vice activity in their neighborhoods. As it had during the Prohibition era, Harlem had become a central focus of anti-vice patrolling mainly to protect white people.[92]

Black New Yorkers had also been frustrated by their economic situation in the city. Not only were food costs exorbitant but also their rents. Throughout the Depression and the war, Harlemites and Black leaders had complained about the high costs of food. Black women knew this as patrons of neighborhood stores. In August 1942, the NAACP's study *Food Cost's More in Harlem* echoed their frustrations with statistical evidence.[93] White proprietors often exacerbated these grievances, for not only were some unwilling to hire Blacks, but Harlemites knew that the police occupied their neighborhoods because of the complaints of white businesses. As Earl A. Ballard reminded journalist Carl Lawrence, "We are . . . desirous of having GUILTY PERSONS not the innocent pay for their crimes. We want as much protection for the colored residents as we've been getting for the white business men who after all are making a living as a result of our patronage."[94] Harlemites had also witnessed labor struggles in the city and across the nation, especially A. Philip Randolph's March on Washington Movement, which held an event at Madison Square Garden in June 1942. Tenant activism, especially the Consolidated Tenants' League, responded to poor housing conditions, high rents, and widespread evictions. Angered with their mayor, Black New Yorkers understood that these matters were not solely found in the city's private housing market.[95] They were political decisions embedded in liberal governance and the city's commitment to racial residential segregation.

In early June 1943, the La Guardia administration contracted the Metropolitan Life Insurance Company to build Stuyvesant Town, a quasi-public housing complex in lower Manhattan, but it would not be available to Black tenants. La Guardia endorsed residential segregation and white New Yorkers' preference for it. While this revealed the mayor's complicity in segregating public housing for Black New Yorkers, it also reinforced their vulnerability to exploitive landlords. As Charles Williams wrote in January 1943 in *The Nation*, "Harlem, of course, is itself the creation of Jim Crowism, which is only less onerous in New York than in the South," and while it had the city's "worst slums, rents are higher there than elsewhere in the city—this, you are told, is part of the 'tax on being black.'"[96] La Guardia, of course, was fully aware of the housing conditions under which Black New Yorkers lived. Even if he ignored the state's commission and CWCCH's reports, his park commissioner Robert Moses had "engineered an amendment to the 1942 Redevelopment Companies Act specifically to ensure that Met Life would be free to bar Blacks" from the apartment complex.[97]

The Savoy and Stuyvesant Town debacles jointly disclosed the poverty of racial liberalism and highlighted La Guardia's willingness to allow Blacks to pay exorbitant rents and live unprotected in congested, crime-ridden neighborhoods. In this way, the mayor legitimated white New Yorkers' efforts

FIGURE 7.2 A general view of the March on Washington Movement's mass meeting in Madison Square Garden. The movement has put forth an eight-point program that will give the 13,000,000 Black citizens of the United States equal rights and abolish racial discrimination. Bettmann via Getty Images.

to maintain all-white spaces and contain Black migration by any means necessary. Several years before, Alain Locke urged the mayor to use the commission's report to hold accountable previous administrations for the inadequate living conditions that contributed to the Harlem uprising. Now the mayor only had his administration to blame. Less than a week later, anti–Mexican American violence erupted in Los Angeles, jump-starting the Zoot Suit Riots; about a week after that, rioting broke out in Beaumont, Texas. Detroit followed suit the next week.

8 But Nightsticks Never Cure Anything

· ·

The Detroit Riot that began on June 20 and lasted for two days fomented rightful concern across Gotham City. The NAACP's Walter White and Mayor La Guardia investigated the racial explosion in Detroit and tried to put in place measures to prevent the same happening in New York City. La Guardia and White corresponded regularly and assembled a provisional group of Black and white leaders to advise the mayor on how to move forward. White traveled to Detroit and La Guardia dispatched two police officers, one Black and the other white, to that city to look into the matter. Upon return, White sent a letter on June 30 to Black ministers, labor leaders, and club presidents in the city, urging them to control and manage the behavior of their respective Black communities. He hoped that "during the next few critical weeks and months that Negroes will give no cause for racial friction in New York City" and urged them to especially "check lawlessness and bad manners by a minority of irresponsible Negroes, particularly those in their late teens and early twenties." White also assured them of La Guardia's cooperation and noted, "Unlike the spineless Mayor of Detroit, Mayor La Guardia is taking every precaution to avert trouble here." Optimistic, he wrote, "We need have no fear that the police here will act as they did in Detroit."[1] White sent that letter to the mayor, who was so impressed that he drafted his own and sent it to white ministers across the city. On the Fourth of July, Mayor La Guardia asked New Yorkers to sign a "pledge of unity," to bring all citizens together without regard to race, color, and creed against racial hatred, especially "in the midst of a war being fought for democracy." New Yorkers, white and Black, citizens and organizations commended their mayor for his campaign for peace and racial democracy.[2]

But the mayor's "pledge of unity" campaign was a belated response to Black New Yorkers' complaints about police violence. Throughout the summer of 1943, Harlem's councilman Adam Clayton Powell Jr. and the *People's Voice*, along with other Black weeklies, had complained about and mobilized around police brutality and the white press's manufactured "crime wave."[3] On June 24, Powell gave notice that a Detroit-style uprising could happen in Harlem, and if it came to be, it would "rest upon the hands" of Valentine and

La Guardia. Both La Guardia and many Black leaders judged Powell's warnings as the irresponsible actions of an instigator using fear for his own interests as a political path to the November elections. But Powell's broadsides were more than political posturing, and his complaints, regardless of his political aspirations, were well known among Harlemites. Writing in the *People's Voice* a week later, he congratulated La Guardia for finally speaking out but asserted, "NOW HE MUST ACT! Or else he will exactly duplicate the spineless pattern of the Mayor of Detroit."[4] Even young James Baldwin, who had returned to Harlem anticipating his father's death and his mother's confinement in the second week of June, wrote about the problem of policing. He observed, "I had never before been so aware of policemen, on foot, on horseback, on corners, everywhere, always two by two."[5]

After the Detroit episode, over the city's radio station, WNYC, La Guardia stated, "I will not permit, as long as I am Mayor, any minor group to be abused by another group. I will maintain law and order, and I will afford protection to anyone who is attacked as I will prosecute anyone who does the attacking or provoking."[6] No riot occurred in July, but the next month was a different story. On the first and second of August, Harlem experienced its second racial uprising in less than a decade. With Detroit on everyone's mind, La Guardia's control over the riot was impressive. Though Black Harlemites looted and burned businesses, flipped over automobiles, and even attacked whites driving through the district, Valentine's NYPD had managed to restrain itself. Days after, La Guardia would not issue a commission to investigate the riot. The riot and commentary about it had confirmed what white New Yorkers and the white press had admonished all along: that Harlem was crime ridden. Along with this came the now-familiar argument not only that Harlem needed "adequate policing" but also that police should have greater authority to use excessive force. This claim, first taken up by the police in the late 1930s, had become an established truism among many New Yorkers, including Black ones. While there were a range of explanations for the uproar, La Guardia, Valentine, and many of Harlem's Black leaders, including Walter White, blamed it on "hoodlumism." Yet White's theory was more nuanced. The riot, he claimed, was symbolic of Harlemites' anger about the abuse, segregation, and disrespect Black soldiers experienced in the Jim Crow South. It, in other words, was essentially an external problem.

At the Citizens Emergency Conference for Interracial Unity held that September, White, while still critical of "hoodlums," centered the necessity of placing Blacks in positions of power in local government, as did A. Philip Randolph's Citizens' Committee on Better Race Relations. Randolph argued, however, that the riot was more than an act of crime; it was also an expression of a social revolution. The *New York Amsterdam News*, on the other hand, prioritized local politics, particularly the negligence of the La Guardia administration. Just as the narrative of hoodlumism was challenged, the Kings County August Grand Jury submitted a presentment in November charging the mayor with failing to protect the citizens in Bedford-Stuyvesant. Sumner Sirtl, John L. Belford, and others followed with a letter to the governor complaining about crime and demanding that La Guardia be removed from office. These conflicts in Bedford-Stuyvesant, much like the uprising months before, were again connected to the question of police discretion, whites' demands for police protection, and La Guardia's alleged acquiescence to the Black vote.

During the year 1944, citywide discussions of juvenile crime animated local news and even city politics, yet crimes committed by Black youth, as before, were treated differently. Despite the prevalence of juvenile crime across racial lines, white dailies and white New Yorkers framed youth crime as a "negro problem" and demanded police protection on the grounds of protecting white people. These dynamics would play out especially during the summer of 1944, as crimes by Blacks committed against whites mobilized judges, Black and white reformers, and the police to target juvenile crime as principally a problem of Black youth and public safety.

"Hoodlums Didn't Start Riots; 'Twas Jim Crow"

On August 1 just after 7:00 P.M. in the Braddock Hotel on 126th Street and Eighth Avenue, James Collins, a white police officer, tried to arrest Marjorie Polite, a Black woman, for disorderly conduct. Upon observing the officer mishandle Polite, Robert Bandy, a Black soldier of the 703rd Military Police Battalion stationed in New Jersey, came to her defense. Florine Roberts, a nurse and Bandy's mother, visiting him from Middletown, Connecticut, also witnessed what she likely interpreted as Collins manhandling another Black woman. Bandy and Roberts, according to the police report, attacked Collins, and during the struggle, Bandy hit Collins, grabbed his nightstick, and ran. Collins drew his gun and shot Bandy in the shoulder. The officer arrested him and marshaled him to Sydenham Hospital. Thereafter, a crowd gathered and followed the ambulance to the hospital, and soon over 2,000 more arrived. As they waited, they received no news of Bandy's condition from the doctors. Perhaps the news that he had been taken to Bellevue Prison Ward might have thwarted the violence. Then, in the

FIGURE 8.1 A crowd gathers in the street to watch the beginning of a riot in the Harlem section of Manhattan, 1943. Weegee (Arthur Fellig) / International Center of Photography via Getty Images.

confusion and emotion of the incident, someone cried out, "A white police-man killed a Negro soldier." Rumors quickly spread that a Black soldier had been killed in front of his mother by a white police officer. Although the police dispersed the crowd in front of the hospital, others scattered through-out Harlem. Three thousand people, alarmed and angered by the news, gathered at the 123rd Street police station, shouting "threats against the officer who did the shooting."[7]

Shattered glass. Laughter. Gunshots. Thumping. The cacophony of bro-ken glass, of store windows and bottles from above, was heard far and near. Incensed by the rumors of Bandy's death, Black men and women, young and old, working and middle class, threw stones at the store windows; people used makeshift weapons, such as side slabs of beds, to break windows. On the ground, glass, blood, dummies from dress shops, and refuse were found, and in the air was smoke from the many small fires that had been set. William Comager of 158 West 131st Street, who had walked the streets until 2:00 A.M., saw several businesses that had been looted. He remembered arriving at the corner of 131st Street and Seventh Avenue at about 11:30 P.M., seeing people running, and hearing a crash. "It was the window of a beauty parlor." On Seventh Avenue, he saw two beauty parlors, a tailor shop, and an A & P that had their windows shattered. While on his way home, Frederick Wilkerson of West 120th Street, witnessed crowds "running and milling and cursing and breaking in doors." He also heard rumors that a soldier had been shot and later learned that two soldiers were shot.[8]

Once Mayor La Guardia was informed, he immediately drove through Harlem and appealed to the people to "go home and go to bed," but he was ignored. The mayor called Walter White, the secretary of the NAACP, and White and Roy Wilkins took a cab through Harlem and met up with La Guardia at the Twenty-Eighth Precinct police station at West 123rd Street. In the meantime, La Guardia had called the governor for military support. The mayor, White, and Wilkins toured Harlem, urging the crowds to break up and return to their homes. White remembered, as they heard a brick crash into a store window, La Guardia "jumped from the car and screamed at the crowd before the building." Although the mayor's frenzied commands managed to disperse the crowd, White and Wilkins knew La Guardia's "one-man campaign" could not restore calm. White recommended the mayor use city sound trucks, upon which Black celebrities and leaders from Harlem would appeal to the people to go home. La Guardia asked White to invite celebrities and leaders, but to their disappointment, Duke Ellington, Adam Clayton Powell, Joe Louis, and Cab Calloway were "out of the city." Parole Commissioner Samuel Battle; Rev. John H. Johnson, rector of St. Martin's Protestant Episcopal Church; and Ferdinand Smith, secretary of the National Maritime Union, were recruited in their stead.[9]

An hour before midnight, La Guardia closed the Braddock Hotel. The mayor also halted all traffic to Harlem, and shortly before 2:00 A.M., he issued orders for all taverns to be closed. Throughout late Sunday night and early Monday morning, he made five radio broadcasts, appealing to citizens to go home, correcting the rumor that Bandy had been killed, and promising that order would be restored. On Monday, he banned the sale of alcohol from the areas between the North and East Rivers between 100th and 170th Streets and imposed a curfew, extending between 110th and 155th Streets from Fifth Avenue to St. Nicholas Avenue. At the governor's direction, William Ottman, the commander of the New York State Guard,

FIGURE 8.2 Residents of Harlem were quick to volunteer their services to help restore order to the district on August 2, 1943 in Harlem, New York. Major Samuel J. Battle (in uniform) and Edward S. Lewis, executive secretary of the New York Urban League, pin auxiliary arm bands on the volunteers, who will patrol the streets. Mayor La Guardia emphasized that the disturbance was not a race riot. New York Daily News Archive via Getty Images.

ordered 8,000 of the guardsmen to "stand by" in metropolitan armories across the city. Police Commissioner Valentine mobilized 6,000 city and military police officers, City Patrol units, and air-raid wardens in Harlem, and Battle led 1,500 Black volunteers, 300 of whom were women, armed with batons and designated arm bands.[10] Property damage approximated $5 million, 1,485 stores were rampaged and looted, and 4,495 plate-glass windows smashed. Though the riot was larger and more damaging than the 1935 uproar, it paled in comparison to the Detroit Riot, where there were three days of rioting, 760 injured, thirty-four confirmed deaths, and about $2 million in property damage. Blacks sat victim to unhinged white mob violence and police brutality—it was a race riot *and* a police riot.[11]

"Shame has come to our city and sorrow to the large number of our fellow citizens, decent, law-abiding citizens, who live in the Harlem section," lamented La Guardia during his 9:50 A.M. broadcast the morning after the uproar. La Guardia exploited Harlemites' criticisms of intracommunity crime and directed the city's attention toward the "thoughtless hoodlums" and by extension Harlem. Though he described the majority of Harlem as "law-abiding," La Guardia consistently depicted the "disturbance" as a problem intrinsic to the Black community and generously used the term "hoodlum" throughout his broadcast. Whether he agreed with it or not, the mayor knew that "hoodlumism" was pregnant with racial meaning. Thus, by asserting that hoodlums, that is, Black youth, were responsible for breaking the "windows of the stores, looting many of these stores belonging to the people who live in Harlem," La Guardia cemented criminality as a problem of the people "who live in the Harlem section." In this sense, the riot was not really about the hoodlums who happened to live in Harlem but was tethered to Harlem as a place. La Guardia's strategy was no different in 1943 from what it was in March 1935, yet much had changed in the past eight years. La Guardia's response was compared to Detroit's mayor Edward Jeffries's feeble response. La Guardia also masterfully built rhetoric on a whirlwind of broadsides coming from New Yorkers across the racial and ethnic spectrum against Black youth crime in Harlem and throughout the city. Many Blacks, therefore, appreciated La Guardia's appeals to Harlem's decency. He spoke directly to their grievances and reinforced the virtue of their own complaints long made about crime in their community.[12]

La Guardia also trumpeted the behavior of the police, who, he described, "were the most efficient and exercised a great deal of restraint" while managing to make over 300 arrests. While some Harlem residents were injured, "they were injured by their own neighbors throwing missiles and bottles from roof tops." La Guardia's appraisal of the police was also a way to appeal to white New Yorkers. He declared, "The situation is under control. I want to make it clear this was not a race riot." By framing the disturbance as mainly self-inflicted by Harlemites and asserting that the police were "charged with maintaining order," the mayor concealed the roles of police brutality and ignored the exploitive white businesses that Harlem looters directed their animosity at. Conveniently, La Guardia described Collins's mistreatment of and aggression toward Polite and Roberts and the shooting of Bandy as "an unfortunate incident." The mayor warned Harlemites that unlawful behavior would result in arrests and prosecution and promised the "law-abiding" among them food and milk for the children.

FIGURE 8.3 New shift of police lined up in West 123rd Street on August 2, 1943, in Harlem to take over from those who had been on duty all night. At one time during Harlem disorders there were 6,000 cops on duty in that area. New York Daily News Archive via Getty Images.

He again applauded the "quick action of the Police that saved many lives" and ended the broadcast by declaring, "Law and order must and will be maintained in this city." Walter White was right about the mayor. Gotham was no Detroit. La Guardia was different, and so was the NYPD.[13]

In the days and weeks after the uproar, the mayor received considerable praise from across the city and nation for his prompt and prudent response to the uprising but also criticism.[14] The first lady, Eleanor Roosevelt, arriving the Monday after the calm of riot, spoke at Greenwich House, Twenty-Seven Barrow Street. She asked the city not to worsen the problems that caused the riot and stated, "I hope that those who control the riots will keep their heads and behave in a kindly way."[15] Some whites applauded the mayor, but others censured him for aiding and abetting criminal behavior. In his column, "Fair Enough," Westbrook Pegler believed that La Guardia was given more credit than he deserved. According to Pegler, "In the first place, . . . the authority of the police has been systematically undermined in Harlem during La Guardia's time in office." Pegler touted the now familiar narrative that the mayor "put handcuffs on the policemen to hamper them in dealing with offenders who would be slapped down fast and locked up as a matter of routine if the law were faithfully and impartially enforced in Harlem."[16]

White New Yorkers also wrote La Guardia, giving him commendation and condemnation. Beatrice Lindemann "thanked God for" La Guardia's leadership. She recalled how the mayor—"quiet, determined, full of confidence and reassurance"—calmed her after she heard about the attack on Pearl Harbor on December 7, 1941. La Guardia's voice on August 2 once again put her at ease, and she believed that "millions of others had the same reaction." Some expressed appreciation for La Guardia's handling of the uprising but demanded that he address social and economic conditions in Harlem. Mrs. Herman Lass urged the mayor to improve housing conditions and was convinced that "once the Negros in Harlem are given a chance to pay a fair rental for their apartments, a fair price for their food, etc., we will have eliminated the causes for any future 'off the beam' actions on the part of our Negro citizens." Roy Whitman, labor leader, Industrial Insurance Agents Union, Local 30, encouraged the establishment of an interracial committee for the city. Whitman tailored his letter as a critique of racial discrimination and a push for greater municipal resources and improved "race relations." He congratulated La Guardia on La Guardia's prompt and measured response and explained that the mayor's cooperation with Black and labor leaders "prevented a more serious disturbance than occurred." Some white letter writers, however, were not impressed and complained about La Guardia's alleged favoritism to Black people.[17]

One resident from Brooklyn, asked, "Well now that the volcano has erupted, what do you intend to do now with your negro problem?" Echoing journalist Pegler, the letter writer charged, "It is about time we get real honest to goodness, police protection, meaning that the police should be allowed to use their guns. You know the police don't love you (oh yeah?) right now." Another letter writer who signed as "Group of White People" blamed councilman Adam Clayton Powell Jr., claiming that Powell misled the public about the high rents and food prices that Black people paid for. The letter writer asked, "Do not we whites have to pay the same high prices for rent and food on much less than what a great percentage of the niggers are making or how come that the nigger can afford to dress and strut far better than a lot of the whites." White New Yorkers' resentment extended beyond the alleged "crime problem" and the uprising. They used crime as a prism to articulate their own insecurities regarding their own economic situation and vulnerabilities in the housing market. Their criticisms of Blacks' sartorial choices disclosed their own expectations of wartime responsibility as well as their sense of loyalty and envy. White people, the letter complained, were forced to "vacate for niggers," because Blacks voluntarily paid higher rents for housing. The letter writer questioned, "WHAT ARE WE WHITE AMERICANS FIGHTING FOR AND HAVE FOUGHT FOR? TO MAKE AMERICA SAFE FOR THE NEGRO." The letter writer portended violence, "If one race can riot for their so-called rights, so can another and we will," and asserted that there should be "a boundary line." The letter writer asked that La Guardia keep Blacks out of white neighborhoods "in their ridiculous zoot suits and airs of defiance and gaping after every white girl that passes," and to restrict them to Harlem. The letter closed with, "The above applies to the Spics too, as they are the forerunners of the negroes."[18]

Following the lead of La Guardia, Black leaders immediately asserted that the uproar was not a "race riot."[19] Though many civic, religious, reform, and civil rights groups applauded La Guardia's and Police Commissioner Lewis Valentine's management of the "disorder" without excessive force, they also reminded him of the social and economic factors that triggered the commotion. Others focused on the problem of hoodlumism, while others blamed police brutality and the mayor's failure to address these conditions in the city that hobbled the Black community.

Walter White blamed the "disorder" on Harlemites' righteous discontent with the widespread and incessant news of whites' mistreatment of and violence against Black soldiers, especially in military bases in the South splattered over the front pages of Black weeklies across the nation. White lauded La Guardia and Valentine, who "set a new pattern of community relationship." With the aid of the police, and especially the mayor's recruitment of Harlem's Black leadership, "the decent people of Harlem had been rallied to vigorous opposition to the criminal element." It was not a race riot, White insisted, but "festering evils" that turned "human beings into mobbists."[20]

Roy Wilkins, editor of *The Crisis*, followed White's lead. In the September issue, he wrote, "In the minds of Harlemites that Sunday night the gun in the hands of a good New York policeman doing his duty was the gun in the hands of Dixie cops shooting down men in the uniform."[21] Arthur G. Hays, a member of the Mayor's Commission and chairman of the subcommittee on the cause of uproar in 1935, made similar comments as White's in his letter to the *New York Times*. Hays, long a civil rights and civil liberties activist, asserted, "The recent riot, like that of 1935, was an explosion induced by pent-up feelings of resentment." But unlike the NAACP officials, Hays complained about the pattern of police violence in the city and detailed the committee's recommendations to reform the NYPD, noting that, as far as he knew, the "recommendations . . . were ignored."[22] Max Yergan, president of the National Negro Congress, urged "Mayor La Guardia and mayors of thirty other key American cities to 'establish, immediately, local interracial committees, designed to help prevent the occurrence or recurrence of racial outbreaks.'" Yergan asserted that the riot was the result of racial discrimination but also municipal neglect. According to Yergan, "Despite the gratifying fact that the disturbances did not assume the character of a race riot, the wholesale destruction of property and the amazingly quick activation of masses of Harlem citizens on the basis of an unfounded rumor, are vivid and costly indications of the necessity for action on the part of the City Administration."[23] A. Philip Randolph condemned "hoodlumism" but asserted that "Negroes must stand up and fight for their constitutional and economic rights with the ballot . . . and all means lawful and orderly."[24]

Many Black Harlemites, however, blamed hoodlums for the looting and violence that destroyed the jobs and property of Harlemites, as well as sullied the community's respectability. John Newton Griggs, a Black attorney, told the mayor that he misdirected his message to the law-abiding people of Harlem. In 1941, Griggs shared his thoughts on juvenile crime and discipline in schools in the *New York Age*. He wrote to Ludlow W. Werner's column "Across the Desk" and congratulated Werner for his editorial that promoted corporal punishment. Two years later, Griggs advised La Guardia "that the appeal [that should] be used with the people engaged in this disgraceful episode is force." Moral suasion had no place in disciplining this "class of people." Accordingly, he encouraged the mayor to unleash the "'Joe Brown' type and permit them to exercise their own discretion." In the past, Griggs recalled, there was an officer named Joe Brown, whom "hoodlums and street corner loafers" feared. Once they saw Brown on his beat, they promptly fled. Emphasizing the efficacy of punishment, he wrote, "No honeyed words were used to persuade them to move on."[25]

As Griggs's letter also asserted, the Black community interpreted the rioting and looting through the lens of race and community that bespoke of Harlem's community values and reputation. Theodore H. Hernandez, a letter writer to the *New York Amsterdam News*, expressed that the participants "should feel ashamed."[26] Harlemites rejected violent behavior as reckless and irresponsible, especially because they had to pay the cost, symbolically and physically, for the violence. Injustice required a response, but few were convinced that criminal behavior was the right answer. Hernandez asserted that there were no excuses "for what happened in Harlem on a Sunday night." Distinguishing the majority of the law-abiding community from the offending minority, "the hoodlums, the drunken, the criminal element," he asked the readers not to "blame all Harlem for the crime of the relative few." Another letter writer, leaving only the initials L. A. C., blamed Harlem's Black community, especially Black parents, for allowing criminal behavior to wreak havoc on the neighborhood. For too long, parents had ignored their children's poor behavior. Yet now because they turned a blind eye to the misconduct of their "offspring and defend him at any cost . . . now they have done this terrible thing." The letter writer asked, "Whom have they hurt?" Answering their own question, the writer lamented, "Their own race." L. A. C. continued, "The clothes from the cleaning places and tailors were our clothes. . . . The shops they have wrecked are the shops that are giving our people work."[27]

The letter writers believed that the "decent people" needed to take back Harlem and "let the other people of the world know that our race can live in a community decently and in order." L. A. C. was especially concerned about the reputation of Harlem, noting that in most cities "the Black Belt is the Criminal Belt." Harlem *was* different, but it was "on its way to be like the others." Furthermore, as Harlemites had complained in the past, "Our men who should be defending the Negro women were accosting them by placing their knives to their throats and in their sides . . . taking them to parks and roof-tops and raping them."[28] Harlemites understood the uprising as an extension of Harlem's long-discussed and long-debated "crime problem," and while they were critical of the "relative few," they framed it as both an intracommunity affair and a wider social and economic problem. So while L. A. C. doubted that an improved economic situation would address the "moral degeneracy and lack of religion," Hernandez framed the solution as a social and economic problem that might be addressed through "activat[ing] every agency in our community in the cause of a new and hygienic attitude to the trying problems which are not of our making—our newspapers, churches, welfare, fraternal, political and social organizations of one accord."[29]

But many Black New Yorkers and journalists rejected the "hoodlumism" rhetoric. In his column, "Pointed Points," the New York Amsterdam News's S. W. Garlington wrote, "While it is wise to make such emphasis as a deterrent against future outbreaks, we are neither frank nor foresighted if we fail to admit that the riots were attacks by Negroes on the PROPERTY of whites. In this sense, they were race riots, for they expressed the resentment of Negroes against the white world which the Harlem property represented."[30] Dan Burley, also a journalist of the same Black weekly, similarly asserted, "The angle on the riot most of the boys will probably miss is that despite the odious aspect of the thieving, destruction and vandalism present, the outburst was in reality a revolt of the common people against the symbols of white supremacy they contend with every day. Symbols, mind you, not personalities. Otherwise, many whites would have been attacked and a real race riot would have been on."[31]

Writing for the Pittsburgh Courier, J. A. Rogers directed his analysis of the uprising to segregation in the city. With the construction of Stuyvesant Town underway, as well as extortionate rents that Harlemites paid, Rogers compared Gotham City, the "most enlightened city in America," to "some God-forsaken town in Mississippi." Recalling the aftermath of the 1935 uprising, Rogers had then urged Mayor La Guardia and the city council to equalize the rents. The exorbitant rent that landlords fleeced from Black New Yorkers, conditions that residential segregation fostered, deepened their resentment of the pervasive and interlocking racist conditions in the city. Rogers wrote, "This color tax makes me mad every time I have to fork it out and I feel that the sole thing that kept me out of that outbreak Sunday night was because my education and training have made a coward of me. 'The cowardice of culture.' And there are thousands of educated Negroes who feel as I do over rent-gouging." Rogers was not solely writing for himself. "Hoodlums" and "zoot-suiters" were not the lone participants in the uproar, in other words. Blacks of some economic standing, Burley argued, took the circumstances of the occasion as an opportunity to "get even" and threw bricks "with vengeance." Their education, as Rogers admitted, could not shield them from racism and residential segregation.[32] Wilfred H. Kerr, a Brooklynite, believed the uprising "was the direct result of the American system of discrimination, segregation and police brutality against the Negro people." The neighborhood's drugstores, groceries, and meat markets sold Harlemites overpriced and inferior goods. Kerr wrote, "Many good people [were] fed up to the core with the cheating and robbery of the Harlem storekeepers, [and] the laxity and inefficiency of the O.P.A. [Office of Price Administration]."[33] Questioning the efficacy of the La Guardia administration to address the conditions of the Black poor, Rogers claimed that they had no other opportunity to receive justice or revenge except by "exploding from time to time." Segregation in the city, he argued, explained the conditions that produced hoodlums. Black New Yorkers, especially the poor, Rogers asserted, exploded "because they are robbed and dogged around within the law, which law includes the unwritten law of jim crow."[34]

Rogers soberly interrogated criticisms among Harlem's leadership that targeted hoodlums as the perpetrators of the uproar. He encouraged the "better salaried Negroes" to try to understand the combined impact of racial and economic inequality on the Black poor. Noting that Black crime harmed both Blacks and whites, he asked, "Whose fault is it that they are 'hoodlums'?" Rogers urged the readers, "Look at the faces of the hundreds of those arrested Sunday night and you'll see that without exception they belong to the underprivileged, uneducated class, the people who never had a chance."[35] Dan Burley and Rogers questioned Black leaders' connection to the Black working class, especially the youth. Rather than knowing "the little guy way down on the ladder," they alienated working people. Burley asserted that they had scarcely offered the poor concrete solutions, but only held only mass meetings and issued resolutions.[36] Rogers opined, "The fact is that few, if any of these submerged Negroes have ever heard of Walter White or Max Yergan, or the Rev. John Johnson, and when they see these well-fed, well-dressed, cultured Negroes, who are miles above them, among white people, cautioning them to be good, the contempt of these roustabouts for such other Negroes is great." He concluded, "They regard them as enemies, especially as some of them appeared Sunday with white policemen, whom the underprivileged have especial cause to hate." Black leadership's proximity to whiteness, embodied and symbolic, and law

FIGURE 8.4 During the Harlem Riot of 1943, the owner of this clothing store posted signs to make sure people would know that it was a "colored store," that is, that it was owned by an African American, in the hopes it would be undamaged. Bettmann via Getty Images.

enforcement widened their distance from the "submerged," especially as they too often framed political and economic matters as moral ones, such as "cautioning them to be good."[37]

The daily interruption of police violence that Black New Yorkers endured cast a shadow on the public's approval of the NYPD during the uprising. Blacks were victims and witnesses to police brutality, and their memory of police violence had outlasted their initial entanglement with the police. Recounting the Rhythm Club incident, as Ethelred Brown had done months before, Frank Perry, a letter writer to the *New York Amsterdam News*, reminded readers and Harlemites of the racist question and behavior of the police officer, noting that this recent upheaval held much in common with the 1935 uproar, when the rumor of the police killing of Lino Rivera stirred up the ire of the Black community.[38] Perry argued, "The incident which precipitates a riot is not the cause of a riot. Rather, one must look for such causes in a long chain of historical events." Thus, police misconduct in Harlem was more than a local phenomenon. It was tethered, Kerr believed, to the nationwide violence exacted upon Black people. He lamented, "Police brutality is common in Harlem and the shooting of Negro soldiers in the North as well as the South is not uncommon." Harlem's uprising, from this perspective, not only was representative of Black America's frustrations and legitimate rage, but it was one link on a long, powerful chain of collective racism, injustice, and anti-Black violence. As Kerr averred, "Beaumont, Mobile, Los Angeles and Detroit all add up to Harlem. Let no fine drawn distinctions between these other riots and Harlem be made. Their causes are the same."[39] Another letter writer, with the initials B. W., also placed the Harlem uprising in a national and international context but centered the war effort, the violence against Black soldiers, and the need for self-protection. He asked why should a "citizen police shoot a soldier," since the police military were responsible for handling soldiers' misconduct. He reminded readers that Black soldiers fought for this country and urged Black people to arm themselves. He complained, "Why shouldn't we, the Negroes, carry arms. We don't have any chan[c]e for protection. Any police will shoot us down as if we are dogs."[40]

For many Harlemites, the uproar manifested from criminal elements of the community, evoking disappointment and shame. Harlemites and Black New Yorkers had persistently complained that crime was a problem. The riot exposed, for everyone willing to see, that safety was not simply the protection of Black individuals but also about their own community. And yet safety meant more than security from criminal acts. The riot loudly spoke to a broader sense of safety. Black families' patriotism and willingness to send their loved ones off to war to fight for their country and democracy could not shield them from police violence, municipal neglect, economic exploitation, and residential segregation. Despite the efforts of Black leaders to address these issues, they could not. La Guardia's experiment with racial liberalism had imploded.

"A Sort of Revolution of the Common Man"

On August 13, A. Philip Randolph and the Negro Labor Assembly (NLA) held an emergency meeting concerning the riot and adopted resolutions that were later used as the basis for their recommendations to the mayor.[41] In late September, the Citizens' Committee on Better Race Relations (CCBRR) formed after the riot, built upon the resolutions adopted by the NLA, and published them as a pamphlet, *Recommendations for Action*.[42] The CCBRR centered federal and governmental discrimination and segregation. Citing "the inequalities imposed by the federal government," the CCBRR asserted, "All of the inequalities . . . burst forth with what was not just hooliganism or vandalism but a violent and surging protest—actually a sort of revolution of the common man." The CCBRR approached these issues at the federal and local levels and urged La Guardia to call President Franklin D. Roosevelt to issue an executive order to abolish "Jim Crowism" across the nation, including the government and the armed forces. It also recommended that La Guardia create a commission on race relations consisting of representatives of all groups that would address labor issues and social agencies and "recommend for execution the report of the Mayor's own Committee of 1935." The CCBRR wanted Blacks in positions of leadership, including the police department.[43] The CCBRR did not blame "hoodlumism," as Walter White had and would again a month later. Of course, the CCBRR knew La Guardia would do no such thing, but it was a sober reminder to the public and the mayor that he was partly responsible for the rioting. Rather than describe the looters as a "mob," like White, the CCBRR labeled their actions a "protest," as an extension of "a sort of revolution of the common man."

As debate about the rebellion died down, Walter White and the NAACP organized a conference, scheduled for September 25, in response to the riot. Mayor La Guardia opened the conference enumerating the progress the city had made under his administration "toward interracial unity." Affirming his support and respect for the city's Black leadership and that there was more work to be done, La Guardia pledged that he would continue to seek their "advice and counsel." Following the mayor, White immediately condemned hoodlumism and the violence of the riot, describing the riot as "needless destruction of life and property." As White opined, the riot "humiliated and embarrassed the law-abiding citizens of that part of New York City." Harlem's rage was mainly a response to their frustration with "prejudice and violence against Negro soldiers." Only through interracial unity and the erasure of prejudice and bigotry could true democracy come about. As White explained, "I do feel that we have got to break down the indifference, apathy, prejudice and ignorance of each of us about the other, so that we can find a practical means of tackling these problems, not for the benefit of Jews, Negroes, Catholics or foreign born, but for the benefit of all the people."[44]

The conference made eleven "suggestions for immediate action," with the first eight directed at long-standing demands that the NAACP and other organizations had made well before the war. The conference centered interracial unity and collaboration on all political, economic, and social issues, including "full protection of consumers interests in Harlem," "equal employment opportunities for all," affordable housing, adequate health care and education, and child welfare. The conference recommended that a "Negro appointee" be placed on "all municipal policy-making bodies concerned with education, health, police protection, and other community services." Glaringly absent, however, from the conference and the report was a discussion of police brutality. The series of Black street crimes against whites across the city, as well as the publicity around the so-called crime wave, had sullied Black New York's reputation. Consequently, instead of questioning La Guardia's police force's brutality against the Black soldier, the conference focused on the war, the unquestionable loyalty of Black soldiers, and the nation's unyielding commitment to ignoring their contribution to the war effort. White and the conferees flatly ignored the criticisms leveled at La Guardia coming from Black Harlem. White reframed the Harlem uprising as the home front phase of the war for democracy abroad. The "Statement of Resolutions Committee" read, "The first purpose of everyone concerned about the Harlem disturbance of August 1st was to restore law and order." Certainly, the committee's appeal to law and order reflected a broad swath of Black New York. Acknowledging this, the committee explained that the riot was an "unhappy night" and that it was "unanimously and completely deplored." This time, La Guardia had restrained his routinely brutal police force. With preparation, the NYPD had been unusually civil, at least in comparison to the police in Detroit. Without the spectacle of conspicuous police violence, Black people had to take "responsibility for helping to maintain city order and promote racial unity and good citizenship."[45] The plans and recommendations from the Black left and liberals were reinforced partly by the *New York Amsterdam News*.

Beginning in mid-September, over the next eight weeks, the *New York Amsterdam News* published an article per issue about the different issues raised in the La Guardia Commission report to gauge if there had been progress made between the report and the recent uprising. Overall, the *New York Amsterdam News* "believed that . . . most of the basic causes that led to the 1935 riot still remain in Harlem today." Despite all the published surveys on Black New York, including the La Guardia Commission's report, the City-Wide Citizens' Committee on Harlem's reports, and others documenting widespread racial inequality, little had been done. Months before in April, the Black weekly complained about this "classic pattern" of investigating a problem, which "add[ed] nothing new."[46] The Black weekly held La Guardia accountable. Each article reminded readers that the mayor hushed up his own report. A. M. Wendell Malliet, authoring most of the editorials, asserted, "It would have been difficult to accuse the mayor of bad faith to suppressing the report of his commission if he had taken action with Commission's recommendations but, with possible minor improvements in one municipal department or another, there is not the slightest evidence of any social reforms that would prevent the periodic rioting in Harlem."[47]

Rereading the Mayor's Commission's chapter on housing, Malliet still found that "economic and racial barriers . . . held the Negro population within certain limits." The wartime economic recovery, he believed, had "enlarged the problem of housing," and because of the racial barriers, Blacks moved out of Harlem to other neighborhoods in Brooklyn, the Bronx, and Long Island. The *New York Amsterdam News*'s commentary on health, schools, and the police department betrayed the same pattern. Reporting the high rates of venereal disease and syphilis in the early 1940s, the Black weekly explained that the rates represented not a "moral problem" but a "slum problem," a problem of "poverty, overcrowding, ignorance, and lack of health facilities."[48] The conditions, including the inadequate accommodations at Harlem Hospital, were not dissimilar to those documented in the mayor's 1936 commission report. The city had made considerable progress in the school building program, but the La Guardia administration made these improvements in areas that bordered Black and white neighborhoods. Public School (P.S.) 194, at 144th Street between Seventh and Eighth Avenues, was the only school building built since 1935 in the area where the majority of Black Harlem resided, above 135th Street.

In the neighborhoods in Central and Lower Harlem, La Guardia built five schools. According to the Mayor's Commission, P.S. 89, which had been built in 1889 and renovated in 1895, was perhaps the worst school in neighborhood. Malliet lamented that while the Mayor's Commission had recommended that the school "'be condemned and torn down' . . . nothing has been done except a few coats of paint to cover filth and dirt." He questioned the mayor's commitment and explained that if La Guardia had desired to make any significant educational improvements in Harlem, "[the city] would have started at 135th Street and Lenox Avenue, the location of Harlem problem school building No. 1." Malliet pointed out that the commission's most important recommendation was for the mayor to appoint a Black educator to the Board of Education, but it had, he claimed, "never been treated seriously." While other groups, racial and religious, were represented on the board, Blacks were not. He believed that this was a test of the mayor's belief in democracy for Black New Yorkers. And his failure to appoint a Black educator indicated that the mayor's belief in democracy for Blacks was "lip service, nothing more or less." He wondered if it was too much to expect the Department of Education to behave differently, since none of the other city departments had treated Black New Yorkers better. "Jim Crow and segregation," he asserted, "based as they have always been, on race prejudice affect the Negro's life and development in New York City, as it does in almost every other city of the nation."[49]

Commenting on the New York Police Department and the La Guardia administration, the *New York Amsterdam News* concluded that the relationship had not changed and that it remained disappointing. The conviction among Harlemites and Black New Yorkers that the police department was brutal and criminal was unchanged. The police officer, Black and white, was "a hated figure." The Black weekly reported, "The people accuse him of brutality, race prejudice, collusion in keeping the prostitution houses, brothels, gambling dens and policy racket wide open." According to the *New York Amsterdam News*, the NYPD assigned maligned officers to Harlem as punishment. Harlem was "Siberia" for these officers, who arrived with "a persecution-complex and grievances," which made them "unfit" to serve and protect in Harlem. They "may be of questionable character and others of low moral character," rendering them unsuitable to "constitute a force to handle the police problems" of a community that had unique problems within its own "borders and among its own residents." Shifting from police brutality to the treatment of Black police officers, the Black weekly asked why Black policemen were not found in areas outside of the "Black belt" of the city's metropolitan area and why they were not promoted higher than sergeant. "Only on special occasions are Negro policemen seen on lower Fifth Ave. Broadway, Times Square, Park Ave., Madison Ave., and other ritzy sections of the city," the *New York Amsterdam News* reported. The Black weekly, speaking for the Black community, claimed that the recruitment, treatment, and assignment of Black officers seemed to operate "in the interest of the dominant white group."[50]

The *New York Amsterdam News*'s appraisal of the uprising differed from and was complementary with both conferences, but it held most in common with the CCBRR's. As the Black press and letters to the mayor noted, many Black New Yorkers held distaste for the riot. So Walter White's appeals to law and order, as well as the shame that some Blacks felt, faithfully spoke to the sentiments of Black community. Yet Harlemites' criticism of the looting and damage to property must be understood as an expression of their long-standing demands for safety in Harlem and across the city. The relative restraint the NYPD displayed during the conflagration was notable but calculated. La Guardia and Valentine's anticipation and preparation to control the police were a political maneuver, and with the help of White and others, they chose to restrain the NYPD, an approach passed over before the uprising. The absence of police accountability and the inequality in other arenas of local government were precisely the point of the *New York Amsterdam News*'s series' assessment of La Guardia's suppressed report. In its recounting of the report from the vantage point of fall 1943, the Black weekly went further than CCBRR. The topical chapters of the Mayor's Commission's report were much more damning than its recommendations. By presenting the evidence and pointing out the gap between the mayor's rhetoric and his administration's investment in Harlem, the series judged him derelict and responsible for the uprising. Despite White's silence on the inadequacies of La Guardia and his appeals to racial and ethnic unity, the conference's recommendations aligned with the Black weekly's overall argument, but much needed to be done. Rather than critique La Guardia, however, White pursued the NAACP's war objectives and reinforced its loyalty to the mayor.

"One of the Worst Areas in This Entire State"

Weeks after the uproar, Mayor La Guardia's handling of crime and race was tested once again. This time in Brooklyn's "Little Harlem," Bedford-Stuyvesant. In mid-August, Norman R. Silver, an attorney, sent a letter to the grand jury to complain about "hoodlumism." According to Silver's letter, "Residents and business people ha[d] been terrorized, beaten and robbed." Silver's letter jump-started the Kings County August Grand Jury's investigation into crime in the area.[51] In late September at the Bedford Branch of the YMCA, John A. Tracy, chairman of the delinquency committee of the Central Brooklyn Midday Club, demanded the augmentation of the police presence and the arrest and punishment of the "packs of wolves." William S. Webb, district tax supervisor, explained that it was not "'a Negro problem' but one of 'law enforcement,'" and he advocated for stiffer sentences and that "police be given 'a freer hand,'" concluding that "freedom from fear is all right, but at times a little fear goes a long way." Angered by the crime news and disgruntled by the slow progress of the grand jury, Silver wrote a letter to Leon Alexander, the foreman of the grand jury. Like Tracy and Webb, Silver stated, "This is not a social problem but a criminal one and requires prompt criminal enforcement."[52]

On November 15, the August Grand Jury of Kings County submitted a presentment to the court. The presentment, "In the Investigation of Crime and Disorderly Conditions of the Bedford-Stuyvesant Area of Brooklyn," described Bedford-Stuyvesant as a neighborhood in decline. According to the presentment, the neighborhood had changed from "one of the finest residential sections of this borough" to "one of the worst areas in this entire state." Bedford-Stuyvesant had become a place of lawlessness and immorality, where all manner of crime thrived unencumbered. Prostitution and petty and violent crime pervaded the neighborhood. Schoolchildren were unsafe, and respectable residents were afraid to walk the streets before and especially after nightfall. As the presentment described, "At least one church has been robbed. Innocent and law-abiding citizens have been assaulted, robbed, and murdered and insulted both on the public streets and on public conveyance traversing through this area."[53]

Race and Black youth crime, the usual targets of public condemnation, were scarcely mentioned in the grand jury's presentment. The report first alluded to race when it mentioned that respectable Blacks in the neighborhood complained about crime. After describing Bedford-Stuyvesant as a crime-ridden cesspool, the grand jury stated, "The foregoing conditions have been testified to by many, eminent, responsible and trustworthy Colored citizens of this area. They strongly deplore these conditions and have asked and appealed to this Grand Jury to do something about them." The testimonies of Black Brooklynites substantiated the grand jury's claim that crime was not an expression of racism or necessarily characteristic of the "Negro problem." Perhaps anticipating criticisms from the Black community, the presentment stated flatly that street crime was "in no sense a race problem" but "purely a social and law enforcement problem which calls for prompt action and immediate attention." And yet, La Guardia, during his interview with the grand jury, questioned their line of racial reasoning. Quoting the mayor, the presentment read, "'Let's be more frank about it—this is the Negro question we are talking about.' He added, 'I know that the Police Department is making a sincere and honest effort to control it.' He added, 'Well, it is pretty tough; when a neighborhood changes its complexion that way there is bound to be trouble. . . . Some of these younger criminals are pretty bad.'" Rather than denying the role of race and Blackness, La Guardia spoke to the fact of Black crime. The mayor's rejoinder to the grand jury's presentment would later expand upon his administration's explanation for crime. The presentment's infrequent mention of race in the document echoed the color-blind discourse and liberal politics of the La Guardia administration. The appearance of silences on race and Blackness reflected not only a strategy to represent a neutral stance on crime but also how the association between criminality and Black people had been normalized in public discussions of crime in the city.[54]

If the problem of crime in Bedford-Stuyvesant was undeniable, so was the negligence of Mayor La Guardia. The grand jury commended the efforts of police officers, acknowledging their competence and efficiency after the committal of crime. The ubiquity of "disorders and crimes" in the neighborhood therefore was not primarily a problem of policing but a problem of governance. When questioned about crimes, the mayor "admitted that they existed and stated that 'it is a most unpleasant and difficult problem.'" La Guardia reported, however, that Commissioner Valentine had assured him that "the police are trying to stay on top of that situation." The grand jury judged La Guardia derelict because he offered no concrete plan of action. Instead, he "told this Grand Jury that they are powerless to do any more than they have been doing to ameliorate these conditions." Incredulous, the presentment asserted that the mayor held executive power, and therefore La Guardia had the means and the authority to deploy the police department to serve and protect. From the perspective of the grand jury, rather than lacking the power, La Guardia lacked the will to act and ensure the safety of the citizens. As the presentment charged, "It is not enough for Public Officials in possession of power and under an affirmative duty of preserving the peace and preventing crimes, to say that they can do no more under such circumstances."[55]

At the end of the summary of the investigation, the grand jury enumerated eleven recommendations to the mayor. The usual demands, such as more supervised recreation, playgrounds, and police officers in targeted areas, were listed, but the grand jury also demanded that the mayor "take steps to make it unlawful for crowds to congregate in public without a police license" and "to direct the police to take far more vigorous physical action against groups of roaming hoodlums." As a problem of governance and not merely policing, the grand jury wanted to create a police presence nearing a police state in Bedford-Stuyvesant, where "roaming hoodlums" demanded the proper punishment.[56]

The day the Kings County Grand Jury delivered the presentment, La Guardia charged that it was "entirely political!" and the next day, he ordered Police Commissioner Valentine to conduct an investigation of crime conditions in Bedford-Stuyvesant. The mayor commanded Valentine to "study every single charge or insinuation made in that presentment and investigate each one of them thoroughly and completely," because he wanted the "truth, the whole truth and nothing but the truth." Like Harlem after its 1935 uprising, La Guardia and Valentine made "Brooklyn's Harlem [an] Armed Camp." Valentine deployed 420 police officers to the section to interview the residents and the religious community as well as to comb the records of the six precincts in the neighborhood. According to the *PM*, "One out of every sixty persons in Brooklyn's Bedford-Stuyvesant sections is a policeman today." In addition to unearthing the "truth and nothing but," La Guardia hoped the investigation might also offset criticism leveled at him by the Midtown Civic League's petition that had been submitted independently to Governor Thomas E. Dewey before the grand jury's presentment became public.[57]

The Midwood Civic League, led by Sumner A. Sirtl, with the support of over 400 men and women from the area, put the petition together to complain to the governor about La Guardia's failure to protect Bedford-Stuyvesant residents from crime. Commenting on the grand jury's presentment, Sirtl said that it reflected exactly what "the Bedford section have known for a long time," echoing complaints he had made in the late 1930s, as discussed in chapter 5. Along with fearing crime, explained Sirtl, their property values had suffered and investments in homes and mortgages had been lost because longtime homeowners had left their homes "through fear because of inadequate police protection." Monsignor John L. Belford, pastor of the Roman Catholic Church of the Nativity, who had complained for the past ten years that Bedford-Stuyvesant was "a disgrace to the city," also spoke with the *Brooklyn Daily Eagle*. Belford thought the conditions detailed in the presentment were "more drastic than I thought it would be." He believed that "anarchy" existed in the district because of Black youth's disrespect for the police and law and order and the mayor's support of their behavior. Characterizing the bravado of Black youth, Belford described how they might speak to a patrolman: "'If you lay a hand on me I'll complain to the Mayor' and to the teachers, 'I'll have you fired.'" He continued, "The trouble has been the interference of the Mayor. He tells the police to deal gently with the Negro, not to use the nightstick."[58]

Judge Peter J. Brancato of the County Court agreed with the grand jury's demands for more punishment. Brancato, employing the power of the court, had recently done his part to punish Black criminals in the neighborhood. The judge sentenced two brothers, Haywood and Dannie

Gettys, to twenty years to life for murder in the second degree, and ten to twenty years for manslaughter in the second degree, respectively, for killing John Myers in a bar and grill in late May. Explaining his sentencing, Brancato stated, "Where moral suasion falls and crime is rampant, a police-man's unfettered nightstick and good stiff prison sentences by the court are the panacea for a reign of terror." Brancato questioned La Guardia's commitment to stopping crime, especially the reasonableness of his using more than 400 police officers to interview residents and investigate alleged illegal and legal businesses. From Brancato's perspective, the police's nightsticks, not "data-gathering," was the more effective way to repress the "element of youthful hoodlums who disregard law and order." Magistrate Abner C. Surpless of the Felony Court held similar convictions as his counterpart. Surpless recommended a change in policy to discourage defendants from using a knife as an assault weapon. He also believed that the problem of crime in Bedford-Stuyvesant was the consequence of La Guardia abandoning his responsibility. He proposed, "If the Mayor is not going to back up the police, this court, in cooperation with the District Attorney, must let the word out to anyone carrying a knife that there will be a $5,000 bail in the future."[59]

The Black press and Black leadership mobilized to defend themselves against white Bedford-Stuyvesant's attack on the Black community. The Black press generally accepted the presentment's findings that crime harmed the Bedford-Stuyvesant district but asserted that the characterizations were exaggerated. As the *New York Amsterdam News* opined, "It isn't a question as to whether it is 'political', as the Mayor claims, or not: with the [Black] people of Brooklyn it is a matter of law and order." The Black weekly, quoting an anonymous Black minister, asserted "If there are hoodlums in the community, and nobody denies that there are some, the police should drive them out. In fact, they should have been driven out long ago." But the minister, keen to both the presentment's racist underpinnings, despite its race-neutral, color-blind verbiage, and a swath of Bedford-Stuyvesant's white community's racial animosities, asserted, "We are determined, however, that our community shall not become a training ground for 'jungle fighters' or a target range for snipers." The Black press and the Black community, as readers of the white press and the grand jury's presentment, had been hearing and combating this rhetoric for several years. An article headlining the *New York Times*'s front page upheld the idea that the NYPD understood policing Black people and neighborhoods as a license to exact excessive force. Consistently calling the neighborhood "Little Harlem," the daily reported the state of mind of the officers assigned to the neighborhood on La Guardia's fact-finding mission. The *New York Times* stated, "The policemen seemed only sullen when they learned that they had been brought into Brooklyn's 'Little Harlem,' as it has come to be called, merely to conduct what one angrily termed 'a pencil and paper' beat, rather than augment the existing detail to put down hoodlumism with force."[60]

While the grand jury's presentment and the mayor's police department–led investigation appeared to gloss over the question of race and Blackness in Bedford-Stuyvesant, Black leaders and their liberal allies prioritized the roles of race, racism, and the negligence of the La Guardia administration. Walter White focused on the racist ideas undergirding the grand jury's presentment. According to White, the "allegation that the Bedford-Stuyvesant section of Brooklyn is a 'cesspool of filth' in a 'state of lawlessness' [wa]s shocking." He argued, "What else can New York City expect when some of its citizens because of race are herded into ghettos, victimized by bad housing and high rents and over-crowding, denied employment even in war industries which they must pay taxes to operate, and robbed of most of the incentive which causes others not so restricted to become decent citizens?" Jim Crow conditions in the city, White asserted, explained the problem of crime in Bedford-Stuyvesant. The Black community was committed to law and order, but they "want neither a 'kid gloves' nor a 'muss em up' policy."[61]

Bedford-Stuyvesant's Black community rejected the "anti-Negro" report. Black women were especially vocal. Speaking with *PM* reporter Evelyn Seeley, Mrs. Ada B. Jackson of 454 Halsey Street said she believed the report was an attempt to wreck interracial unity in the community. The president of P.S. 35's Parent-Teachers Association, head of the Stuyvesant-Bedford-Williamsburg Schools Council, and vice president of the United Parents Association, Jackson said the report was "a means to distract us from the real solution of our problems," charging that "the press uses it to smear our race." The report did not represent the views of the Black community—it was "definitely a lie." The Women Voters Council, an organization of 500 Black women, asked Bishop Thomas Molloy to remove Monsignor John L. Belford from the parish because they believed he was "a menace to the community." Mrs. Margaret V. Brown, the president of the council, noted that there were excellent priests in the neighborhood and named Monsignor Campion and Father James W. Asip of St. Peter Claver's Church, which had been founded for Blacks. She also pointed out that unlike Belford's church, the Church of the Holy Rosary, which had been predominantly white, "kept its doors open to the Negro population as it grew and ministered to their needs." She believed that the problem of the community could be addressed only through interracial solidarity. She reached out to President Henry Cashmore, the borough president, after the uprising in August to jump-start such an initiative, but he "did not reply."[62]

The City-Wide Citizens' Committee on Harlem (CWCCH) argued that the grand jury ignored the social and economic plight of the Black community and, more significantly, that the grand jury incriminated the entire Black community. The CWCCH stated plainly, "The Kings County Grand Jury statement constitutes on the face of it a severe indictment of the Negro community in the Bedford-Stuyvesant area." In addition to centering Blacks as the target of the presentment, the CWCCH also focused on governance and the La Guardia administration. La Guardia, the CWCCH asserted, shunned reports demonstrating the need for greater municipal investment from various private and public welfare agencies. In 1941, Department of Parks Commissioner Robert Moses and Paul Blanshard, then the executive director of the Society for the Prevention of Crime, in separate reports pointed out that the Bedford-Stuyvesant and South Jamaica areas had inadequate recreation and support for park employees. In the report, Moses stated, "Brooklyn today is still slightly worse off than the other boroughs from the point of view of neighborhood recreation. The need for additional playgrounds in Greenpoint, Williamsburg, Bedford-Stuyvesant, Park Slope, East New York, Brownsville, and Flatbush is attested by park, police, school, prosecuting, probation, and other authorities."[63]

The mayor "tossed the ball over to the church groups. We hope that they toss it right back to him" and asserted that the responsibility to remedy the situation "is still the responsibility of the Mayor and the City administration." Rather than delegating the responsibility to the churches, the CWCCH demanded that the mayor appoint an interracial, interfaith committee to investigate, make recommendations, and set up procedures for compliance. Incensed, the CWCCH claimed that La Guardia had consistently evaded the demands of various civic and neighborhood associations and coalitions, such as the Council against Intolerance in America, the Citizens Emergency Conference for Interracial Unity, and the Better Race Relations Committee, in Harlem that asserted that the mayor should appoint a committee with enforcement power. Because of La Guardia's evasiveness, harkening back to 1936 and the Black community's yearlong complaints about the mayor's failure to release his commission's report and the police occupation of Harlem, the CWCCH made "an appeal to you [La Guardia] through the press because it has been impossible from month to month for our group or any other group concerned with these issues to get an appointment with you or receive an answer to a letter."[64]

On November 20 the police commissioner delivered the *Report of the Police Commissioner to the Mayor* to La Guardia. The report, according to the *New York Times*, denied some of the charges of the grand jury and "refute[d] others." Admitting that crime in the district remained a problem, the report revealed that there were less crimes and more arrests in 1943 as compared to previous years. In the arena of juvenile delinquency, in the first ten months of the year, arrests were 32.4 percent higher than in 1942 and 53.4 higher than in 1941. Valentine's report explained that the "police have been aware of trouble potentialities in this area for some years due to the various social and economic transformations" in Bedford-Stuyvesant and that it had expanded law enforcement "to forestall any possibility of severe outbreak."[65] The expansion of the Black population, especially the disproportionate increase of Black youth, in the neighborhood contributed to juvenile delinquency, explained Valentine's deputy inspector William M. Kent. "Delinquency," he emphasized, "is a social problem." The movement of "underprivileged races" into the area led to overcrowding and the deterioration of housing conditions. While the presentment marked a rise in offenses, it did not explain why there was a rise. Kent made it plain that the causes were outside the realm of the police, and in fact, it was the Juvenile Aid Bureau's (JAB) efforts that prevented juvenile crime from getting worse.[66]

Employing statistics to disprove the presentment's claim that crime was widespread and that the mayor was responsible, Valentine's report reestablished the legitimacy of the police. According to Kent, the JAB held that there were several "agencies" responsible for crime prevention. The first was the home "with the Father the head, and the Mother, the heart," the second the neighborhood, and the final two were school and the church. He noted that the JAB cooperated with all the agencies. The bureau set up Neighborhood Councils, stationed in three of the ten centers in Bedford-Stuyvesant, and had "cooperated with [the schools, churches and] all Municipal and private social and welfare agencies." Thus, while the presentment demanded an increase in police presence, Valentine's report demonstrated that through the JAB law enforcement was deeply embedded in Black social, cultural, and religious life. Indeed, more than disproving the mayor's malfeasance, Kent argued not only that the police had anticipated crime and taken preemptive measures but also that it was law enforcement that kept crime at bay. While it endeavored to undermine the presentment's conclusions, the report reinforced the grand jury's color-blind framing of

Black youth crime or, as La Guardia called it, "the Negro question." In less neutral terms, by singling out the "underprivileged races," the NYPD made explicit what white Bedford-Stuyvesant had thought and mobilized around all along—that white people needed more protection and more policing to control Black people. At the same time, the NYPD's report enhanced its own legitimacy by directing blame toward other areas of government and social and cultural institutions of the city. Accordingly, as Kent notes, "If all the foregoing agencies played the part that they should play there would be little need for the Police Department to step in."[67]

The next day, the Midtown Civic League held a meeting attended by about 500 people, including some Black residents of Bedford-Stuyvesant, at the Bedford Branch of the Young Men's Christian Association at Bedford Avenue and Monroe Street. Monsignor Belford once again held Mayor La Guardia responsible for the crime in the district but also explained that landlords had rented their homes for low rents. The cheap rents, he claimed, attracted people who were "not desirable neighbors. They didn't care how they behaved or how their children behaved, as long as they didn't get arrested." As conditions became worse, complained Belford, whites in Bedford-Stuyvesant asked for police protection but were made to feel like their safety was not the police's priority. Belford stated, "We went to the captains of the precincts, but they told us that the cops were badly needed for strikes and other duties. Out of 100 policemen stationed in each precinct 60 to 65 were really available."[68]

Two speakers, unexpectedly, triggered an uproar. David Liebman of 297 Wyckoff Avenue, Brooklyn, an off-duty patrolman in plain clothes, explained that he worked in the Bronx, at the Simpson Street Station, where he encountered similar cases of "mugging" by "sunburnt elements," that is, by Black people. Liebman believed that an education and a decent home life might "cure" the conditions. He also employed the NYPD's discourse of police discretionary constraint. Liebman stated, "If we had more policemen we would be able to do a better job. The Mayor should investigate why the morale of the Police Department is at its lowest ebb in ten years." While Liebman's comments seemed measured, as compared to Belford's, they took for granted the general tone of meeting, that is, that La Guardia was responsible for the crime situation and that Black hoodlums were culpable for not only neighborhood crime but also, as Belford put it, making the neighborhood "unfit for human habitation." By supporting the expansion of the police presence, Liebman also endorsed Belford's and the presentment's demands for punishment. Repulsed by the speakers and attendants expressing demands for the punishment of Black youth, Henry S. Ashcroft, a Black attorney and probation officer, tried to pivot the discussion around the Black community's efforts to obtain better housing, schools, and recreation. In the midst of hisses and boos, he protested that the audience had been "treated to a fine tirade against the Negro race." Returning to the common theme of policing, he lamented, "We hear a great deal about police being shackled [but] what these speakers seem to want is to have the police use clubs as they please." This was followed by cries of "No."[69]

Along with the CWCCH and the NAACP, the New York City chapter of the National Lawyers Guild and Judge Nathan R. Sobel joined the Black community in its criticism of the grand jury's presentment. The National Lawyers Guild's report, written by Paul O'Dwyer, chairman of the Committee on Constitutional Liberties, and Samuel Rosenwein, executive secretary of the New York Chapter of the National Lawyer's Guild, stated that the presentment did "violence to basic concepts of orderly administration of justice and paves the way for incitement and provocation." The presentment should be criticized for what it said and for what it left out—that segregation, high rents, the horrible housing conditions under which Blacks lived, and discrimination in the war industries explained the conditions that thrived in Bedford-Stuyvesant. The report disputed the grand jury's presentment point by point, especially its recommendation that the police adopt a "muss 'em up" attitude. O'Dwyer and Rosenwein also regretted the recent espousal of punishment advocated by other public officials. They wrote, "From judges on the bench there have come vitriolic attacks on Negro offenders and the admonition that sentences will be unusually severe in their cases."[70]

In early December, Walter White asked Kings County judge Nathan R. Sobel to invite Black leaders to speak to the December Kings County Grand Jury. Sobel invited Henry Ashcroft to speak because he was "shouted down" before he could finish his comments at the meeting at the YMCA. On December 6, after the grand jury was sworn in, Sobel delivered a speech to the assembled body. Like White, the CWCCH, and the NLG before him, the judge highlighted the racial undertone of the August grand jury's presentment and the unequal distribution of resources, high rents, and discrimination Black people faced in New York City. Sobel questioned if the August grand jury really believed that Mayor La Guardia ordered police officers to not use their night sticks and contended that he was certain that La Guardia had never given such an order. "If Mayor La Guardia sought to protect the people of Bedford-Stuyvesant from abuse by police authorities, then he was serving," Sobel explained, "the same purpose as a Grand Jury." He concluded, "More policemen—yes; more Negro policemen in particular! But nightsticks never cure anything. Poverty is still poverty; hunger is still hunger; discontent is still discontent."[71]

After he completed his speech, Sobel left time for Ashcroft to share his thoughts about the presentment, the meeting, and the conditions for Blacks in Bedford-Stuyvesant. Ashcroft was thankful for the opportunity to speak to the grand jury and explained why he was invited and how he came to learn about the meeting held at the YMCA. Ashcroft's speech asserted the Black community's respectability and detailed the problems of crime, housing, discrimination, and the dearth of resources Black citizens had access to in Brooklyn. While Ashcroft's comments were representative of White's and those of others, he also expressed how the August grand jury presentment and the meeting harmed Black Brooklynites' dignity. He lamented, "The colored people residing in the real Bedford-Stuyvesant district have had their pride hurt, their sensibilities wounded, their intelligence overlooked and their daily livelihood endangered as a result of the incisive and acid language of the August Grand Jury's presentment." While he centered his comments on the social and economic aspects, he emphasized that "the colored people stand unalterably for the maintenance of law and order and the proper exercise of the police function without let or hindrance or discrimination based upon color, poverty or ignorance." Ashcroft ended his comments with observations that prioritized the safety of Black citizens in the district and encouraged interracial comity:

1. Repressive measures never solved social problems in any group, anytime, anywhere.
2. Any attempt to isolate minority population groups from the mainstream of community life, thought and effort, is injurious to the mental and social health of the community.
3. The need for the establishment of an officially sponsored interracial committee, charged with the responsibility of furthering cooperation and harmony among all elements of this city's population, is more apparent now than ever before.[72]

· · · · · ·

The Bedford-Stuyvesant moral panic overshadowed demands for more police in other parts of the city. Since mid-September, James A. Gumbs, the owner of the apartment building at 453 West 166th Street, and his attorney

Lloyd E. Dickens complained to the police about white youth vandalizing his building.[73] Blacks occupied all of the apartment buildings on 165th between Edgecombe and Amsterdam Avenues, but slowly the racial "boundary" was moving north. On October 14, whites threw bricks through the windows. Gumbs called the police, but they "refused to act and they told [him] the only thing they can do is send a policeman after an incident has happened" and "informed [him] that they cannot protect [the] property and the tenants in it from being further molested," impelling him to write a letter to the mayor.[74]

The bricks shattered the windows of the Lythcotts, a family of four: Alphonso, his wife Bernice, and their two sons, Alphonso Jr., two years old, and Leonard, one. Alphonso, the superintendent of the building, stated that the incidents were "directed at the Negro tenants and himself." Whites tore up and burned the signs that read "Newly Open for Colored Tenants" on three separate occasions. On October 8, after the last white family vacated the building, he said "hoodlums" broke into empty apartments and smashed the radiators and fixtures.[75] White gangs directed their frustrations and hate toward property *and* Black people. The Lythcotts were especially concerned because their children would be vulnerable to bricks coming through the window, since they slept in the room that faced the front of the building. Attorney Dickens said, "A gang of white boys set fire to an automobile belonging to a Negro repairman." When the repairman caught one of them, "a crowd of about 35 white neighbors" threatened him, and the policeman told him that "he caught the wrong boy and turned the lad loose." Afraid for her well-being, Mrs. Rosalee Crank, another resident, felt so "terrorized that she left her home and stayed all night in a hotel." Thereafter, Dickens sent telegrams and letters to the mayor, the district attorney's office, and the press. La Guardia ordered the police to protect Black tenants on the block, because the "block situation . . . threatened to develop into a major interracial clash, and give the city its second riot this year," suggested the *New York Amsterdam News*. Dickens warned "that unless something was done he feared the tenants planned to take the matter into their own hands." Whites also vandalized Building 461 on the same block with Black tenants, which was boarded up. They wrote a message on the building with orange paint that read, "The Nigers [*sic*] stink."[76]

For years, the Black press had complained about white youth crime and gang violence in Washington Heights. In March 1942, the *People's Voice* reported that "Negro tenants of 461 and 467 West 164th Street—the only two Negro-occupied houses in the block—are suffering indignities and property damage from white hoodlums." The families complained about the violence,

FIGURE 8.5 A mother holds her child behind broken glass in a door window, Harlem, 1943. Weegee states, "This tragic picture is of that evil thing, race hatred. Mrs. Bernice Lythcott and her one-year-old son Leonard look out through a window through which hoodlums threw stones." Weegee (Arthur Fellig) / International Center of Photography via Getty Images.

but the police were slow to respond. White youth shattered windows and anonymously knocked on doors. The vandalism had been going on since September 1941, and the police assigned a detail there, but after the November election, they departed. One tenant's infant "escaped death . . . when an iron pipe, thrown through her window, just grazed the baby's arm." According to the *People's Voice*, "The renewal of the trouble ha[d] caused alarm among the Negroes, most of whom fear for the safety of themselves and their children."[77]

In the midst of the Bedford-Stuyvesant moral panic and white youth vandalism, the *New York Amsterdam News* issued a clarion call about gang violence in the city. Characterizing white Brooklyn's outcries about crime, the Black weekly contended that they painted "a picture of Frankenstein escapades," questioning "why in the blazes of Hades this much effort isn't put on getting more recreation facilities for the area; bettering the current 'poor school' system; lowering the exorbitant rents and the hundreds of other things that would definitely quell delinquency."[78] Gang violence, however, was a problem of law enforcement, parental responsibility, and the lapse of moral edification. Tommy Watkins of the *New York Amsterdam News* wrote the gangs, "both white and colored," lacked "respect or understanding of the law and even of the simplest conceptions of human behavior in a modern society. . . . [They took] advantage of the wartime economy in which the police department is being decimated by the draft and the domestic front is in an unsettled condition." This posed serious problems for all New Yorkers, across class, race, ethnicity, and religion, since gang violence was not a "Negro problem," as the white press and the NYPD argued. Nonetheless, police targeted Black youth and Black people as if they were all criminals, despite scholarly evidence that juvenile crime increased in the city and across the nation for most groups. The mayor prioritized the safety of white New Yorkers. If he ignored whites' demands, La Guardia would have undermined the majority of the city's electorate. Police protection for Black New Yorkers, therefore, was separate and unequal. La Guardia's response to white youth violence in Washington Heights paled in comparison to his administration's campaign in Bedford-Stuyvesant. While he appeared to support Blacks in Brooklyn, he mobilized the police force to protect his administration. While Blacks in Washington Heights feared for their lives from white gangs, La Guardia, as the *PM* observed, made "Brooklyn's Harlem" an armed camp.[79]

The next summer, these dynamics would play out in Brooklyn. In early May, just before seven in the evening, Patrolman Abraham Fine broke up a fight among four Black men at 328 Tompkins Avenue near Quincy Street.

Fine grabbed one of the men, William B. Ford, aggressively, and Miss Helen Clayton, a Black woman, yelled, "Witness the brutality of the police toward Negro people! Let this man go!" As a crowd eventually gathered, growing to nearly 400 people, according to the *New York Amsterdam News*, others chastised Fine's belligerence, and then Mrs. Essie Davis "lunged at Fine . . . and scratched his face before being subdued." Ford and Clayton were arrested for disorderly conduct and Davis for felonious assault. As the people dispersed, they admitted to the Black weekly that they supported the police efforts to halt criminal activity in their neighborhood but objected to the "spasmodic outbursts of brutality by cops who have apparently let the recent Grand Jury crime report, lead them on." As one Black woman explained, "We don't mind the police getting the hoodlums and taking care of them. They deserve it. But some of the cops think everybody is a hoodlum and start beating them before they discover the trouble."[80]

"Won't Be Safe for Any White People"

Throughout the remainder of the La Guardia administration, deep racial tensions festered around juvenile crime and gangs and interracial strife in the city. These tensions between Blacks and whites, adults and youth, occurred in their neighborhoods and on public transportation. As police and civilian violence persisted, the citywide problem of juvenile crime and gangs gained greater public attention. During the spring and summer of 1944, the *New York Times* featured a range of stories on youth crime and the city's and communities' responses to it. Students at Benjamin Franklin High School suggested recreational activities but also "teen canteens" for them to meet in the evenings. Josephine, a student, the *New York Times* reported, believed "the causes for juvenile delinquency comes from the parents." She blamed parents for being overprotective, especially as it related to girls going out at night. The *New York Times* also reported on the problems in the truancy system, that the Children's Court was understaffed, and that there was a dearth of facilities for Protestant and Catholic children. Despite these problems, businessmen, clergy, and social workers joined the Juvenile Aid Bureau and formed Citizens Coordinating Councils in eighty-one patrol precincts to erase juvenile delinquency. The citizens' group adopted two resolutions: the creation of a community council and a civilian representative for each precinct. The civilian representative would coordinate with the captain and unit commander of the JAB. Although juvenile delinquency was recognized as a citywide problem, the white press and the police criminalized Black youth and treated them principally as a threat to white New Yorkers' safety.[81]

In late February, the *New York Times* printed an editorial by John Edgar Hoover, the director of the Federal Bureau of Investigation, about the need for the nation to create a "third front" against juvenile delinquency. Hoover described juvenile crime as a nationwide problem and acknowledged the roles of the war, instances of "'latchkey' youngsters," and the desire for freedom and excitement among the youth. Hoover, however, encouraged greater parental and community responsibility and disclosed stories of youth misconduct: "Ruth" from Illinois stole $1,000 from her employer and went on a spending spree; and then "Jack" in Indiana, too young to enlist, paraded around in a navy uniform and told stories of his adventures during the war; and then there was the "real trouble," such as "muggings," where a nameless youth of fourteen years of age robbed a man on the street with a toy gun. The mugger commanded, "Let me have every damn thing you have or I will kill you." Although no name, city, or race was associated with the child, with the label "mugging" long tethered to Black youth, at least in New York City, the director had managed to distinguish youth crime along racial lines.[82] Throughout the remainder of the year, the white and Black press faithfully reported on cases of juvenile crime and gang violence. Race, Blackness, and space remained staples of the white press's crime reportage. The *New York Times* racialized crime, as it had before, either by identifying criminal acts by "negro hoodlums," "negro gangs," and "zoot suiters" or by the neighborhoods, such as "Harlem" and "Little Harlem."[83]

On June 11, fifteen Black teenagers "terrorized more than a hundred passengers" on the Brighton Beach Line on the Brooklyn-Manhattan Transportation (BMT) subway. Shortly after nine in the evening, the teens boarded a crowded car at the Prospect Park Station and began parading through the cars yelling, "This is D-day for the colored folks, white trash get off," according to the *New York Times*. They pushed and provoked passengers until John Montero, near the Park Place Station, ordered "the boys to quiet down, that their conduct was beyond endurance." One of the boys punched him on the chin, and Montero fell to the ground, where he was shot twice, in his left wrist and left hip. Thereafter, as the police neared the station, the assailants escaped, and Montero was rushed to the Jewish Hospital. Although Montero's injuries were minor, some white New Yorkers viewed the incident as an all-out attack on white people.[84] Only a week before, seven Black youth were arrested for harassing "women passengers [and] . . . snatch[ing] their purses" on the Tompkins Avenue trolley car. Magistrate Alfred Lindau dismissed the charges of disorderly conduct against the boys but withheld judgment of the girls because, dressed in identical outfits of black shirtwaists and white skirts, they belonged to an "organization," they told the police, known as the "Vigilantes." Days later, Matthew J. McLaughlin, a Bronx Democrat, promised that if he was reelected in November, he would support a bill posting police patrols on the subway trains, because the trains were "fields of prey for all types of undesirables." Not yet a year after the 1943 Harlem rebellion and only six months after the Bedford-Stuyvesant scare, white New Yorkers, incensed by what they viewed as anti-white violence, once again condemned Mayor La Guardia for failing to protect white people.[85]

The flood of letters written to La Guardia by white Brooklynites expressed their anger about the seemingly frequent attacks upon white passengers. Mr. V. G. Flountine stated that he was "extremely angry over the BMT affair. If you and your negro loving friends in the police Dept don't do something very soon this city won't be safe for any white people."[86] Mrs. E. S. Millay, a witness to the commotion on the BMT, believed that it would take the murder of a white citizen for La Guardia to properly respond. She advised him to post plainclothes officers on the trains over the weekends, but she also wanted Blacks punished, stating "some kind of sentence should be meted out. Somehow punishment was not meant for this class." Mrs. Millay felt that Blacks were pampered but white men found no justice in the city's criminal justice system. She writes, "Let a white man place a bet on a horse and he goes to jail for a year or more. What does constitute a crime in your mind, Mr. Mayor." Taking note of the mayor and Police Commissioner Valentine's campaign against mobsters and their bookmakers, she asserted, "Let some of the men who did such a thorough job on bookmakers do something to put fear in the hearts of the Negroes. They have no fear because they go unpunished."[87] Philip Drago, another white letter writer, describing his letter as "a complaint which . . . the seven million white people are thinking or would be thinking if they all read this article in the news," agreed with the need to punish Black perpetrators. Initially wary of stereotyping Black people as criminals, he thought it was "an accident or something," after his wife was attacked on the train. Yet after reading the newspapers, he complained that "it is getting worse by the hours not days" and urged La Guardia to do something "quick and put these people in the[ir] place."[88]

White Brooklynites' demands mirrored the last three years of criticisms whites directed at the mayor. The Harlem Riot of 1943 and the grand jury presentment evoked fear and anger among many white New Yorkers, and they believed that the mayor's lethargic response to Black crime threatened the livelihood of the white race. Many whites, ignoring or sympathizing with the violence of white juveniles and gangs, felt unsafe and vulnerable to Black people. As Drago explained, "I'm sure you can do something to protect us white people because we are not looking for fights as these people are doing at every opportune moment they insult the white, try to rape a woman." This crime talk among white people recast whites as double victims, as the prey of Black predators and, according to Mrs. Millay, the target of La Guardia's war on crime. These demands for safety and punishment evinced more than the recent news of the BMT attack. The NYPD neglected, as Millay stated, to "put fear in the hearts of the Negroes." For some white New Yorkers, whites were unsafe because of the laxity of law and order. Yet Drago, reworking southern whites' justification for lynchings, warned, "I'm a law-abiding citizen and expect that you and the Police Force . . . can . . . protect the people from such happenings as this[.] I don't like to hear of this or of riots but that is how riots start when the law cant stop them then the people take the law into their own hands."[89]

That same week, a gang of approximately 200 whites on June 16 brandishing baseball bats, knives, and pipes roved the Fort Greene Public Housing Project in Brooklyn and attacked Black children, women, and men. Seeking revenge because Blacks had allegedly sexually assaulted a white woman in Fort Greene Park and attacked white people on the BMT the week before, they stoned and injured three Black boys: Virgil Carte, fifteen years old; Henry Jones, fourteen; and Leonard Sawyer, fifteen, in front of Eight Monument Walk in the housing project. The police apprehended and arrested only two of the throng, Anthony Caramanica, twenty-two, and Fred De Gregoria, eighteen, both from Brooklyn.[90] According to the *PM*, the gang yelled, "Lynch 'em!" "Kill the Black bastards!" The white gang targeted a recreation center in the housing complex, where each Friday, a youth group met for "juke-box dancing." On that Friday, however, the housing project's baseball committee and the Cub Scouts met at the recreational center, including mothers with their small children. The doors were locked and the rioters "thrust [a baseball bat] through the glass pane of the door." Thereafter, the baseball manager opened the door and urged the rioters to leave, explaining that only women and children were in the recreational center. The manager recalled, "I never saw so many baseball bats on any ball field . . . and you could see knives flashing in the light." He believed that most of the rioters were between eighteen and twenty with a "scattering of younger kids and older men." They said, "Colored folks were getting too uppity and had to be put in their place."[91]

After the commotion at the housing project, an interracial collective of tenants organized "in defense of their right to live without . . . the violence of racial conflict." The executives of the Fort Greene Tenants Association, comprising 500 of the 3,500 families in the housing project, formed a volunteer night patrol, and they planned mass meetings to inform the residents of the relevant issues and to establish relationships with churches, schools, clubs, welfare organizations, and other relevant neighborhood associations. The tenants' association assigned two unarmed men who, if necessary, would contact the police or Navy shore patrols to assign law enforcement to different areas of the housing complex. Mrs. Belle Sundeen, an executive of the tenants' association, explained that the tenants mobilized to protect their homes and racial unity during the war effort. Acknowledging that racial unity would not be "an easy thing," Sundeen explained, "These are our homes and we want to live in peace and harmony with our neighbors." She noted that most of the families living in the Fort Greene housing project were war workers or had an immediate family member serving in the armed forces and "that white and colored are fighting for the same kind of world." The memory of the recent Harlem uproar and the various melees across the nation also prompted the tenants to organize. She explained, "We're going to do everything we can to see that this kind of thing—or something worse—doesn't happen again."[92] In an editorial, "Time for Action," *PM*'s Tom O'Connor commended the efforts of the civic-minded and patriotic tenants "for their prompt and intelligent action," for they understood that the root of the problem was "prejudice and misunderstanding." O'Connor asked if La Guardia would ever "wake up to the fact that race tension in New York City is a frightful danger" and questioned what had become Valentine and the mayor's standard response: "assigning more cops to danger points is no cure for the disease." Citing recent occurrences of interracial conflict across the city, O'Connor opined that racism was firmly rooted in the city. Like Sundeen, he was concerned about hoodlumism, among Blacks and whites, and asked "what's holding" the mayor from action, since the escalation of racial violence might trigger a "major race war."[93]

While covering white and Black youth crime, the Black press followed the white press's lead. The *New York Times*'s headline about Black youth crime on the BMT read, "8 Young Negro Hoodlums," while the *New York Age* labeled them "hoodlums."[94] In the case of white youth, the *New York Times*'s headline referenced the Black victims: "3 Negro Boys Stoned in Row in Brooklyn: 200 Rowdies Provoke Trouble in Fort Greene Park Area." The

New York Times not only omitted the race of the aggressors in the headline but also described them as "rowdies," certainly an unfavorable term yet one that had less political and racial salience in the city's crime reportage.[95] The *New York Amsterdam News* and the *New York Age*, however, labeled white youth "white hoodlums." For years the Black press, the NAACP, and various liberal and left organizations criticized the white press, especially the *New York Times*, for solely identifying the race of the perpetrators or would-be perpetrators when they were Black. In the spring of 1943, because of that activism, the *New York Times*'s and other white dailies' crime reportage temporarily withheld race as a descriptor. The Black press's racially explicit headlines were both an indictment of the white press's reversal in crime reportage and reengagement with its past efforts to detach race from crime. By identifying whites as "hoodlums," the Black weekly, at least for its Black readership, broadened the criminal stamp to include whites, an editorial practice that was generally missing in the white press.[96]

The NYPD responded to all of these cases of juvenile crime in Brooklyn. In his June 18 article, the *New York Times*'s Emanuel Perlmutter opened with, "As a result of recent outbreaks of racial violence caused by young Negro hoodlums on subway trains and trolley cars serving the Prospect Park district of Brooklyn, the Police Department has taken extraordinary measures to protect the area." Assistant Chief Inspector John R. Ryan assigned a special squad of sixteen detectives to the area between Prospect Park and Franklin Avenue and asked them to "give attention to rapid-transit and trolley facilities on their way to and from work." Police officers were placed on twenty-four-hour weekend guard and ordered to trail trolley cars that left Prospect Park with white and Black youth. Additionally, a special unit of BMT patrolmen were detailed to Coney Island, posted at five stations between Prospect Park and Franklin Avenue. Franklin Avenue, the *New York Times* reminded readers, "is located in the heart of Brooklyn's 'Little Harlem.'" Perlmutter devoted most of the article to the police investigation of the youth who attacked John Montero on the eleventh. While the white daily gave more space to Black juvenile crime, the police gave considerable attention to finding the Black youth. Perlmutter described the police work as "painstaking detective work" and detailed step-by-step how they found and arrested four youths.[97]

Extra police from three stations were assigned to Fort Greene to pursue the white youth. Of the more than 100 gang members, the police apprehended two, a lackluster performance of police work considering the NYPD's sweeping response to the two cases of Black youth crime on the

BMT. Perlmutter briefly mentioned the white gang that attacked Black youth in Fort Greene public housing, but the Black press provided more context of the motives of the two men, Caramanca of 296 Van Buren Street, Brooklyn, and De Gregoria of the U.S. Navy, 142 Clinton Avenue, Brooklyn. While the *New York Times* described the white attacks in neutral terms, the Black press interviewed the police to explain Caramanca and De Gregoria's reasons for the attack.[98] Accordingly, Perlmutter stated that they were arrested because of "several encounters between Negro and white youths."[99] At the court hearing, Caramanca told Magistrate Surpless that the night before the raid, his sister had been walking past the housing project and a group of Black youth insulted her. Magistrate Surpless questioned, "Don't you know that you should have reported the matter to the police? Don't you know that you should have written a letter to the Mayor?" The judge then granted them suspended sentences. Tommy Watkins, the journalist who covered the story for the *New York Amsterdam News*, complained, "All of which leaves Brooklyn's 123,000 Negroes in a dither. This didn't happen below the Mason-Dixon line. Twas right here in Brooklyn which, for your information is located way up in the NORTH."[100]

"Negroes Are Attacking and Killing Other Negroes"

On May 1, Walter White, concerned about juvenile delinquency in Harlem and the potential of another riot during the summer of 1944, wrote a memorandum to Ella Baker, Thurgood Marshall, and Roy Wilkins, inviting their feedback about the formation of a community-based bureau as a preventive measure. White believed that Blacks were angrier about the mistreatment of Black soldiers "than [they] . . . w[ere] last year this time, because there has been more of it." While acknowledging that not much could be done until the cause was "removed," steps might be made, he explained, to "allay hysteria which might be helpful and might even enable us to go through the summer without a riot." He hoped to establish a temporary bureau, open twenty-four hours a day to investigate and dispel rumors and to use Black leadership, the Black press, and Black celebrities, such as "Cab Calloway, Duke Ellington, Ella Fitzgerald and whatever other heroes this young group may have," to impress upon the community to reject hoodlumism and consider the negative consequences of another riot. White also suggested that they might use block leaders to target specific areas and "tie-up with Mayor's Committee and with city departments so that the committee would have at least semi-official status and authority to call on City departments for information and help." He wanted an authentic group of Harlemites that "should consist of people resident in and known to the Harlem community, speaking as the voice of Harlem."[101]

In a memo dated May 12 to Walter White and Roy Wilkins, Ruby Hurley, the national youth council director, expressed her deep concern about the "increasing outbreaks of violence perpetrated by our young people in the greater New York area." Framing the problem in "sociological facts," she believed that the problem was more "parental and community rather than juvenile." The impact of the war and the impoverished situation of the Black family left, she asserted, "almost indelible marks on the unfortunate children." Julia Baxter, a staff member of the NAACP, in her June 8 memo to White, agreed with Hurley's suggestion that the NAACP might concentrate on Black youth crime. Baxter expanded White's initial goal from investigating and, if necessary, correcting rumors and preventing another uproar to establishing a police presence and a social reform infrastructure to combat juvenile delinquency and parental negligence. Baxter was concerned about "the outbursts of surly belligerency on the part of Harlem youth," which, combined with the warm weather, might instigate "zoot suiters in Harlem which may reach riot proportions." Juvenile crime in Harlem and across the city was centrally a community problem rather than a racial problem. Trouble-ridden Black youth had exploited rumors of police brutality and the killing of Black soldiers, she believed, to unleash "the discontent that has become so much a part of their being." Baxter was especially concerned about intraracial Black crime. She writes, "Within the past month at least fifteen of the crimes committed in Harlem have been highlighted and brought to the attention of the reading public of the city—robberies, muggings, rapings, stabbings and murder. Negroes are attacking and killing other Negroes."[102]

The murder of nine-year-old Margaret Patton in the school yard at Public School 119 brought this problem into high relief. On May 9, Patton was fatally stabbed with a knife by Madeline Kirkland, an eleven-year-old. Arlene "Peggy" Foster, Kirkland's accomplice, held Patton from the back. Kirkland and Foster had attacked Patton as revenge because she "snitched" on them. Patton had told her teacher that Kirkland had stolen $60 from her mother and records from Miss Fanny Cohen, the principal, and that she was "approached the wrong way" by one of her classmates. About 2,000 people attended Patton's funeral at the Memorial Baptist Church on 115th Street in Harlem, and at least 15,000 mourners passed through the Griffin Funeral Home at 134th Street and Seventh Avenue to view Patton's body. This was the first time that Harlemites had taken the district's juvenile crime problem seriously, according to journalist Carl Dunbar Lawrence of the *New York Amsterdam News*. He wrote, "Patton carried a wallop Harlem has seldom experienced in recent years and surpassed in general interest even the murder of young Bobby Forbes," who was killed in 1939. The Reverend W. Willard Monroe, Harlem's "top 'funeral preacher,'" wrote Lawrence, blamed Black youth crime on Black mothers. Monroe directed his Mother's Day funeral sermon at "one of the chief causes of juvenile delinquency . . . 'barfly mothers.'"[103] He preached, "I am going to give you a piece of my mind. Some of you are sitting there in tears, probably grief-stricken over a tragedy like this. Don't worry about Margaret. She's all right. She's resting. But you careless mothers are not all right." He continued, "You're worried and you have a right to be concerned because you know and I know that many of you are not living right at home."[104]

Community concern about juvenile delinquency within Harlem and the recent slaying of Patton in May prompted the Harlem Committee to expand its program beyond riot prevention and prioritize the safety of the Black community. This shift from mainly providing corrective and moral persuasive information to combating rumors signaled the conviction among many civic-minded Harlemites that a riot might be avoided by refocusing on crime prevention and punishment. Throughout the remainder of May and early June, NAACP officials, mainly Walter White, Wilkins, and Baxter, discussed the scale, the objectives, and the organization of a Harlem-wide coordinated committee. They invited a wide array of Harlem's Black and white leaders from the neighborhood's vast civic, religious, labor, and cultural institutional life and held three meetings on June 9, 19, and 29 and a confidential one with Mayor La Guardia on June 30.[105]

Gang violence among Blacks and especially publicity about it in the white press reinforced the work of the committee and the need to rein in juvenile delinquency. On June 22, Judge Louis Goldstein had two Black gangs, the Robins and the Beavers, in his courtroom to witness the sentencing of one of their members. The two gangs along with another, the Marauders, had almost caused a riot on May 20, when innocent citizens were assaulted with weapons, explained Goldstein. He warned, "These gangs of young loafers and hoodlums have and are creating serious disturbances which have created a dangerous and menacing situation on various public conveyances, in subways, in our parks and on our streets." With all eyes on the judge, the gang members, Police Captain John McGoey, and Rev. Thomas S. Harten, Black pastor of the Holy Trinity Baptist Church, watched Goldstein sentence sixteen-year-old Joseph Parker to ten to twenty years in Sing Sing Prison for first-degree assault on Joseph Foster, also sixteen years old. Parker confronted and shot Foster in the stomach on March 28 at the corner of Tompkins and Jefferson Avenues in Brooklyn for refusing to admit his gang affiliation. After the sentencing, Goldstein stated to the gangs, "I had you brought here for the sole purpose of giving you a sound warning of what will happen to you if you commit any vicious crime. At the same time, I beg of you, for your own good, that you turn over a new leaf at once by disbanding and divorcing yourselves from any of these so-called gangs." He told them to "become decent, respected and law-abiding young men for the good of your own future and the happiness of your parents and friends." The judge also asked the captain to speak, and he explained that the police only wanted to help not arrest them, and Pastor Harten encouraged them to "cultivate respect for and to be courteous to others." From his point of view, playgrounds were inadequate, for "there must be religious and spiritual influence in the home."[106]

At the confidential meeting on June 30, the Committee on Delinquency in Harlem proposed a program that prioritized four areas: legislation, policing, social reform, and media. They wanted a curfew extended throughout the city and a law fining and potentially imprisoning delinquent parents. To shape public discussions on crime, the committee wanted to monitor crime reportage involving the Black community. The committee would request "the white press to refrain from reporting crime under the designation of Negro crime, and to refrain from publishing stories that might lead to a disturbance." The Black press, however, would "stress the necessity of parents giving greater supervision to their adolescent children." The civic-minded would protect Harlemites from hoodlums and "let the community know that the Negroes in Harlem will stand behind the Police Force in the performance of its duties and will not speak up for criminals." The committee also wanted to create canteens, where youth would meet for recreation with adult supervision, which would be coordinated with an expanded Juvenile Welfare Council. Social agencies would give block parties and invite athletes, entertainers, and others to talk with gang members. The overall emphasis was on providing supervised recreation, surveillance, and punishment. The committee wanted the La Guardia administration to appoint more Black detectives and temporary police officers and the Navy to augment the Shore Patrol in Harlem. As George Gregory, the assistant chairman of the committee, wrote, "It is generally agreed that there is not now and has not been, except during the disturbance of last August 1st, adequate police coverage of Harlem. We, therefore, advocate increased police protection of life and property in this community." The committee proposed a $120,000 budget for the year.[107]

La Guardia explained that "it would be impossible for the City to back the cost of the plan" but would pledge a contribution of $1,000 if the committee raised $5,000 from contributions of $5 or less. The mayor also rejected the curfew, "object[ing] strongly to the [youth] being taken to police stations" because he did not want them to feel like they were being forced off the streets. He suggested taking youth found in the streets after eleven in the evening to centers where they could be retrieved by their parents and requested that the committee create a subcommittee to coordinate the plan with William M. Kent, the deputy police commissioner. The mayor explained that he was open to expanding the police presence in Harlem and contacting the Navy about augmenting the Shore Patrol, which was needed across the city. He stated that the "city [wa]s anxious to appoint temporary patrolmen," but for the appointment of plainclothes Black officers, the committee would have to consult with Police Commissioner Valentine. La Guardia supported the committee's goal of monitoring and cooperating with the press, but only the Black press. He believed that "the Negro press should 'crack down hard' every time a member of the Negro race did something that brought degradation to the whole race." The mayor viewed the role of the white press differently from the committee. While he did not oppose the committee's corresponding with them about crime, the mayor stated, "Decent Negroes should not be too sensitive about the matter, pointing out that the Italian race had received the same type of abusive treatment in the years past, and read two items from the June 30 press re: Italian gangsters." Committee members corrected him, highlighting that "no mention was made of the fact that they were Italian."[108] Gregory submitted a temporary plan, enumerating the recommendations mentioned above. La Guardia stated that if the committee agreed with the plan, then it should contact Judge Jackson, who would function as a liaison between the committee and local government.

Even as La Guardia expressed his commitment to the Black community and law and order, he only went so far. Despite the white press's herculean cultural power to shape public perceptions of crime, the mayor ruled out challenging the white press, as he at the same time articulated Black crime as essentially a Black problem rather than a problem of the city. But the mayor remained supportive of expanding police presence in Black neighborhoods, as Valentine had done on several occasions since the Harlem uprising of 1935. When it came to the white press, La Guardia appeared to embrace a color-blind sense of crime reportage, that is, the idea that the white press reported on all groups equally. Of course, the Black press among other liberal and leftist organizations had mobilized to stop the white press's zealous practice of binding crime to "negro crime." No religious or racial group found its identity or neighborhoods tethered to crime in the news the way that Blacks had. For La Guardia, all groups engaged in crime and his agenda was to fight crime with the police and parents, so for the mayor, Black parents and the Black press had to do their part. La Guardia's appeal to color-blind reportage, even as he differentiated between the Black press and mainstream press, was symptomatic of his racial liberalism. Nonetheless, the Delinquency Committee, despite its endorsement of fines and prison sentences for negligent parents, distinguished Black criminal activity from the ways the white press manufactured and shaped white New Yorkers' perceptions of Black crime. For Black communities across the city, especially in Harlem and Bedford-Stuyvesant, these perceptions of Black crime had become a political bludgeon that not only reinforced stereotypes of Black criminality but also sanctioned police brutality.

· · · · · ·

By the end of summer of 1944, Walter White's and especially Julia Baxter's predictions would be proven wrong. Neither Harlem's nor Bedford-Stuyvesant's "surly" youth or zoot-suiters incited a riot. The NAACP's anti-crime campaign, like those since the late 1930s embracing rehabilitation and punishment, was doubly critical of crime in the Black community and the white media's criminalization of the Black community. Yet the Committee on Delinquency in Harlem was different from the anti-crime campaigns from yesteryear. Persisting mistreatment of Black soldiers, the Harlem Riot of 1943, and the political and judicial attacks upon Bedford-Stuyvesant's Black community attenuated the fears of Black "hoodlumism" among Black liberals. The confluences of these conditions, especially Black intracommunity crime, put Black liberals in a vulnerable and perhaps desperate position, prompting them to more loudly and publicly than before assert the Black community's commitment to a punitive-oriented law-and-order policy. Yet this commitment did not mean that the committee and the Black community at large were uncritical of the white press or police abuse. Black Brooklyn's response to the grand jury presentment, as well as its army of white judges, civic organizations, and religious leaders calling for more police and punishment, was illustrative of the double bind that Black New

Yorkers confronted as they faced an evolving police state that targeted the Black community, especially Black youth.[109] The Black community had long framed Black crime—no different from crime for any other racial, ethnic, or religious group—as a social and economic problem. But racial discrimination and segregation—as the *New York Amsterdam News*, the Citizens Emergency Conference for Interracial Unity, the City-Wide Citizens' Committee on Harlem, and the Citizens' Committee on Better Race Relations argued collectively—explained Black New Yorkers' social and economic situation. Thus, in order to ensure their safety, the Black community fought crime on multiple fronts and challenged racist caricatures of crime created by the white press and especially the NYPD.

The Harlem Riot of 1943 and especially the Kings County August Grand Jury presentment were a tipping point that powerfully cemented the NYPD's discourse on Black crime. Since the late 1930s, the NYPD had spun the narrative that the mayor restrained police discretion, which many white New Yorkers, citizens and the press, accepted at face value. The police blamed the "crime wave" and the compromised safety of whites on the La Guardia administration and the Black community. These manufactured arguments of suppressed police discretion were a compelling riposte to the Mayor's Commission report that contended that police aggression was the result of the NYPD's "heritage of wrong police psychology." Over the course of time, the police's narrative shifted critiques of and activism against police brutality to discussions of Black criminal behavior and masked whites' insecurities about the settlement of Black people in formerly all-white neighborhoods. The Harlem Riot of 1943, as well as the police's narrative of restraint under the leadership of La Guardia and Valentine, exposed and corroborated for many white New Yorkers, and some Blacks, the consequences of prohibiting police from suppressing Black crime in the city's largest Black district. Three months later, the grand jury's presentment again fortified the narrative and the problem of Black crime in the city's emerging Black "ghetto," Bedford-Stuyvesant. In spite of this, the Black community tried to distinguish police brutality from "adequate policing." But these patterns of "disorder," as well as the clarion calls of judges and politicians for unimpeded police aggression during the summer of 1944, legitimated not only demands for punishment but also the expansion of the city's police force.

Throughout the fall of 1944 and 1945, La Guardia and Valentine's last year serving the city in their capacities as mayor and police commissioner, police occupation remained their singular solution to addressing allegations of Black crime from white New Yorkers across the city. In early September, in a letter signed "An American Citizen," the letter writer from the Bronx complained that La Guardia failed to "clean up the great evil going on" in the city by "colored people," because "their votes is more important than the crimes they commit." In late March 1945, another letter writer, signed "A Resident of this vicinity," asked the mayor to "look into a situation that is going on in the neighborhood known as Washington Heights where law and order seem to never have existed."[110] Throughout the spring and summer, white civic groups, the dailies, and public officials in Stapleton, Staten Island, called upon Valentine to increase the police presence there to offset unsubstantiated crimes committed by Black soldiers, including the sexual assault of a white woman, stationed at the army's Fox Hills cantonment. By mid-March, La Guardia and Valentine responded aggressively and detailed over 200 police, detectives, and military police to the area.[111]

Months later in late September, the white dailies alleged that white and Black students at Benjamin Franklin High School in East Harlem "boiled over into a spectacular street battle." That afternoon and the next, police were stationed at the high school. On the day of the fight, the police only arrested Black youth, who were surrounded by white students and adults. Thereafter, after a meeting with the principal, a group of white mothers sent a petition to La Guardia requesting that a "separate white and Negro school be established in the area." These demands across the city for police protection and punishment overlapped with complaints from white citizens and public officials about shortages in the police departments. From Colonel Leopold Philipp and the Uptown Chamber of Commerce in Harlem and Sumner Sirtl and the Midtown Civic League in Bedford-Stuyvesant in the 1930s to Magistrate Abner Surpless and Senator John J. Dunnigan in the early forties, white New Yorkers had tethered Black crime to "crime waves" to exert pressure on La Guardia and public officials to augment the police force. Throughout the La Guardia era, this array of white civic leaders, judges, and politicians in concert with the white press constituted an influential political bloc that promoted aggressive policing.[112]

No longer defending himself against allegations of being weak on Black crime nor needing to appeal to Gotham's diverse electorate, Mayor Fiorello H. La Guardia took a bolder law-and-order stance, as he approved certifications to expand the police department by 3,000. As the mayor gave his last speech in late November 1945 to a new class of provisional policemen to be sworn in, he advised them on being responsible police officers and how to handle themselves during the war on crime. He warned them not to get involved in politics, declaring that it "has been out of the department since I'm here and it's going to stay out." But even as he observed the reform he brought to the New York Police Department, La Guardia urged the rookies to punish criminals. He exhorted, "Anytime you walk into a situation in which firearms are being used in the commission of crime, be quick to trigger. You've got a nightstick. You've got a gun. They're not meant to be ornamental. When you know there's a crime being committed and there's a criminal in the place, go in with your gun in your hand. Go in shooting."[113]

Epilogue

· ·

On April 17, 1964, several Black kids tipped over a fruit stand in Harlem. Overhearing the commotion, the police chased them, in pursuit they pulled out their guns, and upon catching them began pummeling them. Frank Stafford, a thirty-one-year-old Black salesman, brazenly asked the two police officers, "Why are you beating him (a child) like that?" They answered with their fists and batons. James Baldwin tells this story of police violence—of basic disregard for Black children and adults, as episodes of the "Little Fruit Stand Riot," captured in Truman Nelson's *The Torture of Mothers*, a book detailing the case of the Harlem Six and their mothers. The police arrested the youths, Wallace Baker (nineteen), Donald Hamm (eighteen), Walter Thomas (eighteen), Willie Craig (seventeen), Ronald Felder (eighteen), and Robert Rice (seventeen) for the killing of Margit Sugar, a white woman, and the wounding of Frank Sugar, her husband, owners of a used department store on Three West 125th Street on April 29. In July of 1965, the court convicted them of first-degree murder, first-degree attempted murder, and robbery. The police had initially arrested Baker and Hamm on the seventeenth for intervening like many others on the behalf of the kids. At the police station, Stafford among others endured the third degree: "About thirty-five [police officers] started beating, punching us in the jaw, in the stomach, in the chest, beating us with a padded club—spit on us, call us niggers, dogs, animals—they call us dogs and animals when I don't see why we are the dogs and animals the way they are beating us. Like they beat me they beat the other kids and the elderly fellow. They throw him almost through one of the radiators. I thought he was dead over there." That "elderly fellow" was Fecundo Acion, a forty-seven-year-old Puerto Rican sailor. When he asked the same question as Stafford, "the cop turn[ed] around and smash[ed] him a couple of times in the head." Like Tommy Aikens, the victim of police violence before the uprising in March 1935, Stafford had to wear an eye patch. The police had been beaten him so horribly that the doctors at Bellevue Hospital had to remove his eye, because it "endanger[ed] the good eye."[1]

Baldwin's recounting painted a picture of Harlemites' lived experience in what Baldwin called an "occupied territory." Baldwin based his essay

"A Report from Occupied Territory" not only on Nelson's book but also, as he described it, "On what I myself know, for I was born in Harlem and raised there." For decades Baldwin had chronicled stories of white racism in and outside the South, but his reportage on Harlem was intimately personal. As he wrote, "I also know, in my own flesh, and know, which is worse, in the scars borne by many of those dearest to me, the thunder and fire of the billy club, the paralyzing shock of spittle in the face, and I know what it is to find oneself blinded, on one's hands and knees, at the bottom of the flight of steps down which one has just been hurled."[2] In 1960, he wrote similarly in "Fifth Avenue, Uptown," in *Esquire* magazine that the police "represent the forces of the white world." He stated "Rare, indeed, is the Harlem citizen, from the most circumspect church member to the most shiftless adolescent, who does not have a long tale to tell of police incompetence, injustice, and brutality. I myself have witnessed and endured it more than once." Baldwin's description of Harlem as an "occupied territory" was not hyperbole. Echoing Black Harlemites' charges about police occupation in 1936, Baldwin explained that the policeman "moves through Harlem . . . like an occupying soldier in a bitterly hostile country; which is precisely what, and where, he is, and is the reason he walks in twos and threes." For Baldwin, the case of the Harlem Six was not an exceptional case of police corruption and brutality but a requisite and a long-standing condition of white domination. As he wrote, pithily, "The only way to police a ghetto is to be oppressive."[3]

Baldwin's "A Report from Occupied Territory" was published in July 1966, two years after the Harlem Uprising of 1964, which many contemporaries and historians pinpoint as the result of the shooting of James Powell, a Black fifteen-year-old, by white policeman Lieutenant Thomas Gilligan on July 18. Harlem erupted during the presidential election race between Democratic president Lyndon Baines Johnson and his Republican rival Senator Barry Goldwater of Arizona, whose calls for law and order conflated civil rights and civil disobedience with crime and disorder. In response to the explosion in Harlem, President Johnson pronounced "the immediate overriding issue in New York is the preservation of law and order," as his administration transitioned from the war on poverty to the war on crime. After winning the election, Johnson signed the Law Enforcement Assistance Act (LEAA) in March 1965, which subsidized state and municipal law enforcement agencies. The LEAA intensified the already volatile relationship between Black communities and law enforcement and set the stage for the Watts Uprising in August 1965 and other rebellions across the nation throughout the 1960s and the 1970s.[4]

Like his liberal political predecessor Mayor La Guardia, President Johnson policed the crises that produced the occupied territories that Baldwin had been writing about since the 1940s. By reading Baldwin, it is clear that the uprising several months after the Little Fruit Stand Riot was tied to a much longer and deeper history than the killing of Powell or even the case of the Harlem Six. Baldwin noted, "What I have said about Harlem is true of Chicago, Detroit, Washington, Boston, Philadelphia, Los Angeles and San Francisco—is true of every Northern city with a large Negro population. And the police are simply enemies of this population. They are present to keep the Negro in his place and to protect white business interests, and they have no other function." He also understood how police occupation was linked to national politics as a frustrated adviser to the John F. Kennedy and the Johnson administrations that called upon him seeking advice about whether the "unemployed, unemployable Negroes who are going to be on the streets all summer will cause us any trouble." Instead of pointing to Black youth crime, Baldwin pointed out the pattern of racism excluding Blacks from labor unions, the lack of economic investment in jobs, the separate and unequal educational system, and the complicity of the city, state, and federal government.[5]

In July 1967, Johnson formed the President's National Advisory Commission on Civil Disorders, known as the Kerner Commission, after its chair Governor Otto Kerner Jr. of Illinois, to investigate the cause of the uprisings and recommend solutions. The Kerner Commission, documenting white civilian racism, government neglect and discrimination, and widespread police violence, echoed the findings of La Guardia's commission's report. Turning a blind eye to his commission's report, Johnson signed and Congress passed the Omnibus Crime Control and Safe Streets Act of 1968, creating the Law Enforcement Assistance Administration and entrenching the federal infrastructure for the modern carceral state. Several decades before, Mayor La Guardia provided a roadmap for subsequent public officials to exercise liberal law and order.

The police occupation of Harlem in the aftermath of the Harlem Uprising of 1935 jump-started a pattern of policing that Black New York would endure throughout the remainder of the twentieth and the twenty-first centuries. As *The Politics of Safety* demonstrates, well before the uprising in 1935 and the fictitious racialized crime waves of the 1940s, police violence was unwavering. Mayor La Guardia's promise to protect Black neighborhoods in 1936 went unfulfilled, yet his argument that his police officers needed protection from Black Harlemites operated as an official policy and a justification for criminalizing Black protest against police brutality. La Guardia's liberalism—despite the mayor's public proclamations—sanctioned state violence against Black New Yorkers. In New Deal New York, white mobilization for safety, demands for the expansion of the police force, and unfettered police discretion to use coercive force legitimated and formalized aggressive policing and punitive practices that were already informally in use. In 1964, these policies would become law when the State of New York passed no knock and stop-and-frisk laws because of the outcries of whites about Black crime *before* the Little Fruit Stand Riot. Although juvenile crime spiked—not only in New York but across the nation—under the La Guardia administration because of the war, the NYPD, white New Yorkers, and the white press targeted and centered Black youth street crime as a political issue of public safety. Like President Johnson decades later, La Guardia, amid Black freedom struggles for better housing, jobs, education, and overall political accountability, prioritized the safety of whites. At the same time, his administration denied the fact that Black neighborhoods lived under intermittent police occupation, and as a result of this, Black citizens endured the daily indignities of disrespect, intimidation, and violence.

In this political milieu, Black resistance against police violence struggled to bring about safety for the community and meaningful police accountability in the 1930s and 1940s. Nonetheless, Black New Yorkers organized and coordinated protests, expanding the range of core issues that made up the city's postwar freedom struggles. Although Blacks had always resisted police brutality, police occupation of Harlem after the 1935 uprising and the augmentation of police presence across the city pushed them to prioritize mobilization against police brutality as a critical political and movement issue. In the postwar era, Blacks continued their tradition of interrogating the lawfulness of police discretion by depicting police violence as a form of lynching. Comparable to the *New York Amsterdam News*'s description of the third degree as "an indoor, lynching, or near-lynching bee sanctioned openly by authority" in 1926, Harlem councilman Benjamin Davis's office published a pamphlet called *Lynching Northern Style: Police Brutality* in 1947 that exposed how the lack of disciplinary action gave license to the police to punish Black citizens. Despite this Black mobilization, beyond the city's occasional, grudging defensive response to police brutality, the police maimed and killed Black people. The Black community tirelessly organized to halt intracommunity Black crime. These efforts, to fight police violence and the police withholding protection, were mainly hidden within the veil of the Black community and the Black press.[6]

When these issues crossed the color line, the NYPD, white civilians, and the white press used them as grist for the mill to cement the narrative of Black youth as a threat to white New Yorkers. Even when Black youth initiated their own efforts to curtail "Negro juvenile crime," police punitive practices and policies continued. As historian Carl Suddler notes, "The police controlled the crime and delinquency rates, [and] decided who was presumed criminal."[7] Police power emerged not only from the enlargement and militarization of police departments but fundamentally from its authority to define Black communities as a threat to the social order and its discretion to employ coercive force. In 1965 and 1966, John Cassese, the leader of the Patrolmen's Benevolent Association (PBA), wielded the discourse of discretionary constraint to pass a referendum to eradicate the Civilian Complaint Review Board (CCRB). Campaigning in support of William F. Buckley, the Conservative Party's candidate for mayor against the eventual victor, Democrat Robert F. Wagner, Cassese warned, noted one historian, that "the objective of Black New Yorkers was to weaken the police so that Black criminals would not be punished." Although Cassese's efforts did not result in Buckley's winning the mayoralty race, a year later Cassese and the PBA effectively abolished the CCRB. In contrast to the argument that unencumbered police discretion would make all New Yorkers safe, Black neighborhoods remained unprotected from criminals, those with and without police badges.[8]

Consequently, since the late nineteenth century, Black communities in New York City and other metropolises engaged in crime prevention and crime fighting. This anti-crime work emerged out of neighborhood uplift, self-determination, and criticism of racism in the public and private sectors. Whether it was W. E. B. Du Bois's demands that whites curb racism or Black Philadelphia reformer James S. Stemons and his League of Civic and Political Reform's efforts during the Progressive era to rally whites and Blacks around crime prevention and crime fighting, anti-crime work has been a pivotal site of Black activism in the long Black freedom struggle. This work has come in many forms, including the protective work of Victoria Earle Matthews's White Rose Mission founded in 1897, one of the first settlement houses run by and for Black women in the city, as well as the preventive work of Black probation officer Grace Campbell. But not all members of the race were protected or treated equally. Oftentimes Black reformers unjustly targeted Black parents, especially Black women. Black leaders' support of laws penalizing Black parents and especially Reverend Monroe blaming the untimely death of nine-year-old Margaret Patton on "barfly mothers" in 1944 at the child's funeral services are illustrative. Thus, within this tradition of Black activism for safety, conservative, anti-working-class, and misogynist elements resided.[9]

Whether this work occurred independent of or within the city's criminal justice system, Black New Yorkers' anti-racist work undergirded their anti-crime work. Blacks' demands for equitable protection were an indictment of police racism and exposed how the police rendered protection as a racialized "separate and unequal" service in Gotham's criminal justice system. Thus, Blacks' notion of law and order—articulated ahead of the 1960s—differed considerably from whites', La Guardia's, and the NYPD's. As Blacks called for support from the city's Juvenile Aid Bureau and local government more broadly, they put forth a trenchant analysis of Jim Crow policing that disclosed how cops forcefully protected white businesses in Black neighborhoods but denied that same protection to Blacks. Black activism against crime therefore called for a more nuanced conceptualization of law and order that did not conflate police violence—or what would later be known as Valentine's "muss 'em up" crime policy with "adequate policing." The campaign led by the *New York Age*'s Fred Moore for justice for Herbert Dent, a victim of the third degree in the summer of 1922, exemplified Black New Yorkers' simultaneous support for law enforcement and the safety of the Black community.

Black New Yorkers' bottom-up approach to anti-crime work and law and order in the 1930s and 1940s included understanding Black crime as a manifestation of structural problems. The commission hearings in spring of 1935 and the report described the uprising as the product of racism in the areas of housing, recreation, health, education, and employment and pointed to white racism and the negligence and the unaccountability of public officials, including Police Commissioner Lewis J. Valentine. Black leaders and the Communist Party upheld the report's censure of the La Guardia administration when they condemned the mayor for not implementing the recommendations and maligned the yearlong presence of the police as a "police army of occupation" in the summer of 1936. La Guardia and Commissioner Valentine followed this policy of policing the crises throughout the remainder of their tenure together in public office. In 1939, the New York State Temporary Commission's report bore out the Mayor's Commission's findings, when it stated, "Although increased preventive and correctional facilities for more effective and expeditious handling of cases would materially reduce the volume of delinquency and crime among the State's Negro population, the removal of the basic and deep-rooted contributory factors . . .

is a more fundamental approach to the whole problem." This "more fundamental approach" acknowledged that while the expansion of the state's carceral capacity might help, intentional policies and practices to make the
political system equitable were the more appropriate path for transformative change. This approach would "undoubtedly result in a tremendous social saving to all communities . . . and would afford the Negro citizens of
the State greater equality for sharing with the general population of the
State opportunities for self-support, economic, and cultural development."[10]
Subsequent reports by the City-Wide Citizens' Committee on Harlem in
the wake of the so-called crime waves and widespread commentary and
criticism directed at the mayor in the aftermath of the uprising of 1943 and
the Kings County Grand Jury's presentment highlighted the incongruity between the Black community's long-standing demands for the eradication of
racial discrimination and the La Guardia administration's public policy of
criminalizing poverty and policing the crises.

Still in the twenty-first century, the criminalization of Black youth and
police complaints about discretionary constraint, what has been recently
dubbed "de-policing," have functioned as powerful weapons to delegitimize
Black protest against police brutality.[11] As the killing of Trayvon Martin in
2012 and the George Zimmerman case in 2013 demonstrate, the narrative of
the threat of Black youth crime to white communities still lives with us.
Zimmerman's killing of Martin was sanctioned, in part, by his defense
team's efficacy at persuading the jury that widespread Black crime in San-
ford's gated community in Florida authorized Zimmerman to pursue and
fatally shoot an unarmed Martin to protect the white community, especially its vulnerable women and children. The police, too, continue to wea-
ponize challenges to police discretion to criminalize Black protest. In the
aftermath of the Ferguson uprising in 2014, Sam Dotson, then St. Louis's
police commissioner, and county chief Jon Belmar claimed that rising
crime rates were the result of the so-called Ferguson Effect, that is, officer
fatigue and stress from the protests and riot training to control the civil
unrest. As a result of the Ferguson Effect, warned Dotson, "the criminal element is feeling empowered by the environment."[12] Police departments
across the nation have taken up variations of this rhetoric, including New
York City's police union leaders. In 2019, Patrick Lynch, the president of the
Police Benevolent Association, urged "all New York City police officers to
proceed with the utmost caution in this new reality, in which they may be
deemed 'reckless' just for doing their job." Lynch's warning, a reprisal to the
firing of veteran Officer Daniel Pantaleo, whose chokehold contributed to

the death of Eric Garner, recapitulated charges the NYPD had been making since the Progressive era.[13]

Although the tragic death of Martin and the acquittal of Zimmerman laid the foundation for the Black Lives Matter Movement, the anti-racist movement for safety began more than a century before. The various local, state, and federal investigations of policing—from the Chicago Commission's report in 1919 to the Department of Justices' Investigation of the Ferguson Police Department in 2015—have powerfully exposed that law enforcement has long operated as an institution of harm. These investigations have all come from the political work—the protests, the litigation, the letter-writing, the marching, and sometimes the uprisings—that constitute Black organizing and activism around safety. While the La Guardia commission's hearings and its report called for neither the defunding of the police nor its abolition, Harlemites and the report's recommendation for civilian oversight and cooperation with the NYPD demonstrated a vision of eradicating harm that centered the safety of the Black community. This continued throughout the 1930s and 1940s, as Black and white liberals and leftists called for police protection and municipal support for root-cause issues.

From desegregating police departments and forming their own police associations, such as the New York City Guardians Association in 1943, to creating grassroots organizations, such as the Black Panther Party for Self-Defense in Oakland, California, in 1966 and Harlem Mothers S.A.V.E. (Stop Another Violent End) in 2006, African Americans even at great risk and failure have had to experiment and build alternatives to policing and the criminal justice system.[14] During the William J. Clinton presidency, as Black politicians supported the controversial 1994 crime bill, they also asked for legislation supporting full employment, equitable education, drug rehabilitation, and police accountability. Much like the La Guardia administration, the Clinton administration and the Democratic Party engaged in the liberal policy of "selective hearing." During both administrations, "when Blacks ask[ed] for better policing, legislators" and public officials heard "more policing."[15] Since the summer of 2021, a year after international protests and months after the conviction of Derek Chauvin for the murder of George Floyd, liberals and conservatives have called for the expansion of police departments and increased budgets to combat the "crime waves" sprawling across the nation's cities and suburbs while support for police reform legislation languished in Congress.[16] It is no surprise, considering Black communities' long and numerous efforts to reform police departments from the inside and out, that over the last two decades or so anti-prison and anti-police violence activists and organizers have called for the abolition of prisons and police departments. As Mariame Kaba has argued, prison and police abolitionists aspire to create a safe society that reduces harm, and to do that, organizers must experiment and create institutions and programs for meaningful social transformation.[17] But as long as we equate the police with security, and the police continue to define criminal activity and leverage coercive force to control it—authority that is given to them by citizens—Black communities will remain unsafe and vulnerable to public officials unwilling to prioritize and protect Black life.

Acknowledgments

I could not have written this book without the wisdom and teaching of my grand aunt, known famously among my closest and oldest friends as Aunt Rose. She taught me about the "politics of safety." I spent maybe thousands of hours watching various police shows with her. From *Matlock* to *Law and Order*, Aunt Rose and I loved crime procedurals, and she had all kinds of comments about criminal behavior and policing. She also loved to read the newspapers. She read the *New York Amsterdam News*, the *New York Daily News*, and the *New York Times*. We talked about police brutality, David Dinkins, and New York City politics. In 1986, we talked about the killing of Michael Griffith in Howard Beach and criminalization of the "Exonerated Five" in 1990. She had these talks with me not to politicize me, but because she was concerned about my safety—from police violence and crime. Our conversations have remained with me and have shaped the writing of the book.

For some reason, I was under the impression that writing my second book would be easier. It wasn't. So much has happened since I began the project in 2013. The writing of the book overlapped with the emergence of the Movement 4 Black Lives (M4BL). Watching widespread anti-Black police violence, the atrocities of racial capitalism, and the governmental negligence that the M4BL has battled in real time during a pandemic has helped me better understand what I was trying to do and make sense of in my own work. It has also humbled me. Talking with scholars Carl Suddler and Hasan Jeffries also informed my work during this time, as we all discussed the history of policing in the country, especially New York City, and how our own memories of police violence in the 1980s and 1990s still live with us.

The book began at the College of Wooster. While there I was fortunate to have the support and encouragement of the Department of History, as well as colleagues in other departments and programs: Christa Craven, Amber Garcia, Matthew Krain, Lee McBride, Philip Mellizo, Amyaz Moledina, and Tom Tiernay. I am also grateful for the laughter and support I continue to receive from what I call the "COW diaspora." It is a blessing to get a call, a visit, and even a Zoom meeting with you all: Kabria Baumgartner, Raymond Gunn, Barbara Thelamour James, Leah Mirakhor, Charles Peterson, and Leslie Wingard. In addition to mentorship and overall support, the College of Wooster also provided several subventions for research, travel, and writing, including the Ralston Endowment Fund for Faculty Development and the Henry Luce III Fund for Distinguished Scholarship.

Upon my arrival at Fairfield University, I was immediately welcomed to the History Department by the chair Patricia Behre and members of the department. Sunil Purushotham, since the day you picked me up at the hotel on my visit, we have been fast friends and, indeed, as soon as I come to the third floor, you're the first person I look for. LOL. Silvia Marsans-Sakly, thank you for being my book accountability partner. It has been wonderful writing our books together. The scholars in the Black Studies program, especially Kris Sealey, Rachelle Brunn-Bevel, Elizabeth Hohl, and Johanna Garvey have been gracious mentors and advisers and patient with me as I tried to direct the program and complete the book. I must also thank Kris Sealey and Dave Wooley for welcoming me into their home for birthday celebrations, and various holidays, and introducing me to their brilliant kids. I am thankful for my sisters and colleagues, Tanika Simpson, LaTasha Smith, and Stephanie Storms, introducing me to New Haven's cultural life. The music, theater, and film have brought balance to my life. Thank you for forcing me to leave my computer.

Jeanne Theoharis and Komozi Woodard came into my academic life at the perfect time. I have learned so much from you as historians and mentors and from your work but also from the ways that you have brought so many scholars together. I got the opportunity to participate in and witness this as part of the 2015 NEH Summer Faculty Seminar, "Rethinking Black Freedom Studies in the Jim Crow North," that you two directed. The deep dive into the scholarship and the opportunity to meet revered scholars such as Matthew Delmont, Eric Gellman, Karen Miller, Brian Purnell, and Clarence Taylor helped me think about my work in new ways. While I learned a lot, I laughed more. Who said historians (and sociologists and literature scholars) are boring? I had so much fun kicking it in Bronxville with my fellow seminarians: Ujju Aggarwal, Mary Barr, Balthazar Beckett, Stefan Bradley, Say Burgin, Kristopher Burrell, Tahir Butt, Natanya Duncan, Aliyah Dunn-Salahuddin, Ayesha Hardison, Laura Hill, Hasan Jeffries, Peter Levy, Crystal Moten, John Portlock, Verdis Robinson, and Lynell Thomas. Brother Purnell, my fellow New Yorker and New York historian, I really appreciate your close reading of my work, especially your ability to see my work in the context of the city's longer Black freedom struggle. I have often gone back to review your comments on my essay. They were instrumental in helping me conceptualize the framework of the book.

The book project would not have been possible without the knowledge and generosity of the librarians and archivists at the College of Wooster, the Rare Book and Manuscript Library and the Oral History Research Office at Columbia University, the Library of Congress Reading Room, the New York City Municipal Archives, the New York Public Library, the Schomburg Center for Research in Black Culture, and the Stephen A. Schwarzman Building.

I want to thank Debbie Gershenowitz and JessieAnne D'Amico at the University of North Carolina Press. Debbie, thank you for your patience. It has been a long journey since 2009 (I think), but we finally got to work together, and it has been a pleasure. Your consistent support has been unmatched. I am grateful for your long-standing support and your many readings and great feedback on the manuscript. I am also indebted to the two anonymous readers and, of course, the brilliant Simon Balto, who read the book and offered many insightful suggestions.

I also want to thank several scholars who have provided support as readers, mentors, or peers: Davarian Baldwin, Stefan Bradley, Amrita Chakrabarti Myers, N. D. B. Connolly, Pero Dagbovie, Erica Armstrong Dunbar, Johanna

Fernandez, Marisa Fuentes, Ayesha Hardison, LaShawn D. Harris, Cheryl D. Hicks, Hasan Jeffries, Randal Jelks, Charles McKinney, Khalil Muhammad, Donna Murch, Carla Murphy, Brian Purnell, Thomas Sugrue, Brandi Thompson Summers, Jeanne Theoharis, Michael O. West, Kidada Williams, and Komozi Woodard. To my New York City sisters, Tiffany M. Gill, "the book whisperer," and LaShawn D. Harris, without fail, you two consistently brought humor, wisdom, and grace to my daily life. Though you doubted my Bronx credentials because of my Harlem roots, I appreciate you and refuse to support either Brooklyn (Dr. Gill) or the Bronx (Dr. Harris) as the better or worse borough in the city. In different ways, your examples as scholars, teachers, and friends have helped me understand the people whom I've written about and have inspired me through song, food, and friendship to complete the project.

From the very beginning, my friends and family's support has been inestimable. I want to thank Charles Peterson, Timothy Johnson, Grant and Eva Vega-Olds for their unwavering friendship and tomfoolery. My Baltimore family, Kamau, Lisa, Dara, and David Sennaar, and my New York family, Jamal Ketcham, Malik Ketcham, Evelyn Fernandez-Ketcham, Elio Fernandez, and Jamilah, Shania, and KaylaRose Ketcham have been my foundation. Family time, sports, coffee, Prince, crime procedurals, and as always talking about politics and culture have gotten me through starting a new job, moving back to the East Coast, and writing another book. Thank you.

Notes

Introduction

1. James Baldwin, "Me and My House . . . ," *Harper's Magazine* 211: 1266 (November 1955), 54.

2. Stuart Hall, Chas Critcher, Tony Jefferson, John Clarke, and Brian Robert, "Preface to the Second Edition," in *Policing the Crisis: Mugging, the State, and Law and Order* (New York: Palgrave Macmillan, 2013), xi.

3. Kali N. Gross, *Colored Amazons: Crime, Violence, and Black Women in the City of Brotherly Love, 1880–1910* (Durham, N.C.: Duke University Press, 2006) and *Hannah Mary Tabbs and the Disembodied Torso: A Tale of Race, Sex, and Violence in America* (New York: Oxford University Press, 2016); Cheryl D. Hicks, *Talk with You like a Woman: African American Women, Justice, and Reform in New York, 1890–1935* (Chapel Hill: University of North Carolina Press, 2010); Khalil G. Muhammad, *Condemnation of Blackness: Race, Crime, and the Making of Modern Urban America* (Cambridge, Mass.: Harvard University Press, 2010); LaShawn D. Harris, *Sex Workers, Psychics, and Numbers Runners: Black Women in New York City's Underground Economy* (Urbana: University of Illinois Press, 2016); Tera E. Agyepong, *The Criminalization of Black Children: Race, Gender, and Delinquency in Chicago's Juvenile Justice System, 1899–1945* (Chapel Hill: University of North Carolina Press, 2018); Carl Suddler, *Presumed Criminal: Black Youth and the Justice System in Postwar New York* (New York: New York University Press, 2019); and Douglas J. Flowe, *Uncontrollable Blackness: African American Men and Criminality in Jim Crow New York* (Chapel Hill: University of North Carolina Press, 2020).

4. For recent engagement with policing, see Special Issue, "African Americans, Police Brutality, and the U.S. Criminal Justice System: Historical Perspectives," *Journal of African American History* 98, no. 2 (Spring 2013): 200–76; and "Special Section: Urban America and the Police since World War II," edited by Christopher Lowen Agee and Themis Chronopoulos, *Journal of Urban History* 46, no. 5 (September 2020): 951–1116; Christopher Agee, *The Streets of San Francisco: Policing and the Creation of a Cosmopolitan Liberal Politics, 1950–1972* (Chicago: University of Chicago Press, 2014); Elizabeth Hinton, *From the War on Poverty to the War on Crime: The Making of Mass Incarceration in America* (Cambridge, Mass.: Harvard University Press, 2016); Max Felker-Kantor, *Policing Los Angeles: Race, Resistance, and the Rise of the LAPD* (Chapel Hill: University of North Carolina Press, 2018); Clarence Taylor, *Fight the Power: African Americans and the Long History of Police Brutality in New York City* (New York: New York University Press, 2018); Simon Balto, *Occupied Territory: Policing Black Chicago from the Red Summer to Black Power* (Chapel

Hill: University of North Carolina Press, 2019). An older body of scholarship that has also influenced this work includes Jill Nelson, *Police Brutality: An Anthology* (New York: W. W. Norton, 2000); Dwight Watson, *Race and the Houston Police Department, 1930–1990* (College Station: Texas A&M University Press, 2005); Leonard N. Moore, *Black Rage in New Orleans: Police Brutality and African American Activism from World War II to Hurricane Katrina* (Baton Rouge: Louisiana State University Press, 2010); and chapters on police brutality and attention to policing as central to the Black freedom struggle; see Martha Biondi, *To Stand and Fight: The Struggle for Civil Rights in Postwar New York City* (Cambridge, Mass.: Harvard University Press, 2003); Robert O. Self, *American Babylon: Race and the Struggle for Postwar Oakland* (Princeton, N.J.: Princeton University Press, 2003); Karl E. Johnson, "Police-Black Community Relations in Postwar Philadelphia: Race and Criminalization in Urban Social Spaces, 1945–1960," *Journal of African American History* 89, no. 2 (Spring 2004): 118–34; Matthew Countryman, *Up South: Civil Rights and Black Power in Philadelphia* (Philadelphia: University of Pennsylvania Press, 2006); Donna Murch, *Living for the City: Migration, Education, and the Rise of the Black Panther Party in Oakland, California* (Chapel Hill: University of North Carolina Press, 2010).

5. Naomi Murakawa, *The First Civil Right: How Liberals Built Prison America* (New York: Oxford University Press, 2014); Agee, *Streets of San Francisco*; Hinton, *From the War on Poverty*; and Felker-Kantor, *Policing Los Angeles*; Michael W. Flamm, *Law and Order: Street Crime, Civil Unrest, and the Crisis of Liberalism in the 1960s* (New York: Columbia University Press, 2005). Also see Muhammad's *Condemnation of Blackness* regarding a Black law-and-order politics.

6. Michael Fortner, *Black Silent Majority: The Rockefeller Drug Laws and the Politics of Punishment* (Cambridge, Mass.: Harvard University Press, 2015); James Forman Jr., *Locking Up Our Own: Crime and Punishment in Black America* (New York: Farrar, Straus and Giroux, 2017). Noel K. Wolfe, a historian, has also contributed to this scholarship; see "Battling Crack: A Study of the Northwest Bronx Community and the Clergy's Coalition Tactics," *Journal of Urban History* 43, no. 1 (January 2017): 18–32. For a nuanced appraisal of the drug crime crisis and the Black community's response by a historian, see Donna Murch, "Crack in Los Angeles: Crisis, Militarization, and Black Response to the Late Twentieth-Century War on Drugs," *Journal of American History* 102, no. 1 (June 2015): 168–72. Murch frames the Black response within the context of police violence but also discusses how Blacks supported both punitive and what she calls an "anti–drug war sentiment" that explained the drug crisis in socioeconomic and political terms related to Reagan-era politics.

7. Scholarship on Mayor Fiorello H. La Guardia has mainly examined how the mayor managed the two uprisings. Consequently, the multiple relationships among whites, Blacks, the police, and the criminal justice system have escaped this scholarship. See Dominic J. Capeci Jr., *The Harlem Riot of 1943* (Philadelphia: Temple University Press, 1977). Although he covers La Guardia's three administrations, Capeci mainly limits discussions of policing and crime to their roles in shaping conditions before and after the riot. For other scholarship that offers more general information on the uprising, see Thomas Kessner, *Fiorello H. La Guardia and the Making of Modern New York* (New York: McGraw-Hill, 1989); Alyn Brodsky, *Great*

Mayor: Fiorello La Guardia and the Making of the City of New York (New York: St. Martin's, 2003).

8. Quote from Karen R. Miller, *Managing Inequality: Northern Racial Liberalism in Interwar Detroit* (New York: New York University Press, 2015), 9. Self, *American Babylon*, 13–14. Self describes New Deal liberalism, as the New Deal program's "institutions, and its commitment to a modified welfare state," and racial liberalism, as "racially equal opportunity in social and political life, as well as some state intervention to achieve an 'equal playing field.'" See also Daniel Martinez HoSang, *Racial Propositions: Ballot Initiatives and the Making of Postwar California* (Berkeley: University of California, 2010). For an important discussion of the variability of northern liberalism as part of a racial system outside the South, see Brian Purnell and Jeanne Theoharis's "Introduction" in *The Strange Careers of the Jim Crow North: Segregation and Struggle outside of the South*, edited by Brian Purnell and Jeanne Theoharis with Komozi Woodard (New York: New York University Press, 2019), 9–10.

9. Cheryl Greenberg, *"Or Does It Explode?": Black Harlem and the Great Depression* (New York: Oxford University Press, 1997), 42; Clyde V. Kiser, "Diminishing Family Income in Harlem: A Possible Cause of the Harlem Riot," *Opportunity: Journal of Negro Life* (June 1935): 172.

10. Elmer Anderson Carter, "The A. F. of L and the Negro," *Opportunity: Journal of Negro Life* (November 1929): 335; and William Green, "Correspondence," *Opportunity: Journal of Negro Life* (December 1929): 381.

11. Thomas Kessner, *Fiorello H. La Guardia and the Making of Modern New York* (New York: McGraw-Hill, 1989), 171.

12. Mason B. Williams, *City of Ambition: FDR, La Guardia, and the Making of Modern New York* (New York: W. W. Norton, 2013), 161, 182, 205.

13. *A Report of the New York Urban League*, box 32, folder: New York Urban League Study 1935 (Revision), Part 1, Series 4, Department of Industrial Relations, National Urban League Records, Collection of the Manuscript Division, Library of Congress, 4.

14. "Rev. A. Clayton Powell Bars Father Divine from Abyssinian Baptist Church Protest Meeting against Discrimination in Relief," *New York Age*, December 22, 1934, 1.

15. Greenberg, *"Or Does It Explode?,"* 114–39; Roi Ottely, *New World A-Coming: Inside Black America* (Boston: Houghton Mifflin, 1943), 113–21.

16. Shannon King, *Whose Harlem Is This, Anyway?: Community Politics and Grassroots Activism during the New Negro Era* (New York: New York University Press, 2015).

17. Hall et al., "Preface to the Second Edition," xii.

18. Greenberg, *"Or Does It Explode?,"* 126–28.

19. Here, I'm building on historian Mason B. Williams's discussion of the growing political enmity between local and national electoral politics, as a result of La Guardia's connection to Roosevelt. Williams, *City of Ambition*, 222–28, 209. Williams is quoting columnist Arthur Krock, who criticized Harry Hopkins and the Works Progress Administration.

20. Hall et al., "Preface to the Second Edition," xii.

21. For a discussion of the discursive framings and strategies of liberals outside the South to manage Black protest, see Jeanne Theoharis, *A More Beautiful and Terrible History: The Uses and Misuses of Civil Rights History* (Boston, Mass.: Beacon, 2018).

22. Muhammad, *Condemnation of Blackness*, 9. Muhammad writes, describing "race liberals," "The shift from a racial biological frame to a racial cultural frame *kept* race at the heart of the discourse." For the connection between racial liberalism and Black criminality during World War II and especially the postwar era, see Murakawa's book on liberal law and order, *The First Civil Right*, 8–15; 32–37. *The Politics of Safety* builds on Murakawa's work, but *The First Civil Right* centers the postwar era and federal liberal law and order; on the other hand, The *Politics of Safety* gauges the La Guardia administration's response to Black crime and Black uprisings, so this work offers a local variation.

23. Purnell and Theoharis, "Introduction," 8.

24. Hall et al., "Preface to the Second Edition," xii.

25. On the primary and secondary definers of the news, see Hall et al., *Policing the Crisis*, 60–63.

26. Suddler, *Presumed Criminal*, 70–84. Thus, as historian Thomas Sugrue has argued regarding urban politics in Detroit, *The Politics of Safety* spotlights the vulnerability of the New Deal coalition from the very beginning. For anti-Black white mobilization and violence around housing in the early postwar era, see Thomas J. Sugrue, "Crabgrass-Roots Politics: Race, Rights, and the Reaction against Liberalism in the Urban North, 1940–1964," *Journal of American History* 82, no. 2 (September 1995): 551–78; and Arnold Hirsch, *Making the Second Ghetto: Race and Housing in Chicago, 1940–1960* (Chicago: University of Chicago Press, 1998).

27. Edward J. Escobar, *Race, Police, and the Making of a Political Identity: Mexican Americans and the Los Angeles Police Department, 1900–1945* (Berkeley: University of California Press, 1999), 286.

28. All quotes from Hall et al., *Policing the Crisis*, 61.

29. For "autonomous police discretion," see Agee, *Streets of San Francisco*, 8.

30. Stuart Hall, *The Fateful Triangle: Race, Ethnicity, Nation* (Cambridge, Mass.: Harvard University Press, 2017), 47. Hall's comments on racial discourse, "What matters historically is that these meanings then organize and are inscribed within the practices and operations of relations of power between groups."

31. Martin J. Murray, *Panic City: Crime and the Fear Industries in Johannesburg* (Stanford, Calif.: Stanford University Press, 2020), 30; and Escobar, *Race, Police,* 286.

32. For Harlem uprisings, policing, and Black activism in the 1930s and 1940s, see Capeci Jr., *Harlem Riot of 1943* and Greenberg, *"Or Does It Explode?."* Capeci and especially Greenberg provide excellent background to the social and political conditions that shaped the Harlem uprisings, but neither examines police brutality beyond its role as a catalyst to the uproar. More significantly, policing of Black neighborhoods is not placed within the context of interracial conflict. For police

brutality, see Marilynn S. Johnson's *Street Justice: A History of Police Violence in New York City* (Boston: Beacon, 2006); Biondi, *To Stand and Fight*; Barbara Ransby, "Cops, Schools, and Communism: Local Politics and Global Ideologies—New York in the 1950s," in *Civil Rights in New York City: From World War II to the Giuliani Era*, edited by Clarence Taylor (New York: Fordham University Press, 2011), 32–51; and Taylor, *Fight the Power*. Johnson's sweeping narrative mainly treats police violence as a trigger to the uprising and the immediate aftermath, while Taylor foregrounds Black organized responses to police brutality; for policing and the criminalization of Black youth, see Luis Alvarez's *The Power of the Zoot: Youth Culture and Resistance during World War II* (Berkeley: University of California Press, 2008) and Carl Suddler's *Presumed Criminal: Black Youth and the Justice System in Postwar New York* (New York: New York University Press, 2019). For Black activism, see Greenberg, *"Or Does It Explode?"*; Johnson, *Street Justice*; Mark Naison, *Communists in Harlem during the Depression* (University of Illinois Press, 2004); Farah Jasmine Griffin, *Harlem Nocturne: Women Artists and Progressive Politics during World War II* (New York: Basic Civitas, 2013); Taylor, *Fight the Power*; Suddler, *Presumed Criminal*; for other works addressing Black politics in the areas of Black activism, policing, or collective violence during the 1930s and 1940s outside New York City, see Balto, *Occupied Territory*; Beth Tompkins Bates, *The Making of Black Detroit in the Age of Henry Ford* (Chapel Hill: University of North Carolina Press, 2014); Victoria W. Wolcott, *Race, Riots, and Roller Coasters: The Struggle over Segregated Recreation in America* (Philadelphia: University of Pennsylvania Press, 2012); Ann Collins, *All Hell Broke Loose: American Race Riots from the Progressive Era through World War II* (Santa Barbara, Calif.: Praeger, 2012); Dominic J. Capeci Jr. and Martha Wilkerson, *Layered Violence: The Detroit Rioters of 1943* (Jackson: University of Mississippi, 2009); Escobar, *Race, Police*; Hirsch, *Making the Second Ghetto*.

33. Gross, *Colored Amazons*, 62. Of course, this is not an effort to conflate the Black elite's responses to Black women with Black men or Black boys and girls, for that matter.

34. Hicks, *Talk with You*; Arthur Browne, *One Righteous Man: Samuel Battle and the Shattering of the Color line in New York* (Boston, Mass.: Beacon, 2015); and King, *Whose Harlem*.

35. For moral suasion and self-defense in New York City as a form of safety in the twentieth century before the Great Depression, see Marcy S. Sacks, *Before Harlem: The Black Experience in New York City before World War I* (Philadelphia: University of Pennsylvania Press, 2006); Hicks, *Talk with You*; King, *Whose Harlem*; for Black resistance in the postwar era, including calls for more police, organized protest, and litigation, see Taylor, *Fight the Power*; and Suddler, *Presumed Criminal*. Also see the biography on Battle, Browne, *One Righteous Man*.

36. Heather Ann Thompson, "Why Mass Incarceration Matters: Rethinking Crisis, Decline, and Transformation in Postwar American History," *Journal of American History* 97, no. 3 (December 2010): 706.

37. For "Jim Crow policing," see Shannon King, "A Murder in Central Park: Racial Violence and the Crime Wave in New York during the 1930s and 1940s," in *The*

Strange Careers of the Jim Crow North: Segregation and Struggle outside of the South, edited by Brian Purnell and Jeanne Theoharis with Komozi Woodard (New York: New York University Press, 2019), 45. For an example in the urban south see Jeffrey S. Adler, *Murder in New Orleans: The Creation of Jim Crow Policing* (Chicago: University of Chicago Press, 2019).

38. Randall Kennedy, *Race, Crime, and the Law* (New York: Vintage Books, 1997), 29.

39. W. Marvin Dulaney, *Black Police in America* (Bloomington: Indiana University Press, 1996), 13.

40. Muhammad, *Condemnation of Blackness*, 229. Muhammad describes this form of Black activism among race relations experts and social scientists as "writing crime into class." He writes, "Structural inequality . . . became the primary basis for explaining Black criminality."

41. Forman Jr., *Locking Up Our Own*, 12.

42. For Juvenile Aid Bureau, the Police Athletic League, and the juvenile justice work of Jane Bolin, see Suddler, *Presumed Criminal*, 13–38; for a biography of Bolin, see Jacqueline A. McLeod, *Daughter of the Empire States: The Life of Judge Jane Bolin* (Urbana: University of Illinois Press, 2011); for crime prevention and protection of Black women, see Hicks, *Talk with You*.

43. "Law and order" has mainly been framed as a political and crime policy of the state; see Flamm, *Law and Order*; Murakawa, Hinton, and Felker-Kantor cited above. As *The Politics of Safety* demonstrates, Black New Yorkers not only employed the term "law and order" but also used it to make sense of "crime" and policing in multiple ways. This work, of course, is not the first to demonstrate the various ways Blacks responded to crime. See note 2, above.

44. Scholars, especially social scientists since the 1960s, have framed these earlier forms of collective violence as pogroms (mob violence), communal riots (interracial violence), or commodity riots (violence upon property). Others writing about the postwar era, especially the 1960s, termed collective forms of violence as "riots," a spontaneous disorder of mass criminality; "rebellions" or "uprisings," as forms of collective action with definable political objectives. Peter Levy, *The Great Uprising: Race Riots in Urban America during the 1960s* (New York: Cambridge University Press, 2018), 1–13; Elizabeth Hinton, *America on Fire: The Untold History of Police Violence and Black Rebellion since the 1960s* (New York: Liveright, 2021), 1–16. For further discussion of riots and uprisings see Capeci Jr., *Harlem Riot of 1943*, 169–84; Dominic J. Capeci Jr., "Foreword: American Race Rioting in Historical Perspective," in *Encyclopedia of American Race Riots*, edited by Walter Rucker and James Nathaniel Upton (Westport, Conn.: Greenwood, 2006), xix–xlii; Heather Thompson, "Urban Uprisings: Riots or Rebellions," in *The Columbia Guide to America in the 1960s*, edited by David Farber and Beth Bailey (New York: Columbia University Press, 2001), 109–17; Donna Murch, "The Many Meanings of Watts: Black Power, Wattstax, and the Carceral State," *OAH Magazine of History* 26, no. 1 (January 2012): 37–40; Kwame Holmes, "Beyond the Flames: Queering the History of the 1968 D.C. Riot," in *No Tea, No Shade: New Writings in Black Queer Studies*, edited by E. Patrick Johnson (Durham, N.C.: Duke University Press, 2016), 303–22.

Chapter 1

1. "Harlem, N.Y., Scene of Big Riot," *Indianapolis Recorder*, July 28, 1928, box I: C362, folder: Harlem, NYC, 1928, National Association for the Advancement of Colored People Records, Manuscript Division, Library of Congress (hereafter, NAACP Records, LOC).

2. "2300 Negroes Fight 150 Harlem Police," *New York Times*, July 23, 1938, 1.

3. "Harlem, N.Y., Scene of Big Riot."

4. "Newspapermade Riots," *New York Age*, August 4, 1928, 4.

5. "Why 3,000 Harlem Citizens Rebelled against the Authority of the Police Department," *New York Amsterdam News*, July 25, 1928, 1.

6. "2300 Negroes," 1, 2.

7. "No Mob Rule for New York," *New York World* (New York City) July 24, 1928; "Four Policemen Hurt in Harlem in Racial Riot," *New York Herald Tribune*, July 23, 1928, box I: C362, folder: Harlem, NYC, 1928, NAACP Records, LOC.

8. "No Mob Rule for New York." For more on the commotion in 1928, see Shannon King, *Whose Harlem Is This, Anyway?:Community Politics and Grassroots Activism during the New Negro Era* (New York: New York University Press, 2015), 177–83.

9. "Control the Police," *New York Amsterdam News*, August 1, 1928, 1.

10. Richard A. Leo, *Police Interrogation and American Justice* (Cambridge, Mass.: Harvard University Press, 2009), 41–77; Marilynn S. Johnson, *Street Justice: A History of Police Violence in New York City* (Boston: Beacon, 2003), 114–48.

11. Robert M. Fogelson, *Big-City Police* (Cambridge, Mass.: Harvard University Press, 1977); Christopher Lowen Agee, *The Streets of San Francisco: Policing and the Creation of a Cosmopolitan Liberal Politics, 1950–1972* (Chicago: University of Chicago Press, 2014), 8–9.

12. My conceptualization of "liberal law and order" derives from a reading of Khalil G. Muhammad's classic, *Condemnation of Blackness: Race, Crime, and the Making of Modern Urban America* (Cambridge, Mass.: Harvard University Press, 2010). In *Condemnation of Blackness*, Muhammad introduces what might be dubbed the first moment of liberal law and order. Before historians centering the post–World War II era published about "liberal law and order," Muhammad presented a cast of Black and white historical actors—civic leaders and social scientists as well as mayors, district attorneys, and police commissioners—who approached the criminal justice system through a liberal formulation that generally, at least publicly, rejected the inherent criminality of Blacks. Muhammad also illustrates how African Americans inaugurated a more community-oriented form of policing. Describing the work of the League of Civic and Political Reform (LCPR), a crime prevention and crime-fighting organization founded by James Stemons, he writes, "By basically calling for community policing before it became a staple in the arsenal against inner-city crime, the [LCPR] represented a practical response to Du Bois's earlier proposition that the 'duty of the Negroes' in Philadelphia should 'first be directed toward a lessening of Negro crime.'" For quote, see Muhammad, *Condemnation of Blackness*, 187. My formulation of "liberal law and order" is also shaped by Karen R. Miller's

Managing Inequality: Northern Racial Liberalism in Interwar Detroit (New York: New York University Press, 2014), 9 and Naomi Murakawa's *The First Civil Right: How Liberals Built Prison America* (New York: Oxford University Press, 2014).

13. Daniel Czitrom, *New York Exposed: The Gilded Age Police Scandal that Launched the Progressive Era* (New York: Oxford University Press, 2016), 103–4.

14. Fogelson, *Big-City Police*, 37, 20.

15. Frank Moss, *The Story of the Riot* (New York: Citizens' Protective League, 1900), 2. For more on the 1900 race riot, see Herbert Shapiro, *White Violence and Black Resistance: From Reconstruction to Montgomery* (Amherst: University of Massachusetts Press, 1988), 93–98; Cheryl D. Hicks, *Talk with You like a Woman: African American Women, Justice, and Reform in New York, 1890–1935* (Chapel Hill: University of North Carolina Press, 2010), 53–90; King, *Whose Harlem*, 1–2.

16. Moss, *Story of the Riot*, 37, 38–39, 48, 50–51.

17. Moss, *Story of the Riot*, 3, 4.

18. "Attorney General Moves to Curb Lawless Law Enforcement, Scoring 'Drives' on Crime—Canada Created Precedent in 'Hot Pursuit' Cases," *New York Times*, April 14, 1929, 61.

19. Czitrom, *New York Exposed*, 42–44; "Queries from the Curious and Answers to Them," *New York Times*, July 4, 1909, 54; Dan Barry, "Cheats, Swindlers and Ne'er-Do-Wells: A New York Family Album," *New York Times*, February 9, 2018, www.nytimes.com/2018/02/09/nyregion/cheats-swindlers-and-neer-do-wells-a-new-york-family-album.html.

20. "He Rules through Fear," *New York Times*, December 10, 1893, 13.

21. "Police Chiefs Tell of Past Adventures," *New York Times*, May 17, 1908, SM7; Thomas Byrnes, "The 'Third Degree' Its Successful Use by the Police in Detecting Criminals," *New York Tribune*, October 8, 1908, Sunday Magazine 3; J. North Conway, *The Big Policeman: The Rise and Fall of America's First, Most Ruthless, and Greatest Detective* (Guilford, Conn.: Lyons, 2019), 3–4.

22. Samuel Walker, *A Critical History of Police Reform: The Emergence of Professionalism* (Lexington, Mass.: Lexington Books, 1977), 58.

23. For autonomous police discretion, see Agee, *Streets of San Francisco*, 8.

24. Quotes from "Condemns The Third Degree," *New York Times*, April 16, 1910, 8; "Life Saved by Third Degree," *New York Times*, April 11, 1910, 18. One letter writer, Frank S. Fitch, believed that lawyers manufactured stories of police abuse to free their clients. Fitch, "Third Degree," *New York Times*, April 21, 1910, 10.

25. "The Third Degree," *New York Times*, April 17, 1910, 10.

26. Edward Marshall "American Police Are Regarded with Suspicion," *New York Times*, November 27, 1910, 1.

27. For a broader analysis of the conflict between the NYPD, magistrates, and the Gaynor administration, see Johnson, *Street Justice*, 100–107.

28. "Attacks the Mayor for the Crime Wave," *New York Times*, March 23, 1911, 1.

29. "Attacks the Mayor," 1.

30. "Corrigan's Attack Raises a Storm," *New York Times*, March 24, 1911, 4; "300 Mulberry St. Passes into History," *New York Times*, November 28, 1909, 18.

31. "Corrigan Wrong, They Say," *The Sun*, March 24, 1911, 1.

32. "Go to Albany to Fight Grady Bill," *Star-Gazette*, Elmira, New York, June 24, 1911, 3.

33. "Anti-Mugging Bill Passed," *The Sun*, June 14, 1911, 2; Quote from "Vetoes 'Anti-Mugging' Bill," *New York Times*, June 29, 1911, 1.

34. J. W. G., "Mayor Gaynor's Police Reforms in New York," *Journal of the American Institute of Criminal Law and Criminology* 1, no. 2 (July 1910); Arthur W. Towne, "Mayor Gaynor's Police Policy and the 'Crime Wave' in New York City," *Journal of the American Institute of Criminal Law and Criminology* 2, no. 3 (September 1911): 375, 376; Quote from J. W. G., "Veto of the New York Anti-mugging Bill," *Journal of the American Institute of Criminal Law and Criminology* 2, no. 3 (September 1911): 344.

35. Edwin R. Keedy, "The 'Third Degree' and Trial by Newspapers," *Journal of the American Institute of Criminal Law and Criminology* 3, no. 4 (November 1912): 502–5; Frank D. Casassa, "Using the Beneficent Third Degree," *Washington Post*, March 28, 1915, M4; and A. C. Sedgwick, "The Third Degree and Crime," *The Nation* 124, no. 3232 (June 15, 1927): 666–67.

36. "Whalen to Head Police," December 9, 1928, 2; "Whalen Orders Clean-up: Tells Police to Shut Broadway Clubs," *Daily News*, December 20, 1928, 10; "Whalen Rushes Vice War in Bootleg Crime Drive," *Daily News*, December 21, 1928, 2, 6.

37. "Strong Arm Squads Go Out, Gangsters Run to Cover; 60 More Speakeasy Raids," *New York Times*, January 4, 1929; "Police Methods," *New York Times*, January 12, 1929, 11; "Business Men Pay Tribute to Whalen," *New York Times*, January 23, 1929, 3.

38. Quotes from "Whalen, Back, Asks 'Facts' on Traffic: Commissioner Says He Is Ready to Right Any Wrongs in Theatre Rules," *New York Times*, February 25, 1929, 1, 11; "Returning Whalen Likes His Traffic," *Daily News*, February 25, 1929, 14; "Back on the Job," *New York Times*, February 27, 1929, 15.

39. Quote from "Hays Hits Whalen War on Criminal," *Brooklyn Daily Eagle*, March 12, 1929, 24; "Assails 1,350 Arrests in Garment Strike," *New York Times*, March 13, 1929, 62; quotes about aggressive policemen from "Whalen Sees Crime as Huge Problem," *New York Times*, March 16, 1920, 14; and "figment of the imaginations" in "Again Asks Crime Study," *New York Times*, March 19, 1929, 16.

40. "The Third Degree," *New York Times*, February 17, 1930, 16; "Wickersham Board Hits 'Third Degree' and Brutal Police," *New York Times*, August 11, 1931, 1; "New York Officials Deny Being Brutal," *New York Times*, August 11, 1931, 11; and "The Third Degree," *New York Times*, February 11, 1932, 20.

41. For works by journalists, see Ernest Jerome Hopkins, *Our Lawless Police* (New York: Viking Press, 1931) and Emanuel H. Lavine, *Third Degree: A Detailed and Appalling Exposé of Police Brutality* (New York: Vanguard Press, 1930); quote from "Wickersham Board Hits 'Third Degree,'" 1; National Commission on Law Observance and Enforcement, *Reports, Volume IV, No. 11. Report on Lawlessness in Law Enforcement* (Washington, DC: U.S. Government Printing Office, 1931), 22–23.

42. *Report on Lawlessness in Law Enforcement*, 87–88.

43. *Report on Lawlessness in Law Enforcement*, 88. On the failure of the Wickersham report to consider race and racism, see Johnson, *Street Justice*, 136; Muhammad, *Condemnation of Blackness*, 266.

44. "Man Hunt On in Black Belt for Negro Slayer of 2 Detectives," *New York Daily News*, January 7, 1922, 2; "Boddy, Caught in Philadelphia, Admits He Killed Detectives," *New York Daily News*, January 10, 1922, 2; "Negro Man Killer Taken in Bed Here at Pistol's Point," *Philadelphia Inquirer*, January 10, 1922, 1.

45. "Boddy, Caught in Philadelphia," 1.

46. "'First Degree Murder' Verdict by Jury in Luther Boddy Trial," *New York Age*, February 4, 1922, 1.

47. Court of Appeals of the State of New York. The People of the State of New York, Respondent, against Luther Boddy, Defendant-Appellant. Record on Appeal, vol. 98, 1922, 427–29; for the discussion of deniable physical abuse, see Leo, *Police Interrogation*, 48–50.

48. "Eyewitnesses Say Boddy Did Not Kill Cops," *Chicago Defender*, January 21, 1922, 3.

49. "Warning to Policemen: Those That 'Beat Up' Prisoners Make Your Work Dangerous," *Negro World*, January 21, 1922, 11; and "Boddy Testifies to Police Beating," *New York Times*, January 27, 1922.

50. W. E. B. Du Bois, "Opinion," *The Crisis* (March 1922), 199.

51. "Luther Boddy Paid Death Penalty, Night of Aug. 31," *New York Age*, September 9, 1922, 1.

52. "Negro Thug Killed in Fight at Station," *New York Times*, June 28, 1922, 19; "Sleuths Held in Blameless in Death of Negro," *Daily News* (New York, New York), June 28, 1922, 4.

53. All quotes from "Negro Thug Killed," 19; "Negro Who Shot Policeman Killed in Police Station," *Evening World* (New York, New York), June 27, 1922, 1.

54. "Are the Police Unnecessarily Brutal in Treatment of Prisoners at the West 135th Street Station," *New York Age*, July 1, 1922, 1, 5.

55. "Are the Police Unnecessarily Brutal," 5.

56. "Police Brutality Is Subject of Criticism," *New York Age*, July 8, 1922, 5.

57. "Many Cases Indicate Epidemic of Brutality as Practiced by Members of Police Force," *New York Age*, July 15, 1922, 1.

58. "Many Cases Indicate Epidemic," 1.

59. "Police Brutality Is Subject," 5.

60. "Additional Developments in the Matter of Police Brutality Indicate Need of Change," *New York Age*, July 22, 1922, 2.

61. "Additional Developments," 2.

62. Leo, *Police Interrogation*, 55, 63.

63. For Black protest against police brutality in Harlem during the New Negro era, see King, *Whose Harlem*, 154–74; David F. Krugler, *1919, the Year of Racial Violence: How African Americans Fought Back* (New York: Cambridge University Press, 2015).

64. King, *Whose Harlem*, 171.

65. "Additional Developments," 2.

66. "Additional Developments," 1.

67. "City and County Authorities Are Asked to Investigate Beating to Death of H. Dent," *New York Age*, July 29, 1922, 1.

68. "Dist. Atty. Banton Promises Action," *New York Age*, August 5, 1922, 1, 2.

69. "Attorney Hoffman Takes Up Dent Killing with Banton," *New York Age*, September 2, 1922, 1; "Banton Urged to Act in Herbert Dent Case" *New York Age*, September 23, 1922, 1.

70. "Banton Tries to Shift Burden in Matter of Dent Investigation," *New York Age*, September 30, 1922, 2.

71. "Eyewitness Tells the Story of Beating Herbert Dent to Death," *New York Age*, November 11, 1922, 1.

72. "Eyewitness Tells the Story," 2.

73. "District Attorney Banton Will Not Act in Dent Case," *New York Age*, December 30, 1922, 1.

74. "Hoffman Again Puts Dent Killing up to Dist. Atty.," *New York Age*, January 27, 1923, 5.

75. "Negro Thug Killed in Fight at Station," *New York Times*, June 28, 1922, 19.

76. Letter to Honorable Panger from St. William Grant, November 11, 1928, New York City Indictment No. 174626, Calendar No. 52964. Municipal Archives of the City of New York.

77. "Magistrate Bushel Expresses Doubt of 'Riot' Witness' Guilt," *New York Amsterdam News*, August 29, 1928, 2.

78. People against St. William Grant, Statement of George Webber, 16th Squad. Made to Assistant District Attorney Morris H. Panger. October 31, 1928, 3, New York City Indictment No. 174466, Calendar No. 52962, September 27, 1928, Municipal Archives of the City of New York.

79. People against St. William Grant, 3 and *New York Amsterdam News*, August 22, 1928.

80. According to the *New York Amsterdam News*, Donald and Grant were members of the Universal Improvement Association. See "U.N.I.A. Head Scores Police Brutality," *New York Amsterdam News*, September 5, 1928, 1; "Hon. E. B. Knox, American Leader, Discusses Our Plans and Policies at Garvey Day Memorial Meeting," *Negro World*, September 15, 1928, 2–3. For a biography of St. William Grant, see Robert A. Hill, *The Marcus Garvey and Universal Negro Improvement Association Papers* 7 (Berkeley: University of California Press, 1992): 309–10.

81. "Magistrate Bushel," 2.

82. "Magistrate Bushel," 2; King, *Whose Harlem*, 181–82.

83. "Magistrate Bushel," 2.

84. "Lawless Policemen," *New York Amsterdam News*, October 17, 1928, 16.

85. "Police Terrorism," *New York Amsterdam News*, March 13, 1929, 16; King, *Whose Harlem*, 183–85.

86. "Police Brutality Seen as Man Dies in Prison," *New York Amsterdam News*, March 5, 1930, 1; "Cop's Brutality Alleged in Case of Benj. Chase," *New York Age*, March 8, 1930, 1; "Believe Beating Caused Man's Death," *Norfolk New Journal and Guide*, March 8, 1930, 1.

87. "The Third Degree," *New York Amsterdam News*, August 18, 1926, 20.

Chapter 2

1. Lewis J. Valentine, *Night Stick: The Autobiography of Lewis J Valentine, Former Police Commissioner of New York* (New York: Dial, 1947) 15–16, 17.

2. "Patrolman Shoots Negro Student as He Flees after Clash over Seat in Elevated Train," *New York Times*, September 10, 1929, 1; "Police Shooting Inquiry Ordered," *New York Telegram*, October 19, 1929, newspaper clippings, Cases Supported, Ralph Baker, October 1–29,1929, Papers of the NAACP, Part 8: Discrimination in the Criminal Justice System, 1910–1955, Series A: Legal Department and Central Office Records, 1910–1939, ProQuest History Vault (hereafter cited as Cases Supported, Ralph Baker).

3. James Weldon Johnson, Secretary to the Hon. Grover A. Whalen, Commissioner of Police, September 10, 1929; James Weldon Johnson, Secretary to the Hon. Charles J. Dodd, District Attorney, Kings County, September 11, 1929, Cases Supported, Ralph Baker, September 10–16, 1929; "Shot Negro, Suspended," *New York Times*, September 11, 1929, 8.

4. Walter White to Dr. Roberts, September 10, 1929, Cases Supported, Ralph Baker, September 10–16, 1929.

5. William Hallock Johnson, President to Walter White, Secretary NAACP, September 12; Walter White, Assistant Secretary to Dr. Johnson, September 13, 1–2, Cases Supported, Ralph Baker, September 10–16, 1929; Wm Hallock Johnson to Mr. Walter White, September 17, 1929, NAACP, Cases Supported, Ralph Baker, September 17–30, 1929.

6. William Pickens to Mr. Johnson, Mr. White, Mr. Bagnall, September 20, 1929, Cases Supported, Ralph Baker, September 17–30, 1929.

7. Beta Chapter, Omega Psi Phi Fraternity, Lincoln University to Walter White, September 2?; Epsilon Sigma Chapter of the Phi Beta Sigma Fraternity, NAACP, Cases Supported, Ralph Baker, September 17–30, 1929.

8. "N.A.A.C.P. Calls upon Kings Authorities to Jail Patrolman," *New York Amsterdam News*, September 18, 1929, 1; Statement made by Ralph Baker, at the St. John Hospital, Brooklyn, New York, September 16, 1929; William Fontaine, affidavit, September 11, 1929, Cases Supported, Ralph Baker, September 10–16, 1929.

9. Gladys Brendhagen, affidavit, September 12, 1929, Cases Supported, Ralph Baker, September 10–16, 1929.

10. "N.A.A.C.P. Calls upon Kings Authorities to Jail Patrolman," *New York Amsterdam News*, September 18, 1929, 1; "Demand Punishment of Cop Who Shot Lincoln 'U' Student," *Norfolk New Journal and Guide*, September 21, 1929, 10.

11. "Cops Cleared in Shooting of College Student," *New York Age*, October 25, 1929, 1; "Shooting Cop Unfit to Have Revolver, Declares N.A.A.C.P.," *Afro American*, November 2, 1929, 5.

12. Quote from "Court Cleanup Demanded," *Daily News*, December 22, 1929, 4; Louis Ruppel, "Rudich off Magistrate's Bench," *Daily News*, January 1, 1930; "Mayor Refers Rudich Case to Bar Ass'n," *Brooklyn Daily Eagle*, January 4, 1930, 1.

13. Walter White, Acting Secretary, to Hon. William McAdoo, Chief Magistrate, City of New York, January 11, 1930, 2, Cases Supported, Ralph Baker, January 5–22, 1930.

14. Walter White, Acting Secretary, to Hon. William McAdoo, 2–3.

15. "Bar Group Plans to Clear Rudich, Tip as Quiz Ends," *Brooklyn Daily Eagle*, January 24, 1930, 1; "No Full Bar Probe of Rudich's Conduct," *Brooklyn Daily Eagle*, January 23, 1930, 3; "Rudich Prober Toastmaster at His Dinner," *Brooklyn Daily Eagle*, January 28, 1930, 1; Quotes from "Rudich Is Upheld; To Be Reappointed," *New York Times*, January 30, 1930, 18; Quotes from Archer in "Report Admits Judge Erred in Shoplift Case," *Brooklyn Daily Eagle*, January 29, 1930, 17.

16. Walter White to Magistrate McAdoo, January 30, 1930, 2, Cases Supported, Ralph Baker, January 23–31, 1930.

17. "McAdoo Orders Arrest of Cop Rudich Released," *Brooklyn Daily Eagle*, February 4, 1930, 3; "Warrant Out for Arrest of Officer Who Shot Student," *New York Amsterdam News*, February 5, 1930, 1; "Cop's Arrest in Colored Youth Shooting Ordered," *Daily News*, February 5, 1930, 17.

18. "Policeman, Freed by Rudich, Is Held," *New York Times*, February 6, 1930, 20.

19. Walter White to Dr. George E. Haynes, February 6, 1930, Cases Supported, Ralph Baker, February 1–6, 1930; "NAACP Brings Arrest of 'Trigger' Officer," *Pittsburgh Courier*, February 15, 1930, 4; "Magistrate Reserves Decision till March 1 in Student Shooter's Case," *New York Amsterdam News*, February 19, 1930, 7; Walter White to Hon. George E. Brower, February 8, 1930, Cases Supported, Ralph Baker, February 7–14, 1930; George E. Brower to Mr. Walter White, February 10, 1930, Cases Supported, Ralph Baker, February 7–14, 1930.

20. Walter White to Hon. George E. Brower, February 27, 1930, 2–3, Cases Supported, Ralph Baker, February 17–28, 1930.

21. Walter White to Hon. George E. Brower, March 5, 1930, Cases Supported, Ralph Baker, March 1–20, 1930.

22. "Patrolman Lowe Held for Grand Jury in Shooting of Lincoln 'U' Students," *New York Amsterdam News*, March 12, 1930, 1; "White Policeman Held for Grand Jury for Shooting of Student," *New York Age*, March 15, 1930, 1.

23. William T. Andrews to Mr. Ellis Williams, March 11, 1930, Cases Supported, Ralph Baker, March 1–30, 1930; Walter White to Members of the Lincoln University Alumni Association, March 14, 1930, 2, Cases Supported, Ralph Baker, March 1–30, 1930; "Absolves Policeman of Assault Charge," *New York Times*, March 26, 1930, 21; "Policeman Freed in Assault Case," *New York Amsterdam News*, April 2, 1930, 18; "Jury Frees N. Y. Cop Who Shot Collegian," *Chicago Defender*, April 5, 1930, 1.

24. "Policeman, Freed by Rudich," 20.

25. Thomas Kessner, *Fiorello H. La Guardia and the Making of Modern New York* (New York: McGraw-Hill, 1989), 132, 186–90.

26. Kessner, *Fiorello H. La Guardia*, 161–63.

27. Quote from "La Guardia Insists Walker New Rothstein," *Times Union* (Brooklyn, N.Y.), October 28, 1929, 42; Louis Ruppel, "Mayor-Rothstein Tieup Refuted by

Date Checkup," *Daily* (New York), October 29, 1929, 8; Louis Ruppel, "La Guardia Throws New Tax Grenades," *Daily* (New York), October 3, 1929, 6.

28. "Critics of Delaney Plan on Buses to Get Hearing: Berry Expected to Defend His Report Tuesday," *New York Herald Tribune*, October 17, 1931, 14.

29. "$631, 366, 297 Budget O/K/'d: Walker Wins Fight with Berry," *Brooklyn Daily Eagle*, November 1, 1931, 2

30. Quote found in Kessner, *Fiorello H. La Guardia*, 219, 217.

31. Mason B. Williams, *City of Ambition: FDR, La Guardia, and the Making of Modern New York* (New York: W. W. Norton 2013), 114.

32. Kessner, *Fiorello H. La Guardia*, 234–45.

33. "Machine Rule the Issue," *New York Age*, October 28, 1933, 4.

34. "La Guardia Friend of Negro, De Priest Says," *New York Amsterdam News*, November 1, 1933, 3.

35. "Police Commissioner O'Ryan Takes Office," *Spring 3100* 4, no. 11 (January 1934): 4.

36. Arthur Watson, "There Is a Santa! N.Y. Gets Real New Deal!," *Daily News* (New York), December 24, 1933, 2.

37. Jack Miley, "La Guardia Pays Debt to O'Ryan," *Daily News* (New York), December 20, 1933, 37; Kessner, *Fiorello H. La Guardia*, 275; Marilynn S. Johnson, *Street Justice: A History of Police Violence in New York City* (Boston: Beacon, 2006), 165.

38. Martin Sommers, "Striking Taximen Beat Drivers and Fares, Smash Cabs," *Daily News* (New York), February 4, 1934, 2.

39. "Anti-Austria Riot Chokes 5th Avenue," *Daily News* (New York), February 15, 1934, 2, 6; "4000 Radicals Battle 300 Police in Anti-Dollfus Riot on 5th Av.," *New York Herald Tribune*, February 15, 1934, 8.

40. "Rioting Marks Taxi Strike," *Star-Gazette* (Elmira, N.Y.), March 22, 1934, 1.

41. Fred Pasley, "King Mob Captures Town as La Guardia Ties Hands of Cops," *New York Daily News*, March 23, 1934, 3, 43.

42. O'Ryan's quote in Kessner, *Fiorello H. La Guardia*, 354; for more on commissioner O'Ryan see Johnson's *Street Justice*, 168–69.

43. "Drivers Accept New Taxi Plan," *Los Angeles Times*, March 27, 1934, 2.

44. "5,500 Attend Holy Name Breakfast," *Spring 3100* 5, no. 2 (April 1934): 11.

45. "Jury Scores Mayor for Taxi Riots," *Daily News*, April 12, 1934, 6.

46. "Mayor Rebukes Taxi Grand Jury," *New York Times*, April 13, 1934, 20.

47. "Moorish Leader Shot, Cops Rapped," *New York Amsterdam News*, March 24, 1934, 11; "Jurors Sift Shooting of Moorism Leader," *New York Amsterdam News*, March 31, 1934, 11.

48. "Jurors Sift Shooting," 11.

49. "Moor Wounded Battling Cops on Policy Raid," *Daily News*, March 11, 1934, 34; "Jury to Visit Man Shot in Gaming Raid," *Daily News*, March 29, 1934; "Take Evidence in Shooting of Moorish Leader, David Fletcher, in Hospital," *New York Age*, April 14, 1934, 12; "Mayor Scored by Grand Jury for Home Raid," *Brooklyn Daily Eagle*, April 16, 1934, 3; "Two Cops Freed in Shooting over Gambling Charge," *Daily News*, April 17, 1934; "Wounds Kill Cops' Victim," *New York Amsterdam News*, June 23, 1934, 1.

50. "Second Woman Attacked in Home by Hammer Man," *Daily News*, April 13, 1934, Brooklyn Section 3; "Mother of Seven Injured in Third Hammer Attack," *Daily News*, May 9, 1934, Brooklyn Section 3; "Hammer Attack Suspect Is Held," *Brooklyn Daily Eagle*, May 26, 1934.

51. "Suspect Held for Assaults," *New York Amsterdam News*, June 2, 1934, 3; quotes in "The Negro Hunt," *New York Amsterdam News*, June 2, 1934, 8.

52. "'Negro' in the Headlines," *New York Age*, June 2, 1934, 6.

53. "'Negro' in the Headlines," 6.

54. Quote from "Clyde Allen to Be Tried," *New York Amsterdam News*, August 18, 1934, 11; "Negro Is Convicted of Hammer Attack," *New York Times*, October 17, 1934, 5; "Clyde Allen Convicted in 'Gorilla Man' Case," *New York Amsterdam News*, October 20, 1934, 1; quote on guilt in "Clyde Allen Claims He Was Tricked by Police," *New York Age*, October 20, 1934, 12; "Hammer Man Gets 17 to 35 Years," *Brooklyn Daily Eagle*, November 27, 1934, 13; "Kings Colored Hammer Fiend Gets 17 ½ Yrs.," *Daily News*, November 28, 1934.

55. James A. Miller, Susan D. Pennybacker, and Eve Rosenhaft, "Mother Ada Wright and the International Campaign to Free the Scottsboro Boys, 1931–1934," *American Historical Review* 106, no. 2 (April 2001): 387–430.

56. "5,000 Fight the Police in Harlem Streets," *New York Times*, March 18, 1934, 1; "Cop Brutality Charge in Red Rioting Probe," *Daily News*, March 19, 1934.

57. "5,000 Fight the Police," 2.

58. "5,000 Battle Cops at Meet for Nine Scottsboro Boys," *Daily Worker*, March 19, 1934, 2.

59. "Harlem Police Face Dismissal or Suspension for Tear Gas Attack on Scottsboro Meeting," *New York Amsterdam News*, March 24, 1934, 2; "5,000 Battle Cops," 2.

60. "Police Investigate Rioting in Harlem," *New York Times*, March 19, 1934, 36.

61. "5,000 Battle Cops," 2; "Harlem Police Face Dismissal or Suspension," 2.

62. "Valentine Scores Use of Tear Gas," *New York Times*, March 22, 1934, 13.

63. "Cops Attacked Peaceful Meet, Inquiry Shows," *Daily Worker*, March 23, 1934, 1.

64. "It's Time to Act," *New York Amsterdam News*, March 24, 1934, 1.

65. Quotes from Chief Inspector, Lewis J. Valentine to Police Commissioner, John F. O' Ryan, Alleged Misconduct of Members of This Department at an Open Air Meeting, Lenox Avenue and 126th Street, Borough Manhattan, March 17, 1934, March 26, 1934, Office of the Mayor, Fiorello H. La Guardia Records (hereafter, La Guardia Records), Series: Subject Files: reel 77, New York City Municipal Archives (hereafter, NYCMA), 5–6; and Police Commissioner, John F. O'Ryan to The Honorable, Fiorello H. La Guardia, Mayor, March 29, 1934, La Guardia Records, Series: Subject Files: reel 77, NYCMA.

66. "Action Delayed in Cop Brutality Probe," *New York Amsterdam News*, May 12, 1934, 2.

67. "Action Delayed," 2.

68. "Two Policemen Cleared," *New York Times*, September 8, 1934, 4.

69. "Cops Cleared of Brutality Charges Here," *New York Amsterdam News*, September 15, 1934, 1.

70. "O'Ryan Must Go," *New York Amsterdam News*, September 15, 1934, 1.

71. "General O'Ryan's Statement on Difference with Mayor," *New York Times*, September 25, 1934, 16.

72. "O'Ryan Out, Valentine to Boss Force," *Brooklyn Daily Eagle*, September 21, 1934, 14.

73. "New Deal, Leniency, to Guide Valentine," *Daily News*, September 22, 1934, 2.

74. Valentine, *Night Stick*, 21, 29.

75. "Mayor Brands O'Ryan Police Charges False," *Daily News*, September 26, 1934, 18.

76. "Thank You, Mr. Mayor," *New York Amsterdam News*, September 29, 1934, 8.

77. Lyman S. Moore, "Municipal Government and Labor Disputes," *American Political Science Review* 31, no. 6 (December 1937): 1121.

78. Valentine, *Night Stick*, 20–21.

79. "Police Get Orders to Terrorize Thugs," *New York Times*, November 27, 1934, 1; "'Rough Stuff for Thugs' Valentine Edict to Cops," *New York Daily News*, November 27, 1934, 10; "Beat Up All Thugs, Police Are Ordered," *Brooklyn Daily Eagle*, November 26, 1934, 1; "Valentine Adds 'Discretion' to 'Muss Up' Order," *New York Herald Tribune*, November 28, 1934, 15.

80. Lewis J. Valentine, "Editorially Speaking," *Spring 3100* 5, no. 10 (December 1934): 3.

81. "Mayor Upholds Police Order to Muss Em Up," *Brooklyn Daily Eagle*, January 21, 1935, 3.

82. "Mayor to Back Cops Who Muss 'Em Up," *Daily News*, January 28, 1935, 20. The police commissioner also legitimated this policy for what he perceived as ethical reasons. Gangsters, who had not earned an honest wage, therefore were also appropriate prey because they were fashionably attired. "Styles Rules Underworld: Topics of the Times," *New York Times*, November 28, 1934, 20.

83. "Cop Accused of Brutal Attack on Boy," *New York Amsterdam News*, October 6, 1934, 3.

84. "N.Y. Pastor Would Remove Police Commissioner," *Afro American*, December 15, 1934, 12.

85. "Crime and Punishment," *New York Amsterdam News*, February 23, 1935, 8.

86. For police brutality and the labor movement and radicals, see Johnson, *Street Justice*, 172–80. She writes that the Valentine era stood "as a watershed in the history of police-community relations." For quote, see Johnson, *Street Justice*, 179.

Chapter 3

1. "Grabbing Knife Just a Whim to Riot Starter," *New York Herald Tribune*, March 21, 1935, 2.

2. "Police Shoot into Rioters," *New York Times*, March 20, 1935, 15.

3. "Harlem Race Riot: 1 Dead; Cops Fire," *New York Daily News*, March 20, 1935, 4.

4. *The Complete Report of Mayor La Guardia's Commission on the Harlem Riot of March 19, 1935* (New York: Arno, 1969), 6.

5. Adam Clayton Powell Sr., *Riots and Ruins* (New York: Richard R. Smith, 1945), 67.

6. Quote from "Police Shoot into Rioters," 15. The detail about the ambulance is found in "Harlem Race Riot," 4, but not in the *New York Times* account.

7. "Harlem Riot Damage Is Figured at Half Million," *Afro-American*, March 30, 1935, 2.

8. "Police Shoot into Rioters," 15. For the cause of the riot, see Cheryl Greenberg, "The Politics of Disorder," *Journal of Urban History* 18, no. 4 (August 1992): 395–441.

9. "1 Dead, 7 Shot, 30 Injured as Harlem Crowds Riot over Boy, 10, and Hearse," *New York Herald Tribune*, March 20, 1935, 9.

10. "1 Dead, 7 Shot, 30 Injured," 1.

11. "650 Police Patrol Harlem to Block Renewed Rioting," *New York Herald Tribune*, March 21, 1935, 1.

12. "Police End Harlem Riot," *New York Times*, March 21, 1935, 16.

13. Edna Ferguson, "Loot Frenzy of Mob Bared in Riot Terror," *Daily News*, March 21, 1935, 4.

14. "Police End Harlem Riot," 16; "One Dead, Scores Hurt, in N. Y. Riot," *Chicago Defender*, March 23, 1935, 1, 3.

15. Cheryl Greenberg, *"Or Does It Explode?": Black Harlem and the Great Depression* (New York: Oxford University Press, 1997), 4; "Harlem Riot Damage," 2; "One Dead, Scores Hurt," 1; "One Killed Scores Hurt in Harlem Riot," *The Sun*, March 20, 1935, 1; "Harlem Riot Was Very Tough on Window Glass: $147,315 Paid for Breakage," *Pittsburgh Courier*, April 6, 1935, A3; "Two Inquiries Under Way; Four Dead; Many Hurt," *Pittsburgh Courier*, March 30, 1935, 1.

16. "Police End Harlem Riot," *New York Times*, March 21, 1935, 1; "Mayor Lays Riot to Vicious Group," *New York Times*, March 21, 1935, 16.

17. "Police End Harlem Riot," 1.

18. "12 Indicted in Riot," *New York Times*, March 22, 1935, 1; Mark Naison, *Communists in Harlem during the Depression* (New York: Grove,1984), 142; Frank Donner, *Protectors of Privilege: Red Squads and Police Repression in Urban America* (Berkeley: University of California Press, 1990), 48; Mark Solomon, *The Cry Was Unity: Communists and African Americans, 1917–1936* (Jackson: University of Mississippi, 1998), 272–75; Marilynn S. Johnson, *Street Justice: A History of Police Violence in New York City* (New York: Beacon, 2003), 149–80, 186–91; for radical repression in Depression-era Chicago, see Simon Balto, *Occupied Territory: Policing Black Chicago from the Red Summer to Black Power* (Chapel Hill: University of North Carolina Press, 2019), 71–90.

19. "Harlem's Stores Ask Soldier Guard," *New York Times*, March 21, 1935, 16.

20. "12 Indicted in Riot," 13.

21. Telegram, To Honorable Mayor F. H. La Guardia from Eugene Walsh, March 20, 1935, Office of the Mayor, Fiorello H. La Guardia Records, Series: Subject Files, box 167, folder 5, New York City Municipal Archives (hereafter, NYCMA).

22. "12 Indicted in Riot," 2. See Shannon King, *Whose Harlem Is This, Anyway?* (New York: New York University Press, 2015) and Naison, *Communists in Harlem*.

23. Imes letter in "What Our Readers Say of the Riot," *New York Amsterdam News*, April 6, 1935, 8; Theophilus Lewis, "Harlem Sketchbook," *New York Amsterdam*

News, April 6, 1935, 8; and Claude McKay, "Harlem Runs Wild," *The Nation*, April 3, 1935. See Greenberg, *"Or Does It Explode?,"* 115–39 and "Politics of Disorder," 402–6; Traci Parker, *Department Stores and the Black Freedom Movement: Workers, Consumers, and Civil Rights from the 1930s to the 1980s* (Chapel Hill: University of North Carolina Press, 2019), 54–82; Lizabeth Cohen, *A Consumers' Republic: The Politics of Mass Consumption in Postwar America* (New York: Vintage Books, 2003), 41–53.

24. To Chairman, Mayor's Committee to Investigate Harlem Conditions from Harlem Section, International Labor Defense, March 25, 1935; To Chairman of Mayor La Guardia Committee to Investigate Economic Conditions in Harlem from Mike Walsh, International Labor Defense, March 25, 1935, Office of the Mayor Fiorello H. La Guardia Records, box 24, folder 5, NYCMA.

25. To the Honorable Fiorello La Guardia from Henry K. Craft, Executive Secretary, March 23, 1935, 1, 2. Fiorello H. La Guardia Records, Series: Subject Files, reel 76, NYCMA.

26. The Chicago Commission on Race Relations, *The Negro in Chicago: A Study of Race Relations and a Race Riot* (Chicago: University of Chicago Press, 1922), 640.

27. To Mrs. Eunice Hunton Carter, Secretary, Committee on Investigation of the Harlem Riot, from Walter White, March 26, 1935, Office of the Mayor, Mayor Fiorello H. La Guardia Records, Subject Files, box 167, folder 6, NYCMA. Walter White propagandized what historian Shannon King has dubbed "New York exceptionalism." See King, *Whose Harlem*, 3; for a book-length exploration of this, see Andrew M. Fearnley and Daniel Matlin, *Race Capital? Harlem as Setting and Symbol* (New York: Columbia University Press, 2018).

28. To Honorable Mayor from Mrs. D. J. Williams, March 23, 1935, 1, Fiorello H. La Guardia Records, Series: Departmental Correspondence, box 34, folder 6, NYCMA.

29. To Honorable Mayor from Mrs. D. J. Williams, March 23, 1935, 1 and 2, Fiorello H. La Guardia Records, Series: Departmental Correspondence, box 34, folder 6, NYCMA.

30. To Honorable Mayor from Mrs. D. J. Williams, March 23, 1935, 2.

31. To Mrs. Eunice Hunton Carter from Helen Mohamed, March 23, 1935, Fiorello H. La Guardia Records, Series: Departmental Correspondence, box 34, folder 6, NYCMA; To Honorable Mayor F. La Guardia from Calista F. Turner, August 21, 1935, La G, Series: Departmental Correspondence, box 34, folder 6, NYCMA. On consumerism as the basis of Black protest in Harlem, see King, *Whose Harlem*, 33. For a broader history, see Davarian Baldwin, *Chicago's New Negroes: Modernity, the Great Migration, and Black Urban Life* (Chapel Hill: University of North Carolina Press, 2007); Parker, *Department Stores and the Black Freedom Movement*; Cohen, *Consumers' Republic*.

32. To the Committee Investigating Conditions in Harlem from Argyle Stoute, April 11, 1935, 1, Fiorello H. La Guardia Records, Series: Departmental Correspondence, box 34, folder 6, NYCMA.

33. To Gentlemen from Anonymous, May 6, 1935, Fiorello H. La Guardia, Series: Departmental Correspondence, box 34, folder 6, NYCMA; To Hon. F. H. La Guardia from Anonymous, March 21, 1935, Fiorello H. La Guardia Records, Series: Subject

Files, reel 76, NYCMA; To Mayor La Guardia from a White Woman with Brothers and Sisters Living in That Section, March 20, 1935, 1, 2.

34. King, *Whose Harlem*, 17–23.

35. Jeff Kisseloff, *You Must Remember This: An Oral History of Manhattan from the 1890s to World War II* (Baltimore: Johns Hopkins University Press, 1999), 190.

36. Quotes from King, *Whose Harlem*, 164–69. For interracial conflict and crime in New York in the late nineteenth century see Marcy S. Sacks, "'To Show Who Was in Charge': Police Repression of New York's Black Population at the Turn of the Twentieth Century," *Journal of Urban History* 31, no. 6 (September 2005): 799–819.

37. Connected to Tammany Hall's political machine, the NYPD understood "protection" as an aspect of electoral politics. Furthermore, La Guardia's recent support of trade unions and laborers and his gestures toward the CP and Harlem's Black community during the police riot in 1934, as discussed in chapter 2, reinforced his reform credentials and antagonized the NYPD. Crime in Harlem, as it was across the city, was controlled by white gangsters. For discussions of the police and political machines, see Robert M. Fogelson, *Big-City Police* (Cambridge, MA: Harvard University Press, 1977), 17–39, 74; on white organized crime, see Robert Weldon Whalen, *Murder, Inc., and the Moral Life: Gangsters and Gangbusters in La Guardia's New York* (New York: Fordham University Press, 2016); LaShawn Harris, *Sex Workers, Psychics, and Numbers Runners: Black Women in New York City's Underground Economy* (Urbana: University of Illinois Press, 2016); Shane White, Stephen Garton, Stephen Robertson, and Graham White, *Playing the Numbers: Gambling in Harlem between the Wars* (Cambridge, Mass.: Harvard University Press, 2010). For the rise of the Democratic Party's political machine in the early 1930s Chicago, see Balto, *Occupied Territory*, 62–90.

38. Quote from "Says Cops Could Have Prevented N.Y. Riot," *Chicago Defender*, April 6, 1935, 1; "Eugene Gord on Analyses Causes of the Harlem Riot," *Afro-American*, April 6, 1935, 16; and "Mayor Places Radicals' Foe on Riot Body," *New York Amsterdam News*, April 6, 1935, 1.

39. "Mayors Places Radicals' Foe," 2 and "Eugene Gord on Analyses Causes," 16.

40. "Censorship Is Handicap to Riot Probe," *Norfolk New Journal and Guide*, April 13, 1935, 10.

41. "Censorship Is Handicap," 10; "Governor Lehman Demands End of Harlem Slums," *New York Amsterdam News*, April 13, 1935, 1.

42. "Governor Lehman Demands End," 2.

43. "Mayor Places Radicals' Foe," 2; "Eugene Gord on Analyses Cause," 16; Bessye J. Bearden "Says Cops Could Have Prevented N.Y. Riot," *Chicago Defender*, April 6, 1936, 2.

44. "Harlemites Insist Beating of Youth Preceded Riot," *Afro-American*, April 13, 1935, 12.

45. "Police Scored at Mayor's Harlem Riot Investigation," *Norfolk New Journal and Guide*, April, 27, 1935, 4.

46. "Police Scored," 4 and "Brutality Hit at Riot Probe," *New York Amsterdam News*, April 27, 1935, 1.

47. "Brutality Hit at Riot Probe," 1; "Jeers and Boos Halt Committee Probing Riots," *Afro-American*, April 27, 1935, 12; "Negroes Accuse Police at Hearing," *New York Times*, April 21, 1935, n4; "Police Scored," *Norfolk New Journal and Guide*, April, 27, 1935, 4.

48. "Jeers and Boos," 12 and "Police Scored," 4. Thereafter, the *New York Times* and the Black weeklies end Welsh's story differently. The *New York Times* and the *Norfolk* imply that Welsh was allowed to remain as long as he made "no other insult," and the *New York Amsterdam News* and the *Afro-American* stated that he left.

49. "Lieut. Battle on Grill at Police Brutality Hearing," *Afro-American*, May 25, 1935, 10.

50. "Crowds Boo N. Y. Cops in Hearing about Brutality," *Afro-American*, May 11, 1935, 12; "Hobbs Slaying Action Sought," *New York Amsterdam News*, June 8, 1935, 3; "Five Deaths in Six Months Due to Social, Economic Struggles, I.L. D. Claims," *Norfolk New Journal and Guide*, July 13, 1935, a3.

51. "Calls on Dodge to Investigate Killing of Negro," *Daily Worker*, March 25, 1935, 1.

52. "Ford Presses C.P. Demand for Inquiry," *Daily Worker*, March 26, 1935, 1; quotes from Cyril Briggs, "Eye-Witnesses Tell of Harlem Murder," *Daily Worker*, March 26, 1935, 2.

53. "Police Killer of Laurie Also Murderer of Boy," *Daily Worker*, March 28, 1935, 2.

54. "Brutality Hit at Riot Probe," *New York Amsterdam News*, April 27, 1935, 1; "Jeers and Boos," 12; "Negroes Accuse Police at Hearing," *New York Times*, April 21, 1935, n4; "Police Scored," 4.

55. "Use Boycott, Picket Firms, Thomas Urges," *New York Amsterdam News*, April 20, 1935, 1.

56. "Use Boycott," 5.

57. "Harlem Investigation Uncovers Many Startling Things," *Atlanta Daily World*, May 24, 1935, 1, 2. For more on the Black response to poor school conditions and the commission's report, see Thomas Harbison, "'A Serious Pedagogical Situations': Diverging School Reform Priorities in Depression-Era Harlem," in *Educating Harlem: A Century of Schooling and Resistance in a Black Community*, edited by Ansley T. Erickson and Ernest Morrell (New York: Columbia University Press, 2019), 60–67.

58. "Housing in Harlem Sharply Debated," *New York Times*, May 23, 1935, 27.

59. "Governor Lehman Demands End of Harlem Slums," *New York Amsterdam News*, April 13, 1935, 1–2; "The Housing in Harlem," *New York Amsterdam News*, April 13, 1935, 8.

60. Bessye J. Bearden, "New York Comish Investigates Work of Home Relief Bureau," *Chicago Defender*, May 4, 1935, 2.

61. "Memorandum: On the Case of Victor Suarez-Precinct 26-Adminstrator by the Sub-Committee on Relief of the Mayor's Commission on Conditions in Harlem," Mayor's Commission on Conditions in Harlem Discrimination Negro Employment, box 3146, 04, microfilm, NYCMA; To Honorable A. Philip Randolph from Edward Corsi, May 16, 1935, Mayor's Commission on Conditions in Harlem, box 3146, folder 1, microfilm, NYCMA.

62. The firing of Suarez was followed in July 1936 by La Guardia's appointing a Black leader, Rev. John H. Johnson of St. Martin's Church, to the Emergency Relief Bureau. "Praiseworthy Appointment," *New York Age*, July 11, 1936, 6.

63. *Report of Subcommittee Which Investigated the Disturbance of March 19th*, May 29, 1935, 2, Fiorello H. La Guardia Records, Series: Subject Files, reel 76, NYCMA.

64. *Report of Subcommittee*, 8, 9.

65. *Report of Subcommittee*, 14; "2 Grand Juries Won't Indict Cop Who Killed Boy," *Baltimore Afro-American*, June 15, 1935, 12; "Policeman Faces $25,000 Suit in Brutality Case," *New York Amsterdam News*, June 8, 1935, 1; "Hobbs Slaying Action Sought," *New York Amsterdam News*, June 8, 1935, 3.

66. *Report of Subcommittee*, 18, 12.

67. *Report of Subcommittee*, 18.

68. *Report of Subcommittee*, 18, 19.

69. *Report of Subcommittee*, 20.

70. "Defends Harlem Police," *New York Times*, August 16, 1935, 2; "Catholic Priest Hit for Views on 'Cop Brutality,'" *Afro-American*, August 24, 1935, 12.

71. "Catholic Priest Hit," 12.

72. "Fears Harlem Riots if Cops 'Wear Gloves,'" *Daily News* (New York, New York), August 19, 1935, 164.

73. To Honorable F. H. La Guardia from Colonel Leopold Philipp, the Uptown Chamber of Commerce, August 14, 1935, 2, Office of the Mayor, Fiorello H. La Guardia Records, Subject Files, reel 76, NYCMA.

74. To Honorable F. H. La Guardia from Colonel Leopold Philipp, the Uptown Chamber of Commerce, 3.

75. To Honorable F. H. La Guardia from Colonel Leopold Philipp, the Uptown Chamber of Commerce, 2, 3.

76. St. Clair Bourne, "In This Corner," *New York Age*, August 31, 1935, 5; "Ofay Business Men Hit Commissioner's Report," *Afro American*, August 24, 1935, 12.

77. To Mr. Arthur Garfield Hays from the Police Commissioner, Lewis J. Valentine, September 28, 1935, 1, Subject Files, reel 83, La Guardia Records, NYCMA.

78. Naomi Murakawa, *First Civil Right: How Liberals Built Prison America* (New York: Oxford University Press, 2014), 43 and 44. Murakawa argues that liberal law and order makes a division between legitimate and illegitimate force. The latter was reflected in private, arbitrary violence and the former "exercised when the state followed predictable rules," such as the NYPD's nondiscrimination policy. But, as Murakawa contends, "Carceral violence was so lethal precisely because it was not arbitrary." For a discussion of liberal law and order in the postwar era see Max Felker-Kantor, *Policing Los Angeles, Race, Resistance, and the Rise of the LAPD* (Chapel Hill: University of North Carolina Press, 2018).

79. To Mayor from Edmond B. Butler, City of New York Emergency Relief Bureau, Home Relief Division, Memorandum, May 7, 1936, 1, 4, Fiorello H. La Guardia Records, Series: Subject Files, box 167, folder 15, NYCMA. For statistical discourse, see Khalil G. Muhammad, *Condemnation of Blackness: Race, Crime, and the Making of Modern Urban America* (Cambridge, Mass.: Harvard University Press, 2010).

80. To Honorable F. H. La Guardia, Mayor from Lewis J. Valentine, the Police Commissioner, City of New York, April 30, 1936, 2 and 3, Fiorello H. La Guardia Records, Series: Subject Files, reel 76.

81. To Honorable F. H. La Guardia, Mayor from Lewis J. Valentine, the Police Commissioner, City of New York, April 30, 1936, 4 and 6, Fiorello H. La Guardia Records, Series: Subject Files, reel 76.

82. Quote from Murakawa, *First Civil Right*, 43. For a different framing of the report and the mayor's commissioners' responses, see Dominic J. Capeci Jr., *Harlem Riot of 1943* (Philadelphia: Temple University Press, 1977), 4–7. Capeci offers a balanced appraisal of the report's criticisms and the commissioners' critiques of the report. While he reads this as a difference in views or quoting the mayor "owing to the conflict of facts," I read this as an aspect of the violence of racial liberalism.

83. "Howe Urges Patience for Harlem Reforms," *New York Amsterdam News*, March 21, 1936, 2.

84. Quotes from "'Daily' Bares Mayor's Hushed Report on Harlem Hospital Death, Disease," *Daily Worker*, April 6, 1936, 1–2; "Commission's Report Hits Harlem Hospital," *New York Amsterdam News*, April 11, 1936, 1, 5; "Discrimination Caused Harlem Riot," *Pittsburgh Courier*, April 18, 1936, A3.

85. Anthony M. Platt, *The Politics of Riot Commissions, 1917–1970* (New York: Macmillan, 1971), 162; Confidential Memo to Mayor La Guardia from Dr. Alain Locke, Office of the Mayor, Fiorello H. La Guardia Records, Subject Files, 1934–1945, reel 76, 1, 2. NYCMA.

86. "La Guardia for Curbing Whites, Night Orators," *New York Amsterdam News*, June 27, 1936, 1.

87. *The Complete Report of Mayor La Guardia's Commission on the Harlem Riot of March 19, 1935* (New York: Arno, 1969); "Discrimination Caused Harlem Riot, Report," *Pittsburgh Courier*, April 18, 1936, A3.

88. *Complete Report*, 35.

89. *Complete Report*, 57.

90. *Complete Report*, 63.

91. Quote from King, *Whose Harlem*, 93.

92. *Complete Report*, 70–71.

93. *The Negro in Harlem: A Report on Social and Economic Conditions Responsible for the Outbreak of March 19, 1935*, 108; *Complete Report*, 121.

94. *Complete Report*, 133; *Negro in Harlem*, 118.

95. *Negro in Harlem*, 107.

96. Alain Locke, "Harlem: Dark Weather-Vane," in *Survey Graphic: Magazine of Social Interpretation* (August 1936), 458.

97. Locke, "Harlem," 459, 494–95.

98. To Mayor Fiorello La Guardia from Oswald Garrison Villard, September 26, 1936; To Mr. Oswald Garrison Villard from F. H. La Guardia, September 29, 1936; To Mayor Fiorello La Guardia from Oswald Garrison Villard, September 30, 1936, La Guardia Records, Series: Subject Files, reel 76, NYCMA.

99. Thomas Kessner, *Fiorello H. La Guardia and the Making of Modern New York* (New York: McGraw-Hill, 1989); 375; Alyn Brodsky, *Great Mayor: Fiorello La Guardia*

and the Making of the City of New York (New York: St. Martin's, 2003), 320. Kessner explains that La Guardia did not want to "weaken his efforts to attack the rackets, including those based in Harlem, and it would bring him in conflict with Valentine." Brodsky echoes Kessner's explanation. Kessner, Brodsky, Capeci, and Janet L. Abu-Lughod have pointed out that though La Guardia did not release the report, the mayor did appoint Blacks to key government positions and initiated the building of public housing and two schools and other programs. Black Harlem, however, saw La Guardia's political response as Locke foretold "as concessions" rather than "the beginning of a new program." Janet L. Abu-Lughod, *Race, Space, and Riots in Chicago, New York, and Los Angeles* (New York: Oxford University Press, 2007), 151.

Chapter 4

1. Adam Clayton Powell Jr., "Soapbox: 'It Can't Happen Here,'" *New York Amsterdam News*, April 11, 1936, 12; "Cop to Face $25,000 Suit in Brutality," *New York Amsterdam News*, June 8, 1935, 1.

2. *The Complete Report of Mayor La Guardia's Commission on the Harlem Riot of March 19, 1935* (New York: Arno, 1969), 122.

3. "Queens Ministers Flayed Civic Inactivity," *New York Amsterdam News*, August 10, 1935, 13.

4. This chapter centers the multiple forms of Black protest and mobilization against police brutality. From mass meetings and self-defense to activist journalism and litigation, Black New Yorkers used whatever means necessary to protect themselves. For Black protest in the early twentieth century before the Great Depression, see Marcy S. Sacks, *Before Harlem: The Black Experience in New York City before World War I* (Philadelphia: University of Pennsylvania Press, 2006); Cheryl D. Hicks, *Talk with You like a Woman: African American Women, Justice, and Reform in New York, 1890–1935* (Chapel Hill: University of North Carolina Press, 2010); Shannon King, *Whose Harlem Is This, Anyway?: Community Politics and Grassroots Activism during the New Negro Era* (New York: New York University Press, 2015). For a different approach to Black protest against police brutality, see Clarence Taylor, *Fight the Power: African Americans and the Long History of Police Brutality in New York City* (New York: New York University Press, 2018), 3. According to Taylor, before the 1940s, Black protest was sporadic, "and few Black New York ministers in the early twentieth century turned to street demonstrations, rallies, or other forms of protest to confront police practices." Because of Taylor's narrower approach, it is unclear from his work what brought about the shift from sporadic protests to more organized forms. This chapter addresses exactly that change over time.

5. "Police Still on Riot Duty," *New York Amsterdam News*, March 30, 1935, 1.

6. "Cop Apologizes, Is Freed in Attack Case," *New York Amsterdam News*, August 10, 1935, 12.

7. "Police Still on Riot Duty," 1; "Brooklynites Demand Negro Police after 2 Riots," *New York Amsterdam News*, July 20, 1935, 1 and 2.

8. "Brooklynites Demand Negro Police," 2.

9. "Cop Apologizes," 12.

10. "Brooklynites Demand Negro Police," 2.

11. "Memo to Mr. Valentine," *New York Amsterdam News*, July 13, 1935, 12.

12. "Cop Faces Trial for Striking School Girl," *New York Amsterdam News*, March 14, 1936, 4; "Cop Faces Trial in Schoolgirl Assault," *New York Amsterdam News*, March 21, 1936, 14.

13. "Harlem Action Forces Assault Charge against Policeman," *Daily Worker*, April 1, 1936, 2.

14. "Harlem Action," 2; "Cop Accused of Brutality," *New York Amsterdam News*, April 4, 1936, 1, 2.

15. "Harlem Action," 2; "O.K. Fraenkel Utility to Prosecute Harlem Officer," *Daily Worker*, April 15, 1936, 3.

16. "Harlem Police Trying to Gag Eyewitnesses," *Daily Worker*, April 2, 1936, 2; "Policeman Faces Trial for Assault," *Daily Worker*, April 20, 1936, 3; "Assault Trial of Policeman Is Postponed," *Daily Worker*, April 22, 1936, 4; "ILD Demands Police Lineup in Assault," *Daily Worker*, April 24, 1936, 3; Quote from "McNeil Case Witness Firm in Testimony," *Daily Worker*, April 27, 1936, 3.

17. "Harlem Police Terror Case Put Off Again," *Daily Worker*, May 1, 1936, 4.

18. "Cops to Stay Is Valentine's Terse Decree," *New York Amsterdam News*, May 30, 1936, 19.

19. "Child Victim of Police Gun Near Death," *Daily Worker*, May 13, 1936, 1. Quotes from "Negro Child, Police Victim, Near Death," *Daily Worker*, May 15, 1936, 2.

20. "Valentine Upholds Police Rule," *Daily Worker*, May 27, 1936, 2; "Cops to Stay," 1.

21. "Police Brutality Case Is Put Off," *New York Amsterdam News*, April 11, 1936, 1; "Scottsboro Lawyer to Prosecute Cop," *New York Amsterdam News*, April 18, 1936, 1, 2; "Cop Will Face Assault Trial," *New York Amsterdam News*, May 9, 1936, 1, 2; and "Cop Set Free Despite Fight," *New York Amsterdam News*, June 20, 1936, 3. All quotes from "Harlem Plans Fight on Police Brutality," *Daily Worker*, June 17, 1936, 3.

22. "Harlem Is Up in Arms against Brutal Cops," *Sunday Worker*, May 31, 1936, 16.

23. "Cops to Stay," 1, 2.

24. "Police Unleash New Terror against Harlem Anti-Fascists," *Daily Worker*, May 20, 1936, 1.

25. William R. Scott, "Black Nationalism and the Italo-Ethiopian Conflict 1934–1936," *Journal of Negro History* 63, no. 2 (April 1978): 118–34; "Italo-Ethiopian War Starts War," *New York Amsterdam News*, September 28, 1935, 20; "Harlem Drive upon Italians Stirs Disorder," *Daily News* (New York, New York), October 4, 1935, 2; "Harlem's War Fervor Sinks to Mere Talk," *Daily News* (New York, New York), October 5, 1935, 6.

26. "Cops to Stay," 2.

27. "Time to Reconsider," *New York Amsterdam News*, June 6, 1936, 12.

28. "Negro Congress Group Protests Police Attack," *Daily Worker*, June 13, 1936, 4; "Protest Brooklyn Police Brutality," *New York Amsterdam News*, July 4, 1936, 10.

29. "Police Occupation," *New York Amsterdam News*, June 13, 1936, 12; Charles Augustin Petioni, "Mostly False and Dishonest," *New York Amsterdam News*, June 13, 1936, 12.

30. Ebenezer Ray, "Dottings of a Paragrapher," *New York Age*, June 13, 1936, 6.

31. "Lehman Given Protests over Brutal Police," *New York Amsterdam News*, June 20, 1936, 7.

32. "How Long, Mr. Mayor?," *New York Amsterdam News*, June 27, 1936, 12.

33. "'Cops Will Play Fair,' Mayor Tells Harlem," *Daily News* (New York, New York), July 1, 1936, 6; "Print Report on Harlem Group Asks," *Daily Worker*, July 1, 1936, 1.

34. "Mayor Promises to Confer Often on Harlem Situation," *New York Amsterdam News*, July 25, 1936, 11.

35. "Mayor Promises," 11.

36. "Negro Boy, 7, Is Killed as Police Shots Go Wild," *Daily Worker*, June 8, 1936, 1; "Police Terror in Harlem," *Daily Worker*, July 14, 1936, 8.

37. "Cops to Stay," 1; "Withdrawal of Extra Police Sought by Club," *New York Age*, July 25, 1936, 1; "How about Some Action?," *New York Age*, August 1, 1936, 6; Quote from "Harlem Sets up Group to Press Demands on City," *Chicago Defender*, August 15, 1936, 20.

38. "Protest B'Klyn Police Terror," *New York Amsterdam News*, August 15, 1936, 10; "District Attorney Geoghan Gets Protest in Police Brutality Case in Brooklyn," *New York Amsterdam News*, November 14, 1936, 12.

39. "How about Some Action?," 6.

40. "How about Some Action?," 6.

41. "La Guardia's Long, Hard Road," *New York Amsterdam News*, October 10, 1936; and "State Your Intentions, Mr. La Guardia," *New York Amsterdam News*, December 19, 1936.

42. Decades later, writer James Baldwin would describe the large presence of police in Black neighborhoods as "occupied territories." James Baldwin, "A Report from Occupied Territory," *The Nation*, July 11, 1966, 39–43.

43. To Hon. Lewis J. Valentine, Police Commissioner of the City of New York from Theophilus Johnson, February 26, 1937; Unaddressed from Charles Houston, January 2, 1937, box I: C278, folder 15: Police Brutality, 1937, New Jersey, New York, State, and City, National Association for the Advancement of Colored People Records, Manuscript Division, Library of Congress (hereafter, NAACP Records, LOC).

44. "Hurl New Police Brutality Charge," *New York Amsterdam News*, March 27, 1937, 12.

45. Letter to NAACP from Walter Ross, box I: C278, folder 15: Police Brutality, New Jersey, New York, State and City, NAACP Records, LOC.

46. From James St. John, undated, box I: C278, folder 15: Police Brutality, New Jersey, New York, State and City, NAACP Records, LOC.

47. From James St. John, June 22, 1937, box I: C278, folder 15: Police Brutality, New Jersey, New York, State and City, NAACP Records, LOC.

48. "Charges Cop Invaded Home" *New York Amsterdam News*, October 9, 1937, 1, 19.

49. Adam Clayton Powell Jr., "Soapbox," *New York Amsterdam News*, November 27, 1937, 13.

50. Powell Jr., "Soapbox," 13.

51. "Slain by Cops, Youth Seems to Be Innocent," *New York Amsterdam News*, December 25, 1937, 1.

52. "Slain by Cops," 1.

53. "Police Declare Swett 'Suicide,'" *New York Amsterdam News*, May 1, 1937, 10; Archie Waters, "Examination of 'Suicide' Set Back," *New York Amsterdam News*, May 29, 1937; "To Disinter Body of Albert Moore," *New York Age*, June 5, 1937, 1; "Judge Grants Disinterment to Moore Kin," *New York Amsterdam News*, June 6, 1937, 11.

54. "Judge Grants Disinterment to Moore Kin," *New York Amsterdam News*, June 5, 1937, 11; "Moore's Death Is Still a Mystery" *New York Amsterdam News*, June 19, 1937, 10; "Civic Group to Continue Moore Issue," *New York Amsterdam News*, June 26, 1937, 11.

55. "Detective Beaten by Prisoner Dies," *Philadelphia Tribune*, November 11, 1937, 10; "Still Hold Man in Cop's Death," *New York Amsterdam News*, November 13, 1937, 4; "Cop Death, Unwelcome Suitor in Hospital," *Afro-American*, November 13, 1937, 22; "Cop-Biter Held," *New York Amsterdam News*, December 4, 1937, 4; "Irked Brooklyn Citizens Ask Cop Probe," *New York Amsterdam News*, January 1, 1938, 13; "Boro Questions Suicide Death," *New York Age*, January 1, 1938, 7; "Detective Arthur J. DeMarrais," *Spring 3100* 8, no. 10: 10.

56. "Amityville Sleuths on Still Hunt Kill Man by Shot in Back," *Brooklyn Daily Eagle*, September 30, 1937, 5.

57. "An Old, Old Story Not Improved by Repetition" and "Negro Running from Officer Shot in Back, Dies Instantly; Officer Claims 'Self-Defense,'" *Afro-American Echo*, October 25, 1937, 1, 2; To Counselor Charles H. Houston from Mary E. Nowell, November 10, 1937, box I: C278, folder 15, NAACP Records, LOC; "North Amityville Holds Another Protest Meeting," *Long Island Sun*, November 19, 1937; To Counselor Charles H. Houston from Mary E. Nowell, November 27, 1937, box I: C278, folder 15, NAACP Records, LOC.

58. To Honorable Martin W. Littleton, District Attorney of Nassau County from Charles H. Houston, Special Counsel, February 10, 1937, box I: C278, folder 15, NAACP Records, LOC; Jacqueline A. Mcleod, *Daughter of the Empire States: The Life of Judge Jane Bolin* (Urbana: University of Illinois Press, 2011), 36–38; Carl Suddler, *Presumed Criminal: Black Youth and the Justice System in Postwar New York* (New York: New York University Press, 2019), 30–38.

59. McKinley McClurin, State of New York County of Nassau, affidavit, November 19, 1936, box I: C278, folder 15, NAACP Records, LOC.

60. Rosa Smith, State of New York County of Nassau, Affidavit, December 4, 1936, 1, box I: C278, folder 15, NAACP Records, LOC.

61. Pauline Blanchard, State of New York County of Nassau, Affidavit, November 19, 1936, 1, box I: C278, folder 15, NAACP Records, LOC.

62. Jeff Holsey, State of New York County of Nassau, Affidavit, January 1937, 1, box I: C278, folder 15, NAACP Records, LOC.

63. Martha Moore, State of New York County of Nassau, Affidavit, January 1937, 1, box I: C278, folder 15, NAACP Records, LOC.

64. Jeff Holsey, State of New York County of Nassau, Affidavit, 1.

65. Martha Moore, State of New York County of Nassau, Affidavit, 2.

66. To Honorable Martin W. Littleton from Charles H. Houston, 1.

67. To Charles H. Houston, Special Counsel from Martin W. Littleton, District Attorney, Office of the District Attorney of Nassau County, Mineola, New York, February 15, 1937, 1–2, box I: C278, folder 15, NAACP Records, LOC.

68. William Hufnegel vs. James Samuel, Charge: Assault 3rd Degree, Before: Hon. Jacob Eilperin, Chief Magistrate, June 21, 1939, June 22, 1939, 8, James Samuel assault case in Brooklyn, New York, involving police brutality, Papers of the NAACP, Part 8: Discrimination in the Criminal Justice System, 1910–1955, Series A: Legal Department and Central Office Records, 1910–1939, ProQuest History Vault (hereafter, James Samuel assault case); "Refuses to Apologize to Cop, Is Freed," *New York Amsterdam News*, November 25, 1939, 22.

69. James Samuel assault case, 5, 8.

70. "Refuses to Apologize," 22; James Samuel assault case, 5, 8.

71. "Refuses to Apologize," 22.

72. Marian McDonell Affidavit, August 1937, 1, 2, Marian McDonell disorderly conduct case from New York City, August 1–December 31, 1937, Papers of the NAACP, Part 8: Discrimination in the Criminal Justice System, 1910–1955, Series A: Legal Department and Central Office Records, 1910–1939, ProQuest History Vault (hereafter, Marian McDonell disorderly conduct).

73. Marian McDonell Affidavit, August 1937, 3, Marian McDonell disorderly conduct.

74. Thurgood Marshall, Assistant Special Counsel, to Commissioner Louis J. Valentine, Police Department, August 25, 1937, 1, 2, Marian McDonell disorderly conduct; Thurgood Marshall, Assistant Special Counsel, to Commissioner Louis J. Valentine, Police Department, September 7, 1937, 1, 2, Marian McDonell disorderly conduct.

75. Thurgood Marshall, Assistant Special Counsel, to Commissioner Louis J. Valentine, Police Department, September 20, 1937, 1, Marian McDonell disorderly conduct.

76. Thurgood Marshall, Assistant Special Counsel, to Commissioner Louis J. Valentine, Police Department, September 20, 1937, 1–5, Marian McDonell disorderly conduct.

77. Thurgood Marshall, Assistant Special Counsel, to Mayor Fiorello La Guardia, Municipal Building, New York City, September 24, 1937, 1–2; Memorandum to Thurgood Marshall, in re: Marian McDonell Case, October 20, 1937; Thurgood Marshall to Inspector Michael A. Wall, Manhattan Borough Office, October 29, 1937, 1; Michael A. Wall, Inspector, to Thurgood Marshall, November 4, 1937, 1, all Marian McDonell disorderly conduct.

78. From Marian McDonell to Mr. T. Marshall, Asst. Attorney of NAACP, December 21, 1937, 1–2; From Thurgood Marshall, Assistant Special Counsel, to Miss Marian McDonell, 205 West 145th Street, December 22, 1937, 1, all Marian McDonell disorderly conduct.

79. From Mayor Fiorello H. La Guardia to Mr. Thurgood Marshall, Assistant Special Counsel, December 8, 1937, 1, Marian McDonell disorderly conduct. See "An

Open Letter to the Police Commissioner," *New York Age*, January 13, 1940, 1; "Accuse Woman of Knifing Cop," *New York Amsterdam News*, August 9, 1941, 1; "Hold 4 Women Involved in Subway Attack Which Stirred 'Police Brutality' Battle," *New York Amsterdam News*, October 4, 1941, 12.

Chapter 5

1. "Something Must Be Done?," *New York Age*, January 14, 1939, 6.

2. Carl Dunbar Lawrence, "Killer of Forbes Must Die," *New York Amsterdam News*, December 9, 1939, 2.

3. Demographics from the *New York Times* from Craig S. Wilder, *A Covenant with Color: Race and Social Power in Brooklyn* (New York: Columbia University Press, 2001), 178; "Center Will Help Brooklyn 'Harlem,'" *New York Times*, November 15, 1941, 34; V. A. S., "Brooklyn's 'Harlem' Problem," *New York Herald Tribune*, November 21, 1941, 18. For more on the Midtown Civic League, see Wilder, *Covenant with Color*, 198.

4. Harold X. Connolly, *A Ghetto Grows in Brooklyn* (New York: New York University Press, 1977), 58.

5. "Inconsistent in Playground Fight," *New York Amsterdam News*, April 10, 1929, 10.

6. Connolly, *Ghetto Grows in Brooklyn*, 58–60; for early efforts to prevent black settlement and residential segregation in Bedford-Stuyvesant, see Wilder, *Covenant with Color*, 181–96; Brian Purnell, *Fighting Jim Crow in the County of Kings: The Congress of Racial Equality in Brooklyn* (Lexington: University Press of Kentucky, 2013), 8–11; Michael Woodsworth, *Battle for Bed-Stuy: The Longer War on Poverty in New York City* (Cambridge, Mass.: Harvard University Press, 2016), 52.

7. "Rev. W. S. Blackshear Bars Negroes from St. Matthews; Woman Leaves in Tears," *Brooklyn Daily Eagle*, September 16, 1929, 1.

8. "Grace Church Forms Merger," *Brooklyn Daily Eagle*, June 24, 1937, 3; "Grace Church Ruling Delayed," *Brooklyn Daily Eagle*, June 29, 1937, 4; "Answers Clayborn on Sale of Church," *Brooklyn Daily Eagle*, July 8, 1937, 4.

9. "Midtown League to Preserve Area," *Brooklyn Daily Eagle*, June 16, 1937, 8.

10. "Warns of Race Row on Church," *Brooklyn Daily Eagle*, July 6, 1937, 17. See Connolly, *Ghetto Grows in Brooklyn*, 68–73.

11. "Answers Clayborn," 4.

12. "Presbytery Approves Bethel Purchase," *New York Amsterdam News*, July 17, 1937, 11. On Blacks' efforts to combat claims of their depreciating property values in the 1920s and 1930s, see Stephen Grant Meyer, *As Long as They Don't Move Next Door: Segregation and Racial Conflict in American Neighborhoods* (Lanham, Md.: Rowman and Littlefield, 2001), 51–52. For an important intervention on how whites thinking on race changed with transformations in federal housing policy, property, and suburbanization, see David M. P. Freund, *Colored Property: State Policy & White Racial Politics in Suburban America* (Chicago: University of Chicago Press, 2007) and see historian Keeanga-Yamahtta Taylor's discussion of how the degradation of Black

urban life was conflated with Black people, *Race for Profit: How Banks and the Real Estate Industry Undermined Black Homeownership* (Chapel Hill: University of North Carolina Press, 2018), 25–29.

13. "More Police Urged in Bedford Section," *Brooklyn Daily Eagle*, January 16, 1937, 11.

14. "Midtown League Circulates Petition for More Police," *Brooklyn Daily Eagle*, January 18, 1937, 1.

15. "3,000 in Bedford Ask More Police," *Brooklyn Daily Eagle*, January 20, 1937, 9; "Says Boro Needs 1200 More Cops," *Brooklyn Daily Eagle*, January 27, 1937, 14.

16. "Demands Meeting with Ingersoll on Need of Police," *Brooklyn Daily Eagle*, February 10, 1937, 30; "Midtown Civics Asks More Police," *Brooklyn Daily Eagle*, February 18, 1937, 2; "Midtown League Scores La Guardia on Cop Shortage," *Brooklyn Daily Eagle*, March 26, 1937, 11.

17. "Midtown District Asks More Police," *Brooklyn Daily Eagle*, September 13, 1937, 24; "Cop Sirens Give Thugs Chance to Flee, Civic Group Protests," *Brooklyn Daily Eagle*, October 27, 1937, 5.

18. "Police Take Action to Curb Holdups," *Brooklyn Daily Eagle*, November 15, 1937, 5.

19. "Cops Give Up Spare Time to War on Crime," *Brooklyn Daily Eagle*, November 17, 1937, 12.

20. "Battle 'Crime Wave,'" *New York Amsterdam News*, November 20, 1937, 2.

21. "50 Policemen Map Drive to Halt Beatings," *New York Amsterdam News*, November 27, 1937, 11

22. "Rector Protests Local Conditions," *Brooklyn Daily Eagle*, December 4, 1937, 8.

23. "Valentine Bid for Cops Praised and Assailed," *Brooklyn Daily Eagle*, December 6, 1937, 4; "More Police to Be Demanded at Borough Civics Meeting," *Brooklyn Daily Eagle*, December 12, 1937, 9; "Consolidated Civics Demand More Police," *Brooklyn Daily Eagle*, December 16, 1937, 5.

24. "League Starts Terror War to Combat 'Crime,'" *New York Amsterdam News*, December 11, 1937, 11.

25. Alfred A. Duckett, "Monsigneur Belford Once More Attacks Negroes of Borough at Mass Meeting," *New York Age*, December 25, 1937, 1. For "muss 'em up" policing, see chapter 1.

26. Marvel Cooke, "Brooklyn," *New York Amsterdam News*, January 29, 1938, 11; "Ask Police Commissioner for More Cops in Borough," *New York Age*, November 12, 1938, 5. For more on Sirtl, see Wilder, *Covenant with Color*, 195–98; Clarence Taylor, *Reds at the Blackboard*, 80.

27. Alfred A. Duckett, "Shows Whites Far in Lead Wednesday's Crime Review," *New York Age*, January 22, 1938, 1.

28. Shannon King, *Whose Harlem Is This, Anyway?* (New York: New York University Press, 2015), 17–22.

29. Cheryl D. Hicks, *Talk with You like a Woman: African American Women, Justice, and Reform in New York, 1890–1935* (Chapel Hill: University of North Carolina Press, 2010), 188.

30. King, *Whose Harlem*, 146–47; Committee of Fourteen, *Annual Report for 1928*, 33, box 86, Committee of Fourteen Records, Manuscript and Archives Section, New York Public Library.

31. Unsigned letter to Reverend Imes, July 1935, Fiorello H. La Guardia, Series: Departmental Correspondence, box 35, folder 8, New York City Municipal Archives; *The Complete Report of Mayor La Guardia's Commission on the Harlem Riot of March 19, 1935* (New York: Arno Press, 1969), 133.

32. Carl Suddler, *Presumed Criminal: Black Youth and the Justice System in Postwar New York* (New York: New York University Press, 2019), 21–25.

33. "Realtor Recommends Junior Police Force," *New York Amsterdam News*, February 8, 1936, 3.

34. For the Black community's demands for police protection, particularly Black police officers during the New Negro era in New York City, and the Juvenile Park Protective League, see Shannon King, *Whose Harlem*, 39–40, 47. See Tera Eva Ageyepong's discussion of the Black child-saving movement in Chicago, *The Criminalization of Black Children* (Chapel Hill: University of North Carolina Press, 2018), 22–35. "Society to Blame for Crime-Wave," *New York Age*, February 8, 1936, 7; "They Can Learn Plenty," *New York Amsterdam News*, March 18, 1939, 10; "Sgt. Chisholm Gets Promotion," *New York Age*, March 14, 1936, 1; and "Police Plan Junior Police Club," *New York Age*, July 11, 1936, 2.

35. Edythe Robertson, "What the Play Streets and the Juvenile Aid Bureau Are Doing This Summer for Your Children," *New York Age*, August 7, 1937, 5; "Patrolman Charles Jones Speaks about Delinquency," *New York Age*, November 27, 1937, 3. The issue of child delinquency was also raised in the Mayor's Commission's report and stated that while rates were higher for Black children than whites, the rates were the result of socioeconomic factors and the dearth of public and private resources open to Black youth. For more on child delinquency see Earl R. Moses, "Community Factors in Negro Delinquency," *Journal of Negro Education* 5, no. 2 (April 1935): 220–27. An issue of the *Journal of Negro Education* was devoted to Black youth and education: E. Franklin Frazier, "The Negro Family and Negro Youth," *Journal of Negro Education* 9, no. 3 (July 1940): 290–99; and Mary Huff Diggs, "The Problems and Needs of Negro Youth as Revealed by Delinquency and Crime Statistics," *Journal of Negro Education* 9, no. 3 (July 1940): 311–20.

36. "Can't Stop Crime," *New York Amsterdam News*, February 6, 1937, 4; Thelma Berlack-Boozer, "Aids Delinquent: Bureau Helps Wayward Ones," *New York Amsterdam News*, August 14, 1937, 11 and "Broken-Home Children," *New York Amsterdam News*, October 9, 1937, 12.

37. "Police Protection Is Protested in Borough," *New York Amsterdam News*, November 6, 1937, 12.

38. "Harlem's 'Most Robbed' Block Gets Weary," *New York Amsterdam News*, January 15, 1938, 6.

39. Jeff Kisseloff, *You Must Remember This: An Oral History of Manhattan from the 1890s to World War II* (Baltimore: Johns Hopkins University Press, 1999), 333.

40. "Harlem Booms Joe Louis for U.S. President," *Afro-American*, July 2, 1938, 15.

41. "2,000 Cops and Fire Hose Keep Harlem Peace," *Daily News*, June 23, 1938, 2; "Harlem Celebrants Toss Varied Missiles," *New York Times*, June 23, 1938, 14; and "Negroes Fill Streets of Harlem in Celebration of Louis Victory," *New York Herald Tribune*, June 23, 1938, 22.

42. "Too Much Enthusiasm," *New York Age*, July 2, 1938, 6.

43. "Local Lawlessness," *New York Amsterdam News*, September 10, 1938, 6. See political scientist Naomi Murakawa's critique of liberal law and order. Murakawa explains that despite liberal and conservative law and order advocates differing approaches, they both "accepted Black aggression as the center of the debate." For quote, see Murakawa, *The First Civil Right: How Liberals Built Prison America* (New York: Oxford University Press, 2014), 53.

44. Archie Seale, "Around Harlem," *New York Amsterdam News*, January 7, 1939, 13.

45. "A Perennial Problem," *New York Amsterdam News*, January 21, 1939, 6.

46. "Crime in Harlem," *New York Amsterdam News*, January 28, 1939, 6.

47. "Hopes to Force Valentine Out of Job, Says Baldwin," *New York Daily News*, January 20, 1939, 2; "Baldwin Cites Twenty-Seven 'Dives'—Cops Rip List to Bits," *New York Daily News*, January 22, 1939, 2C.

48. "Crime in Harlem," 6. Ebenezer Ray, "A Paragraph's Dottings," *New York Age*, February 4, 1939, 6.

49. "6 in 4 Days . . . Murder Record!" and "Switchblade Knife: A Family Story!," *New York Amsterdam News*, February 11, 1939, 1.

50. "It Is Our Duty," *New York Amsterdam News*, February 18, 1939, 6; "Disgusted Reader," *New York Amsterdam News*, February 25, 1939, 6; Harold Austin "Letters to the Editor: Sensational Journalism," *New York Age*, January 28, 1939, 6; "Black-listing Harlem," *New York Age*, April 8, 1939, 6, and Effie Robinson Jackson to Honorable F. H. La Guardia, April 14, 1939, box I: C305, folder 3, National Association for the Advancement of Colored People Records, Manuscript Division, Library of Congress (hereafter, NAACP Records, LOC).

51. "Ban Switchblades," *New York Amsterdam News*, January 21, 1939, 6.

52. For a discussion of the use of film and documentary for Black youth in Harlem, see Lisa Rabin and Craig Kridel, "Cinema for Social Change: The Human Relations Film Series in the Harlem Committee of the Teachers Union, 1936–1950," in *Educating Harlem: A Century of Schooling and Resistance in a Black Community*, edited by Ansley T. Erickson and Ernest Morrell (New York: Columbia University Press, 2019), 103–8.

53. Lewis Chisholm to Friend, February 3, 1939, box I: C305, folder 3, NAACP Records, LOC; Crime Conference, February 10, 1939, 1, 2, box I: C305, folder 3, NAACP Records, LOC; "Switchblade Sale Rapped in Campaign," *New York Amsterdam News*, February 18, 1939, 1, 20; "Assembly Has Bill Banning Switchblades," *New York Amsterdam News*, March 25, 1939, 1; "Switchblade Now in City Council," *New York Amsterdam News*, April 1, 1939, 1; "Committee Organized to Work on Solution of Increasing Juvenile Delinquency," *New York Age*, February 18, 1939, 1; Ebenezar Ray, "'Switchblade' Outlawed Dottings," *New York Age*, 1939, 6; "Switchblade Bill Wins Here," *New York Amsterdam News*, April 8, 1939, 1. Scholars, following

Michel Foucault's "carceral continuum," have criticized the overlapping practices and networks among the police, schools, and other institutions. Foucault, *Discipline and Punish: The Birth of the Prison* (New York: Vintage Books, 1991), 293–308. Historian Elizabeth Hinton describes this as the "diffusion of crime control techniques into the everyday lives of low-income African Americans." Elizabeth Hinton, *From the War on Poverty to the War on Crime: The Making of Mass Incarceration* (Cambridge, Mass.: Harvard University Press, 2016), 16. See also Katherine Beckett and Naomi Murakawa, "Mapping the Shadow Carceral State: Toward an Institutionally Capacious Approach to Punishment," *Theoretical Criminology* 16, no. 2 (May 1, 2012): 221–24; Julilly Kohler-Hausmann, *Getting Tough: Welfare and Imprisonment in 1970s America* (Princeton, N.J.: Princeton University Press, 2017).

54. I use the word "vulnerability" to get at how the *Amsterdam News* espoused the protection of Black women as an expression of masculinity. See Hicks, *Talk with You* and Farah J. Griffin's "'Ironies of the Saint': Malcolm X, Black Women, and the Price of Protection" in *Sisters in the Struggle: African American Women in the Civil Rights-Black Power Movement*, ed. Bettye Collier-Thomas and V. P. Franklin (New York: New York University Press, 2001).

55. "B'klyn Police Try to Dodge Rape Probe in Vicious Attack," *New York Amsterdam News*, March 11, 1939, 1; and "Police Seize Alleged Rapist," *New York Amsterdam News*, April 22, 1939, 13.

56. "They Can Learn Plenty," 10; "Police Trail Alleged Rape Case Suspect," *New York Amsterdam News*, March 25, 1939, 2; and "Police Seize Alleged Rapist," 13.

57. St. Clair Bourne and Marvel Cooke, "The Truth about Harlem Crime," *New York Amsterdam News*, March 4, 1939, 1, 5; St. Clair Bourne and Marvel Cooke, "The Truth about Harlem Crime," *New York Amsterdam News*, April 8, 1939, 11.

58. St. Clair Bourne and Marvel Cooke, "The Truth about Harlem Crime," *New York Amsterdam News*, April 1, 1939, 11.

59. St. Clair Bourne and Marvel Cooke, "The Truth about Harlem Crime," *New York Amsterdam News*, March 11, 1939, 7. Milligan, a seventeen-year-old, died defending his friends in a fight.

60. St. Clair Bourne and Marvel Cooke, "The Truth about Harlem Crime," *New York Amsterdam News*, April 29, 1939, 17. For the emergence of Black gangs in early twentieth-century New York City, see King, *Whose Harlem*; for a sample of recent scholarship on race and gangs, see Eric Schneider, *Vampires, Dragons and Egyptian Kings*; and Andrew Diamond, *Mean Streets*.

61. St. Clair Bourne and Marvel Cooke, "The Truth about Harlem Crime," *New York Amsterdam News*, March 18, 1939, 11.

62. Leon E. DeKalb "Juvenile Delinquency . . . Community Problem," *New York Amsterdam News*, December 2, 1939, 5.

63. Leon E. DeKalb, "Blame Unhappy Home Life for Delinquency," *New York Amsterdam News*, December 16, 1939, 11 and "Guidance of Child Is Up to Parents," *New York Amsterdam News*, January 9, 1940, 4.

64. See Hazel V. Carby, "Policing the Black Women's Body in an Urban Context," *Critical Inquiry* 18, no. 4 (Summer 1992): 738–55; Michelle Mitchell, *Righteous Propagation: African Americans and the Politics of Racial Destiny and Reconstruction*

(Chapel Hill: University of North Carolina Press, 2004), 141–72. See also E. Franklin Frazier, "The Negro Family and the Negro Youth," *Journal of Negro Education* 9, no. 3 (July 1940): 290–99; E. Franklin Frazier, *The Negro Family in the United States* (Chicago: University of Chicago, 1968).

65. For discussion of intracommunity Black crime, crime prevention, and crime fighting in the late nineteenth and early twentieth century, see Kali N. Gross, *Colored Amazons: Crime, Violence, and Black Women in the City of Brotherly Love, 1880–1910* (Durham, N.C.: Duke University Press, 2006); Cynthia M. Blair, *I've Got to Make My Livin': Black Women's Sex Work in Turn-of-the Century Chicago* (Chicago: The University of Chicago Press); Khalil G. Muhammad, *Condemnation of Blackness: Race, Crime, and the Making of Modern Urban America* (Cambridge, Mass.: Harvard University Press, 2010); Hicks, *Talk with You*; King, *Whose Harlem*; LaShawn D. Harris, *Sex Workers, Psychics, and Numbers Runners: Black Women in New York City's Underground Economy* (Urbana: University of Illinois Press, 2016).

66. "Along the NAACP Battlefront" *The Crisis*, July 1941, 231.

Chapter 6

1. "Crime Outbreak in Harlem Spurs Drive by Police," *New York Times*, November 7, 1941, 1.

2. St. Clair Bourne and Marvel Cooke, "The Truth about Harlem Crime," *New York Amsterdam News*, March 18, 1939, 11.

3. "Negro Prowler in Apartment across the Hall from Mayor's," *New York Herald Tribune*, November 10, 1941, 1.

4. Sometimes Blacks are accompanied by Puerto Ricans.

5. "Crime Outbreak in Harlem," 1; For a conceptualization of "white space," see Elijah Anderson, "The White Space," *Sociology of Race and Ethnicity* 1, no. 1 (2015): 10–21.

6. Katheryn K. Russell, *The Color of Crime: Racial Hoaxes, White Fear, Black Protectionism, Police Harassment, and Other Macroaggressions* (New York: New York University Press, 1998), 3. Dominic J. Capeci Jr., "Fiorello H. La Guardia and the Harlem 'Crime Wave' of 1941," *New York Historical Society* 64 (January 1980): 28. This chapter builds on some of Capeci's insights, but I begin the story in the 1930s and center the politics of safety. This approach aids in exploring the roles of whites, the white press, and the NYPD in contributing to the rhetoric and myth of the "crime wave." Capeci points out that "inadequate municipal funds and war priorities prevented La Guardia from taking any immediate steps to improve the conditions under which multitudes of Black residents lived" and believed that "considering all the complex factors, La Guardia deserves recognition as one of the most sincere civil rights advocates in public office and as the most liberal mayor in New York's history." I do not wholly disagree with these claims, though many Black New Yorkers blamed La Guardia and racial discrimination in city government for their living conditions, not simply wartime priorities. More significantly, Capeci is generally silent on police violence and its consequences for Black New Yorkers, though he admits they criticized law enforcement and that "La Guardia was the NYPD's staunchest

supporter." This chapter unearths how La Guardia's liberalism effectively coexisted with and abetted police violence.

7. For white violence and police cooperation linked to housing and commercial recreation in New York City, see Marcy S. Sack, "'To Show Who Was in Charge': Police Repression of New York City's Black Population at the Turn of the Twentieth Century," *Journal of Urban History* 31, no. 6 (September 1, 2005): 799–819; Shannon King, "'Ready to Shoot and Don't Shoot': Black Working-Class Self Defense and Community Politics in Harlem, New York, during the 1920s," *Journal of Urban History* 37, no. 5 (August 8, 2011): 757–74; Douglas J. Flowe, *Uncontrollable Blackness: African American Men and Criminality in Jim Crow New York* (Chapel Hill: University of North Carolina Press, 2020, 58–93; Arnold Hirsch, *Making the Second Ghetto: Race and Housing in Chicago, 1940–1960* (Chicago: University of Chicago Press, 1998); Victoria W. Wolcott, *Race, Riots, and Roller Coasters: The Struggle over Segregated Recreation in America* (Philadelphia: University of Pennsylvania Press, 2012), 39–46; Simon Balto, *Occupied Territory: Policing Black Chicago from the Red Summer to Black Power* (Chapel Hill: University of North Carolina Press, 2019), 96–101.

8. Max Felker-Kantor, *Policing Los Angeles: Race, Resistance, and the Rise of the LAPD* (Chapel Hill: University of North Carolina Press, 2018), 5. For police discretion, see Christopher Lowen Agee, *The Streets of San Francisco: Policing and the Creation of a Cosmopolitan Liberal Politics, 1950–1972* (Chicago: University of Chicago Press, 2014).

9. Roy Wilkins, "Crime Smear," *The Crisis*, December 1941, 375.

10. For "rights talk," see Thomas Sugrue, "Crabgrass-roots Politics: Race, Rights, and the Reaction against Liberalism in the Urban North, 1940–1964," *Journal of American History* 82, no. 2 (September 1995): 562–64.

11. For liberal law and order, see Felker-Kantor, *Policing Los Angeles*; Agee, *Streets of San Francisco*; Elizabeth Hinton, *From the War on Poverty to the War on Crime: The Making of Mass Incarceration* (Cambridge, Mass.: Harvard University Press, 2016); and for conservative law and order, Michael W. Flamm, *Law and Order: Street Crime, Civil Unrest, and the Crisis of Liberalism in the 1960s* (New York: Columbia University Press, 2005).

12. See Stuart Hall, Chas Critcher, Tony Jefferson, John Clarke, and Brian Roberts's *Policing the Crisis: Mugging, the State, and Law and Order* (New York: Palgrave Macmillan, 2013).

13. "Crime Outbreak in Harlem Spurs Drive by Police," *New York Times*, November 7, 1941, 1; Fiorello H. La Guardia to the Board of Estimate, November 13, 1941, Office of the Mayor, Fiorello H. La Guardia Records (hereafter, La Guardia Records), Series: Subject Files: reel 76, New York City Municipal Archives (hereafter, NYCMA).

14. "Crime Outbreak in Harlem," 1.

15. "Extra Police Assigned to Park," *PM*, November 9, 1941, 18; "Valentine Adds 250 Policemen to Park Patrol," *New York Herald Tribune*, November 8, 1941, 13; "250 More Police in Harlem to Stamp Out Crime Wave," *New York Times*, November 8, 1941, 1.

16. "250 More Police in Harlem to Stamp Out Crime Wave," *New York Times*, November 8, 1941, 1.

17. "Extra Police Assigned," 18.

18. See Hall et al., *Policing the Crisis*.

19. "Police Is Not Enough," *New York Herald Tribune*, November 11, 1941, 24; "2 Negroes Rob, Beat Salesman; Others Look On: Newest Victim of Harlem 'Muggings' Saves Money but Loses Diamond Ring," *New York Herald Tribune*, November 28, 1941, 40; "Harlem Crime Drive by Police Nets 8 Arrests," *New York Herald Tribune*, November 9, 1941, 46. Black leaders not only focused on socioeconomic issues but also condemned the label "crime wave." Thus, even as this daily reports the perspectives of the Black community, its use of the language "Harlem crime drive" and "wave of violence" undermines the content of the article.

20. "Hoodlums Hunted in Fatal Stabbing," *New York Times*, November 3, 1941, 21 and "Crime Outbreak in Harlem," 1; Sugrue, *Crabgrass-roots Politics*.

21. Anne E. Kolodney to Mayor F. H. La Guardia, November 8, 1941, La Guardia Records, reel 76, NYCMA; Gertrude E. Blanchard to Mayor La Guardia, November 1, 1941, La Guardia Records, reel 76, NYCMA; Apartment 7 A, 58 West 71st, New York City, November 7, 1941, La Guardia Records, reel 76, NYCMA, and George Belmont to the Honorable Fiorello La Guardia, November 8, 1941, La Guardia Records, reel 76, NYCMA.

22. Thomas Curtin to the Honorable Fiorello H. La Guardia, November 7, 1941, La Guardia Records, reel 76, NYCMA.

23. Khalil G. Muhammad, *Condemnation of Blackness: Race, Crime, and the Making of Modern Urban America* (Cambridge, Mass.: Harvard University Press, 2010).

24. "Mayor Rejects Ringel View on Harlem Crime," *New York Herald Tribune*, November 30, 1941, 43.

25. From LT to Hon. Fiorello H. La Guardia, Mayor, November 10, 1941, La Guardia Records, reel 76, NYCMA.

26. From "The Real American" to Mayor La Guardia, December 2, 1941, La Guardia Records, reel 76, NYCMA.

27. Edwin Fadiman to Mayor F. H. La Guardia, November 3, 1941, reel 76, NYCMA.

28. Unnamed, undated, La Guardia Records, reel 76, NYCMA.

29. "Crime Outbreak in Harlem Spurs Drive by Police," *New York Times*, November 7, 1941, 1.

30. Police Reporter, "Voice to the People: 'His Harlem Answer,'" *New York Daily News*, November 14, 1941, 37.

31. Unnamed, undated, La Guardia Records, reel 76, NYCMA.

32. James H. Hubert, Executive Director, to Mayor F. H. La Guardia, November 17, 1941, 1, La Guardia Records, reel 76, NYCMA.

33. Blacks' intracommunity discussions of crime in the Black press, therefore, included not only criticizing criminal behavior but also supporting crime prevention. Blacks also interpreted these discussions of crime and crime prevention around gender and especially around the behavior of Black women and their

management of the household. But Blacks' protest against White depictions of Black crime represented what Muhammad calls "writing crime into class," whereby Black reformers and activists and some white liberals argued that structural inequality and police racism explained Black crime. Muhammad, *Condemnation of Blackness*, 228–29.

34. See chapter 3 for whites' perceptions on crime in the aftermath of the Harlem Riot and the commission's subcommittee report on police brutality and chapter 4 on police violence and occupation of Harlem.

35. "Blitzkrieg on Harlem," *New York Amsterdam News*, November 15, 1941, 8.

36. "Blitzkrieg on Harlem," 8.

37. Roy Wilkins, "The Watchtower" and C. B. Powell, "The Mighty White Press," *New York Amsterdam News*, November 15, 1941, 9 and 1. For criticism of the World's Fair, see "Blacklisting Harlem," *New York Age*, April 8, 1939, 6.

38. All quotes from "Statement by the NAACP Board of Directors," box II: A298, folder 4, Harlem, Crime Conferences, 1–3, National Association for the Advancement of Colored People Records, Manuscript Division, Library of Congress (hereafter, NAACP Records, LOC); *State of New York, Second Report of the New York State Temporary Commission on Condition of the Colored Urban Population, to the Legislature of the State of New York*, no. 69, February 1939; "'Crime Wave' Publicity Causes Wide Activity in an Effort to Find a Solution to Problem," *New York Age*, November 22, 1941, 1; "NAACP Asks Mayor LaGuardia to Call Conference Soon on Conditions in Harlem," *New York Age*, November 22, 1941, 1; "Condemns Widespread Publicity of Harlem as Crime Center" and "Mayor's Report on Riot Asked," *New York Amsterdam News*, November 15, 1941, 1, 15; "Cites Need for More Negro Policemen in Harlem Area," *New York Amsterdam News*, November 22, 1941, 28; "Says Program to Aid Harlem Must Have Full Cooperation," *New York Amsterdam News*, December 20, 1941, 14; "Why This Juvenile Crime?" and "Jobs Cited as Greatest Need in City's Fight against Delinquency," *New York Amsterdam News*, December 27, 1941, 6, 13. For "Bigger Thomas," see Richard Wright's Introduction: "How Bigger Was Born" and *Native Son* (New York: Harper & Row, 1989). For Richard Wright and "Bigger Thomas," see Daryl Michael Scott, *Contempt and Pity: Social Policy and the Image of the Damaged Black Psyches, 1880–1996* (Chapel Hill: University of North Carolina Press, 1997), 98–100; Naomi Murakawa, *The First Civil Right: How Liberals Built Prison America* (New York: Oxford University Press, 2014), 51–53; for La Guardia's belated attempt to offer economic assistance and social services, see Capeci Jr., "Fiorello H. La Guardia," 14–16.

39. Carl Lawrence "Cites Need for More Negro Policemen Harlem Area," *New York Amsterdam News*, November 22, 1941, 28. For Black police officers, see *One Righteous Man: Samuel Battle and the Shattering of the Color Line in New York* (New York: Beacon, 2016); Marilynn S. Johnson, *Street Justice: A History of Police Violence in New York City* (New York: Beacon, 2003), 203; W. Marvin Dulaney, *Black Police in America* (Bloomington: Indiana University Press, 1996), 22, 69.

40. Ludlow W. Werner, "Across the Desk," *New York Age*, November 22, 1941, 6.

41. Ebenezer Ray, "About People and Things," *New York Age*, November 15, 1941, 6. For a recent social history addressing Black masculinity and intraracial crime

in New York City, see Douglas J. Flowe, *Uncontrollable Blackness: African American Men and Criminality in Jim Crow New York* (Chapel Hill: University of North Carolina Press, 2020).

42. Dorothy Simons to Mayor La Guardia, undated, La Guardia Records, reel 76, NYCMA.

43. Adele Wist to Mayor La Guardia, November 10, 1941, La Guardia Records, reel 76, NYCMA; H. Wigden to Hon. Lewis J. Valentine, November 22, 1941, La Guardia Records, reel 76, NYCMA.

44. "The Thirtieth Precinct," *New York Amsterdam News*, February 15, 1941, 16. The *New York Amsterdam News* had made a similar complaint about the inaction of the Thirtieth Precinct in 1938. "Police in New Crime Campaign on Sugar Hill," *New York Amsterdam News*, November 19, 1938.

45. A Negro Resident to Honorable Fiorello La Guardia, October 2, 1941, Mayor of the City of New York, La Guardia Records, reel 77, NYCMA.

46. H. Wigden to Hon. Lewis J. Valentine, November 22, 1941; Adele Wist to Mayor La Guardia, November 10, 1941.

47. Adele Wist to Mayor La Guardia; H. Wigden to Hon. Lewis J. Valentine, November 22, 1941; and Anna L. Moore, President of Dunbar Housewives League, to Honorable Fiorello H. La Guardia, November 19, 1941, La Guardia Records, reel 76, NYCMA. On Jim Crow policing, see Shannon King, "A Murder in Central Park: Racial Violence and the Crime Wave in New York during 1930s and 1940s," in *The Strange Career of the Jim Crow North: Segregation and Struggle Outside of the South*, edited by Brian Purnell and Jeanne Theoharis with Komozi Woodard (New York: New York University Press, 2019).

48. Lawrence D. Reddick, "In Harlem," *New York Amsterdam News*, November 22, 1941, 8.

49. Margaret C. Byrne to Roy Wilkins, November 14, 1941, box II: A368, folder 2, Citizens Committee on Harlem, 1943, 1, NAACP Records, LOC.

50. "Defends Harlem Publicity: Court Says Newspapers Seek to Protect Public," *New York Times*, November 20, 1941, 29.

51. "'Crime Wave' Publicity Causes Wide Activity in an Effort to Find a Solution to Problem," *New York Age*, November 22, 1941, 1.

52. "Whites Join in Fight on Local Conditions," December 7, 1941, *New York Amsterdam News*, 1, 15.

53. "Harlem Center of Neglect, Says Leader of 'Crime Stop' Drive," *New York Amsterdam News*, January 3, 1942, 12.

54. *The Story of the City-Wide Citizens' Committee on Harlem*, May 23, 1943, box II: A368, folder 3, Citizens Committee on Harlem, 1943, 1, NAACP Records, LOC.

55. Citizens' Committee Reports on Living Conditions in New York's Harlems at Freedom House, box II: A368, folder 2, Citizens Committee on Harlem, 1941–42, 2–3, NAACP Records, LOC; *Story of the City-Wide Citizens' Committee*, 5.

56. *Report of the Subcommittee on Housing of the City-Wide Citizens' Committee on Harlem*, box II: A368, folder 3, Citizens Committee on Harlem, 1943, NAACP Records, LOC.

57. State of New York, *Second Report of the New York State Temporary Commission on the Condition of the Colored Urban Population* (Albany, N.Y.: J. B. Company Printers, February 1939), 74, 75.

58. State of New York, *Second Report,* 79.

59. *Report of the Sub-committee on Housing,* 3.

60. *Report of the Sub-committee on Housing,* 4.

61. *Report of the Sub-committee on Housing,* 7, 7–13.

62. City-Wide Citizens' Committee on Harlem, New York, *Report of the Subcommittee on Crime and Delinquency of the City-Wide Citizens' Committee on Harlem,* 2, 4–5, Schomburg Center for Research in Black Culture.

63. Minutes of Meeting of the Executive Board of the City-Wide Citizens' Committee on Harlem, October 8, 1942, box II: A368, folder 2, City-wide Citizens' Committee on Harlem, 1941–42, 3, NAACP Records, LOC; "Urge City to Withhold Millions from Jim Crow Charities," *New York Amsterdam News,* April 18, 1942, 2; "City Rules No Cash for Biased Institutions," *New York Amsterdam News,* April 25, 1942, 1; "City to Deny Funds to Charities Which Are Discriminatory" and "To Curb Juvenile Delinquency," *New York Age,* April 25, 1942, 1, 6.

64. Minutes of Meeting of the Executive Board of the City-Wide Citizens' Committee on Harlem, October 8, 1942, box II: A368, folder 2, NAACP Records, LOC; "Withdraw City Aid to Jim Crow Orphanages," *New York Amsterdam News,* November 7, 1942, 1, 4. For juvenile justice, see Carl Suddler, *Presumed Criminal: Black Youth and the Justice System in Postwar New York* (New York: New York University Press, 2019); Dennis A. Doyle, *Psychiatry and Racial Liberalism in Harlem, 1936–1968* (Rochester: University of Rochester Press, 2016); and Gerald Markowitz and David Rosner, *Children, Race, and Power: Kenneth and Mamie Clark's Northside Center* (Charlottesville: University Press of Virginia, 1996). For La Guardia's efforts to enforce the Race Discrimination Amendment, see Capeci Jr., "Fiorello H. La Guardia and the Harlem 'Crime Wave' of 1941," 22–24.

Chapter 7

1. "'Mugging Night Sticks' Are Withdrawn from Sale at Macy's," *New York Amsterdam News,* May 8, 1943, 1, 2.

2. "'Mugging Night Sticks' Are Withdrawn from Sale at Macy's," 1.

3. "'Crime Wave' Arrest Found Unjustified by Sessions Judge," *New York Age,* January 24, 1942, 1; Carl Lewis, "Free Crime Wave Martyr," *New York Amsterdam News,* January 24, 1942, 1; "Thief Loots Home Next to Mayor's in 'Crime Region,'" *New York Times,* November 10, 1941, 1; and "Less Park Crime, Valentine Holds," *New York Times,* November 11, 1941, 25.

4. Inez Cavanaugh, "NY Telegram Begins New Smear Series," *New York Amsterdam News,* May 9, 1942, 5. For more on law enforcement and reformers pushing crime out of white neighborhoods into Black ones in New York City, see Kevin Mumford, *Interzones: Black/White Sex Districts in Chicago and New York in the Early Twentieth Century* (New York: Columbia University Press, 1997); Elizabeth Clement, *Love for Sale: Courting, Treating, and Prostitution in New York City, 1900–1945* (Chapel Hill:

University of North Carolina Press); Khalil G. Muhammad, *Condemnation of Blackness: Race, Crime, and the Making of Modern Urban America* (Cambridge, Mass.: Harvard University Press, 2010); and Shannon King, *Whose Harlem Is This, Anyway?: Community Politics and Grassroots Activism during the New Negro Era* (New York: New York University Press, 2015); for the numbers game, see Shane White, Stephen Garton, Stephen Robertson, and Graham White, *Playing the Numbers: Gambling in Harlem between the Wars* (Cambridge, Mass.: Harvard University Press, 2010); LaShawn Harris, *Sex Workers, Psychics and Numbers Runners: Black Women in New York City's Underground Economy* (Champaign: University of Illinois Press, 2016).

5. Tommy Watkins, "White Man Lures Girl, 9, to Cellar, Attacks Her," *New York Amsterdam News*, August 29, 1942, 1; Roy Wilkins, "The Watchtower," *New York Amsterdam News*, September 26, 1942, 7.

6. Lucille Grant, "Crime in Harlem?: Letters to the Editor," *New York Amsterdam News*, August 29, 1942, 6.

7. "Crime in Harlem," *New York Amsterdam News*, September 12, 1942, 6.

8. Carl Lawrence, "Harlem Roundup," *New York Amsterdam News*, October 17, 1942, 19.

9. "Crime in Harlem," 6. For the Chicago Committee of Fifteen and the Chicago Crime Commission, see Kevin J. Mumford, *Interzones: Black/White Sex Districts in Chicago and New York* (New York: Columbia University Press, 1997); Cynthia M. Blair, *I've Got to Make My Livin': Black Women's Sex Work in Turn-of-the-Century Chicago* (Chicago: University of Chicago Press, 2010); see Nora C. Krinitsky, "The Politics of Crime Control: Race, Policing, and Reform in the Twentieth-Century Chicago," PhD diss., University of Michigan, 2017; Simon Balto, *Occupied Territory: Policing Black Chicago from the Red Summer and Black Power* (Chapel Hill: University of North Carolina Press, 2019).

10. Carl Lawrence, "Harlem Roundup," *New York Amsterdam News*, September 19, 1942, 15.

11. "Crime in Harlem—II," *New York Amsterdam News*, September 19, 1942, 6.

12. "Crime in Harlem—IV," *New York Amsterdam News*, October 3, 1942, 6.

13. Anonymous, "Praises Article," *New York Amsterdam News*, September 19, 1942, 7.

14. Walter L. Thomas, "The People Speak: Urged for Harlem Fight to End Crime," *New York Amsterdam News*, October 3, 1942, 6.

15. Thomas, "People Speak: Urged for Harlem Fight," 6.

16. Carl Lawrence, "Harlem Roundup," *New York Amsterdam News*, September 26, 1942, 15.

17. Brewster, "On Harlem Crime," *New York Amsterdam News*, October 3, 1942, 6.

18. "We Ask the Question," *New York Amsterdam News*, October 17, 1942, 7.

19. Alfred A. Duckett, "Police Commissioner Gets Complaint on Brutality," *New York Age*, July 26, 1941, 7; Alfred A. Duckett, "Postscript to Comm. Valentine in re 'Macon St. Crapshooters,'" *New York Age*, August 2, 1941, 7.

20. Alfred A. Duckett, "Offering the Mayor Our Support," *New York Age*, August 23, 1941, 7.

21. "Brooklynites Assail 'Police Brutality' at Rally," *New York Amsterdam News*, March 15, 1941, 10; Civic Groups Rally against "Police Brutality," *New York Amsterdam Star-News*, February 22, 1941, 10.

22. "Convict 110 Lb. Man for Assault on 2 Hefty Cops," *Chicago Defender*, April 19, 1941, 3. The Black press was suspicious of the police's story. Although Officers Shannon and Long claimed that Weaver pulled a knife on them and was convicted of simple assault, the Black press consistently mentioned Weaver's weight to question whether he could physically assault them. Although Weaver's weight changed from 110 to 135 pounds from one editorial to the next in the *Amsterdam News*, the Black weekly also questioned the alleged assault based on the fact that Weaver confronted "two fully-armed policemen." In reporting Weaver's conviction, the *Chicago Defender* similarly questioned the officers' charge describing them as "hefty" in the title of the article.

23. "Brutality Charge Lodged against Officer by Woman," *New York Amsterdam News*, July 12, 1941, 5; "Bronxites Rally behind Woman Who Charges Cop Slapped Her," *New York Amsterdam News*, July 26, 1941, 3.

24. "Accuse Woman of Knifing Cop," *New York Amsterdam News*, August 9, 1941, 1; "Hold 4 Women Involved in Subway Attack Which Stirred 'Police Brutality' Battle," *New York Amsterdam News*, October 4, 1941, 12.

25. "On Police Brutality," *New York Amsterdam News*, October 18, 1941, 8.

26. Maurice Dancer, "Harlem Tense after Police Shoot Boy, 14," *Chicago Defender*, December 6, 1941, 1; "Man Dies of Gun Wounds; Youth Shot by Policeman," *New York Age*, December 6, 1941, 1.

27. Dancer, "Harlem Tense," 1; "Harlem Boy, 14, Ignores Cop's Command, Shot," *Daily News*, December 1, 1941, 6.

28. "400 Boroughites Watch Near-Riot," *New York Amsterdam News*, May 2, 1942, 18.

29. "Hearing Held for Cops Facing Brutality Charges during Raid," *New York Amsterdam News*, May 16, 1942, 18.

30. Hulan E. Jack to His Honor Fiorello H. LaGuardia, May 9, 1942, Office of the Mayor Fiorello H. La Guardia Records, Series: Subject Files, 1934–45, reel 76, New York City Municipal Archives (hereafter, NYCMA).

31. J. Robert Smith, "Mob Menaces Cops in Slaying Mental Patient Shot to Death: 2,000 Angry Harlemites Swarm around Harlem Hospital Area," *New York Amsterdam News*, May 16, 1942, 1; From Commanding Officer, Sixth Division to the Police Commissioner, May 12, 1942, Office of the Mayor, Fiorello H. La Guardia Records, Subject Files, 1934–45, reel 77, NYCMA. See also Dominic J. Capeci Jr., *Harlem Riot of 1943 The Harlem Riot of 1943* (Philadelphia: Temple University Press, 1977), 26; and Charles V. Hamilton, *Adam Clayton Powell, Jr.: The Political Biography of an American Dilemma* (New York: Cooper Square, 2002), 122–24.

32. J. L. C., "Mounted Cop, Gun in Hand Quelled Mob," *People's Voice*, May 16, 1942, 35.

33. Smith, "Mob Menaces Cops," 4.

34. Quote from J. L. C., "Mounted Cop, Gun in Hand Quelled Mob," 35; Smith, "Mob Menaces Cops," 1.

35. Lionel C. Barrow to Lewis J. Valentine, Police Commissioner, May 13, 1942; Walter White to Hon. F. H. La Guardia, Mayor, May 15, 1942, Office of the Mayor, Fiorello H. La Guardia Records, Subject Files, 1934–45, reel 77, NYCMA.

36. To Mr. Mayor from Edwin Washington, May 18, 1942, 2; To F. La Guardia from Ernest N. Barringer, May 23, 1942, 2, Office of the Mayor, Fiorello H. La Guardia Records, Subject Files, 1934–45, reel 77, NYCMA.

37. Lewis Valentine to La Guardia, "attached circular," May 15, 1942, Fiorello H. La Guardia Records, Subject Files, 1934–45, reel 77, NYCMA.

38. Conversation between Mr. Lester Stone and Adam Clayton Powell Jr., May 16, 1942, Fiorello H. La Guardia Records, Subject Files, 1934–45, reel 77, NYCMA.

39. From Asst. Lt. Schulbersky, Criminal Alien Squad to Commanding Officer of Criminal Alien Squad, Mass Meeting Protesting the Killing of One Wallace Armstrong by a Patrolman of This Department, May 17, 1942, Fiorello H. La Guardia Records, Subject Files, 1934–45, reel 77, NYCMA.

40. From Asst. Lt. Schulbersky.

41. J L. C., "Mounted Cop," 35.

42. W. Thomas Watson, "Harlem's Police Expected Trouble," *People's Voice*, May 23, 1942, 37.

43. Roy Wilkins, "The Watchtower," *New York Amsterdam Star-News*, May 23, 1942, 7.

44. Quote from "Harlemites Visit DA's Office in Armstrong Slaying Case," *People's Voice*, May 30, 1942, 3; Carl Dunbar Lawrence, "Greyhound Cop Kills Passenger," *New York Amsterdam Star-News*, March 7, 1942, 1; "Brutal Slaying Sifted by D.A.," *New York Amsterdam Star-News*, May 23, 1942, 1; "Grand Jury Absolves Cop of All Blame in Fatal Shooting Case," *New York Age*, July 25, 1942, 1.

45. "Magistrate Surpless on a Limb," *New York Amsterdam News*, January 2, 1943, 6.

46. "Mayor Is Condemned on 'Mugging' Cases," *New York Times*, January 17, 1943.

47. Magistrate Abner C. Surpless from Walter White, January 19, 1943, box II: A454, folder 6, New York City, General, 1940–44, National Association for the Advancement of Colored People Records, Manuscript Division, Library of Congress (hereafter, NAACP Records, LOC).

48. Mr. Walter White from Magistrate Abner C. Surpless, January 22, 1943, box II: A454, folder 6, New York City, General, 1940–44, NAACP Records, LOC.

49. Magistrate Abner C. Surpless from Walter White, February 1, 1943, box II: A454, folder 6, New York City, General, 1940–44, NAACP Records, LOC.

50. Mr. Walter White from Magistrate Abner C. Surpless, February 6, 1943, box II: A454, folder 6, New York City, General, 1940–44, NAACP Records, LOC.

51. Magistrate Abner C. Surpless from Walter White, February 10, 1943, box II: A454, folder 6, New York City, General, 1940–44, NAACP Records, LOC.

52. "Agree Upon Bill for Extra Police," *New York Times*, February 4, 1943, 24.

53. Quotes from "Crime Wave Here Blamed on Mayor by Dunnigan," *Brooklyn Citizen*, February 23, 1943, 1; "Blame Mayor for Spread of Crime Wave," *Brooklyn Daily Eagle*, February 23, 1943, 1; "Mayor Denies Crime Wave Threatens City,"

Brooklyn Daily Eagle, February 24, 1943, 3; "Dewey Approves Temporary Cops," *Daily News* (New York, New York), March 6, 1943, 49.

54. From John A. Morsell to Editor of the *New York Times*, March 18, 1943, box II: A220, folder 7, NAACP Records, LOC.

55. From Edwin L. James to Mr. John A. Morsell, March 22, 1943, box II: A220, folder 7, NAACP Records, LOC.

56. Roy Wilkins, Assistant Secretary to Mr. Edwin L. James, Managing Editor, the *New York Times*, March 24, 1943, box II: A220, folder 7, NAACP Records, LOC.

57. Wilkins to Mr. James, 2–3; "Pastor's Son Stabbed by 'Muggers' as He Protects Girls against Gang," *New York Times*, March 15, 1943, 1. Wilkins's letter mentions the article "Two More Muggers in Harlem Spur Police to Added Precautions," *New York Times*, March 16, 1943, 1, which was likely the title from an earlier edition of the March 16 issue. I used "Mugger Stabs Woman on Bronx St. Two Earlier Attacks Spur Police" from the late city edition, which is located on the front page and covers the same content as the earlier article.

58. Wilkins to Mr. James, 3–4; and "Wave of Crime in Harlem Denied," *New York Times*, March 23, 1943, 21.

59. Wilkins to Mr. James, 4–5.

60. Edwin L. James, Managing Editor to Mr. Roy Wilkins, Asst. Secretary, National Association for the Advancement of Colored People, March 26, 1943, 1–2.

61. Roy Wilkins to Mr. Edwin L. James, Managing Editor, March 29, 1943, 1.

62. Wilkins to Mr. James, March 29, 1943, 2–3.

63. Wilkins to Mr. James, March 29, 1943, 3.

64. "Memorandum to Metropolitan Press Relative to the Manner in Which Crime Committed by Negroes Is Now Being Reported," undated, box II: A220, folder 7, 2–3, NAACP Records, LOC.

65. Walter White to Commissioner Lewis J. Valentine, Police Department, April 9, 1943, 1–2, box II: A220, folder 7, NAACP Records, LOC.

66. Mr. Arthur Hays Sulzberger, President, *New York Times*, from Walter White, April 9, 1943, 1–2, box II: A220, folder 7, NAACP Records, LOC.

67. "Faked Mugging Story," *New York Times*, April 9, 1943, 23; Sulzberger, president, *New York Times*, from Walter White, 1–2.

68. Lewis J. Valentine, the Police Commissioner, City of New York to Mr. Walter White, Secretary, National Assn. Advancement of Colored People, April 10, 1943, 1, box II: A220, folder 7, NAACP Records, LOC.

69. Memorandum to Judge Delany, Reverend John H. Johnson, Henry Craft, John Beecher, Dr. Peyton Anderson from Walter White, April 12, 1943, 1; Walter White to Mr. Kent Cooper, General Manager, the Associated Press, April 10, 1943, 1–3; Walter White to Mr. Walter M. Dear, President, American Newspaper Publishers Association, April 21, 1943, 1–2, box II: A220, folder 7, NAACP Records, LOC.

70. Memorandum for Mr. James from A. H. S., April 10, 1943; To Mr. Sulzberger from E.L. J., April 10, 1943, New York Times Company Records, Arthur Hays Sulzberger Papers (hereafter, Sulzberger Papers), Series II, box 212, folder 12, Negroes, 1943 Mar–May, Stephen A. Schwarzman Building.

71. Mr. Walter White, National Association for the Advancement of Colored People, from Arthur Hays Sulzberger, Publisher, *New York Times*, April 13, 1943, 1.

72. Roy Wilkins, Assistant Secretary, National Association for Advancement of Colored People from Alan J. Gould, Associated Press, Executive Assistant, April 16, 1943, 1.

73. Meyer Berger, draft of editorial on mugging in New York City, April 1943, 1, Sulzberger Papers, Series II, box 212, folder 12, Negroes, 1943 Mar–May, Stephen A. Schwarzman Building.

74. Berger, draft of editorial on mugging in New York City, 2–4.

75. Dear Mr. Sulzberger, from Meyer Berger, April 16, 1943, Sulzberger Papers, Series II, box 212, folder 12, Negroes, 1943 Mar–May, Stephen A. Schwarzman Building; memorandum for Mr. Sulzberger from E. L. James, April 17, 1943, Sulzberger Papers, Series II, box 212, folder 12, Negroes, 1943 Mar–May, Stephen A. Schwarzman Building; memorandum for Mr. Sulzberger from Charles Merz, April 28, 1943, Sulzberger Papers, Series II, box 212, folder 12, Negroes, 1943 Mar–May, Stephen A. Schwarzman Building. See W. Thomas Watson, "More Delinquency among Whites than Negroes," *New York Amsterdam News*, August 21, 1943, 11.

76. "The Dailies vs. Harlem," *New York Amsterdam New*, April 3, 1943, 10.

77. T. H. Fernandez, "The People Speak: Flays White Press for Harlem Smear," *New York Amsterdam News*, April 10, 1943, 11.

78. Fernandez, "People Speak," 11.

79. "Press on the New Rampage in Campaign to Smear," April 3, 1943, *New York Amsterdam News*, 10.

80. "Mugger Scare Backfires; Editors Hit by N. Y. Judge," *Chicago Defender*, April 24, 1943, 3. For military service, see Thomas A. Guglielmo, *Divisions: A New History of Racism and Resistance in America's World War II Military* (New York: Oxford University Press, 2021) and Matthew F. Delmont, *Half American: The Epic Story of African Americans Fighting World War II at Home and Abroad* (New York: Viking, 2022).

81. Minutes Harlem Conference, Harlem YMCA, February 20, 1943, 1–4, box II: A298, folder 4, Harlem Crime Conference, NAACP Records, LOC.

82. Minutes Harlem Conference, 2.

83. Minutes Harlem Conference, 1; Dear Walter from Elmer A. Carter, Unemployment Insurance Appeal Board, Department of Labor, New York State, 342 Madison Avenue, New York City, February 19, 1943, box II: A298, folder 4, Harlem Crime Conference, NAACP Records, LOC.

84. Minutes Harlem Conference, 2; Recommendations from Harlem Crime Conference, February 20, 1943, 1, box II: A298, folder 4, Harlem Crime Conference, NAACP Records, LOC.

85. "The Dailies vs. Harlem," *New York Amsterdam News*, April 3, 1943, 10.

86. "Solving Harlem's Problem," *New York Amsterdam News*, April 17, 1943, 10.

87. Rev. Ethelred Brown, "Minister Assails Police Brutality," Letter to the Editor, *New York Amsterdam News*, April 3, 1943, 10.

88. Brown, "Minister Assails Police Brutality," 10.

89. Frank D. Griffin, "Press on New Rampage in Campaign to Smear" in "Letters to the Editor," *New York Amsterdam News*, April 3, 1943, 10.

90. "Solving Harlem's Problem," 10.

91. Capeci Jr., *Harlem Riot of 1943*, 138–39; Nat Brandt, *Harlem at War: The Black Experience in WWII* (Syracuse, N.Y.: Syracuse University Press, 1996), 170–71.

92. "Prostitution Curb Is Urged on Police," *New York Times*, September 24, 1943, 14. For Black protest around the Savoy, see Dominic J. Capeci Jr., "Walter F. White and the Savoy Ballroom Controversy of 1943," *Afro-Americans in New York Life and History* 5, no. 2 (July 31, 1981), 13–32.

93. National Association for the Advancement of Colored People, *Food Costs More in Harlem: A Comparative Survey of Retail Food Prices* (New York: National Association for the Advancement of Colored People, 1942), box II: A298, folder 8, Food Costs in Harlem, 1942, Feb–Aug, NAACP Records, LOC; Arnold Beichman, "Harlem Pays More Money for Less Food," *PM*, February 23, 1942, 6 and *The People's Voice*, February 28, 1942, 14; "Expose Price Violations in New York," *Chicago Defender*, August 29, 194, 6; "Pledges Action on Food Costs," *New York Amsterdam Star-News*, September 19, 1942, 4; "Wants City Council to Act on Harlem's High Cost of Food," *New York Age*, October 3, 1942, 2. Also see Mason B. Williams, *City of Ambition: FDR, La Guardia, and the Making of Modern New York* (New York: W. W. Norton, 2013), 340–49 for La Guardia's response to the city's shortage of meat and his interactions with the Office of Price Administration.

94. Carl Lawrence, "Harlem Roundup," *New York Amsterdam News*, September 26, 1942, 15.

95. Cheryl Greenberg, *"Or Does It Explode?": Black Harlem and the Great Depression* (New York: Oxford University Press, 1997), 202–3; David Lucander, *Winning the War for Democracy: The March on Washington Movement, 1941–1946* (Urbana: University of Illinois Press, 2014); J. Robert Smith, "March on Washington Drive Draws Nationwide Response," *New York Amsterdam Star-News*, June 7, 1941, 1; "March-on-Washington to Garden on Tuesday," *New York Amsterdam Star-News*, June 13, 1942, 1. On housing activism, see Ronald Lawson and Mark Naison, *The Tenant Movement in New York City, 1904–1984* (New Brunswick, N.J.: Rutgers University Press, 1986); "'Beale Street' Survey Bares Housing Evils," *New York Amsterdam Star-News*, July 26, 1941, 11; "Tenants Call Landlord Gyp and Win Redress," *New York Amsterdam Star-News*, April 11, 1943, 5; Eugene Gordon, "Launch Negro Housing Program," *Daily Worker*, May 27, 1942, 5.

96. Charles Williams, "Harlem at War," *The Nation*, January 16, 1943, 86.

97. Quote from Martha Biondi, "Robert Moses, Race, and the Limits of an Activist State," in *Robert Moses and the Modern City: The Transformation of New York*, edited by Hilary Ballon and Kenneth T. Jackson (New York: W. W. Norton, 2007), 117.

Chapter 8

1. Walter White Letter to Harlem and Brooklyn Ministers, Club Presidents, and Labor Organization, box II: A507, folder 2: Racial Tensions, Letters to Ministers

and Clubs, June 30, 1943, National Association for the Advancement of Colored People Records, Manuscript Division, Library of Congress (hereafter, NAACP Records, LOC).

2. Warren Hall, "Mayor in Race Appeal," *Daily News*, July 5, 1943, 11.

3. "Council Asked for Probe of Riot Inciters," *New York Daily News*, June 25, 1943, 10. Clarence Taylor, *Fight the Power: African Americans and the Long History of Police Brutality in New York City* (New York: New York University, 2019), 9–33.

4. Adam Clayton Power Jr., "Soapbox," *People's Voice*, July 3, 1943, 5.

5. James Baldwin, "Me and My House . . . ," *Harper's Magazine* 211: 1266 (November 1955), 57–58.

6. "Mayor La Guardia in Warning against Race Trouble Here," *New York Age*, July 3, 1943, 1.

7. Chappy Gardner, "Hoodlums Wreck 500,000 in Property: Leaders Say Harlem Riot Set Ground Back 20 Years," *Philadelphia Tribune*, August 7, 1943, 1; "Rumors of Soldier's Killing Caused Frenzied Mob to Riot," *New York Amsterdam News*, August 7, 1943, 4; and Seymour Peck, "Reporter Tells of Being Swept Along by Waves of Rioting over Harlem," *PM*, August 3, 1943, 6.

8. "Eyewitnesses Tell Same Story of Spreading Rumor," *PM*, August 3, 1943, 6.

9. Walter White, *A Man Called White* (New York: Arno Press and New York Times, 1969), 236, 237; Roy Wilkins, *Standing Fast: The Autobiography of Roy Wilkins* (New York: Viking, 1982), 183–84; "Rumors of Soldier's Killing," 4.

10. "Harlem Is Orderly with Heavy Guard Ready for Trouble," *New York Times*, August 3, 1943, 1, 10; "Mayor in Command of Harlem Forces," *New York Times*, August 3, 1943, 9; "6 Dead in Harlem Riot," *Chicago Defender*, August 7, 1943, 1, 4.

11. Nat Brandt, *Harlem at War: The Black Experience in WWII* (Syracuse, N.Y.: Syracuse University Press, 1996), 207; Max Herman, "Detroit (Michigan) Riot of 1943," in *Encyclopedia of American Race Riots*, edited by Walter Rucker and James Nathaniel Upton (Westport, Conn.: Greenwood, 2006), 160; and Dominic J. Capeci Jr. and Martha Wilkerson, *Layered Violence: The Detroit Rioters of 1943* (Jackson, Miss.: University of Mississippi, 2009), 94.

12. Mayor F. H. La Guardia, For Immediate Release, City of New York, Office of the Mayor, August 2, 1943, 1–2, Office of the Mayor, Fiorello H. La Guardia Records, Subject Files, 1934–45, reel 77, New York City Municipal Archives (hereafter, NYCMA).

13. Mayor F. H. La Guardia, For Immediate Release, 1–2.

14. "Mayor in Command of Harlem Forces," *New York Times*, August 3, 1943, 9.

15. "First Lady Asks Coolness," *New York Times*, August 3, 1943, 8.

16. Westbrook Pegler, "Fair Enough," *Atlantic Constitution*, August 5, 1943, 16.

17. To Hon. F. H. La Guardia, City Hall, New York, N.Y. from Beatrice Lindemann, August 3, 1943, 1; To Mayor Fiorello H. La Guardia, City Hall, New York City from Mrs. Herman Lass, 1410 Avenue I, Brooklyn, N.Y., August 3, 1943; To the Honorable Fiorello La Guardia, Mayor of the City of New York, City Hall, New York from Roy Whitman, President, General Organizer, Industrial Insurance Agents Union, Local 30, 5 Beekman St., New York, 1, Office of the Mayor, Fiorello H. La Guardia Records, Subject Files, 1934–45, reel 77, NYCMA.

18. Dear Mayor La Guardia from Brooklyn, August 3, 1943, 1; To Mayor F. La Guardia, Gracie Mansion, N.Y. City from Group of White People, Manhattan, August 3, 1943, 1. Office of the Mayor, Fiorello H. La Guardia Records, Subject Files, 1934–45, reel 77, NYCMA.

19. "Mayor in Command of Harlem Forces," *New York Times*, August 3, 1943, 9.

20. Walter White, "People and Places," *Chicago Defender*, August 13, 1943, 15.

21. Roy Wilkins, "The Harlem Riot," *The Crisis*, September 1943, 263.

22. Arthur G. Hays, "Riots in Harlem Analyzed," *New York Times*, August 6, 1943, 14.

23. "30 Mayors urged to Set Up Racial Boards to Avert Riot," *Chicago Defender*, August 14, 1943, 24.

24. A. Philip Randolph, "Randolph Hits Hoodlumism, Asks Probe of National Racial Tension," *New Leader*, August 7, 1943, 1.

25. Hon. Fiorello H. La Guardia, City Hall from John Newton Griggs, August 2, 1943, La Guardia Records, reel 77, NYCMA; Ludlow W. Werner, "Across the Desk," *New York Age*, May 3, 1941, 6 and November 22, 1941, 6.

26. Theodore H Hernandez, "Hoodlumism, Started Disturbances—Reader," *New York Amsterdam News*, August 14, 1943, 13.

27. Hernandez, "Hoodlumism, Started Disturbances," 13 and L.A.C., "The People Speak: Parents Shortcomings Helped Start Riots," *New York Amsterdam News*, August 14, 1943, 10.

28. L.A.C., "Parents Shortcomings Helped Start Riots," 10; and Hernandez, "Hoodlumism, Started Disturbances," 13.

29. Hernandez, "Hoodlumism, Started Disturbances," 13. In "Group Violence: A Preliminary Study of the Attitudinal Pattern of Its Acceptance and Rejection: A Study of the 1943 Harlem Riot," *Journal of Social Psychology* 19, no. 2 (May 1, 1944): 320, sociologist Kenneth B. Clark's found that of sixty-seven subjects interviewed, 20 percent condoned the uprising, 40 percent rejected it, and 10 percent neither condoned or rejected it.

30. S. W. Garlington, "Pointed Points," *New York Amsterdam News*, August 21, 1943, 11.

31. Dan Burley, "Dan Burley's Back Door Stuff: . . . And They Went Wild as They Plundered Harlem," *New York Amsterdam News*, August 14, 1943, 16.

32. J. A. Rogers, "Rogers Says: New York Riot Was Born Out of Desperation: Need Preventive Action Now," *Pittsburgh Courier*, August 14, 1943, 7.

33. Wilfred H. Kerr, "Hoodlums Didn't Start Riots; 'Twas Jim Crow,'" *New York Amsterdam News*, August 14, 1943, 13.

34. Rogers, "Rogers Says: New York Riot Was Born Out of Desperation," 7.

35. Kerr, "'Hoodlums Didn't Start Riots,'" 7; J. A. Rogers, "Rogers Says: Sermonizing Will Not Do: The Cause of Rioting Must Be Given Close Study," August 21, 1943, 7 and "Rogers Says: New York Riot Was Born Out of Desperation," 7.

36. Burley, "Dan Burley's Back Door Stuff," 16.

37. Rogers, "Rogers Says: New York Riot Was Born Out of Desperation," 7.

38. Frank Perry, "My! My! How Times Has Changed," *New York Amsterdam News*, August 21, 1943, 10.

39. Kerr, "'Hoodlums Didn't Start Riots,'" 13.

40. B. W., "As One Reader Thinks about Police, Prejudice," *New York Amsterdam News*, August 14, 1943, 13.

41. "The Mayor Gets Anti-Riot Plans," *New York Amsterdam News*, August 28, 1943, 13; "Mayor Urged to Name Negro to His Staff, and on Board of Education and Police Dept.," *New York Age*, August 28, 1943, 1.

42. "Committee Charges Mayor Refused to See Them to Receive Recommendations on Riot," *New York Age*, September 25, 1943, 1; "Harlem Riot Probe Asks 10-Point Remedial Plan," *Chicago Defender*, September 25, 1943, 7; Ludlow W. Werner, "Across the Desk: Special Privileges," October 9, 1943, *New York Age*, 1943; "Still Divided, Still Ineffective," *New York Amsterdam News*, October 16, 1943, 12A, col. 1.

43. Citizens' Committee on Better Race Relations, *Recommendations for Action*, 1, 2, box II: A506, folder 9, NAACP Records, LOC.

44. *Report of the Citizens Emergency Conference for Interracial Unity*, September 25, 1943, published by the Executive Committee, pursuant to Conference Resolutions, 7, box II: A506, folder 5, NAACP Records, LOC.

45. *Report of the Citizens Emergency Conference for Interracial Unity*, 9.

46. "The Dailies vs. Harlem," *New York Amsterdam News*, April 3, 1943, 10.

47. A. M. Wendell Malliet, "Causes of Harlem's Two Riots Known; Awaits Action by City Heads," *New York Amsterdam News*, September 18, 1943, 5.

48. A. M. Wendell Malliet, "Suggested Solutions for Harlem's Housing Problem," *New York Amsterdam News*, September 25, 1943, 7; "Harlem Health Conditions Explored in Mayor's Report," *New York Amsterdam News*, October 16, 1943, 4.

49. "Harlem's School Situation Compared with 1935 Study," *New York Amsterdam News*, October 23, 1943, 4.

50. "Policemen's Hostile Tactics Outlined by Mayor's Report," *New York Amsterdam News*, October 2, 1943, 5; "Is Harlem 'Siberia' of the Police Dept.?," *New York Amsterdam News*, January 28, 1939, 1; "Harlem Revealed as a Siberia to Which Police Are Demoted," *New York Herald Tribune*, December 7, 1941, 1.

51. "Stories of Fear and Crime Bared in Bedford Area," *Brooklyn Daily Eagle*, August 19, 1943, 2; "Police Called in Jury's Probe of Bedford Area," *Brooklyn Daily Eagle*, August 23, 1943, 1.

52. "Nightstick Held Answer to Brooklyn Hoodlums," *Brooklyn Daily Eagle*, September 21, 1943, 3; "Warns He'll Ask Dewey to Probe Bedford Crime," *Brooklyn Daily Eagle*, September 22, 1943, 2.

53. Presentment of the August 1943 Grand Jury of Kings County: In the Investigation of Crime and Disorderly Conditions of the Bedford-Stuyvesant area of Brooklyn, 2, box II: A220, folder 2: Crime New York City, Bedford-Stuyvesant, 1943–1944, NAACP Records, LOC.

54. Presentment, 3–5.

55. Presentment, 1, 3a, 4.

56. Presentment, 6a and 7.

57. "Brooklyn's Harlem Made Armed Camp by Mayor," *PM*, November 17, 1943, 10; "Tells Valentine to Get Facts on Bedford Crime," *Brooklyn Daily Eagle*, November 16,

1943, 1; "420 Police Are Sent to Brooklyn Area for Crime Study," *New York Times*, November 17, 1943, 19.

58. "Tells Valentine," 5.

59. "Grand Jurors Recalled for New Action on Bedford Crime Wave," *Brooklyn Daily Eagle*, November 22, 1943, 3, 1.

60. "Cops Itch to Mop Up Brooklyn," *New York Amsterdam News*, November 20, 1943, 1, 2; "420 Police Are Sent," 1.

61. Statement by Walter White, Executive Secretary, National Association for the Advancement of Colored People, regarding Kings County Grand Jury, November 17, 1943, box II: A220, folder 2: Crime New York City, Bedford-Stuyvesant, 1943–1944, NAACP Records, LOC; The City-Wide Citizens' Committee on Harlem Answers Kings County Grand Jury Presentment, 1, box II: A220, folder 2: Crime New York City, Bedford-Stuyvesant, 1943–1944, LOC.

62. Evelyn Seeley, "Brooklyn's Harlem Calls Crime-Wave Charge Vicious," *PM*, November 21, 1943, 12; Evelyn Seeley, "Brooklyn's Harlem's Women to Ask That Mgr. Belford Be Removed," *PM*, November 25, 1943.

63. Nancy Davids, Public Relations Department, "The Citizens' Committee on Harlem Points to Past Reports on Bedford-Stuyvesant Situation as Substantiating Its Criticism of the Mayor and the City Administration," November 21, 1943, Algernon D. Black Papers, 1932–1979, Series I: Catalogued correspondence, box 7, 1–2, Rare Book and Manuscript Library, Bartle Library, Columbia University.

64. Davids, "Citizens' Committee on Harlem," 2.

65. Lewis Valentine, *Report of the Police Commissioner to the Mayor, November 20, 1943*, Office of the Mayor, Fiorello H. La Guardia Records, Series: Subject Files: Bedford, Stuyvesant, Grand Jury Presentment, box 22, folder 13, 49 and 50, NYCMA; "Police Minimize Crime in Brooklyn in Report to Mayor," *New York Times*, November 26, 1943, 18.

66. Valentine, *Report of the Police Commissioner*, 56.

67. Valentine, *Report of the Police Commissioner*, 59.

68. "Valentine Acts to Punish Cop Critic of Mayor," *Brooklyn Daily Eagle*, November 22, 1943, 3.

69. "Brooklyn Meeting Calls on Governor to Remove Mayor," *New York Times*, November 2, 1943, 1; "Here Is Ashcroft Talk Howled Down at Rally," *Brooklyn Daily Eagle*, November 23, 1943, 20.

70. "Kings Grand Jury Presentment on Bedford-Stuyvesant Condemned," *New York Guild Lawyer* 1, no. 4 (December 1943): 1, 6.

71. "Kings County Judge Nathan R. Sobel Today Delivered the Following Charge to the Members of the December Grand Jury," box II, A220, folder 2: Crime New York City, Bedford-Stuyvesant, 1943–1944, NAACP Records, LOC; J. A. Rogers, "Rogers Says," *Pittsburgh Courier*, December 18, 1943, 7.

72. Henry Ashcroft speech to Members of the December Panel, December 6, 1943, 5, box II: A220, folder 2: Crime New York City, Bedford-Stuyvesant, 1943–1944, NAACP Records, LOC.

73. "Vandals Damage House," *New York Times*, October 17, 1943, 16; "Police Called to Give Negroes 'Freedom from Fear,'" *PM*, October 18, 1943, 12; "Police

Smash Plot to Drive Negroes from Heights," *New York Amsterdam News*, October 23, 1943, 2.

74. "Police Called to Give Negroes 'Freedom from Fear,'" *PM*, October 18, 1943, 12.

75. "Police Called," 12.

76. "Police Smash Plot," 2; "Police Called," 12.

77. "Hoodlums Rampant in Washington Heights," *People's Voice*, March 14, 1942, 3.

78. Quotes from "They're Really Painting a Terrific Gates Ave. Yarn," *New York Amsterdam News*, October 2, 1943, 15; Tommy Watkins, "Brooklyn 'Kids' Wage Gang War," *New York Amsterdam News*, October 9, 1943, 13; and "The Problem Must Be Tackled Right!!," *New York Amsterdam News*, October 9, 1943, 14.

79. Watkins, "Brooklyn 'Kids,'" 13; "Delinquency Here Again Increase," *New York Times*, August 13, 1943, 19, 22; "Juvenile Gangs Terrorize Harlem," *New York Amsterdam News*, October 16, 1943, 1A. For scholarly commentary on child delinquency during the war, see Eleanor T. Glueck, "Wartime Delinquency," *Journal of Criminal Law and Criminology* 33, no. 2 (July–August 1942): 119–45; Thorsten Sellin, "Child Delinquency," *Annals of the American Academy of Political and Social Sciences* 229 (September 1943): 157–63; and Edwin J. Lukas, Guest Editor, "Questions and Answers," *Journal of Criminal Law and Criminology* 36, no. 4 (November–December 1945): 271–76.

80. "Near-Riot Hits Uptown Area," *New York Amsterdam News*, May 6, 1944, 1-B.

81. Quotes from "Youth Ideas Seek Delinquency Cure," *New York Times*, July 22, 1944, 17; "Delinquents' Care Held Failing Here," *New York Times*, June 27, 1944, 21; "New Units Fight Delinquency Here," *New York Times*, February 25, 1944, 14; Catherine Mackenzie, "Youngsters 'in Trouble,'" *New York Times*, March 19, 1944, SM23; Dorothy Gordon, "As the Youngsters See Juvenile Delinquency," *New York Times*, August 6, 1944, Sunday Magazine 16; Eric C. Schneider, *Vampires, Dragons, and Egyptian Kings: Youth Gangs in Postwar New York* (Princeton, N.J.: Princeton University Press, 2001), 51–77; quote below, 77. Schneider writes that citizens "discovered" gangs before public officials who were late to discovering them and that "official recognition of the gang problem came with the formation of the New York City Youth Board in 1947." Instead, as this book also argues, public officials and citizens focused on race, race riots, juvenile crime, and war, but Schneider overstates this by framing this as a matter of "discovery." Judges recognized gangs and sometimes gave Black gangs longer sentences than white ones. Thus, although Police Commissioner Valentine publicly rejected the presence of street gangs, judges publicly did so, often through a racial lens.

82. John Edgar Hoover, "A 'Third Front'—against Juvenile Crime," *New York Times*, February 27, 1944, SM8.

83. Though the explosion in juvenile delinquency and gangs occurred in the postwar era, many of these discussions began in earnest at the end of the war, particularly how youth crime might contribute to a crime wave. Bradford Chambers, "Boy Gangs of New York: 500 Fighting Units," *New York Times*, December 10, 1944, SM16; "Harlem Gang Is Seized," *New York Times*, May 21, 1944, 35; "Two Harlem Girls Shot: Bullets Come from Boy Gangs Battling in Streets," *New York Times*, June 7, 1944, 21. There were cases when white youth crime was also indicated by

neighborhood, though these neighborhoods were not criminalized to the same degree as Harlem. For example, see "Policeman Shoots Boy, Youth in Hospital after Gang Row in Inwood Hill Park," *New York Times*, September 7, 1944, 25.

84. Quotes from "Passenger on BMT Train Shot for Objections to Rowdy Acts of 8 Young Negro Hoodlums," *New York Times*, June 12, 1944, 21; and "Hoodlums in Brooklyn Board Train, Shoot Man in Altercation," *New York Age*, June 16, 1944, 1.

85. Quote from "3 Girl Rowdies Guilty," *New York Times*, June 9, 1944, 10; and "Young Rowdies Arraigned: 3 Girls, 4 Boys Face Court for Trolley-Car Disturbance," *New York Times*, June 6, 1944, 19; "Would Urge State Bill for Subway Police Patrols," *Brooklyn Daily Eagle*, June 15, 1944, 1.

86. His Honor the Mayor from Mr. V. G. Flountine, June 12, 1944, Office of the Mayor, Fiorello H. La Guardia Records, Subject Files, 1934–45, reel 77, NYCMA.

87. Hon. Mayor H. H. La Guardia from Mrs. E. S. Millay, June 16, 1944, Office of the Mayor, Fiorello H. La Guardia Records, Subject Files, 1934–45, reel 77, NYCMA. For La Guardia's war against gangsters, see *Robert Weldon Whalen, Murder, Inc. and the Moral Life: Gangsters and Gangbusters in La Guardia's New York* (New York: Empire State Editions, 2016), 75–96; Thomas Kessner, *Fiorello H. La Guardia and the Making of Modern New York* (New York: McGraw-Hill, 1989), 350–68.

88. My Dear Mayor from Philip Drago, Fiorello H. La Guardia Records, reel 77, NYCMA.

89. Hon. Mayor H. H. La Guardia from Mrs. E. S. Millay, June 16, 1944; and My Dear Mayor from Philip Drago.

90. "3 Negro Boys Stoned in Row in Brooklyn: 200 Rowdies Provoke Trouble in Fort Greene Park Area," *New York Times*, June 17, 1944, 14.

91. Tom O'Connor and Maurice Dawkins, "Ft. Greene Tenants Band to Prevent Race Conflict," *PM*, June, 1944, 16.

92. O'Connor and Dawkins, "Ft. Greene Tenants Band."

93. Tom O'Connor, "Time for Action," *PM*, June 19, 1944.

94. "Passenger on BMT Train," 21; "Hoodlums in Brooklyn," 1.

95. "3 Negro Boys Stoned," 14.

96. Tommy Watkins, "White Hoodlums War on Negroes in Borough Park," *New York Amsterdam News*, June 24, 1944, 1B; "Extra Policemen Sent to Brooklyn When White Hoodlums Chase, Beat Negroes in Fort Greene Section," *New York Age*, June 24, 1944, 1.

97. Emanuel Perlmutter, "Police Put Watch on Race Violence," *New York Times*, June 18, 1944, 38.

98. Perlmutter, "Police Put Watch," 38; Watkins, "White Hoodlums War," 1B; and "Extra Policemen Sent," 1.

99. Perlmutter, "Police Put Watch," 38.

100. Watkins, "White Hoodlums War," 1B.

101. Memorandum, from Mr. White to: Mr. Wilkins, Mr. Marshall, Miss Baker, May 1, 1944, box II: A506, folder 8: Racial Tension Harlem, NAACP Records, LOC.

102. Memorandum, to Mr. White and Mr. Wilkins from Mrs. Hurley, May 12, 1944, box II: A506, folder 8: Racial Tension Harlem, NAACP Records, LOC; Memorandum,

to Mr. White from Julia E. Baxter, June 8, 1944, 1, folder: Baxter, Julia E., 1944–1945, Papers of the NAACP, Part 17, Group II, Series A, ProQuest, History Vault.

103. "15,000 See Body of Slain Girl," *New York Amsterdam News*, May 20, 1944, 1A.

104. "15,000 See Body," 12B.

105. Memorandum, from Mr. White to Mrs. Hurley, Miss Baxter, May 24, 1944; Letter to Mr. Ludlow Werner from Walter White, Invitation to Dinner to "avert repetition of last summer's riot" June 3, 1944; To Sara Speaks from Walter White, June 22, 1944, box II: A506, folder 8: Racial Tension Harlem, NAACP Records, LOC.

106. "Rival Negro Gangs Attend Sentencing," *New York Times*, June 23, 1944, 21.

107. Minutes of Confidential Meeting with Mayor La Guardia, June 30, 1944, 4 P.M. at Rectory of Monsignor McCann, 1–2, box II: A506, folder 8: Racial Tension Harlem, NAACP Records, LOC.

108. Minutes of Confidential Meeting, 1, 4–5.

109. Carl Suddler, *Presumed Criminal: Black Youth and the Justice System in Postwar New York* (New York: New York University Press, 2019).

110. Dear Mr. Mayor from an American Citizen, September 7, 1944, 1; and Hon. Fiorello La Guardia, City Hall, New York from A Resident of this vicinity, March 24, 1945, La Guardia Records, Series: Subject Files: reel 77, NYCMA.

111. Emily Brooks, "'Rumor, Vicious Innuendo, and False Reports': Policing Black Soldiers in Wartime Staten Island," *Journal of Urban History*, 1, 9, January 26, 2020.

112. "2,000 High Students Battle in Race Riot," *Daily News*, September 29, 1945, 4.

113. "La Guardia Moves for More Police," *New York Times*, November 30, 1945, 25; Quotes from "New Police Told to 'Go in Shooting,'" *New York Times*, December 2, 1945, 20.

Epilogue

1. James Baldwin, "A Report from Occupied Territory," *The Nation*, July 11, 1966, 39. For more on the Harlem Six, see Carl Suddler, "The Color of Justice without Prejudice: Youth, Race, and Crime in the Case of the Harlem Six," *American Studies* 57, no. 1 (2018): 57–78.

2. Baldwin, "Report from Occupied Territory," 40.

3. James Baldwin, "Fifth Avenue, Uptown," *Esquire*, July 1960, 76.

4. Elizabeth Hinton, *From the War on Poverty to the War on Crime: The Making of Mass Incarceration* (Cambridge, Mass.: Harvard University Press, 2016), 56; and Elizabeth Hinton, *America on Fire: The Untold History of Police Violence and Black Rebellion since the 1960s* (New York: Liveright, 2021).

5. Quotes from Baldwin, "Report from Occupied Territory," 41 and 40, respectively.

6. For Black protest against police brutality from the postwar era to the present, see Martha Biondi, *To Stand and Fight: The Struggle for Civil Rights in Postwar New York City* (Cambridge, Mass.: Harvard University Press, 2003), 72–73; Clarence Taylor, *Fight the Power: African Americans and the Long History of Police Brutality in New York City* (New York: New York University Press, 2018); and Carl Suddler,

Presumed Criminal: Black Youth and the Justice System in Postwar New York (New York: New York University Press, 2019).

7. Quotes from Suddler, *Presumed Criminal*, 123.

8. Quote from Taylor, *Fight the Power*, 135.

9. For this early work on crime prevention and fighting, see Khalil Muhammad's *Condemnation of Blackness: Race, Crime, and the Making of Modern Urban America* (Cambridge, Mass.: Harvard University Press, 2010) discussion of the anticrime work of W. E. B. Du Bois and James S. Stemons and Cheryl D. Hicks's *Talk with You like a Woman: African American Women, Justice, and Reform in New York, 1890–1935* (Chapel Hill: University of North Carolina Press, 2010) on Grace Campbell.

10. State of New York, *Second Report of the New York State Temporary Commission on the Condition of the Colored Urban Population* (Albany: J. B. Company Printers, February 1939), 145.

11. Stephen Rushin and Griffin Sims Edwards, "De-policing," *Cornell Law Review* 102, no. 3 (March 2017): 721–82.

12. Christine Byers, "Crime Up after Ferguson and More Police Needed, Top St. Louis Area Chiefs Say," *St. Louis Post-Dispatch*, November 15, 2014, www.stltoday .com/news/local/crime-and-courts/crime-up-after-ferguson-and-more-police -needed-top-st-louis-area-chiefs-say/article_04d9f99f9a9a-51be-a231-1707a57 b50d6.html.

13. Erik Ortiz, "Police Union Suggests Work Slowdown after NYPD Officer Is Fired in Eric Garner's Death," *NBC News*, August 20, 2019, www.nbcnews.com/news/us -news/police-union-suggests-work-slowdown-after-nypd-officer-fired-eric-n1044486.

14. Interview of Mariame Kaba by Damon Williams and Daniel Kisslinger, "Community Matters, Collectivity Matters," *Airgo*, July 2020, in *We Do This 'Til We Free Us: Abolitionist Organizing and Transforming Justice*, ed. Tamara K. Nopper (Chicago: Haymarket, 2021), 166.

15. Quotes from Elizabeth Hinton, Julilly Kohler-Hausmann, and Vesla M. Weaver, "Did Blacks Really Endorse the 1994 Crime Bill?," *New York Times*, April 13, 2016, www.nytimes.com/2016/04/13/opinion/did-blacks-really-endorse-the-1994 -crime-bill.html.

16. David A. Graham, "Biden Doesn't Have an Answer to America's Crime Spike," *The Atlantic*, June 24, 2021, www.theatlantic.com/ideas/archive/2021/06 /biden-americas-crime-spike-gun-violence/619282/; and Zack Smith and Cully Stimson, "Biden's Hypocritical Efforts to Stem the Wave of Violence Crime Fall Short," *Daily Signal*, June 24, 2021, www.dailysignal.com/2021/06/24/bidens-hypocritical -efforts-to-stem-the-wave-of-violent-crime-fall-far-short/; Mike DeBonis, "Policing Deal Remains out of Reach on Capitol Hill as the Anniversary of George Floyd's Death Approaches," *Washington Post*, May 19, 2021, www.washingtonpost.com /politics/police-reform-congress/2021/05/19/401ffd70-b8cd-11eb-a5fe-bb49dc89 a248_story.html.

17. Kaba, Williams, and Kisslinger, "Community Matters, Collectivity Matters," 166–67.

Index

Italicized page numbers refer to illustrations.

final year in office, 282–84; on Golden Gate Ballroom meeting (1942), 212–13; Harlem, police occupation of, 127, 190; Harlem Riot report, failure to release, 105, 106–7, 112, 125–26, 190, 197, 231, 253–54, 256; interracial cooperation/assistance to Black community, 143, 209; intervention in police affairs, 57–59, 67–68, 143, 180; law-and-order stance, 7, 283–84, 290–91; letters asking for justice, 211; Mayor's Commission report, 163; NAACP conference (1943), 252–53; New Deal programs, 5–6, 45, 76; police complaints concerning, 10; on police victimhood, 20–21; political agenda, 5–6; *Report of the Police Commissioner to the Mayor,* 263–64; response to Braddock Hotel rioting, 240–45; response to Detroit Riot, 236–37; response to Grand Jury presentment, 257–58; response to Harlem Riot (1935), 73–74, 80; response to O'Connell/Keelan incidents, 175; response to Scottsboro meeting complaints, 64, 67–68; riot behavior and use of force, 58–59; Stuyvesant Town, 234; Summer City Hall, Pelham Bay Park meeting, 125–26; taxicab strike, 45, 57–58; urban order vs. racial justice, 45, 105–6, 111–12; Valentine as Police Commissioner, 45–46, 68–72; white anger over subway violence, 271–72; youth violence, 279–81

Lasker, Florina, 123

Lass, Mrs. Herman, 244

Laurie, Edward, 78, 93, 97, 98, 124

Lavell, Louis J., 91

law-and-order: Black vs. white concepts of, 290; calls for, 13–14, 101, 180–81, 188, 206, 256–57; rhetoric of, 20, 162, 201–9

Law Enforcement Assistance Act (LEAA), 286

Law Enforcement Assistance Administration, 287

Lawlessness in Law Enforcement (Wickersham Commission), 29–30, 42

Lawlor, I., 119

Lawrence, Carl Dunbar, 184, 202–4, 234, 278

Lawrence, Louise, 64

Lawrence, Marie, 66–67

Lawson, Maria C., 158

Leach, John N., 37, 66

League of Civic and Political Reform, 289

League of Struggle for Negro Rights (LSNR), 62

Lehman, Herbert, 80–81, 124

Lehr, William, 59–60

Letowsky, Samuel, 117

Levy, Morris, 189

Lewis, Edward, 228

Lewis, George, 119, 120

Louis, Joe, 240

Lewis, Roberta, 131

Lewis, Rosa, 24

Lewis, Theophilus, 82–83

Lexow, Clarence, 22

Lexow Committee, 22

liberalism: La Gaurdia's expression of, 8, 84, 112; New Deal liberalism, 4, 86; as shield for racism, 4, 48, 72, 234–35, 288; varied meanings, 4–5

Liebman, David, 264

Lincoln University, 46, 47–48, 147

Lindau, Alfred, 271–72

Lindemann, Beatrice, 244

Little Fruit Stand Riot, 285, 287

Littleton, Martin W., 135, 137

Locke, Alain, 106, 109, 235

Long, William, 206–7

Louis, Joe, 159–60, *160*

Lowe, Walter (Baker/Lowe case), 46–54

Lundy, Virginia, 134

Luzzatto-Coen, Irene, 54

Lynch, Patrick, 291

Lynching Northern Style: Police Brutality, 288

NAACP, 12, 37, 184; Baker/Lowe case, 47–48, 50, 52–53; conference (1943), 252–53; crime conference, YMCA (1943), 228–30; exchanges with white and Black press, 226–27; *Food Cost More in Harlem* report, 234; Public Relations Committee, 232

Nash, Ann, 118

Nassau County, 134

National Association for the Advancement of Colored People. *See* NAACP

National Commission on Law Observance and Enforcement, 10, 20

National Lawyers Guild, 265

National League for the Protection of Colored Women, 12

National Maritime Union, 240

National Negro Congress (NNC), 127, 206, 207, 246

National Urban League, 156

National War Veterans Association (NWVA), 117, 206

The Negro in Chicago: A Study of Race Relations and a Race Riot, 83–84

The Negro in Harlem (draft subcommittee report), 103, 108–9

Negro Labor Assembly (NLA), 251–52

The Negro World (newspaper), 32

Neidig, Charles, 140–43

Nelson, Truman, 285

Neubauer, William, 61

New Deal liberalism, 4, 86

Newman, Bernard, 78

newspapers: Black press and anti-crime activism, 162–63; Black press and Harlem crime wave, 199–202; Black press' criticism of police, 206–9, 213–14; Black press' criticism of white crime coverage, 217–19; comparisons of Black/white press, 14, 61–62, 279–80; crime coverage, 9–10, 60–62, 176–78; crime coverage, Bedford-Stuyvesant compared with Harlem, 177; crime coverage, frameworks for, 1, 9–10; criticism for overuse of term "mug-

ging", 227–28; interracial coalition to question white press (1943), 198–99; interracial committee on journalism (1942), 222–23; law-and-order rhetoric, 20; stereotypical use of race, 177, 275; white press challenged by Public Relations Committee (NAACP), 232; white press' distorted reportage, 174–75, 181, 183–85, 186, 190, 194, 197–98

New York Age (newspaper): Benjamin Chase incident, 42; campaign for justice for Herbert Dent, 21, 290; Clyde Allen case, 61; complaints concerning police abuse, 206; crime reportage, 19; on "crime wave" rhetoric, 154; criticism of La Guardia, 127; criticism of *New York Amsterdam News,* 164; editorials, 159–60, 246–47; Harlem Riot subcommittee report, 101–2; Herbert Dent incident, 34–35, 36, 37–39; on law and order politics, 147–48; on police occupation of Harlem, 124; Robert Forbes case, 147–48; support for La Guardia, 56

New York Amsterdam News (newspaper): on anti-poverty efforts in Harlem, 230–32; on Bedford-Stuyvesant, 260–61; Black community's pleas for safety, 115; calls to end gang violence, 269; Clyde Allen case, 61; *Complete Report,* 107–8; counternarratives to crime wave mythology, 200–201; coverage of Black crime, 19, 163–64, 166–67, 202–4, 248; "Crime and Punishment" editorial, 71–72; "Crime in Harlem" series, 202–4; criticism of La Guardia and Valentine, 128; criticism of NYPD, 22, 255–56; criticism of white press, 20; criticized for crime reportage, 164; editorials, 118, 123–24; editorials on Black crime, 162–63; editorials on youth crime, 157; on efforts to control Black settlement, 149–50, 154; on Harlem Riot (1935), 250–51; on

Ross, Cecil, 130
Rothstein, Arnold, 55
Rouse, George, 120
Rudich, Mark, 49–50, 51, 54
Ryan, John R., 275

Sala, J. Roland, 227–28
Salem M. E. Church, 105
Samuel, James, 138–39
Sanders, Vera, 131–32
Saunders, Celia C., 95
Savage, Maurice E., 65–66
Savoy Hall, 233
Sawyer, Leonard, 273
Schieffelin, William Jay, 74, 81
Schmeling, Max, 159–60, *160*
schools, public, 95, 228, 229, 254–55
Schupack, Sophie, 6
Scott, Amos M., 31
Scottsboro case and investigation, 45, 62–68, *63*, 119, 120
Seabury Investigation, 45, 56, 111
Seale, Archie, 162
Searle, Robert W., 81, 189, 193
Second Report of the NY State Temporary Commission . . . Colored Urban Population, 191
Seeley, Evelyn, 261
segregation, 107–8, 191, 234, 248–49. *See also* racism and discrimination
Seligmann, Herbert J., 48
Seventeenth Precinct, 139
Seventy-Ninth Precinct, 117
Seventy-Seventh Precinct, 117, 124
Seventy-Third Precinct, 131
sexual assault, 166–67, 201
Shannon, Barney, 206–7
Shannon, James, 116
Shannon, Timothy, 77, 90–91
Shepard, Walter, 132
Shepard, William, 132
Shields (detective), 38
Shore Patrols, 274, 279, 280
Showers, James A., 122
Silver, Norman R., 256–57

Simons, Dorothy, 185–86
Singleton, John A., 170
Sirtl, Sumner A., 148–54, 166, 177, 195, 217, 238, 259, 283
Smirles, Bertha, 60
Smith, Al, 56
Smith, Almira, 70–71
Smith, Ferdinand, 240
Smith, Jackson, 73
Smith, John William, 40
Smith, Patrick, 210
Smith, Rosa, 136
Sobel, Nathan R., 265–66
Social Service Bureau, 189
Society of St. Tammany, 22. *See also* Tammany Hall (Democratic Party political machine)
Solevei, Joseph, 51–52
Solomon, Judge, 121
Solomon, Nathan, 66
South Side House, 115
Spaulter, Maurice, 121, 125
Spector, Frank, 119
Spell, Joseph, 201
Spring 3100 (police department journal), 69, 134
Stafford, Frank, 285
Staten Island, 55–56
St. Augustine Protestant Episcopal Church, 133
Stein, Samuel, 63–64
Stemons, James S., 289
Stepp, India, 208–9
stereotyping and racist tropes, 179, 181, 219, 226–27, 272, 281. *See also* mugging; racism and discrimination
Stern, Magistrate, 120
Stewart, John, 136
St. George's Episcopal Church, 153
Stiegel, Irving, 66
Stier, Albert, 159
St. James Presbyterian Church, 91, 155–56
St. John, James, 130
St. Jude's Community Forum, 156–57

tee investigation, 75; interference in Harlem Riot subcommittee hearings, 90; La Guardia's request to investigate crime in Bedford-Stuyvesant, 258–59; leadership of police force, 68–72, 114; letter from Walter White (April 1942), 223; Marian McDonell case, 140–43; *New York Amsterdam News*' criticism of, 128; *Night Stick* (autobiography), 44; on police violence at Scottsboro meeting, 64–66; promotion of Sergeant Chisholm, 156; reaction to Harlem Riot subcommittee report, 104; *Report of the Police Commissioner to the Mayor,* 263–64; response to Braddock Hotel rioting, 241; response to Harlem Riot (1935), 80–81; response to Harlem Riot subcommittee report, 102–5; response to O'Connell/Keelan incidents, 175; statements against Black youth, 186; use of press coverage, 176; on use of word "mugging," 198, 224

Van Hoesen, Harry, 134
Van Wyck, Robert A., 24
vigilantism, 152, 154–55, 205
Villard, Oswald Garrison, 74, 110–11
Voluntary Defenders Committee (Legal Aid Society), 30

Wagner, Robert F., 289
Walker, James John, 5, 30, 42, 51, 54, 55–56
Walker Memorial Baptist Church, 35
Wall, Michael A., 142
Wallot, Arthur, 60–61
Walsh, Eugene A., 81
Walsh, Mike, 83, 119
Warner, Herman, 159
Washington, Edwin, 211
Washington Heights, 267, 269, 283
Wasservogel, Isidor, 31
Waterson, James B., 91, 92
Watkins, Tommy, 200, 269, 276
Watson, Maude, 208

Watson, W. Thomas, 213–14
Watts Uprising, 286
WAVES (Women's Reserve of the United States Naval Reserve), 233
Weaver, Lindsey, 206–7
Webb, William S., 256
Webber (arresting officer), 40
Weeks, Walter W., 135
Weiss, Leopold, 95
welfare relief, 6, 84–85, 95–96, 179–80
Wells, Ida B., 12
Wells, Irene, 24
Welsh, Edward, 92
Werner, Ludlow W., 184–85, 229, 246–47
Whalen, Grover, 28–29, 30, 47
White, Walter F.: background and "passing" as white, 47–48; on Baker/Lowe case, 50–54; City-Wide Citizens Committee of Harlem (CWCCH), 190; criticism of white press, 198; on "hoodlums", 3; on investigations of police brutality in Harlem, 211, 223–26; on juvenile crime, 228; letter to Eunice Hunton Carter, 84; NAACP conference (1943), 252; Public Relations Committee, 232–33; on racism as root of issues, 261; response to Braddock Hotel rioting, 240, 245–46; Valentine's law-and-order campaign, 215–16; work with La Guardia, 236–38, 244; on youth crime, 276–78
white community: claims of harm against girls and women, 219; complaints about Black crime, 173; containment of Black residential spaces, 9–10, 148–49, 177–78; white mob violence, 36. *See also* newspapers
White Rose Mission/Home for Working Class Negro Girls, 12, 289
white supremacy, 154, 177, 248. *See also* Ku Klux Klan
Whitman, Roy, 244
Wibecan, George E., 116, 118
Wickersham Commission, 20–21, 22, 29–31, 42, 111

Wiesner, Oscar, 208
Wigden, H., 186–87
Wilkerson, Frederick, 240
Wilkins, Roy: criticism of New York Police Department, 233; criticism of white press, 198, 200–201; as editor of *The Crisis,* 246; on Harlem Riot (1935), 81; on intraracial crime, 276, 277, 278; on manufactured "crime waves", 174, 183; on press' criminalization of Black community, 218–22; response to Braddock Hotel rioting, 240; "The Watchtower" column, 214
Williams, Charles, 234
Williams, Mason B., 6
Williams, Mrs. D. J., 84–85, 88
Williams, Patrolman, 129
Williams, Thomas, 95
Wirin, A. L., 64–65
Wissner, Charles E., 149–50
Wist, Adele, 186–88
women: Black women blamed for crime, 202–3, 289–90; mistreatment of, 141–42; safety of Black women, 165–66, 182; safety of white women, 149–50
Women's Reserve of the United States Naval Reserve (WAVES), 233

Women Voters Council, 261
Wood, Lee B., 223
words and terms used in crime reportage, 9–10. *See also* "hoodlumism" label and rhetoric; mugging
World War II, 274; Black soldiers' service, 227, 238; Double V campaign, 11, 202, 213, 227; mistreatment of Black soldiers, 245–46
Wright, Ada, 45, 62–64, 67, 119
Wright, Andy, 62
Wright, Louis T., 47
Wright, Roy, 62

Yergan, Max, 222, 246, 249
Young, C. G., 37
Young Israel of Brooklyn, 29
Young Liberators (YL), 77, 89
Young Men's Christian Association (YMCA), 83, 264
Young Men's Vocational Foundation, 229
youth crime. *See* gangs; Juvenile Aid Bureau (JAB); juvenile delinquency/ crime

Zakutinsky, Abraham, 93, 98
Zimmerman, George, 291, 292
Zoot Suit Riots, 235

Printed in the USA
CPSIA information can be obtained
at www.ICGtesting.com
LVHW091914101123
763623LV00006B/28